## Zed Books of Related Interest

Butchart, A, *The Anatomy of Power: European constructions of the African body*

Campbell, J, *Arguing with the Phallus: Feminist, queer and post-colonial theory: a psychoanalytic contribution*

Hutnyk, J, *The Rumour of Calcutta: Tourism, charity and the poverty of representation*

Kaur and Hutnyk (eds), *Travel Worlds: Journeys in contemporary cultural politics*

Kerridge and Sammells (eds), *Writing the Environment: Eco-criticism and literature*

# Travel Writing and Empire: Postcolonial Theory in Transit

Edited by Steve Clark

Zed Books

LONDON · NEW YORK

*Travel Writing and Empire: Postcolonial Theory in Transit* was first published by Zed Books Ltd, 7 Cynthia Street, London N1 9JF, UK and Room 400, 175 Fifth Avenue, New York, NY 10010, USA in 1999.

Distributed exclusively in the USA by St Martin's Press, Inc., 175 Fifth Avenue, New York, NY 10010, USA.

Cover designed by Andrew Corbett
Set in Monotype Ehrhardt and Franklin Gothic by Ewan Smith
Printed and bound in the United Kingdom by Biddles Ltd, Guildford and King's Lynn

A catalogue record for this book is available from the British Library

ISBN 1 85649 627 9 cased
ISBN 1 85649 628 7 limp

# Contents

# Acknowledgements

I would like to express my gratitude to Paul Harvey and Nigel Leask, to my colleagues at Osaka University and to Warren Chernaik at the Institute of English Studies, University of London, for their support. I would also like to give particular thanks to my editor, Louise Murray, at Zed Books, as well as to Ewan Smith, Anne Rodford, Andrew Corbett, Julian Hosie and Chris Parker for their expertise, professionalism and occasional forbearance throughout the project.

## Notes on the Contributors

Steve Clark is visiting fellow at the School of Advanced Studies, University of London.

T. J. Cribb is a fellow of Churchill College Cambridge.

Gabriel Gbadamosi is a freelance poet and writer based in Brixton.

John Hutnyk is senior lecturer in anthropology at Goldsmith's College, London, and co-editor of the collections *Dis-Orienting Rhythms* and *Travel-Worlds*.

Richard Kerridge teaches at Bath Spa University College. He has recently co-edited a collection on contemporary eco-criticism.

Wendy Mercer is senior lecturer in French at University College London. She is currently preparing a biography of Xavier Marmier.

Ted Motohashi teaches at Tokyo Metropolitan University. He is currently completing a study of representations of the cannibal from Columbus to Marx.

Brian Musgrove teaches at the University of Southern Queensland. He is currently completing a book on the social history of drug literature.

Bridget Orr teaches at Fordham University, New York. She is currently completing a book on English neoclassical drama.

John Phillips is lecturer in post-colonial studies at the University of Singapore, currently preparing a study of crime and justice.

David Taylor teaches at Kyushu University, Fukuoka, and is currently preparing a study of Samuel Beckett.

Katherine Turner teaches at St Peter's College, Oxford. She is currently completing a study of eighteenth-century women's travel literature.

# 1

# Introduction

Steve Clark

Travel writing has taken a mixed and middlebrow form throughout its history, and this gives the genre a peculiar recalcitrance. Anyone can have a go, and usually does. The travel book is unabashedly commercial: it commands large advances, wide distribution and substantial returns. The profit motive is as apparent in the auctioning of Elizabethan logs as in the posthumous proliferation of Chatwin's notebooks; Samuel Johnson paid for his mother's funeral by writing the Abyssinian fable *Rasselas*. Although there has been no shortage of first-rate writers choosing to operate within the form, its force is collective and incremental rather than singular and aesthetic. The tactic of singling out texts such as Kinglake's *Eothen* or Byron's *The Road to Oxiana* as isolated masterpieces simply devalues the vast majority of these narratives.

Arguments for the expiry of the travel book in the post-war period ('travel is now impossible and tourism is all we have left' [Fussell 1980: 41]) have been notably ill-founded. As a popular genre, it has proved strikingly resilient; and in the hands of its most recent exponents, provides a niche for a distinctive kind of postmodern literacy. As Raban (1987) notes, travel writing 'accommodates the private diary, the essay, the short story, the prose poem, the rough note and polished table talk with indiscriminate hospitality' (p. 253): its perennially marginal position both grants a licence for idiosyncratic formal innovation, and allows the production of a self in the course of writing by means of perpetual detours into communal utterance, public codes.

The travel narrative is addressed to the home culture; by its very nature, however, that to which it refers cannot be verified, hence the ready and habitual equation of traveller and liar. This in turn requires the production of counter-balancing stratagems of sensory corroboration and complex decorums of witnessing, whose innovative plain style prefigures and is assimilated into the early novel. Yet this classification of precisely observed particulars remains in close conjunction with parody, high fantasy: the credibility of imaginary voyagers such as More and Swift depends on a kind of hyper-empiricism (McKeon 1987: 102–10).

The dividing line between fact and fiction, documentation and embellishment, is traditionally elusive: the extent of Marco Polo's travels, for instance, remains a hotly contested issue (Wood 1995). The romance origins of the genre preclude any simple opposition. The anthropaphagi in Ralegh serve as devices of authentication through classical allusion; as Hartog observes (1988: 230–7), marvels are necessary, they are what the audience expects.

Autopsy, the appeal to the testimony of the eyewitness, itself may be deconstructed into an illusion of an experiential present embedded in a commentary that necessarily exceeds and transgresses those criteria of authenticity. Seeing presupposes believing. Martin Frobisher's crew find 'a dead fish floating, which had in his nose a horn streight and torquet, of length two yards lacking two inches, being broken in the top ... By the virtue thereof we supposed it to be the Sea-unicorne' (Hakluyt 1925–28: V 144). A modern edition may perhaps gloss this as a narwhal, but for a contemporary reader, such things, like the dimensions of the Great Khan's palace or the average girth of a Midwestern farmer, must be taken on trust and corroborated by hearsay or stereotype, and may themselves eventually become markers of authenticity. The concept of reference needs itself to be contextually defined. Conflicting evidence cannot be readily ascribed to unreliable narration: divergence between travel testimonies is no proof of falsifiability because social rationality may be deduced according to radically divergent protocol (Pagden 1993: 2). Travel reference is to do with world-coherence: the book projects a world, and it is the ethics of inhabiting that alternative domain that are primarily at stake.

Thus the genre presents a problem for academic studies. It seems too dependent on an empirical rendition of contingent events, what happened to happen, for entry into the literary canon, yet too overtly rhetorical for disciplines such as anthropology, sociology, geography or history. For an Enlightenment philosopher such as Locke, travel books served as indispensable data of human diversity (Arneil 1996: 21–44); with the onset of twentieth-century professionalism, its residually fictive elements contaminated the archive. Over the last two decades, however, post-colonial studies has seized upon this very impurity of the form as an exemplary record of cross-cultural encounters between European and non-European peoples. Its powerful and innovative models of reading have made the question of travel inseparable from that of power and desire: asking not only who shall be master, but also what does master want?

Less authoritarian models of transit have been proposed by recent criticism: mobility within pre-European world systems (Abu-Lughod 1989); transnational movements such as the Atlantic triangle resistant to the gravitational pull of the metropolitan centre (Rediker 1987); reconstitution of a female politics of the local (Kaplan 1996); and the phenomenology of diaspora and other forms of enforced migrancy (Brah 1996). To a certain extent, however, travel writing is inevitably one-way traffic, because the Europeans mapped the world rather than the world mapping them. Travellers, merely through their greater access to the technology of transportation, implicitly belong to a more developed culture, and the strong historical connection of exploration with exploitation and occupation, justifiably make them figures to be feared and shunned.

The strong model of travel writing and empire would insist that their texts promote, confirm and lament the exercise of imperial power; and that this ideology pervades their representational practices at every level. As Dorothy Carrington (1947) observed half a century ago, 'if English travel literature tells how Englishmen have looked upon the world, inevitably it tells how they have acted in it. That is the story of the empire', adding with an exemplary clarity perhaps possible only at the moment of imperial demise, 'The object was trade and if necessary conquest' (p. 2). From a contemporary perspective, this 'historical taintedness' (Clifford 1997: 39) may appear to render the whole genre intrinsically invidious: its representations of otherness themselves become a form of incursion and violence, of interest only for its relative explicitness in demonstrating the workings of colonial power. Paradoxically it is this thesis, or variants upon it, that have foregrounded travel writing in recent criticism, with the corollaries of republication, presence on syllabuses, and generally higher profile and respect for its practitioners. Because of post-colonial scholarship, travel writing, particularly in its most racialist and imperialist guises, has become interesting for us again; but usually as a kind of love that dare not speak its name.

Empire is the common preoccupation of the essays in this volume, but their analyses seek to resist the reduction of cross-cultural encounter to simple relations of domination and subordination. The genre obviously overlaps with numerous other discourses of colonialism – bureaucratic instruction, demographic report, geographic mapping, military order, journalistic propaganda (Spurr [1993] acknowledges no distinction) – and the journey itself encodes inevitable ideological aspects: spiritual pilgrimage (Mandeville), mercantile prospectus (Hakluyt), mercenary campaign (Stedman), colonial expedition (Doughty). These do not however exhaust the potentialities of travel writing as a form: the self-reflexivity of the journey/ quest motif; its intricate layering of temporalities; and its allegorical resonances with regard to the traveller's own culture. Even the variant narratives of exile – those of the hostage, migrant or slave – do not preclude the experiences of curiosity and pleasure in new circumstances. If, as Gilroy

(1993) argues, in the black historical experience, 'movement, relocation, displacement and otherness are the norm rather than the exception', it remains necessary 'to refigure the cartography of dispersal and exile' (pp. 111–12), so as to avoid 'the folly of assigning uncoerced or recreational travel experiences only to whites' (p. 133). Interpretation of any specific travelogue must acknowledge not only its complicity, but also its power of refiguration and aspiration towards a more benign ethics of alterity. Travel books tell us something about something, and while structurally one might argue for a constitutive misrecognition, there is at the very least an ethical surplus (Greenblatt's [1991] insistence on wonder arguably idealises this quality, but usefully locates it).

The primary focus of this volume, with the exception of some attention to the Genoese Columbus, and to the French perspectives of Xavier Marmier and Leonie d'Aunet, is undeniably Anglocentric. As justification, one might cite Said's (1993) insistence that 'England of course is in an imperial class by itself, bigger, grander and more imposing than any other' (p. 22); Hassan (1990) on the '(largely British) pedigree' of the 'spirit of quest' (p. 3); or Theroux (1983) on British travel writing as 'a literary version of head-shrinking' (p. 4). I would prefer, however, to stress the diachronic dimension of the genre.

Post-colonial theory has made both the experience and the representation of transit a live and urgent issue: perhaps travel writing in its British variant may partially repay this debt by helping to define a before, during and after of the imperial voice. A strong hermeneutic might argue that the beginning implies the end and vice versa, but this would be to fail to acknowledge clear shifts of convention within a perennially mutating form. Close examination of its generic complexities highlights the contrasts as well as continuities in its internal evolution, which may offer a broader schema of periodisation for empire itself. This may in turn serve to check the post-colonial predilection for undue generality and homology on a global scale, and so facilitate a more nuanced, and perhaps more generous, comprehension of the textuality of imperialism.

This Introduction will begin by offering a brief chronology for both travel writing and empire; examine Said's varying characterisations of transit; look at certain generic resistances to any simplistic equation with the exercise of power; probe the issue of gender in the colonial imaginary; and conclude with individual introductions to the essays.

## Beginnings and Ends

Post-colonial criticism has favoured the textual model of imperialism as a malign system constituted by diffuse and pervasive networks of power.

According to Mary Louise Pratt's *Imperial Eyes* (1992), for instance, the collective European subject displays an 'obsessive need to present and re-present its peripheries and its others continually to itself' (p. 6): a model of power precisely mirrored in the patterns of signification internal to the text. This allows the possibility of reading against the grain to find in-digenous modes of expression and oppressed voices inscribed within the narratives of the conqueror. Every travel account is said to possess this 'heteroglossic function', but textual possibilities are sharply curtailed by clichés of 'the imperialists' inevitable bad faith' (pp. 135, 84): is this true, say, of the missionaries, and does it not posit a degree of foresight that is belied by the sheer ramshackle nature of most colonial beginnings? The staggering collectivity of the 'text of Euroimperialism' must be set against the subsequent admission that the 'material benefits accrued to very few' (in spite of the claim that 'the fruits of empire were pervasive in shaping European domestic society' [pp. 4, 6]). Furthermore, while the production of knowledge in natural history undoubtedly lends itself to a broadly Foucauldian reading, other aspects of the model, such as the production of subjectivity through a variety of forms of institutional apparatus, apply only partially to a colonial situation: at most to elites, with a degree of access to educational facilities, as part of their asymmetrical contract with the interloper.

Narratives of encounter are undeniably dominated by the viewpoint of the mobile culture, yet it is possible to exaggerate the degree of superiority implied. Certainly it is the sheer precariousness of medieval travel that is striking (Helms 1988: 247); and even the early projects of colonisation have an element of self-deluding bluff in them. Britain had no overseas territories at the time of publication of Hakluyt at the end of the sixteenth century; the slash-and-burn tactics of the privateers were directed primarily against other European powers, with the result that native cultures could be seen as potential allies The far-away places of the earth may presuppose a point from which they are defined and taxonomised. And yet in principle travel may be from the periphery to a stronger, if none the less exotic, culture (Herodotus to Egypt; Marco Polo to Cathay); and in a more contemporary guise, to the metropolitan centre: the post-war immigrant to London (Naipaul), the European to New York (Raban), the American to Tokyo (Iyer). If the structural function of the journey is to uncover, bring into relation, there are potential reversals by which the authority of home may be suspended, even repudiated. Travel writing's success as text, repres-entation, may be predicated on what Pratt (1992) terms its 'betrayal' of the imperial project (p. 5), and testimony to failure (in the La Condamine expedition or exploration of the Niger [pp. 18, 71: cf. Fuller 1995: 12]).

For an earlier imperial historiography, the nation-state evolved organically into empire; ironically, post-colonial theory, in rejecting such teleological assumptions, has posited an even more monolithic and omnipotent euro-centrism. Even granted a recent move to greater local discrimination, there is still a striking lack of dialogue with a more traditional historiography of decolonisation. Robert Young (1995), for example, assumes that Latin America is 'not an area where the English have played any great role' (p. 165), despite the well-established point in earlier 'post-colonial theory' on informal empire that British investment in the region, and consequent political influence, was greater than in many territories appropriated (prim-arily to prevent seizure by other European powers), but often extremely lightly administered (Robinson 1990: 50; cf. Pratt 1992: 10): Thesiger (1959) notes two Englishmen were considered sufficient for a Sudanese district of 50,000 square miles (p. 31). On a more theoretical level, one is almost shocked to find the 'in-betweenness' of the post-colonial subject expounded in the historian D. K. Fieldhouse (1984: 18–19).

Whatever the advantages of the textual model of imperialism, its 'syn-chronic essentialism' (Said 1979: 240) has rendered the question of origin unnecessarily vexed. Empire, and the narratives of cultural encounter in which it is encoded, is always ever-present: it becomes irrelevant to ask when it may have begun. If the classical period is bracketed, and the issue restricted to the rise to global predominance of a handful of European maritime nations, plausible suggestions would include the early Portuguese expeditions; more obviously Columbus's voyages; slightly later, the Seven Years War offers the first manifestation of a recognisably imperial strategy on a global scale, founded on British commercial strength consolidated in the early eighteenth century. In its more modern guise, buttressed by Darwinist economics and racialist eugenics, it might be placed as late as the Congress of Berlin and the post-1880 division of Africa.

According to Said (1979), 'from at least the second century BC on, it was lost on no traveller or eastward-looking and ambitious Western potentate, that Herodotus – historian, traveller, inexhaustibly curious chronicler – and Alexander – king, warrior, scientific conqueror – had been in the Orient before' (p. 57). Such a hazy retrospective vista occludes the fact that ancient Persia was politically and militarily stronger than Aeschylus's Greece (p. 21) (just as Dante's Christendom was backward compared to medieval Islam); and Said's recurrent Occidentalism ('the general European effort to rule distant lands and peoples'; 'Europe's special ways of representing') is little help in specifying the precise causes of the ascendancy gained by a handful of Atlantic-coastal nations. There was no automatic given in 1500, 1600, even 1700, that these would triumph (see Wolf 1982): probably the most coherent imperial administration remained the Ottoman (Bayly 1989:19; also note Kinglake's for 'Turks of the proud old school' [1992: 3]). Even during the eighteenth century, it was perfectly possible for Indian rulers to defeat European armies, although usually with the help of technological aid bought in from rivals (though effective control of the continent was achieved by the British after victory at Plassey in 1767).

Thus 'the period of extraordinary European ascendency from the late Renaissance to the present' is by no means 'unbroken or undisputed' (Said 1979: 7). Said's argument is viable only if restricted to 'the period of unparalleled European expansion: from 1815–1914' (p. 41); and even this can be segmented into the late nineteenth-century rush for empire and an earlier free trade policy in the 1840s. High imperialism occupies a relatively brief period from the mid-nineteenth to the early twentieth century; and 'formal conquest, annexation and administration' were by no means even then, as Mills (1991: 1) claims, 'the most common relation'. The 'effort to rule' is often presented as a kind of collective phenomenological a priori, grounded on technological superiority and religious absolutism. Yet this predatory will is difficult to reconcile with more detailed studies conducted by cost-benefit analysis: the circumspection and misgivings connected with the responsibilities of territorial expansion, the relatively late flowering of full-blown jingoist ideologies, the comparative popular indifference to the process of decolonisation. If the English hardly 'conquered and peopled half the world in a fit of absence of mind', as Seeley proposed (1909: 10), it is difficult to discern consistency in their long-term policies: the first British Empire was abruptly terminated with the loss of its prime colony in 1783, and the first stages of decolonisation began with Canada in the 1820s. Imperial free trade, generally seen as the most profitable relation, involved abstention: Said mentions the 'fairly normal and secure connection with the empire' of 'colonial businessmen', but does not see the potential disjunction of attitude. Defining empire in terms of 'prevailing discourse' rather than as a patchwork of discontinuous and at times contradictory interests seems far closer to world-systems theory than imperial history; and Said at certain points even appears to approve of this 'globalised process'. If 'one of imperialism's achievements was to bring the world closer together', then it may, as Gellner argues (1994: 162), be seen as a one-way process of technological transformation, whose injustices were arguably no worse than those internal to the societies it colonised.

The end of empire is similarly debatable. The disengagement of creole and settler colonies from the metropolis from the early decades of the nineteenth century becomes, in Benedict Anderson's argument (1983), the crucible of modern nationalism. A more general consensus would be the period of post-war decolonisation between 1945 and 1960. Even here, the process was far from completed, as the recent handover of Hong Kong makes clear; and a separate argument needs to be made on dependency theory and the continued formative influence of US neocolonialism (de la Campa et al. 1995). Furthermore, most national narratives allow for a post-colonial phase: 'an ancient Roman factory villa in this province of Britain could suddenly after two or three centuries simply with a letting-go of authority ... crumble into ruin' (Naipaul 1987: 292; see also Ahmad 1995). There is no single colonialism, rather differing practices by a variety of cultures over a long historical time-span. Yet, as Nicholas Thomas (1994) comments, post-colonial theory has tended to 'put Fanon and Lacan (or Derrida) in a blender and take the result to be equally applicable for premodern and modern; for African, Asian and American; for metropolitan, settler, indigenous and diasporic subjects' (p. ix). The practical and intelligible decision-making processes of imperial elites are replaced by highly abstract and monocausal explanations whose plausibility reduces in proportion to the amplitude of their claims. The unqualified nature of such a unitary model of empire is its strength as political exhortation, condition as moral diatribe, and limitation as rhetorical criticism; as a consequence, the traveller cannot do other than reproduce its fundamental structures of oppression with varying degrees of blatancy. Yet even in the British context, the period of high imperialism is relatively brief, and contains its own sardonic forms of self-undermining which continue into the odddly evacuated stance of postmodern travelogue.

Pratt's *Imperial Eyes* (1992) poses as its basic question: 'How has travel-writing produced the rest of the world for European readerships at particular points in Europe's expansionist trajectory' (p. 5). The hyperbolic formulation (surely many other practices of representation are involved) suggests that far from 'demystifying imperialism', at the present juncture some greater appreciation of its productive force might be in order: 'the vast discontinuous and over-determined history of imperial meaning-making' may offer further possibilities beyond a tautologous ritual of indictment of its 'redundancy, discontinuity and unreality' (pp. 4, 2). The reception argument also needs to be pinned down far more closely (particularly the class and gender of audiences): who actually reads travel books? If the discovery itself has no existence of its own without the traveller (or other survivor) returning and bringing it into being through texts, this process of 'meaning-making' requires further clarification, particularly if travel writing is to be regarded as 'having produced the rest of the world' for a home audience.

Obviously, there was travel in the ancient world, in the sense of geo-graphical movement between cultures, both in Herodotus's fundamental division between home and abroad, the national self and the collective other, and as Casson (1994) amply demonstrates, in the development of a complex touristic infrastructure (the Greek Pausanias composed the first guidebook in the second century A.D.). It is at the very least arguable, however, whether the precise conjunction of witnessing, testimony and narrativised anecdote characteristic of post-Renaissance European travel writing previously existed.

Raban's (1987) protest – 'Up till now criticism has shunned the travel book' (p. 253; cf. Kowalewski 1992: 1) – has more than a hint of special pleading. Hakluyt has long been central to accounts of the development of English prose, and the form figures prominently in accounts of the evolution of the realist novel (Defoe) and subsequent mutations of romance (Haggard). There appears, moreover, no apparent obstacle to its admission into the post-colonial canon, and it is obvious that texts such as Columbus's *Journals*, Hawkesworth's *Voyages*, and Kingsley's *Travels* are accorded a new prominence from this perspective. What counts as travel writing has been historically variable. Medieval writings flaunt their exotic wonders in contrast to the early modern insistence upon prosaic actuality; high imperial travelogues engage in robust heroics whereas twentieth-century texts assert their whimsical exquisiteness. A genealogy locating its development within the later seventeenth century, anticipated by Hakluyt and Purchas, no longer seems adequate, although a specific market-space probably emerged during that period. In the broadest sense, it might expand to include all forms of textual documentation of cultural interchange; as indeed Pratt (1992: 2) is inclined to take it (analysing native artefacts such as weaving and pottery as counter-narratives).

If travel writing is approached inductively and empirically – which texts continue to be interesting – the productive force of imperial ideology must be acknowledged. The genre may be of interest not because it evades these 'social and perceptual biases' but because it foregrounds them (Kowalewski 1992: 10). The power to generate meaning tends to be reduced to cynical legitimation of more basic and brutal mechanisms of power; but such a characterisation is clearly inadequate. The British Empire, for example, was remarkably unreliant upon, indeed positively abhorred, expensive military action: it was far-flung, run on the cheap, kept ticking over; and, when it could no longer show a profit, promptly disbanded. This ideology may be seen in terms of imposition, something cruelly inflicted, although as a body of institutional practices – political, judicial, educational – it has shown considerable staying-power. Its after-life may appear something sinister, but it is capable of being viewed more positively. If fascism is colonialism practised in Europe (R. Young 1990: 8), then so is the nation-state (Anderson), the advanced education system (Viswanathan) and so on.

The imperial type produced by nineteenth-century educational practices – physically robust, well-trained if unintellectual, a competent administrator and, when necessary, an effective soldier – has been mocked for over a century; but certain ethical qualities here are surely deserving of greater respect. More patient documentation (such as Tidrick 1990) produces a more complex and by no means uniformly unappealing picture of the empire in action. What is most striking is the sense of mission, of entitlement combined with self-denial. The most flagrant ethnocentrism is inseparable from what was strongest and arguably most honourable in the imperial ideal: commitment to collective endeavour, asceticism, resilience and practicality.

All modern British travellers live in awe of the achievements of an earlier overtly imperial generation. However much their chauvinism may be deplored, what is fundamental and creditable in the genre still draws its power in large measure from this self-belief. The belatedness of the contemporary form, the continued defensive allusions to a pre-ironic persona, indicate a continued indebtedness. Post-war travel writing has undoubtedly become more sensitised to ethnic stereotyping and cultural condescension: structurally and generically, however, it refuses to relinquish its basic prerogatives. The certifiably postmodern strategies – duplication of quest, self-mockery, melancholic undertones – cannot detract from a kind of constitutive affiliation. O'Hanlon (1984) reasserts family links with the SAS, however facetiously (p. 3); even a text such as Tete-Michel Kpomassie's *An African in Greenland* defers to that heritage (Bartowski 1995: 62–81). To repudiate the legacy of colonialism would involve not merely a self-indictment but a self-annulment; instead, there is a therapeutic rite of playing the roles through with nonchalant detachment.

The chief fascination of the contemporary travel genre lies in this project of formulating an acceptable, or perhaps less culpable, post-imperial voice. Support for this position will now be sought in the perhaps unexpected quarter of travelling theory.

## Travel Theory versus Travel Practice

Said's *Orientalism* (1979) boldly crosses discipline boundaries, and pays the price of attracting a correspondingly broad range of criticism. In the context of these well-known problematics, the specific analyses of travel writing tend to be overlooked. The book's subject-matter is initially declared to be 'a very large mass of writers, among whom are poets, novelists, philosophers, political theorists, economists and imperial administrators' (p. 2), conspicuously excluding travel writers; there is a similar omission from 'the scientist, the scholar, the missionary, the trader or the soldier' (p. 7); only twenty pages in does the genre finally appear: 'I set out to examine not only scholarly works but also works of literature, political tracts, journalistic texts, travel books, religious and philosophical studies' (p. 23). 'From travellers' tales and not only from great institutions like the various India companies, colonies were created and ethnocentric perspectives secured' (p. 117): a strong, even bizarrely overstated claim, in which 'tales' again appear distinct from literature, very much in the tradition of the travel-lie. And yet 'even the most innocuous travel book ... contributed to the density of public awareness of the Orient' (p. 192).

Such occasional and rather offhand references are by no means unusual. James Clifford (1997) also combines casual disparagement of travel literature '(in the bourgeois sense)' for its 'inextinguishable taint' of 'literariness' (p. 38) with praise of its generic inclusiveness: New Guinea entrepreneur-chief Joe Leahy 'is the sort of figure who turns up in travel books, though not in traditional ethnographies' (p. 26). In Said (1979), however, a more central issue is raised: if 'Orientalism is after all a system for citing texts and authors' (p. 1), the travel genre, with its continuous re-enactment of earlier journeys, becomes not a marginal case but a central paradigm: a startling feat of ideological productivity. It is not necessarily an indictment to say 'even the most imaginative writers ... were constrained in what they could either experience or say about the Orient' (p. 43); it is the very condition of their creativity.

'To be a European in the Orient', hence a traveller, 'always implies being a consciousness set apart from and unequal with its surroundings' (p. 157): despite the inevitable participation in the logistics of travel (such as Cook's tours to Egypt), the 'watcher' is 'never involved, always detached' (p. 103). A tripartite distinction is made between residence for quasi-scientific observation; the adducing of individual style to a comparable official mission; and an individual quest. Yet 'in all cases the Orient is for the European observer a place of pilgrimage' (p. 158): an over-determined term, which conflates empirical reference to the biblical domain; a residual context of medieval journeying; and an internalisation of this as spiritual quest. All three variants offer the Orient 'firstly as spectacle or tableau vivant; then in terms of a comprehensive interpretation (or attempt at it)'; but viewing and commentating are equally pre-inscribed because 'in travel writing the copyist and witness co-exist' (pp. 158, 156).

Said's French terms of reference are readily assimilated to a high 'Romantic idea of restorative reconstruction', and the 'existential vocation' of the 'literary pilgrims' – Chateaubriand, Nerval, Flaubert – is correspondingly cosseted (p. 168). In their work, 'the ego dissolves itself in the contemplation of the wonders it creates, and then is reborn stronger than ever' (p. 170). The self-aggrandisement of their texts provides aesthetic compensation for lack of actual political control (pp. 175–6). The British, in contrast, wielded greater influence in the region; hence their travelogues are regarded as necessarily bound up with the exercise of power. In Said's specific readings, this thesis apparently precludes internal dissonance, or scruple or openness. Lane provides his copious taxomonies at the expense of 'literally abolish[ing] himself as a human subject by refusing to marry into human society' (p. 163), regardless of his erotic attraction and un-moralising tributes to the courtesan-dancers (Lane 1836: II 97); Kinglake exerts 'a public and national will over the Orient' despite *Eothen*'s ironic foregrounding of the most abrasive aspects of 'the being obliged more or less to make one's way by bullying' (Said 1979: 194; Kinglake 1992: 130); Burton's 'individuality perforce encounters and merges with the voice of Empire' (Said 1979: 196) despite the counterpoint of his overtly anti-imperial footnotes ('when in the history of the world do we ever read that such domination made itself popular' [Burton 185: 37n]).

This determinedly reductive account needs to be revised in accordance with Said's expositions of travelling theory, the renewal of intellectual concepts through geographical relocation, altered sites of enunciation. 'Ideas or Ideologies must be reworked to adapt to new cultural conditions' (Said 1984: 226): if this is so for Auerbach, why not for Sir William Jones? An idealised version of theory in transit, however, paradoxically becomes the grounds for a more general indictment of travel as narrative (Thomas 1994: 7). In 'Representations of the Intellectual', for example, 'the pleasure of being surprised, of never taking anything for granted, of learning to make do in circumstances of shaky instability that would confound or terrify most people' is exemplified in Marco Polo, whose 'sense of the marvelous never fails him and who is always a traveler, a provisional quester, not a freeloader, a conqueror or a raider' (Said 1994: 44; contrast Islam 1996). If clemency can be extended to this emissary of European culture, why not to other travellers? As generic definition, 'the double perspective' of the exile who 'sees things both in terms of what has been left behind and what is actual here and now' is surely preferable to positing an interminable reiteration of the archive (Said 1994: 44). In an almost Kiplingesque exhortation, Said insists

> Exile means that you are always going to be marginal, and that what you do
> as an intellectual has to be made up because you cannot follow a prescribed
> path. If you can experience that fate not as a deprivation and as something
> to be bewailed, but as a sort of freedom, a process of discovering in which
> you do things according to your own dictates: that is a unique pleasure.
> (Said 1994: 46)

Delight in one's own unimpeded 'dictates' seems difficult to reconcile with the 'prescribed path' of expulsion by an occupying power; and the forthright individualism of this account of exile also appears to deny the collectivity of diaspora. Political dispossession here actively enhances personal liberty. The enforced journey, the interdiction on return, becomes redemptive, producing the qualities of sprightliness, alertness, a certain malleability from living between cultures: in a fundamental self-reflexivity, encountering new cultures involves greater awareness of one's own; an act of witnessing that enlarges rather than appropriates.

The unexplored conjunction is of the empowered intellectual. Post-colonial theory is eminently recuperable in terms of the self-advancement of a new mobile intelligentsia; itself as much a form of cultural capital as an older narration of discovery (Ahmad 1992: 85–7). One might somewhat caustically claim that Said's version of travelling theory grants to this new elite all the beneficial and privileged perspectives denied to the imperial traveller. I would resist any such facile disparagement of his work on the grounds of intellectual ferment, historical reparation, and the evolution of an ethics appropriate to an increasingly globalised community. However, if its utopian version of the voyage inward is to be spared a demystifying reading, why should not the same degree of exemption be granted to other forms of travel narrative? I now wish to examine certain resistances within the genre to any over-hasty assimilation with the exercise of power.

### 'Notoriously Bad at Saying Why'

Travellers are 'notoriously bad at saying why' (Spufford 1996: 2). They may be distinguished from realist characters through the virtual absence of individual motivation. There are remarkably few direct avowals of either positive impulses of curiosity or invigorating novelty, or negative ones of grief or bereavement (the death of Smollett's daughter, for instance, goes virtually unremarked). The very fact of isolation paradoxically accentuates their exemplary status as a representative social entity. (Reference to companions is avoided even when simple logistics imply quite large-scale expeditions.) The traveller has no inside (cf. Batten 1978: 13); or rather the simple fact of separation from family, home and community makes him or her susceptible to perpetual redefinition through encounter. The hero of adventure is a proleptic concept: a status conferred by challenges to be undergone.

Centring the genre round the figure of the traveller appears to make the form a sub-species of autobiography: 'mere outpourings of a mind full of self' (Burton 1857: I 4); 'a sadly long strain about Self' (Kinglake 1992: 12). Any direct equation of interior development with physical movement, however, should be viewed with suspicion. The narrative voice places the action in the past (although use of present tenses may partially mitigate this); but that past itself has a future which is the temporal progression of the journey, and which can never be regarded as simply synonymous with the older self. Memory and recollection are themselves social and inter-actional: without this continual negotiation, they become vulnerable to the charge of 'self-therapy: the solipsistic attraction of turning a travel account into merely a personal diary, a kind of therapist's couch' (Kowalewski 1992: 9).

Travel as rest-cure is a familiar eighteenth- and nineteenth-century topos (Sterne, Fielding); but the travel writer *qua* travel writer tends not to display personal neurosis. The form resists, if not entirely precludes, such introspection. Its comparative robustness derives from coping with, not necessarily hardship, but voluntarily self-imposed disruption, whose motivation must be sought in broader communal patterns, which precede and envelop the traveller. The invented past through which the writer projects his or her identity remains collective, formed by political and historical sedimentation. Travel paradoxically foregrounds conditioning: part of the fascination of the form is its pre-inscription of role, its accuracy as reflector of cultural status (or lack of it).

On the simplest level, in travel writing there is a transfer of information to an experiential witnessing: what has been absorbed from research or, more cynically, guidebooks, has to be absorbed into structures of anecdote, narratives of self-comprehension and parables of rectified ignorance. On the dramatic level, the ever fallible narrator is seen as misapplying the categories of his home culture. Comedy is intrinsic to the genre: mis-understanding, presumption, and the catalogue of errors and endemic lack of dignity to which any cross-cultural interchange must be sensible.

Yet there is also a counter-empiricist tendency. Set against the gradual and patient accumulation of knowledge through particular experiences, there is the figure of the travel writer who already knows, conscious of the predecessors whose quests may be re-enacted; and with continuous recourse to a broader range of external comparisons. Apparently disconnected anecdote continues to be structured according to culturally instilled norms: most obviously, the frame of classical (and implicitly aggressively imperial-ist) reference of Renaissance travellers (Hulme 1986; Pagden 1993). Even the desire to be different may be seen as part of a historically specific move from the social integration implied by the Grand Tour to the authority of original subjectivity in the post-Romantic period (itself a re-enactment of a finite repertoire of Byronic postures [Buzard 1993a: 120–1]).

Against the thesis of perpetual reconfirmation, however, may be set the fact of departure, initial severance from a home culture. On some level, even the most dyspeptic traveller has a preference for abroad through the mere fact of being there; he or she may fairly be assumed to be untypical through the very fact of journeying, which in narrative terms is always motivated by (thus an admission of) deficiency and lack. This perhaps invites existential or psychoanalytic interpretation; but simpler points may still be made. The traveller was previously ill-adapted to his or her own society; the narrative becomes a plea for readmission.

Travel writing may appear to presuppose a desacralised world-view: even for the pilgrim Mandeville (1967), 'Of Paradys ne can I ne speken propurly, for I was not there. It is fer beyonde, and that forthinketh me, and also I was not worthi' (p. 220). Yet there are stylistic precedents in heavily typological modes (the Authorised Version, Bunyan); and the implicit declaration of leisure and affluence in travel (Rojek 1993) must be set against the possible context of guilt, flight and disgrace (von Martles 1994). Travel may enlarge the mind, but exile degrades, demeans: if the journey is an escape from, one might expect the 'call to pleasure' (D. Porter 1991: 10) to predominate, yet this is subordinated to the element of expiation. If the traveller has penance done, the implicit motivation of the narrative is that he or she penance more must do (Adams 1983: 69). The model of wanderer as exile, sin-bearing, condemned – the medieval denunciation of errancy – becomes a paradoxical source of narrative energy in its refusal of closure.

A proleptic reading is again possible: the traveller, whose mythic resonances must inevitably include the conqueror, the usurper, the enslaver, is guilty of what is to be done. The fact of isolation presupposes the collectivity of prior formation, and the fundamental lack, which necessitates departure and the act of narration, may be regarded as a simple pretext for imperial expansion embedded in a variety of historically specific ideologies: from the feudal knight to the international businessman (Nerlich 1987). The stranger may appear weak, vulnerable, even potentially ludicrous; yet is also typologically inscribed with menace, if not doom: always someone to be suspected, as a spy, an informant, an agitator (Hartog 1988: 313). (Smollett [1979: 215] suggests suitable positions for 'not only a bombardment but even of a cannonade' along the Riviera; German bombers carried out 'Baedeker raids' against prominent landmarks during the Blitz [see Ousby 1990: 4]).

The lacuna of motivation in the western genre of travel writing may itself be read as an encoding of a collective urge to dominate; and certainly the history of European colonialism gives some credence to the positing of a destructive impulse within the interstices of narrative grammar, a genetic pre-programming to destroy. Certain more extreme readings of alterity in the wake of Levinas would argue that there is always a potential violence in the bringing to language: of reduction, of instrumentality, of intrinsic abuse. From such a viewpoint, every journey is an incursion into, potentially threatening, historically catastrophic; better never to have been born than to have travelled thus.

Yet the traveller undergoes and suffers as well as acts and achieves. Captivity narratives are by no means exclusively non-European: for example, the sixteen-year exile of Miles Philips, crew member abandoned by John Hawkins in the West Indies, and enslaved by the Spanish (Hakluyt 1925–28: VI 296–336). Travel itself also has its oddly passive aspects: after all, it is often boring, and requires tolerance of repetition as much as surmounting of ordeals. The narrative impulse of identification is not necessarily one of simple empowerment.

The traveller as hero is one of a number of common features with the genre of romance: quest, obstacles, destination. Rather than elaborate on these affinities, however, I now wish to examine certain dissimilarities that resist any simple reduction to travel writing with the exercise of imperial power.

## Travel as Romance: Power, Contingency and Closure

Romance might appear an implicitly optimistic form: challenges confronted, tasks fulfilled, missions accomplished. In travel writing, however, the solitary and existential aspects of the form predominate: sex, for instance, is more an occupational hazard than desired outcome, and there is no comic pattern of marriage, reproduction and renewal of generations. Even within Frye's (1957) system of modes, the genre may mutate over time into its apparent opposites: tragedy, in terms of the death of the protagonist (Willoughby, Cook); but more customarily satire. The traveller-commentator may deliver bilious comments on the native culture, but readily becomes an object of mirth if not derision. The persona is also implanted, infected, with foreignness. Return embodies elements of defeat with those of triumph: it implies survival and resilience, but also rejection by the foreign environment, even a self-characterisation as a figure of contagion (Helms 1988: 16).

Post-1700, a low mimetic style is set against, but also arguably reactivates, the resonances of a quasi-heroic mode. This necessitates a division in the self-consciousness of the hero, a passive encountering of external circumstances against a deliberate scripting of a life-narrative. There is an element of wilfulness, of self-inflictedness: travel writing appears as much about the invention of difficulty as its circumvention. Typically there is a suspension of goal-directedness, even an element of overt parody: O'Hanlon's self-imposed ordeals are no more intrinsically absurd than Columbus's search for Cathay. The object of pursuit is repeatedly exposed as illusion, but this merely raises the question of the desire for sustaining the deception.

The romance insistence on initial transgression and eventual reward is elided in the travel book: 'The vertue of thinges is in the middes'

(Mandeville 1967: 1). It is necessarily an interim form, authenticating itself both as private record and public documentation, defining a self through a journey (the eighteenth-century preference for editorial rewriting of first-person testimony in third-person narration exacerbates rather than resolves the problem [Adams 1983: 162–3]). The present-tense narration insists on the coincidence of past and present selves, though the hindsight of maturity is present in numerous indirect markers. The relation to the audience can only be present as an afterthought: it is inadmissible to declare the purpose of journeying as 'I travel to write' (Butor 1994: 53).

Unlike the *Bildungsroman*, there is little detail of the early domestic setting: the performative utterance that opens the narrative is 'I went'. Structurally, this is A to B; but A is present only through implicit contrast with subsequent sojourns and destination. Something very strange has always already happened in every travel narrative: the decision to be there, rather than here, and yet still to wish to be heard here. The telling must be on home ground, or at least a voice articulated within the home culture. Conversely, the native can thus never fully know the intruder, whose testimony becomes a kind of secret withheld, a ritual of communal bonding achieved through this very act of exclusion.

This journey may be seen as a refusal, a resistance, or as an expulsion, an ignominious flight. If it is viewed as a means of initiation, of crossing not merely between cultures but also of earning entitlement and status within one's own culture, where is the point of completion? The idea of destination is intrinsically problematic: the round trip, the moment of reinscription is implicit in the production of the book, but seldom developed within the text. The traveller is altered, sometimes changed utterly, but primarily in the sense of being made capable of more travel. Fussell (1980) claims that 'the action, as the quest romance, must be completed' (p. 209); but the genre is characteristically bereft of concluding ruminations, the lessons of experience.

Travellers return: their traces are ephemeral. They must remain in order to comprehend, but the simple fact of temporal residence would remove the original frisson of interrogation of and by the other. Hence a firm demarcation needs to be drawn with settlement literature (Carter 1987), and indeed the duration traditionally required of anthropological fieldwork (Clifford 1997: 58–9). Yet there is a conspicuous reluctance to embark on the homeward journey, and ruthless excision of any actual moment of reincorporation by friends and family. The omission endows the persona with a self-sufficiency within its textual manifestation. The biographical individual may slough off this skin, but the break remains: the lack of continuity between the two realms allows the possibility of extreme reversal. Virtually no reference is made to any future life. We do not and cannot predict what will become of the traveller on account of his or her travels.

Granted this structural lacuna, what could count as success? The temporal dimension of the spatial journey hints at ultimate mortality: arrival at the Heavenly City as a post-mortem state. The traveller is always leaving; both voyaging and narration presuppose continuous deferral; there is always one more destination to this 'unfinished story with an inconclusive plot' (Raban 1986: 503). Anecdote matters more than commentary, digression than sequence. The present voice guarantees past survival; yet in this autobiographical merger of voices, it is possible to detect an elegiac note, a preference for the younger, mobile, strenuous self, an unconsoledness in the maturer reflection. There is a structural principle of loss involved; the condition of utterance is the biological life of the body: 'and now that I am comen hom mawgree myself to reste for gowtes artetykes that me distreynen, that diffynen the ende of my labour ayenst my wille, God knoweth' (Mandeville 1967: 229). Even the modern tourist itinerary with its echoes of medieval pilgrimage in sacred sights, liminal zones, holy relics, possesses something of the same *memento mori* quality: 'so ghastly my countenance, that timorous child had abstained from my house, for fear of the ill consequences of looking at me' (Fielding 1997: 141). The story appears to confirm survival, but publication itself, though a form of immortality, may be seen as a kind of animus against the living self. The traveller *qua* traveller is a textual figment, synonymous with the duration of the tale, the voice of the dead.

These sombre allegorical resonances at the very least qualify any simplistic equation of travel with enhancement of power. Rather, as Dennis Porter (1991) comments, 'it is difficult to avoid reading into the repeated demand for the new, a desire for the end' (p. 11). At this point, support could be sought in the thesis of sublimation as the 'animating force behind empire-building, love's loss as empire's gain' (see Hyams 1990: 10). Simply demographically, a strikingly high number of British colonial administrators married late, if at all, and remained childless; though the alternative French tradition of approved concubinage should be noted (pp. 214–15). On a personal level travel implies not gratified desire, but continuous sacrifice, even, one might speculate, a manifestation of the Freudian death-drive.

The heroic qualities of the traveller – resilience, physical courage, intrepidity – would also seem to categorise the figure as implicitly male. The masculinist bias of genre studies such as Butor, Fussell and Raban is matched if not exceeded by the androcentric emphasis of much post-colonial theory (Wolff 1995). Its use of psychoanalysis primarily in terms of collective intentionality has the side-effect of excising discussion of sexual desire, and all question of gender-specificity. There is notoriously little consideration of the issue in Bhabha (1994a); Dennis Porter (1991) restricts his discussion to male writers, thereby evading the problem; even Trin T. Minh-ha (1996) avoids any specifically feminine variant of a Lacanian model. I now wish to examine this apparent gender imbalance in relation to a broader colonial imaginary.

### 'What are the Women Like?'

According to Richard Burton (1853), this was inevitably 'the first question of mankind to the wanderer' (vol. I, p. 85): a circuit of exchange which may appear exclusively masculine. Men have undeniably travelled more, and left more records of their journeys; but this does not imply an intrinsic exclusion of women from the genre. Female travel writers were a comparative rarity before the nineteenth century, and almost exclusively aristocratic. As well as the question of access to financial resources, basic literacy would have provided a sharp cut-off point, and the importance of the simple issue of physical security should not be underestimated. Thereafter the numbers increase rapidly, not merely as accompanying wife or mother, but also in the professional roles of writer, missionary and nurse (Melman 1991).

Travel writing clearly lends itself to the extrapolation of a dubious sexual archetypalism: 'The Spermatic Journey' (Leed 1991: 217–37) is perhaps the most egregious example, but, as Karen Lawrence (1994) observes, 'to varying degrees, all the studies of adventure and travel cited above encode the traveller as a male who crosses boundaries and penetrates spaces; the female is mapped as a place on the itinerary of the male journey' (p. 2). Frye (1976) stresses the feminine element of guile in romance, craft over force (pp. 66–8); Zweig (1974) sees the lady as performing a necessary magical initiation (p. 68). Narrative roles at the level of depth structure, however, tend not merely to reinforce stereotype – knight pursues damsel – but actively to excise the figures of mother and wife and so repress all contact with the female body. (Though arguably it re-emerges in such motifs as the eroticisation of landscape [Spurr 1993: 170–83].)

There is an obvious oedipal resonance to the journey: the moment of departure represents the son's refusal to stay within the *oikos* or household and so defy paternal authority by embarking on a rite of passage from adolescence to adulthood. Part of the pleasure of the genre might lie in its abandonment and disavowal of certain bonds – kinship, marital, family – which normally appear all-constraining. Travel might thus be seen, in highly abstract terms, as a refutation of the father, and a denial of intimacy with the mother: the necessary condition of entry into language and access unto law.

Yet if the traveller may seem to undertake a self-begetting, a rebirth in terms of his own narrative self-constitution, many traditional areas of masculine authority are annulled: absence of control over the domestic domain; removal from accustomed areas of work-expertise; and vulnerability to unpredictable encounters. (Spufford [1996: 104] argues that Arctic expedition feminises the male traveller by making him more aware of co-operative virtues, the domestic space of the tent; Fuller [1995: 171] notes the 'visible surrender of the body in suffering'.)

Raban (1987) identifies the novel with the 'institution of the family', lives outside of which are 'inherently minor or tragic or aberrant' (p. 224). Travel writing, in contrast, is founded upon an almost irresistible imperative to abandon home, wife and children. (Wollstonecraft is nowhere more transgressive than in acknowledging her daughter's presence.) This might be expected to produce a hedonist ethos, if only through negative definition, and the travel genre is traditionally associated with licentious wandering: the sexual promiscuity of the picaro (Nashe); the erotic Utopias of Pacific voyages (Bougainville); the premeditated indulgence of the Grand Tour (Boswell); the erotic reverie of the orientalist (Flaubert); the homosexual freedom of the interwar Mediterranean ambience (Douglas). Plentiful examples of libertine conduct can be found: and one can argue for the editing out of the colonial mistress as simple stylistic decorum (for example, the economic basis to Stedman's [1992] 'Surinam marriage' with his native lover, Joanna [p. 21]). More usually, however, despite the frequent worldliness of the injunction to travel (Chesterfield demands his illegitimate son take mistresses), the convention is one of abstinence. Travellers seldom pursue seduction, and are surprisingly unamenable to being seduced; even Burton feels obliged to exclude his own sexual adventurism from the text.

There seems an accentuation of puritanism within the home culture as if the male traveller wished to escape not only sexual desire but even the desire for desire. The intrinsic logic seems to involve not merely the deferral or displacement of pleasure, but its nullification: an implicit vow of celibacy for the duration of the journey. (Waugh [1930] recasts his honeymoon trip so as to exclude all mention of his bride: the ethnographic taboo on sexual contacts in the field is equally stringent [Clifford 1997: 71–2].) The generic premise that the traveller will show interest in and be exposed to the world necessarily subordinates erotic or familial ties to accidental and contingent encounters. There is an equalisation, a reduction of everything and everyone to raw material, that is flagrant and brutal: 'the dangerous morality of an existence of temporary pick-ups and friendships, of people dropped as soon as met, of the indifferent, deep egoism of moving for moving's sake' (Raban 1986: 183). The categorising onlooker subordinates all interest in others to a kind of primal narcissism: the

importance of the journey takes precedence over all other human attachments, a love of self that permits the removal of all alternative ties. One
could by extension read the book itself as the long-deferred message. But
the extraordinary denial of expressions of human affection as a condition
for embarking upon the quest remains bizarre, almost frightening; the
journey becomes the search for and the reconfirmation of the loss of love,
and consequent redirection of an almost libidinal intensity upon the self.

Masculinity is thus neither endorsed nor enhanced by the role of
traveller, which displays a comparative sexlessness, certainly a lack of
affectivity in personal relations. This absence of interiority allows the
persona to embody European culture and its attendant urge to appropriate
and erase, or, less dramatically, to categorise and comprehend; the evacuation of individuality enacts submission to the imperial mission. Again,
the cost exacted is far more striking than any apparent rewards; the primary
object of aggression is the self.

In *Discourses of Difference*, Sara Mills (1991) defines her central question
as 'how was this colonial strength' (perhaps a questionable term) 'negotiated
in texts by women who were conventionally seen not to be part of the
colonial expansion?' (p. 1). The initial segregation is historically questionable. Femininity is bound up with empire well before conventions of inter-
marriage or concubinage fell victim to nineteenth-century racial taxonomies
and the advent of the memsahib (Chaudhuri and Strobel 1992). Elizabethan
imperialism pays continuous tribute to the Virgin Queen (Montrose 1991);
eighteenth-century ideologies of domesticity enthusiastically draw upon
the colonial imaginaries of tea, coffee and sugar (Nussbaum 1995).

For an earlier phase of gender studies, female travel writing was exemplary for its transposition of the romance conventions of heroic agency
on to the woman traveller, providing her with a rare opportunity to display
the qualities of the male adventurer (Frawley 1994). Furthermore, if
imperial ideology is regarded as a masculine domain, it becomes possible
to celebrate the female traveller as in flight from domestic oppression
rather than as complicit in domination abroad. Occasional recourse to a
more traditional chivalric rhetoric makes an appeal for protection which
the simple logistics of the genre overwhelmingly refutes. Freya Stark (1982)
in Arabia thanks the RAF for gallantly airlifting her out (pp. 287–8), but
the getting-there and the qualifications for coping – linguistic, physical –
remain her own.

An element of doubling is always present: the persona of adventurer
may be inhabited, but always with a degree of circumspection. She who
travels presupposes she who remains: Penelope sedente. Femininity is
preserved in inauspicious circumstances not only in Mary Kingsley's pre-
occupation with dress in the African jungle, but also by default in Robyn

Davidson's (1980) 'obsession with social graces and female modesty' when menstruating in the Australian desert (p. 206). If the desire to depart may plausibly be seen as a repudiation of femininity on a number of levels – maternal embrace, conjugal fidelity – the female traveller is at the very least a site of generic contradiction.

Mills's commitment to discourse theory poses an immediate and acute methodological problem: how can one preserve the interpretative force of the model (one never in Foucault applied to a colonial context) without eliding the constitutive category of gender? The mapping of power on to patriarchy desexualises both structures, with the result that the initial category of 'texts by women' itself appears to dissolve. Formal criteria for viewing women's travel writing 'on its own terms' (Mills 1991: 6) are surprisingly difficult to establish. They cannot be located in varying authority of testimony: the problem of 'exaggeration and falsehood' (p. 13) is intrinsic to the genre, and status may be accorded by other factors (such as Montagu's use of classical allusion). Similarly, the confessional aspects of an autobiographical narrative need not be predominantly female (p. 19): if anything, the enforced discretion on sexual matters (which Mills herself later stresses [p. 81]) would seem to contradict it. Scandal and notoriety are relegated to extra-textual occurrences: though the claim to respectability of the narrative is contradicted by the condition of restless exile which may itself be regarded as an intrinsic violation of propriety. There is a pronounced reluctance to foreground corporeal embodiment, which would emphasise physical vulnerability: hence the omission of anecdotes of harassment, and even the familiar tropes of gendering of landscape (pp. 101–2, 82). The greater sense of 'personal involvement' (p. 21) may be empirically attributed to women travellers being less likely to have professional status, whether military, diplomatic, commercial or expeditionary observer, and correspondingly less likely to be involved in warfare, politics, business or science.

Mills claims that women's travel writings are 'counter-hegemonic' in so far as they 'disclose and critique from the margins' (p. 23). This poses an immediate question of comparative privilege – even 'travelling without protection signifies colonial control of territory' (p. 22) – and also a more general problem of complicity with imperial ideology. What is most ingratiating ('humour, self-deprecation, statements of affiliation, and descriptions of relationships' [p. 22]) is most insidious in so far as it successfully deflects attention from underlying structures of domination. The female traveller is as ambivalent a figure as her male counterpart; indeed, the same qualities viewed from different perspectives can produce antithetical valuations. Kingsley's text, far from being neglected and slighted, was widely influential in its proselytising for free trade and an interventionist policy in

West Africa. Her control over her native bearers is formidable but racialist, perhaps formidable because racialist; and raises the question of the status of such prejudice in the broader (and customarily ungendered) imaginary of colonial desire. (Nandy [1983] attributes the greater female aggression against natives to their resentment over the homoerotic bonds formed with the male colonisers [pp. 9–10].)

Nevertheless, Mills (1991) argues that women's travel writing is 'more tentative than male writing', more empathetic, other-directed, and so more inclined to present 'people as individuals' (p. 3). Affective bonds, however, may easily be recuperated as ideological mechanism for example; the tendency to present colonised countries as 'populated by harmless loving children' (p. 22). Women writers cannot simply be assumed to have struggled with, rather than benefited from, the discourse of imperialism (or even, as in the case of Flora Shaw, enthusiastically promoted it [Calloway and O'Hellel 1992]). As for 'textual unease' being 'labelled as bad writing' (Mills 1991: 4), there may be contradictions in the works of Montagu and Stark, but by most criteria these remain good writing: lucid, poised and well-informed.

Foucauldian-based models such as Mills necessarily produce downbeat accounts of the continued embeddedness of female travellers in colonial discourse. There is no miraculous exemption, but nor, of course, should this be expected. Other options might, however, be suggested for dealing with women's travel writing.

First, an alternative phenomenology of female spatiality might be posited as a prelude to the project of a more general geographical revisionism (e.g. Rose 1993). The problem here is that the ideal of relatedness and fluidity is historically grounded in sentimentalist vocabularies. In their own period, these are by no means gender-specific; and far from precluding the abstractions of masculine taxonomy, they often serve as their emotional 'complement' either in the form of descriptive epiphanies or erotic subplots (Pratt 1992: 39; see also Stafford 1984).

A second option would be to concentrate on the reprocessing of gendered representation deriving from travel writing by other cultural forms, and possible resistances in reception (e.g. McClintock 1994). This has the advantage of opening up earlier historical periods and of restoring agency to the woman reader. In bracketing the issue of authorial gender entirely, however, such an approach disavows even the possibility of articulating such distinctively female experiences of travel as pilgrimage, domestic labour and concubinage.

A third would be to resign oneself to the historical limitations of the travel genre, but to celebrate the emancipatory potential of a contemporary ideal of transnational mobility. Merging the post-colonial into the postmodern is no guarantee of a more equitable gender-balance, however; it is worth stressing that Caren Kaplan, after a suitably acerbic commentary on the sexism of Baudrillard's (1988) 'pure travel' (p. 9), eventually opts for a feminist politics of the local (Kaplan: 1996 74–8, 143–87).

A final possibility would be to refuse to relinquish the terms of approbation of an earlier, more mimetic, feminist criticism, the decision taken by most biographically-oriented studies (e.g. Birkett 1989). Mills's (1991) verdict of 'usable but naive' (p. 12) seems insufficiently respectful of simple productivity in making available; and it is unclear why the project of retrieving lost historical voices in order to overcome restrictive stereotypes should now be considered obsolete. The more interesting question, perhaps, is whether, if pride, initiative and endurance are to be celebrated in women's travel writing, the same qualities are deserving of equal commendation in narratives by men?

## The Essays

Brian Musgrove's essay, 'Travel and Unsettlement: Freud on Vacation', offers a genealogy of the near-simultaneous rise of post-colonial studies (in the wake of Said's *Orientalism*, and the famous Essex conferences of the early 1980s) and generic studies of travel writing (whose popularity as a form was greatly enhanced by the best-selling *Granta* special issues). The two perspectives may appear antithetical, both in methodological and political aims; it is argued, however, that the latent presence of formalist criteria continue to determine both new historicist and post-colonial accounts. Drawing on the anthropological schema of Arnold van Gennep, Musgrove proposes a model of liminal passage for the genre which unsettles rather than consolidates cultural authority. In support of this contention, he offers an analysis of Freud's famous essay on the Acropolis not as a psychoanalytic reading of travel, but as a travelling reading of psychoanalysis.

A major locus for travelling theory emerges in postmodern ethnography, notably the work of James Clifford, which attempts to construct both an exemplary ethics and social phenomenology based upon the contemporary experience of travel. In 'Argonauts of Western Pessimism: Clifford's Malinowski', John Hutnyk examines the Californian anthropologist's recent *Routes* (1997), and assesses its impact both on the discipline of anthropology and wider assimilation in cultural studies. An alternative model of transition is proposed that is more responsive to the harsher and more abrasive aspects of the experience of diaspora, migrancy and exile, and which eschews a 'feel-good' cultural relativism in favour of the more stringent insights of a Marxist historiography

John Phillips's 'Lagging Behind: Bhaba, Post-colonial Theory and the Future' explores the presentation of travel in the context of Homi Bhabha's work, whose concepts of hybridity, boundary-crossing, globalisation and locality have proved hugely influential in post-colonial studies. The essay argues that the coherence of Bhabha's project ('the performance of identity as iteration, the re-creation of the self in the world of travel' [Bhabha 1994: 9]) must be assessed as a whole, notably in its awareness of mathematical paradox and extensive debt to Hegelian logic. In the key concept of time-lag, fluctuations of signification are mapped on to broader forms of geographical and historical dislocation, and this new form of temporality, it is argued, directs both the specific itineraries of the migrant and exile, and on a broader level constitutes the condition of postmodernity per se.

The consumption of human flesh has in recent criticism become a test-case of the reliability of European testimony with regard to indigenous cultures. Ted Motohashi's 'The Discourse of Cannibalism in Early Modern Travel Writing' seeks to explore not merely how Columbus's letters discursively took possession of the New World, but also how this epistolary rhetoric depends upon a complex network of binary oppositions and un-stable supplements. The actuality of cannibalism (itself a highly contentious issue) is less important than the division between monstrous Carib and gentle Arawak, which serves both as an expedient pretext for exploitation and an eventual apology for genocide. The schema is subsequently adopted by the English privateers as a means of justifying their piracy against the Spanish; and later transposed as a means of legitimating the appropriation of Ireland. It has long been recognised that the Americas were defined according to imported mythologies such as the nomadic Scythians (who thus had no claim to ownership of land); Motohashi argues for a reverse movement by which the demonisation of the cannibal is re-exported and provides a rationale for English imperialism.

Tim Cribb's 'Writing up the Log: The Legacy of Hakluyt' examines the Elizabethan geographer's compilation of travel writings as prefiguration of empire. Froude's nineteenth-century celebration of a collection of prospectuses for mercantile expansion as the prose epic of the English nation is contrasted with Mary Fuller's recent New Historicist treatment which emphasises its internal frailties and the oddly self-defeating quality of many of its narratives. The methodology of cartography and the log provides the template for a certain kind of realist literature, which is thus deeply implicated in the project of empire. These imperial corollaries deriving from Hakluyt are then traced through the West Indian novelist Wilson Harris's *The Guyana Quartet* that attempts both a reappropriation and reversal of this technology in order to undertake a post-colonial remapping of the Caribbean terrain.

Katherine Turner's 'From Classical to Imperial' offers a comparison of the travelogues of Lady Mary Wortley Montagu and Lady Elizabeth Craven at the beginning and end of the eighteenth century. Their representations of the Ottoman Empire are of particular significance in so far as attitudes to Turkey prefigured later strategies in dealing with India: partition, divide and rule. The female traveller disavows the testimony of earlier male travel writings, by drawing on her own superior access to areas available to male travellers only in the realm of fantasy (Turkish bath, harem). Montagu is not wholly divorced from potential appropriation of the exotic, but these elements remain in a complex equilibrium with her foregrounded gender role and deference at points to a stronger culture, with riches at its disposal and technologies to be learnt (notably inoculation). Craven's recourse to stereotyping and eschewal of her predecessor's amused tolerance of cultural difference exemplifies a more developed colonial ideology, perhaps fore-shadowing the rancour of the nineteenth-century memsahib. The sensibility of the female traveller is itself an acute register of political change

Bridget Orr's '"Stifling Pity in a Parent's Breast": Infanticide and Savagery in Late Eighteenth-century Travel Writing' is concerned with the deployment of travel literature in Enlightenment sociology. The philosophical use of voyage literature is not simply as source material, exemplification; it parallels the cultural policing operations performed by conduct books and misogynist verse, often drawing on the same common archive, notably exotic tropes of Pacific sexuality, to enforce a new ideology of maternity. The issue of infanticide is a crucial aporia in the civility/savagery divide, imaginary virtue and barbarous vice; ethnographic evidence becomes the conduit of sentimental exchange. Of particular note is the importance of factors of reception in what may appear an exclusively masculine discourse: before the nineteenth century, women travelled less frequently and under greater constraints, but gender still determines various of the generic conventions of travel writing. Exemplary homiletic remains haunted by its demonic opposite, and both are equally reliant upon a colonial imaginary.

Wendy Mercer's 'Gender and Genre in Nineteenth-century Travel Writing' offers an account of divergent gender-perspectives on a fieldtrip to Lapland. The core–periphery model is applied within Europe in the increasing subordination of the outlying regions; here conducted by another European empire, the French, regrouping for expansion after the losses of the Napoleonic wars. The presence of Leonie d'Aunet and Xavier Marmier on the same polar expedition allows a close comparison of gender differ-entiation in their respective narratives. What emerges from d'Aunet's account is less the fluid identity celebrated in recent feminist theory but certain constraints of corporeal specificity, both in terms of limitations of physical strength and broader pressures of cultural construction. Any too ready collapsing of gender on to power relations must be resisted: the female sphere of writing may itself readily inscribe an imperial ideology, and within the duties and orientation of the male traveller (navigation, surveying) may reside the possibility of a more benign ethics of attentiveness to and respect for cultural others.

In 'Ecologies of Desire', Richard Kerridge deals with the phenomenology of otherness in nature writing, both in high colonial variants and postmodern reworkings. The relationship of imperialism to environmentalism is not uniformly exploitative; ecological techniques evolved among early colonial administrators, and many conservation practices derive from management of big game for hunting. The desire for encounter common to both travelogue and nature writing cannot be reduced to a simple pretext for domination; instead, the body remains a site of numerous anxieties and instabilities, perhaps most familiar in terms of Kristevan abjection. The dual yet antithetical imperatives of intimate knowledge yet hierarchical distance produce a continuous and traumatic renegotiation with the external world that characterises both genres, and may perhaps remain their inescapable limitation.

Gabriel Gbadamosi's 'The Road to Brixton Market' is part travelogue, part reflection on travelogue. Its broad orientation may be situated in the context of three major contemporary debates: the historical formation of black identity through enforced diaspora in the form of slavery and the middle passage across the Atlantic (Gilroy 1993); a post-colonial anger at this neglected underside of the colonial narrative, here termed road rage (Fanon 1963); and the insistence on the inevitable hybridity of a postmodern world (Bhabha 1994). These strands are negotiated in an autobiographical meditation on the voyage inward, the experience of immigration in the post-war world after the decline of the old European empires. Here however, there is no internalised self-accusation, nor proclamation of victimhood; instead, the creativity of these communities is celebrated in their pragmatic exchanges of everyday life, and joyful rediscovery of geographical connections after a brutally disrupted history. In this positive post-colonial vision of infinite circulation, the journey to the imperial centre becomes an enhancing relocation and prelude to continued residence.

David Taylor's 'Bruce Chatwin: Connoisseur of Exile, Exile as Connoisseur' focuses on that celebrity-traveller as exemplary figure of generic expiry and transition to postmodern fragmentation. The central issue is whether the presentation of exile in his writings remains vulnerable to a post-colonial critique. Here the politics become those of style, the sheer exquisiteness of Chatwin's spare, almost crystalline, anecdote; the same rhetorical strategy can be read as both a refusal of the imperial gaze, and as its reintroduction in a more systematic methodological given. In the recurrent motif of cataloguing, of itemisation, there is both an urge to dominance, to decontextualise individual lives and reduce them to specimen, backdrop; and a broader melancholy which may be read politically as a final recognition of separation from empire, with a sense of heroic poignancy in its loss.

Steve Clark's 'Transatlantic Crossings' argues that recent British travel writing about the USA may be read in terms of reversal of power relations. Instead of the familiar motif of American Innocence and European Experience, British travellers are now forced to confront their own demoralised post-imperial identity in their encounter with a newly ascendant and dynamic empire. The journey can be read in cross-cultural terms as a flight from the present and humiliating state of the self and its European heritage: 'the voyage had begun with my running away from London' (Raban 1986: 358). America implies a redemptive narrative, whether in search of Tamla Motown or the Great White Whale, but one that metamorphoses the quester rather than the object. The pursuit is not an implicit assertion of freedom, but the consequence of a prior encoding, producing not only strategies of protective mimicry but also occasional moments of insight and resistance in the post-imperial subject.

The overall intention of this volume is not to reclaim travel writing for the literary, in opposition to the political, but rather to qualify and extend the insights of post-colonial criticism into its broader hegemonic functions. If, as de Certeau insists, every narrative is a travel narrative, the ultimate outcome of those stories remains to be determined.

# Part I

# Methods

**2**

# Travel and Unsettlement: Freud on Vacation

Brian Musgrove

The task of constituting a formalistic approach to travel writing was largely abandoned in the early 1980s; in this chapter I argue that the project might yet illuminate some discursive operations of the travel text. Perhaps I am imagining, or simplistically constructing, unrealised past potentialities. Nevertheless, I want to reappraise the travel text as a site of distress and unravelling that is neither necessarily nor adequately explained by post-colonialisms. In reconsidering travel formally, I also examine anthropological traces and relate them to an unsettled negotiation of subjectivity; an unravelling of value and sense. This approach, I contend, is no less totalising than much post-colonial work, which in any case seems to read travel either as a version of Freud's 'instinct of destruction' – an aggressive agency that destroys the ecology of otherness – or an eroticisation of the foreign, desire without normal limits, which terminates in rape and exploitation on personal and cultural scales.

Ultimately, what I suggest is that a formalist approach to travel is not at all inconsistent with the political objectives of post-colonial readings. In discussing the historical divergence of formal and post-colonial perspectives on travel, from around 1978, and by examining how both new historicist and post-colonial criticisms retain a concern with formalist operations, I want to redirect attention back to the neurotic unknowingness of the travelling euro-subject in a broadly political fashion.

I argue that the formal basis of the travel genre is in the structure of rites of passage, originally schematised by Arnold van Gennep. In travel, the *territorial* passage from one zone to another, the border crossing, represents a critical moment for the identity of the mobile subject. The territorial passage is accompanied by – or even metaphoric of – another movement; the shift from 'seeing with one's own eyes' to discerning the meaning of what is seen. The travel text always supplements the insufficient act of 'witnessing' with epistemological reflection; a process which exposes fundamental morbidities in the ideologies of 'movement' and 'settlement'.

In the end, this is a form of unresolved and unsatisfactory ascesis, whereby the attempt to revise and supplant a pre-existent culture with the travelling-eye-view is not merely a partial but a complete evacuation of the self – an emptying of subjectivity, recognising that the traveller's action of wavering between worlds is potentially annihilating. The 'art of travel' is not, straightforwardly, about the inscription of power over otherness; rather, it is underscored by an anxious sense that to travel is to 'be nowhere'.

The critical perspectives on travel literature that post-colonial readings have produced, the cultural and political specificities which (too often superficially) characterise studies of travel and empire, rely on a generally unarticulated formalism. As a matter of fact, the strategies in new historicist and post-colonial critiques of travel writing can be read in formalist terms, which in turn stress the cultural operations of travel in the construction of a universalised knowledge. At the risk of further universalising the travel genre, and of clinging to an inhibitive retro-methodology, it is worth briefly noting the institutional contest, from the mid-1970s to the mid-1980s, which prepared for and put in place the markers of post-colonial readings and eclipsed (or absorbed) the nascent, formalist approach to travel.

Today, as we have seen in the Introduction, it is virtually impossible to consider travel writing outside the frame of post-colonialism. In many cases now, travel is regarded as a sub-story of the grand narrative of imperialism; in others, travel is the key operation, in language and fact, that makes the colonial adventure possible. This somewhat monocular view, which itself seeks to explain the one-eyedness of eurocentric representations, is underscored by what I would call an environmental concern for the humanist mindscape – 'look how we have blighted worlds of otherness'. (And in so doing, parenthetically observe how we have polluted our own intellectual streams of consciousness.)

Historically, the revival of critical interest in travel writing was co-incident with the rise of post-colonial theory. Both, in their own different ways, were directed at the recuperation of marginal books which were either stylistically or culturally 'left out' of canons. Early texts which catalysed the study of the travel book and the related narratives of imperialism began to attract attention in the mid-1970s: there was Michel Butor's widely cited article 'Travel and Writing' in *Mosaic* (1974), and Brian Street's *The Savage in Literature* (1975). At a more important moment of converging interests – and anticipating future critical divergences – Edward Said's hugely influential *Orientalism* appeared in the same year, 1978, as Charles L. Batten's *Pleasurable Instruction* (a much-used analysis of the formal properties of the travel genre) and Nelson Graburn's suggestive article 'Tourism: The Sacred Journey'. Mary Louise Pratt also tells us that the impetus for her important work on travel and transculturation began in 1978, in a Stanford course co-taught with Rina Berunayor (Pratt 1992: xi).

The paperback reissue of out-of-copyright travel classics, the first-time journeys of the Theroux and Chatwins, the tentative steps towards a poetics of travel and the foundations of post-colonial criticism were happening simultaneously. The development of these intersecting interests was un-surprising. Travel writing is one of the main archives for investigating colonising processes, providing rich source material on the formations of western subjectivities out of the encounter with imagined others. The travel book can also expose transactions of cultural and political power; a power supposedly always purchased at the expense of those imagined others who constitute the zone called 'elsewhere'.

As fresh readings of the imperialist bookshelf offered themselves for curricularisation, renewed attention was also paid to travel – in Paul Fussell's *Abroad* (1980), Philip Dodd's *The Art of Travel* (1982), Percy G. Adams's *Travel Literature and the Evolution of the Novel* (1983) and Bill Buford's first travel special-number of *Granta* (1984). In 1984, as Buford penned an editorial celebrating the cult of movement and mythicising the pathologically mobile Bruce Chatwin, the University of Essex hosted a landmark conference that recast the paradigm for reading travel and contact. Under the rubric 'Europe and Its Others', the University of Essex conference in Colchester was removed by a mere forty miles from Buford's Cambridge base. It was a striking demonstration of the proximity of, and distance between, post-colonial theory and the simplistic generic appreci-ation of travel writing's cultural freedoms.

Travel writing was set to be claimed by either formalism or post-colonialism, and the claims of the post-colonial announced an institutional gravity that could never be matched by trivially 'literary' considerations. After all, the effort to dismantle the ideological apparatuses of imperialism is grander and more challenging than a critique of localised issues; to understand the perverse psychology of orientalising on a big scale is more compelling than knowing why a seasoned traveller-snob like Evelyn Waugh hated tourists. 'The word "tourist" seems naturally to suggest haste and compulsion', Waugh wrote in *Labels*, 'one sheds not wholly derisive tears for these poor scraps of humanity thus trapped and mangled in the machinery of uplift' (Waugh 1930: 44–5). As a rhetorical gesture, this is a formulaic, much-repeated prejudice in the travel genre – a formal demarcation of the identity of the genuine, heroic traveller from the tripper bound by a fixed itinerary. Nevertheless, it takes little critical extension to see in this rhetorical performance an immediate political point: a patrician revulsion at the clamorous order of mass modernity, and a class neurosis over shifting, mobile lines of subjectivity. This is a crisis precipitated by travel and contact within the western subject, whose low others are not always defined in colonial terms.

Where generic readings of travel could be characterised as intro-spectively 'academic' or narrowly author-based, post-colonialisms signalled a mode of relevance to worldly affairs; a promise for that loose baggy monster 'The Humanities' to reinvent itself, and to identify its social utility under the institutional pressures of economic rationalism. Mary Louise Pratt polemicised this, incandescently, in the Preface to *Imperial Eyes*: 'This is a book marked by the global realignments and ideological upheavals that began in the 1980s and continue in the present. It was begun during the anguish of the Reagan–Thatcher years, when demystifying imperialism seemed more urgent than ever, and also more hopeless.' It was a time, too, when 'intense institutional struggles ... over undergraduate humanities curricula' defined the university work-face (Pratt 1992: xi). Set beside such promises and pressures, a book like Fussell's *Abroad*, the first to attempt a drawing-together of strands into something like a contemporary theory of travel writing, was destined to be judged an academic exercise, providing little political gain. The post-structural turn, away from formal-isms, systems and complacent humanisms, seemed to suggest important new functions and social relevances for the art of reading.

The disentanglement of recent critical idioms from more traditional academic practices was not, however, complete or conclusive. In a very perceptive review of Stephen Greenblatt's *Marvelous Possessions*, Greg Manning has suggested how new historicisms – and, I would maintain, post-colonialisms – retain significant elements of formal academic practice and humanist concern. For Manning, they hover between 'a basically structuralist interest in systemic relations [and] a profound suspicion of systems' (Manning 1993: 1). One might argue that these impulses were successive rather than co-existent in Greenblatt's work, which progressively moves away from a model of culture as text (with corresponding homo-logies between, for example, mercantile expansion and Marlovian drama), towards an ethical, even theological, concern with alterity. Manning's parting point, however, remains telling:

> In an age which is trying, however clumsily, to establish post-colonial pos-sibilities for representation, whereby the West might at last stop trampling on the rights of the other, one can see why Greenblatt should be so drawn to the promise of decency. For all the complexity of his analyses, one can only wish things were that simple. (Manning 1993: 84)

Pursuing that argument, there is a revealing moment in the marvellous *Marvelous Possessions* where Greenblatt withdraws briefly from historical complexities to consider the specularity of imperial ownership and the assimilation of otherness to European culture. In so doing, Greenblatt refers to 'the primal act of witnessing around which virtually the entire discourse of travel is constructed'. He continues: 'Everything in the European dream of possession rests on witnessing understood as a form of significant and representative seeing' (Greenblatt 1991: 122). Greenblatt moves on to a discussion of Herodotus (a name claimed equally by historiography, anthropology and sociology) as a founder; an original instrumentality in the discursive shaping of travel writing. By returning to this point of origin and father-figure, and by sliding from 'virtually the entire' to 'everything', Greenblatt momentarily exposes the powerful, residual formalism which underscores much contemporary critical work on travel writing. This particularly tendentious rhetorical slide has, too, a corollary in the new historicist strategy of arguing from the margins of history through key exemplary anecdotes. The anecdote has an ethical, didactic – almost theological – function; it is a fable from which a whole 'fabulised' eurocentric view of other worlds may be extrapolated.

To speak of a discourse configured around a 'primal act' suggests, furthermore, an interest in genre theory which is itself bound up in a search for foundational speech-acts; the quest for a Lévi-Strauss-like homology, where deed becomes word and word is deed, and a 'significant and representative' expressive mode is realised. For Greenblatt, seeing is not merely seeing: it is, in this context, 'witnessing' – an act implying a special social function and gravity. In many ways this is entirely consistent with slightly earlier work on travel writing which, in turn, looked back to critical principles set forth by mythicists like Northrop Frye, to whom a trip was never a trip but always a quest. ('It is part of the critic's business', Frye wrote, 'to show how all literary genres are derived from the quest-myth' [Frye 1957: 105].) Greenblatt's primal speech-act remains marked by the *Genre* connection; his 'witnessing' has an ethico-theological ring, as well as a highly formal sense of the fundamental, Frye-like mythic connections of reading, writing and journeying. The mobile intellect of the travel text serves as the basic exemplum of 'reading and writing culture', suggesting a durable formal homology. This reminds me, in fact, of the structural relation – an inflection of Frye – proposed by Michel Butor:

> there is (at least) the path of the eye from sign to sign, like all sorts of itineraries which can often, but not always, be grossly simplified as the progression along a line from a point of departure to a point of arrival ... The very complex 'words' which are the great sites will be linked by the traveller in a sentence ... [if] travel leads to the composition of a book, this is because in writing a book one is engaged in the act of travelling. (Butor 1994: 3, 15)

In a second revealing moment, this time from Mary Louise Pratt's *Imperial Eyes*, there is a summary discussion of the contiguity, or simultaneity, of travel writing about the non-European world and travels within Europe. Pratt is addressing the application of a centre–periphery trope to different travelling situations; situations apparently discrete in time, geography and cultural context. She writes:

> Readers of European travel books about Europe have pointed out that many of the conventions and writing strategies I associate here with imperial expansionism characterize travel writing about Europe as well. As I suggest at several points in the discussion, when that is so, related dynamics of power and appropriation are likely to be found at work as well. The discourses that legitimate bourgeois authority and delegitimate peasant and subsistence lifeways, for example, can be expected to do this ideological work within Europe as well as in southern Africa or Argentina. (Pratt 1992: 10)

While there is no real objection to the commonplace that imbalanced power relations grounded in nation, race, class or gender are potentially analogous, comments like Pratt's are recognisably problematic. This is particularly so in respect of *Imperial Eyes* – a book about 'witnessing', once again – which takes as its objectives the disunification, the heterogenisation and the rhetorical hybridisation of travel writing. In a somewhat contradictory instant of cross-troping, Pratt reverts to the impulsive globalism which stalks post-colonial theorising. Regarding travel writing as a discourse, a particular configuration of knowledge and experience, post-colonial theories tend to privilege certain inarguably othered territorial contacts: in Africa, the Caribbean, India, the Middle East and, sometimes, South America. But what begins as a limited discursive shaping of travel, located in key places at key times in imperialist history, becomes a vast allegory of knowledge *only*; a reflexive metropolitan epistemology, ultimately, that discovers instances of centralism and oppression structurally-encoded in 'our' cultural history. 'Empire' becomes the ur-myth of 'Literature', the fundamental pattern of the canon and its relation to non-canonical textual others. Post-colonial theories have relied upon a poetics of travel which might not necessarily account for the broader field: what, for example, did it mean *specifically* for a Briton to visit Iceland or Sardinia, take the Grand Tour through France to Italy or, indeed, to explore the extremities of the rural United Kingdom? In these situations it is sometimes quite appropriate, but too often theoretically expedient, to find an imperialising psychology – if not an actual imperial project – at work. The common dynamic of the centre–periphery, employed so effectively in much post-colonial debate, effortlessly reveals parallels in the dominative assumptions of such different texts as Defoe's *Tour through the Whole Island of Great Britain*, Dickens's

*Pictures from Italy* and Robert Byron's *The Road to Oxiana*. To apply a critical trope in this way, however, amounts to something close to high structuralism, whereby situations remote from each other in time, geography and cultural context are brought together in a single and splendidly coherent intellectual field. In terms of scholarship, that kind of cross-troping is at best a short-hand and, at worst, an evasion of historical engagement: to sniff out a colonising tendency in travels to Capri (which, if one reads them, are frequently by homosexuals dodging the law) because it seems to appear synchronically in the Cape of Good Hope (land of the missionary, freebooter and official administrator) is a highly problematic matter.

Greenblatt, again, is instructive here in exposing the simple, formal mapping involved; a mapping to which the subjects of critical attention and the critics themselves are prone:

> The discoverer sees only a fragment and then imagines the rest in the act of appropriation. The supplement that imagination brings to vision expands the perceptual field, encompassing the distant hills and valleys or the whole of an island or an entire continent, and the bit that has actually been seen becomes by metonymy a representation of the whole. That representation is in turn conveyed, reported to an audience elsewhere, and seeing turns into witnessing. (Greenblatt 1991: 122)

This reflexively describes a critical process, not a thoroughly surveyed historical actuality. It reveals a belief in formalised poetics – or, put another way, it celebrates the heroic-intellectual quest to 'explain everything' by knowing and arguing from 'a bit'. 'Seeing', for Greenblatt, becomes 'witnessing'; a kind of religio-legislative omniscience, or omni-science. Likewise, Pratt's John Barrow, lead-player in her article 'Scratches on the Face of the Country', is a representative seer whose identity is critically cast in the type of the Romance Hero. Barrow is 'a kind of collective moving eye' (Pratt 1985: 123) whose visions, along with Livingstone and others, tend to an Edenic or pre-Adamic recuperation of the desolate-foreign. Mr Barrow revivifies and fertilises the African wasteland, making it ripe for imperial exploitation. As both Representative Man and super-annuated Romance Hero, Mr Barrow and his colleagues-in-colonisation come to exemplify a paradigm for the acquisition of knowledge – an epistemological violence, in short, whereby 'information-producing travel accounts' are singularly directed to 'expanding the capitalist world system' (p. 125).

By implication, a formalist or generic reading of travel might readily be considered as cooperative with that expansionist mind-set. Pratt duly discerns a particular critical mode that effectively stresses the poetics of travel and the constitution of the western bourgeois subject: 'an esthetic or literary vein of scholarship has developed, in which travel accounts, usually by famous literary figures, are studied in the artistic and intellectual dimensions and with reference to European existential dilemmas' (Pratt 1992: 10). This dismissively implies that a 'literary' reading is primarily concerned with issues of subjectivity, to the exclusion of political engagement or, indeed, any broader ideological referent.

To examine the limits of this suggestion, we can turn back to the events of 1978. That year, as germinal post-colonial texts and travel studies appeared, anthropologist Nelson Graburn published an article titled 'Tourism: The Sacred Journey'. Briefly, Graburn argued that the modern experience of travel 'has antecedents and equivalents in other seemingly more purposeful institutions such as medieval student travel, the Crusades, and European and Asian pilgrimage circuits'. Alluding to the co-etymology of 'travel' and 'travail' (first codified by Samuel Johnson in his 1755 *Dictionary*) Graburn claimed that even 'sanctioned recreation' was 'often a kind of "hard work"', especially in the rites-of-passage or self-testing types of tourism such as those of youthful travelers' (Graburn 1978: 17). What made Graburn's view anthropologically possible was an appraisal of travel as a key action, theorised in anthropology early this century and forcefully rephrased in the 'myth-ritual school' of literary criticism – a critical mode shadowed by archetypalists like Jung and Joseph Campbell.

The theory, as Graburn's phrase 'rites-of-passage' suggests, came from an anthropological moment that was proto-structuralist. Arnold van Gennep's far-reaching, early twentieth-century observations on passage rites, originally published in 1909, revealed that border-crossings and territorial passages represented a significant variant of the change-of-status scenario. The term 'rites of passage' is often used now as if it constituted a single ritual practice, whereas van Gennep detailed it closely, subclassifying '*rites of separation, transition rites, and rites of incorporation*'. He noted: 'These three subcategories are not developed to the same extent by all peoples or in every ceremonial pattern' (van Gennep 1960: 11). However, if one form of ceremony involved all three types of rite, balanced as equally important constitutive elements, that case would be of peculiar interest; and van Gennep discovered such a case in the territorial passage – 'the magico-religious aspect of crossing frontiers' (p. 15*)*.

Employing a sacred–profane dichotomy like his contemporary Durkheim, van Gennep detailed the demarcation of special zones and the implications of entering them. Of particular interest are his comments on 'neutral zones'. The neutral zone is open and available – like the blank space of 'Darkest Africa', perhaps – and surrounded by 'sacred zones' which are already culturally claimed and encoded:

The neutral zones are ordinarily deserts, marshes, and most frequently virgin forests where everyone has full rights to travel and hunt. Because of the pivoting of sacredness, the territories on either side of the neutral zone are sacred to whoever is in the zone, but the zone, in turn, is sacred for the inhabitants of the adjacent territories. Whoever passes from one to the other finds himself physically and magico-religiously in a special situation for a certain length of time: he wavers between two worlds. (van Gennep 1960: 18)

In post-colonial terms, this immediately suggests a dominant–inferior relation; the mobile possibility of exploitation via the sacralisation, or enchantment, of emptiness. The border-crossing into a neutral zone, however, involves an inversion of value systems: not a lack of identity but a shifting identity, for both landscape and traveller. Landscape and traveller are sites of indeterminacy, so that travel is *not* the simple inscription of an established meaning over a neutralised, identityless other. The travelling subject, wavering between two worlds, is by no means the self-assured colonist; rather, that subject is poised to split and unravel. The process of transition, and its associated liminal rites, were always anthropologically theorised as modes of 'unsettlement' rather than transcendence or occupation. And rather than constructing the world from glimpsed fragments – the intellectual motive-force in Greenblatt's 'primal act of witnessing' – travel and border-crossing signify a geographic and psychic disunification, anticipating a potential confusion of established order whereby disunification becomes cultural dysfunction. Dennis Porter provides a useful gloss on this point:

If, as anthropologists have long since taught us, borders of all kinds are perceived as dangerous as well as exciting places, and are associated with taboos, this is no less true of territorial borders ... something of such an attitude no doubt contributes to the frequent ambivalence to be found in so many works of travel literature [where] the notions of guilt and duty are almost as important as desire and transgression. The acknowledgment of law and obligation, resistance to them and a pervasive sense of guilt, recur with a symptomatic frequency. (D. Porter 1991: 9)

These waverings and psychic conflicts are symptomatic not only of a threatened dismemberment of the individual subject, but also of a whole ideological system – as terms like 'duty', 'law' and 'obligation' imply. In travel, the bourgeois subject is involved in a fundamentally reflexive confrontation with the unsustainable values of 'home'. As Porter, again, notes: 'most forms of travel at least cater to desire: they seem to promise or allow us to fantasize the satisfaction of drives that for one reason or another is denied us at home' (D. Porter 1991: 9). This conclusively underlines

Porter's argument that the desire in travel 'derives from Freud's notion of the libido as updated by Lacan; it embodies the notion of a dynamic but obscure energy within a human subject that insists on satisfactions of a kind the world of objects cannot supply' (p. 8).

As a subject who 'wavers between two worlds', the traveller always finds such satisfactions blocked or out of reach. Moving through a neutral zone, the identity and significance of which is contingent on what is outside it, the traveller can never realize the 'dream of possession'. In contrast, the preferred travel narrative of new historicist and post-colonial criticisms is based on the idea of possession and the ready inscription of stable 'home-values' on the blank page of otherness. This, in turn, assumes a politics of continuity and 'settlement', whereby the border-crossing is unproblematic and the traveller is a confident representative of the paternalist lore of home. Consequently, the travel text's descriptive economies and taxonomies objectify the world; the act of witnessing, as Greenblatt argues with reference to Michel de Certeau, is the foundational rhetorical device which fabricates and accredits the travel text as a recorded understanding of otherness (Greenblatt 1991: 126). With the world thus rendered in concrete terms, as a series of objects under inspection by the travelling gaze, the desires of euro-expansionism can be satisfied.

However, as Meaghan Morris reminds us, the act of witnessing, constituted in both the narrative and descriptive travelogue, must also – and more importantly – be understood as an event that confounds desire. In a critique of the Australian travel writer Ernestine Hill ('an imperialist, a white supremacist and a patriot'), Morris notes a powerful sense of derealisation which impedes the 'dream of possession':

> on the one hand there is something vital about the travel-writer's quest to describe human life ('catch it while you can'), yet on the other, something morbid, even 'doomed', about description. It is an assumption shared by many classic accounts of literary realism, and also by theories of the visual media as a vast descriptive regime for destroying (and for Baudrillard, replacing) 'reality'. (Morris 1988: 172)

What Morris analyses, precisely, is the confusion and unsettlement of a subjectivity that might normally be viewed as centred – imperialist, supremacist, patriotic, unrepentantly and unreflexively chauvinistic. Morris's reading sees the traveller wavering between two worlds: one of the concrete, of the objective, of desire satisfied through the written record of possession; the other is a world of frustration and derealisation, populated by mirages, spectres and ghosts, where the fantasies of possessing and occupying the other – of knowing, with any certainty – simply vanish.

Morris's argument is grounded as much in psychoanalysis as it is in structuralist or formalist procedures, and, as a means of suggesting how the act of witnessing (with the para-legislative certitudes that implies) might be displaced as the basic formal principle of the travel genre, I turn to Freud's essay 'A Disturbance of Memory on the Acropolis'. This essay, dramatising a sophisticated, self-interrogative travelling consciousness in disarray, articulates the doomed ghastliness of 'realising' with which Morris is concerned, as well as the unsettled conflicts of desire and obligation discussed by Dennis Porter. Furthermore, Freud foregrounds the impossibility of extending the known into the zone of 'elsewhere'; that is, he questions the travel experience as a means of simple superimposition or reinscription. There is no continuity in the identity of the travelling subject, and definitely no power to possess or to specularise 'elsewhere' on predetermined conditions.

Writing 'A Disturbance of Memory on the Acropolis', Freud was like any travel writer: recollecting, reconstructing, reflecting critically and morally on the lesson of the journey. Freud wrote the essay in 1936, as a festschrift 'Open Letter to Romain Rolland on the Occasion of his Seventieth Birthday', and in it he recalls an incident which occurred in 1904. And, like any travel text, Freud's essay attempts to bring the immediacy of a past event into a relation with the order and sense of the present; an intellectual operation that, in Freud's case at least, modifies 'the primal act of witnessing' by cross-examining the authenticity of the witness.

Briefly, at the level of narrative, Sigmund was on holiday with his brother. The Freuds travelled to Trieste with the intention of proceeding to Corfu, but were persuaded that Athens would be a more convenient, realisable destination. Freud confesses to a childhood desire to see Athens, but the change of itinerary brings depression, rather than elation. Subsequently, arriving on the Acropolis, Freud finds himself stricken by doubt and a feeling of unreality.

Freud seems to be writing, consciously, against modernist inflections of the rites of passage motif, inflections which mythicised territorial passage as heroic quest. This modernist adjustment of van Gennep's passage rites culminated in the work of Jungians or archetypalists like Joseph Campbell and Northrop Frye. Campbell, particularly, came to regard the figure of 'the hero' as imbricated in 'a magnification of the formula represented in the rites of passage', with the passage from 'the world of common day' into a supernaturalised region of desire and 'wonder' as a test of the hero's decisiveness and majesty (Joseph Campbell 1949: 30). Freud plays with this idea, noting that the travel impulse is grounded in the poverty, limitations and obstructive pressures of 'the world of common day':

My longing to travel was no doubt also the expression of a wish to escape from that pressure, like the force which drives so many adolescent children to run away from home. I had long seen clearly that a great part of the pleasure of travel lies in the fulfilment of these early wishes – that it is rooted, that is, in dissatisfaction with home and family. When first one catches sight of the sea, crosses the ocean and experiences as realities cities and lands which for so long had been distant, unattainable things of desire – one feels oneself like a hero who has performed deeds of improbable greatness. (Freud 1973: 247)

As a sign of the extent to which Freud writes against the impossibly heroic pretensions of mythicism, 'A Disturbance of Memory' is bracketed by a characterisation of the travel writer as baffled, aged and attenuated. Near the beginning of the essay, Freud describes himself as a man whose 'powers of production are at an end ... an impoverished creature, who has "seen better days"'. He concludes by reiterating this view: 'I myself have grown old and stand in need of forbearance and can travel no more' (Freud 1973: 239, 248). If this has some of the 'morbidity' referred to by Meaghan Morris – with Freud as Ancient Mariner, doomed to retell his tale – it also suggests an acute, critical awareness of the problems of 'witnessing' and 'describing'. In an important sense of 'morbidity', the inverted commas on 'seen better days' signify more than a lapse into vernacular; there is an ironic hint that the illusion of 'seeing better' ('witnessing') is mitigated by unsettlement. After all, Freud avers, 'this incident on the Acropolis [has] troubled me so often' (p. 248), and the very unheroic travelling subject can be neither imaginative nor material coloniser of foreign ground. It is, in fact, a split subject, whose desires are confounded in the moment of 'witnessing', or 'seeing better':

When, finally, on the afternoon after our arrival, I stood on the Acropolis and cast my eyes around upon the landscape, a surprising thought suddenly entered my mind: 'So all this really *does* exist, just as we learnt at school!' To describe the situation more accurately, the person who gave expression to the remark was divided, far more sharply than was usually noticeable, from another person who took cognizance of the remark; and both were astonished, though not by the same thing. The first behaved as though he were obliged, under the impact of an unequivocal observation, to believe in something the reality of which had hitherto seemed doubtful ... The second person, on the other hand, was justifiably astonished, because he had been unaware that the real existence of Athens, the Acropolis, and the landscape around it had ever been objects of doubt. What he had been expecting was rather some expression of delight or admiration. (Freud 1973: 241)

With his desire thus frustrated by a world of doubtful objects, and his identity split and confused in the instant of 'witnessing', Freud begins a complex reflection on doubt and displacement. His negotiations with distortions of memory and belief – whether he had or had not doubted the actuality of distant places, the foreign – culminates in a 'feeling of derealisation' ('What *I see here is not real*') which is itself linked to the unsettled passage from seeing to knowing. Eventually, Freud's examination of the depression, doubts and distortions of memory in his Acropolis experience comes to rest in a discussion of transgression and guilt:

> It must be that a sense of guilt was attached to the satisfaction in having gone such a long way: there was something about it that was wrong, that from earliest times had been forbidden. It was something to do with a child's criticism of his father ... as though the essence of success was to have got further than one's father, and as though to excel one's father was still something forbidden. (Freud 1973: 247)

Crossing into territory beyond the reach of the father, beyond the limits of value and sense which characterise home, the traveller wavers – suspended, caught by duties and desires which are irreconcilable. Far from being an occasion for the reinscription of paternal lore, or for a performance of heroic witnessing, travel reveals an emptiness in the belief-system that stands behind the travelling subject. As Freud added: 'The very theme of Athens and the Acropolis in itself contained evidence of the son's superiority. Our father had been in business, and Athens could not have meant much to him. Thus what interfered with our enjoyment of the journey to Athens was a feeling *of filial piety*' (pp. 247–8). For any traveller, home is that which is always necessarily 'in the past', and for Freud travel diminishes that past but can never supply a satisfactory resolution of desire 'in the present'.

Freud's essay contains, or dramatises, a kind of liminal passage rite; a border-crossing from the original event of 'seeing' to an eventual 'knowing'. On one level, Freud's provisional conclusions, his reading of the travel experience, are directed to authenticate the epic science of psychology – a magico–scientific rather than magico–religious wavering. On another, however, what is finally known is that the territorial passage – in its dual senses of 'actual travel' and intellectual movement – is a critical unsettling of belief and value. For Freud, travel exposes potentialities for splitting, contradiction and loss of touch with 'the real'. Formally read in this way, the attempt to master the travel experience and to occupy the terrain of otherness is fundamentally morbid; obstructive of desire and destructive of subjective unity.

Instead of searching out the obvious moments of oppression, arrogance and self-assured chauvinism in the travel text, post-colonial critiques might also focus on the points of unravelling, conflict and uncertainty in the travelling subject. By formally examining the 'unsettlement' of the western subject, we are not necessarily committed to an introspective aesthetic project – deplored by Marie Louise Pratt – that privileges European existential dilemmas and is, therefore, depoliticised and simply formal. New historicist and post-colonial readings themselves depend on formalist tropes and manoeuvres; upon the understanding that formal literary structures, narrative patterns, primal speech-acts and textual claims to validity have a demonstrable relation to 'trampling on the rights of the other'. To employ an alternative point of formalist reference – not 'witnessing' as a mark of imperialising power, but the unsettlement that redefines first-sight in the movement from 'seeing' to 'knowing' – might supply alternative terms for reading texts which seem to legitimise the ideology of occupation and settlement.

# Argonauts of Western Pessimism, Clifford's Malinowski

John Hutnyk

## Part 1

'The institutionalisation of fieldwork in the late nineteenth and early twentieth centuries can be understood within a larger history of "travel"' (Clifford 1997: 64). As James Clifford retells the founding narrative, prior to Malinowski's 1915–19 adventures in the South Seas, anthropologists stayed at home. Only with the professionalisation of the discipline – and keeping science strictly separate from colonial administration (they liked to think) – did anthropologists begin to move (Stagl and Pinney 1996: 122).

Famously, much has been said about rhetorical fabulations in Malinowski, and elaborate commentary is given over to photographs of him in the Pacific, his tent on the beach, himself in his tent; Clifford sees the tent as an icon of 'deep' fieldwork. But he would also have it that Malinowski travels, that he was a 'displaced person' (Clifford 1988: 95) and 'shipwrecked' (p. 10). The reference here is to the English language difficulties of a Polish migrant, but by association the nautical tone deposits the 'founding' father-figure of fieldwork in a South Sea Island scene. Big reputations have been made in this potlatch of metaphor – Clifford himself came to fame editing the agenda-setting text *Writing Culture* with George Marcus (Clifford and Marcus 1986), and much attention to the ways of writing has enriched ethnography and extended the discipline. In the process, however, Malinowski has become a cartoon character. Good to think with, conjured here and there, turned every which way and moved about at will, he struts the Trobriand beach frightening postgraduate students with a year stuck in a tent reading trashy novels. As a rite of passage and ritual incantation, reading Malinowski has become, via Clifford and others, overdetermined. It is important to note that the circumstances of the paradigmatic deep fieldwork scene are more mobile than is often glossed. Malinowski moved back and forth between several islands, between the islands and Australia, and between the villages and the huts of traders, missionaries and magistrates. George Marcus has called Malinowski's years in the Trobriand village one of the initial examples of 'multi-site' ethnography (G. Marcus 1995: 106), although Michael Young has a different view of Malinowski's predicament, saying that travel 'was simple in theory, difficult in practice' and that, boat-bereft as he was, it was easier for him to stay put (M. Young 1984: 23). It might also be wondered just how often the other 'travel' aspects of Malinowski's book, such as the circulation of kula shells, or fascination with canoes, are stressed when the iconic text about 'staying put' to do fieldwork is taught as a vehicle for theoretical debates autonomous from the ethnographic context (G. Marcus 1988: 69–70). Malinowski travels, but with what degree of attention?

Clifford has praised Marcus's advocacy of 'innovative forms' of multi-locale research in more than one place (Clifford 1997: 27, 57; Marcus and Fischer 1986: 94, 186n). Given that multi-site ethnography has become fashionable for advocates of the new experimental moment (which seems to be dragging on and on), it is no surprise that Clifford's latest book celebrates travel as a metaphor for anthropology. In *Routes: Travel and Translation in the Late Twentieth Century*, Clifford sees 'fieldwork as a travel practice' (Clifford 1997: 8). *Routes* elaborates moments of his earlier book, *The Predicament of Culture* (1988), which was subtitled *Twentieth-Century Ethnography, Literature and Art*. The shift in the titles is indicative of a larger move, from twentieth-century modernism (albeit in post-modernist forms) to the 'Late' twentieth century (global and local, dwelling and travelling). From 'predicament' (as in 'stuck'?) to 'on the move' in less than a decade. Now the concerns are with translation, post-colonialism and allegedly post-exoticism. Clifford has been preoccupied with travel from his first book *Person and Myth: Maurice Leenhardt in the Melanesian World* (1982): it is my argument that the more the topic is discussed, the more stuck and stationary he becomes. The diary form that dominates the new book does not move beyond Malinowski, it does not offer a renewal of anthropology, it is – in my assessment – inferior to the earlier work, and, most disappointing of all, it offers no adequate response to the 'predicament' of our, however late, twentieth-century condition. The present commentary is an exploration of these concerns, but one that also seeks to show what can be retained and what is worth reading in this set of texts.

It seems to me that nearly all recent complaints about Clifford mouthed by anthropologists – and there is even more mouthed than written – are often so much sour grapes. It is the case that Clifford's work has shaken the more staid anthropologies, for good or bad it has inspired many, it has raised a host of questions and brought questions raised by others to wider attention. My own problem is largely with the context in which these questions are asked, or, rather, with the necessity to seek out a more radical questioning – one that takes place in a context that matters. The Clifford project, as I view it, is not so disruptive of anthropological modalities as the staid types fear, nor is it so revolutionary as the 'inspired' might think. We can learn much from Clifford, but there is little to it if there is not a programme which will transform the ways we write, read, think and live. The criticisms of Clifford come thick and fast: for collecting (Strathern 1991); for getting surrealism wrong (Price and Jamin 1988); for rehashing Geertz (Whitten 1991); for 'not being an anthropologist' (Nugent 1991: 130) (really? By what criteria?); for patronising women (almost everywhere, but most significantly in the 'companion volume' *Women Writing Culture* edited by Ruth Behar and Deborah Gordon 1995; also Babcock 1993); and for promoting a reflexive dialogic anthropology that is insufficiently aware, or perhaps not capable, of escaping its own artifice, and in danger of being not much more than another 'elitist, intellectualist and essentially Western paradigm for academic knowledge production' (Gledhill 1994: 224). Yet there maybe something to thank Clifford for: a generation of readers, who might have ignored anthropology, now find it intellectually, even politically, stimulating. Another kind of travel connection. Even though the critique of anthropology has its own long history (Hymes, Asad and, tangentially, Said), it was Clifford that helped put the debates on a wider curriculum and awoke other disciplines, such as history and literature, to matters of theoretical importance. It's good copy, Clifford's stuff, whatever limitations there also must be – 'wrong on any number of things' as Ben Ross might say. Similarly, many new and contemporary anthropological readers might not have found a way to Bataille, Leiris, the College of Sociology as part of the social sciences if he had not been such a good publicist (whatever he makes of that history). Even where he is wrong, simplifies or exaggerates, Clifford has the merit, at least, of bringing me back to the debate to try and distinguish, to differentiate and to supplement and extend. This in turn allows discussion of political effects and possible action against racism and imperialism, a salutary move away from endless arguing over whether anthropological truth claims are fiction or not, or that authority tropes rule the page, or don't.

Travel as a metaphor for anthropology, culture, translation and the predicament of late (very late) twentieth-century life *does* deserve evaluation. Let us check the visa requirements.

Clifford begins with travel as a way of bringing the borderlands of ethnography to attention. Certain aspects of the construction of anthropological texts had consistently slipped out of the frame. He offers a list:

(1) The means of transport is largely erased – the boat, the land rover, the

mission airplane. These technologies suggest systematic prior and ongoing contacts and commerce with exterior places and forces which are not part of the field/object. The discourse of ethnography ('being there') is separated from travel ('getting there'). (2) The capital city, the national context is erased. This is what George Condominas has called the *préterrain*, all those places you have to go through and be in relation with just to get to your village or to that place you will call your field. (3) Also erased: the university home of the researcher. Especially now that one can travel more easily to even the most remote sites and now that all sorts of places in the 'First World' can be fields (churches, labs, offices, schools, shoppingmalls), movement in and out of the field by both natives and anthropologists may be very frequent. (4) The sites and relations of *translation* are minimised. (Clifford 1997: 23)

Admittedly, Clifford calls this a partial list. And certainly some of his points might be extended and stressed. The erasure of the university context for anthropological research might especially be noted, as the anthropologist takes the university with him/her in the tent (see Hutnyk 1987: 60), and carries also the institutional apparatus, and entire global network of centres, conference circuits, publishers, bookshops, course guides, canonical texts, disciplinary affiliations, careers and tenure, and so on, along into this 'field'. Clifford's point, however, is sound. The 'field' was never a discrete and bounded scene, however much 'being there' was privileged over 'getting there', or even 'being there on the shelf' (see Hutnyk 1989: 105).

Can travel be the keyword which will open up the various contexts of cultural codification that are hidden in ethnography's realist narratives, and increasingly surrealist inspired ones if we are to follow Clifford? Already in his first chapter of *Routes* he finds it necessary to point out that certain forms of travel have not counted as 'proper travel' and he singles out the need to 'know a great deal more about how women travel' in various traditions and histories (Clifford 1997: 32). As well, we need more on cross-cultural travel, travel that avoids the hotel–motel circuits, immigration, servants who accompany travellers, explorers, guides and, later in a footnote, 'another area of specification I am not yet prepared to discuss: diasporic sexualities and/or sexualised diaspora discourses' (p. 367n [Why not?]). His brief introductory comments on domestic workers from South Asia, the Philippines and Malaysia, whose 'displacement and indenture have routinely involved forced sex' (p. 6) do not succeed as Clifford struggles 'never quite successfully to free the related term "travel" from a history of European, literary, male, bourgeois, scientific, heroic [and] recreational meanings' (p. 33). Just considering the absurdity of including the racist violence and atrocity of the slave trade under any revamped notion of 'travel' would be sufficient to show the likely inappropriateness of general-ising extensions of the travel trope in its Euro-American modes. Referring to 'transatlantic enslavement' as one of the harsh conditions of travel, 'to mention only a particularly violent example' (p. 35), he gathers deportation, uprooting, and other terms under the more inclusive 'diaspora' to which he devotes a useful essay (although still wanting to 'sort out the paradigms' [p. 247]). If it were not for several returns to the governing trope and the ambition to found a 'travelling theory' and a renewed anthropology on the term, perhaps there would be something gained in the association of all those diverse movements under travel: asking if the violence of slavery was travel does at least raise questions about the violences underlying all travel, including that which enables ethnographic projects, such as the colonial power that makes the world safe for ethnographers and tourists (see Phipps 1998).

I think it is worth attempting an evaluation of the general trajectory of this travel trope. Clifford's musings have deservedly come in for some serious scrutiny. Theorising travel has itself become an industry of sorts. And Clifford has become something of an avatar for dispersed members of the cultural studies writing corps. Among others, bell hooks is one who most clearly shows this double gift when she praises Clifford's essay 'Notes on Travel and Theory' (Clifford 1989), for 'his efforts to expand the travel/theoretical frontier so that it might be more inclusive' (hooks 1995: 43). She is also unsparingly critical, showing that the answers to the questions Clifford poses about travel require a 'theory of the journey that would expose the extent to which holding on to the concept of "travel" as we know it [and as Clifford does] is also a way to hold on to imperialism'. She also makes the stark point that '"Travel" is not a word that can be easily evoked to talk about the Middle Passage, The Trail of Tears, the landing of Chinese immigrants, the forced relocation of Japanese Americans, or the plight of the homeless', and – though it should be noted how far hooks's own examples are 'American' ones – that theorising disparate journeying is 'crucial to our understanding of any politics of location' (p. 43). This is no game, however, as hooks points out that 'playing' with the notion of travel may not exactly be the best way to narrate experiences of travel that are about encounters with the terrorism of white supremacy (p. 44).

Clifford wants to 'hang on' to the term travel because of its very 'taintedness' – its 'associations with gendered racial bodies, class privilege, specific means of conveyance, beaten paths, agents, frontiers, documents, and the like' (Clifford 1997: 39). A vocabulary of apparent sin – gender and class as 'tainted' – which redeems travel is akin to what Kaplan calls a 'theoretical tourism [which] constitutes the margin as a linguistic or critical variation, a new poetics of the exotic' (Kaplan 1996: 93). As Kaplan presents it, this is a 'utopian process of letting go of privileged identities and practices [requiring] emulation of the ways and modes of "modernity's" others' (p. 88) and this 'repeats the anthropological gesture of erasing the subject position of the theorist and [perpetuating] a kind of colonial discourse in the name of progressive politics' (p. 88). Perhaps this is also at play in the theoretical advocacy of the travel trope in Clifford, although I would also go further to read a more pervasive 'anthropological gesture' here in the usurping of the 'other's' place of representation as Clifford becomes spokesman (gender intended) for those writers of diaspora and politics of 'travel' he so usefully promotes (this is important in light of Clifford's readings of Paul Gilroy [1993] and Avtar Brah [1996] in his 'diasporas' essay – the institutional and disciplinary overview question is: Why is it that Clifford is the one so well placed, resourced, and circulated to provide the global survey of best new work in the field?). When it comes to presentation of progressive post-colonial, post-exotic Others, Clifford's text does not fall for any of the old manners of representing difference, his version of anthropological ventriloquy occurs through representing himself, and his predicament, *through* that of the other. That this is done on the basis of explicit self-reflexive post-structural high theory credentials may be all the more troublesome.

## Part 2

I want to put Clifford in the fieldwork scene for a moment (there will be justification for dress-ups later). Clifford comments often on photographs; he loves instamatic anthropology. Especially shots of the photogenic Malinowski. In *Routes* the much-conjured-with scene of Malinowski's tent on the beach in the Trobriands is evoked again (Clifford 1997: 20, 54; see also Clifford 1990). The technology of the tent as a marker of presence, in the village, as well as 'its mobility, its thin flaps, providing an "inside" where notebooks, special foods, a typewriter could be kept' (Clifford 1997: 20), also provokes Clifford to ask who is being observed, natives or anthropologist, hiding away behind the canvas (see Dube 1998). He is interested too in the shots of Malinowski in the field in *Coral Gardens and Their Magic*; dressed in white, surrounded by black bodies, in a posture, attitude and style that reminds Clifford of those colonial Europeans dressing formally for dinner in hot sweaty climes (Clifford 1997: 74). Malinowski is not 'going native' here. In *Writing Culture* Clifford takes up the photograph of Malinowski inside his tent: 'Malinowski recorded himself writing' (Clifford and Marcus 1986: 1), but curiously the position of the photographer is not interrogated when Clifford asks 'who speaks? who writes? when and where? with or to whom? under what institutional and historical constraints?' (p. 13). Surely attention to these questions should teach us to read such scenes in a multi-locale way, to see the traces of other travelling Europeans, and of the international extension of the means of representation, at least, in this scene from early twentieth-century Trobriana. The photographs in question must have been taken on a day when Billy Hancock or some other European neighbour was visiting Malinowski (most likely it was Hancock as some of his photographs, better than Malinowski's, were used in *Argonauts* [for more on photographs see Kratz 1994; and Hutnyk 1996: ch. 5]). Yet, whoever the photographer was for sure, we have no guarantee that this was everyday attire and that Malinowski is got up in gear for a sweaty colonial dinner. Well, perhaps, but what is served by such questions? Then again, what did he get up to? After reading the letters (Malinowski and Elsie Masson, in Wayne 1995) there is perhaps reason to suspect the taboo subject of sexual activity in the field, as signalled, but never confirmed, in the 1967 publication of his secret Trobriand jottings, *A Diary in the Strict Sense of the Term*, has become the hidden controversy of Malinowski's stay. He 'pawed' and perhaps more: the *Diary* was censored by his widow before publication (Newton 1993: 7). Of course such exploits could be left out of the written text by a man capable of being simultaneously engaged to daughters of professors in both Melbourne and Adelaide, and possibly others (Wayne 1995: 88, 98). The story of 'pillow-talk' ethnographic instruction on the part of concubines in the field remains a hidden one, even as Clifford cites two recent examples (though leaves one out of the bibliography, referencing only the rather tame Rabinow 1997, omitting Cesura 1982; a steamier episode may be found in Wade 1993). It is perhaps often the case, however, that Malinowski's sex life gets raised beyond its importance.

Whatever the gory details, how the Trobriand books have travelled. Annette Weiner, who also did her fieldwork on Kiriwina in the Trobriands, says, 'No other ethnography has had a more lasting impact' (Weiner 1988: 140), and it has never been out of print. As I have argued in 'Castaway Anthropology', the voyaging of kula structures the book (Hutnyk 1988: 46). 'Argonauts' is the most obvious clue, and Malinowski's thinking can be discerned from the published correspondence between himself and his first wife, Elsie Masson: Jason/Malinowski imagines he would make 'a nice penny' out of the 'golden fleece' of his text (Wayne 1995; Bronio to Elsie, 21 December 1921; 4 April 1922). The influence of Malinowski's Trobriand text has travelled in many directions and justice could not be done in a single chapter to the disciplinary ramifications alone, leaving aside political, social, economic and psychological consequences of the work's itinerary. Malinowski and his protégés came to establish their brand of anthropology world-wide – departmental intrigues there must be – but it very much depended upon the initial success of the *Argonauts*. If he hadn't managed to get *Argonauts* published, Malinowski had decided he was going to go into the margarine business (Wayne 1995: 162; Bronio to Elsie, 4 June 1918). So the text had to be a success and was compared from the beginning to almost every other book: Boon quotes Frazer's preface comparison of *Argonauts* with Cervantes and Shakespeare (Boon 1983: 133), while Conrad, Joyce, Zola, Freud, Kipling and Frazer are recruited in other commentaries (Thornton 1985; Ardener 1985; Clifford 1986; Stocking 1985; Strathern 1987; and Rapport 1990). Already in the letters Elsie Masson was filling Malinowski's head with grand ideas. She imagines the two of them together on a sea voyage: 'You know how Robert Louis Stevenson used to cruise around the South Sea Islands in any old ship, and carry out his work all the while, and wring such a lot of romance and interest besides health out of his life' (in Wayne 1995: 40). Malinowski accepts and appropriates the comparison (Wayne 1995; Bronio to Elsie, 17 January 1918), and also likens his 'writing diary' to the composition of the Arabian Nights (Wayne 1995: 18), anticipating the formulation 'writing culture' by over seventy years. The momentum of *Argonauts* (as vehicle for various debates) was recharged with the publication of the *Diary*. The literary complex multiplies. Clifford takes the *Diary*, with its day-to-day minutiae of novels read, anxieties, prejudice against 'the nigs' and fantasies of sex, and the carefully polished and public *Argonauts* together as one text without forgetting that both are constructed and selective works. Despite the 'unintended for publication' tag attached to the *Diary*, and the hostile or cautiously indifferent reception it received from anthropologists at the time of its release, it now has become, seventy years after it was written, another part of the 'complex intersubjective situation' (Clifford 1986: 145) which also produced *Argonauts*, *The Sexual Life of Savages*, *Coral Gardens* as well as other eruptions of matters Trobriand into anthropological dis- course. 'It is I who will describe or create them' (Malinowski 1967: 140) Malinowski says, and still in 1935, twenty years after his first visit, he was writing up: 'Once again I have to make my appearance as the chronicler and spokesman of the Trobrianders' (Malinowski 1935: v). It would be impossible to track comprehensively the extent to which these texts have now travelled through the various global circuits of discipline, publishing, libraries and gossip.

Of all Malinowski's travel books, though, it is the *Diary* which most appeals to Clifford when he acclaims it as a heteroglot text: 'Malinowski wrote in Polish with frequent use of English, word and phrases in German, French, Greek, Spanish and Latin, and of course [!] terms from the native languages [of which] there were four: Motu, Mailu, Kiriwinian and Pidgin'

(Clifford 1986: 53). Yet celebrations of heteroglossia, especially when found in rehabilitations of previously discarded texts, seem somewhat forced. The current fashion for hybridity and multi-vocal dialogue (Malinowski talking to himself in the jungle) does not exclude the anthropologist, or later the commentator, from the controlling position of authorship as Clifford so often seems to want. Pluralities and multiplicities do not necessarily subvert established orthodoxies of publication and reception. The *Diary*, in Clifford's hands, becomes a record of a fragmenting disassociated self attached, in a process of functionalist therapy, to the *Argonauts* ethnography written several years later (in the Canary Islands): 'One of the ways Malinowski pulled himself together was by writing ethnography. Here the fashioned wholeness of a self and of a culture seem to be mutually reinforcing allegories of identity' (Clifford 1986: 152). This, presumably, is to be contrasted to the 'special poignancy' of the last words of the diary: 'Truly I lack real character' (Malinowski 1967: 53). Clifford adds: 'the arbitrary code of one language, English, is finally given precedence' (Clifford 1986: 53). Later he calls *Argonauts* a 'lie', or rather a 'saving fiction' (Clifford 1988: 99) and suggests that 'To unify a messy scene of writing it is necessary to select, combine, rewrite (and thus efface)' (Clifford 1988: 110).

## Part 3

Much of Clifford's own work takes on the diary form. In a chapter of *Routes* called 'Palenque Log', Clifford offers a travel report of a visit to the site of some Mexican ruins in the state of Chiapas. It is perhaps the influence of Michel Leiris that gives Clifford cause to include weather reports, the news that he has dropped his camera on the bathroom floor, breakfast details and bus itineraries at the beginning of his narrative. Clifford has been reading Leiris for a long time. In *The Predicament of Culture*, the chapter 'Tell Me About Your Trip: Michel Leiris' is devoted to the ethnographic documentation of everything. Leiris's African ethnography from the Mission Dakar-Djibouti tells of both beauty and of the gloriously satisfying morning shit (see Koepping 1989). But more than sixty years later why is this still 'experimental'? Hasn't the convention of travel writing invaded creative ethnography as well, introducing predictable and pedestrian routine to what once were curious or exotic revelations? Is it too demanding to wonder if both travel writing and ethnography need sometimes to be rendered more seriously? Clifford visits the 'jungle walk' at the 'Temple of Inscriptions' and his text documents, in fifteen-minute segments, his 'trip'. Why should we care? (And although his dropped camera jams up, he still manages to take a photograph, it is included in his book, how? Later he writes: 'I'm glad I can't take pictures' and 'Everywhere I glance, it seems, someone is pointing a camera ... hundreds of photos per hour' [Clifford 1997: 224]. I hope this is only an ironic rehearsal of the photogenic self-loathing particular to tourists today.)

We should care about Clifford's trip, not because he is illustrating that the 'ethnographer' is little different from a tourist on a tourist bus snapping happy snaps and buying souvenir T-shirts, but because of the context. Here is Clifford, the producer of books, telling us about his travels in, not insignificantly, Chiapas, in an experimental 'post-exoticist' (Clifford 1997: 90) ethnographic text offered as illustration of contemporary anthropological writing, and he leaves out all but the most trivial reference to politics. At the same time that this report is published, the consequences of a military crackdown on the people of Chiapas, initiated just a few months after Clifford's 'Palenque Log' adventure, visits death and destruction upon the indigenous people, farmers and peasants of the region. Clifford's only substantial comment on the Zapatista 'rebellion' is that it interrupted travel to the ruins at Palenque 'temporarily'. No elaboration on what force was needed to ensure this temporary interruption, no report on the military repressions there, or for that matter the more disturbing actions in nearby Geurrero, nor of the US support for the Mexican regime and so on. Surely at some point the political and military force that enables travel narratives and ethnography should be examined by the self-reflexive scholar who has made a career of telling us that anthropology is founded on power and authority? Later Clifford comments on the exchange value of a fax machine for SubComandante Marcos, and how it is 'not surprising' that the Zapatista uprising was timed to coincide with the implementation of the free trade agreement (Clifford 1997: 322) – this is at least better than some romantic reports on the Zapatistas which suggested that the date was chosen because it coincided with indigenous harvest rituals – but Clifford draws no conclusions beyond noting the 'mysterious' equivalences made between corn in Mexico and corn in Kansas by way of the international market: 'the fact still does not compute' (Clifford 1997: 323; see Spivak 1987: 166–7). This is not to say that the 'independent traveller' (Clifford identifies himself this way three times in the chapter) should have noticed at the time – six months before the uprising – that Zapatista organisers were working among the people (and had been for some years); but certainly pointing to privileges of position – as independent traveller or even as critic – and noting incongruities and contradictions, does not yet amount to an adequate politics. It may be bordering on churlishness to wonder at the timing of Clifford's visit to Chiapas and to link this also to the (un)computed facts of power that include NAFTA, research visas, social science, military control and market trickery. We do not know if he has returned to the troubled region again, but certainly this resonates with other timely anthropological visitations; there will be reason to consider especially Malinowski in the South Seas during the 1914-17 imperialist world war.

Echoes of other famous monographs on time: Lévi-Strauss is evoked when Clifford wonders when was the best time to visit (Clifford 1997: 232); the Palenque arrival story could have come from any of dozens of scene-setting ethnographic scenes – Firth arriving at Tikopia, Evans-Pritchard 'on the heels of a punitive expedition', Geertz invisible in Bali (Clifford 1997: 237; on Malinowski's arrival see Thornton 1985: 13; on Geertz consider how Indonesian politics is invisible in the much-taught Cockfight article [Geertz 1973]). After a day full of minutiae reported as if anyone's day would be available for rendering, only Clifford, professor and author, armed with the resources of the publishing industry, Harvard University Press, past authorisations, the history of anthropology, institutional affiliation with 'hist-con' (the History of Consciousness Program at the University of California), in the West, in the 1990s, gets into print.

Admittedly, Clifford is only one person who produces books (though his research activity is also shared among research assistants, copyeditors, typesetters, binders, packers, truck drivers, salespersons and promotional corps). In the current conditions of academia, however, it is clear that many of those who may have been inspired by Clifford's work could not get academic jobs, especially not in anthropology departments. An entire generation, even two, has not entered the academy at a time when student numbers have increased exponentially and funding plummeted in real terms. The old guard has remained, beset by increased teaching load, administrative duties and commercialisation, bunkered down in defence of their own patch, while in a curiously calculated backlash they attack the postmodern anthropology that Clifford has come to represent.

## Part 4

The front-cover photograph of *Routes* deserves attention, since photographs are the icons of travel stories; necessary accoutrements, markers of real presence (more so than postcards of the very same scenes). The 'subject' James Bosu has been cropped for the cover, although remaining curiously 'hybrid' with traditional 'mind-boggling' headdress and necktie. Clifford 'gravitates towards the incongruous detail' (Clifford 1997: 178), but Bosu's stubbie of beer is kept for the inside enlargement. This doctoring – not necessarily by Clifford, but by design – may well change readings of the image, and it is not without significance that the cover evokes a schoolbook with its background map of the world (or rather, of the West Coast of North America, Clifford's institutional base). In the context of a debate about his Mashpee study in *Predicament*, Clifford has written that the 'invented differences' he values 'are very similar to the products of a transnational capitalism that feeds on impurities, mix and match, unconstrained juxtaposition and import-export' (Clifford 1991: 146). This important point is not, however, countered by fascination with the very mix and match 'invented differences' so denounced. The review of the Wahgi (Highland Papua New Guinea) exhibition that constitutes the chapter 'Paradise' in *Routes* also includes a photograph of the woman Kala Wala, though Clifford mistakenly identifies her earrings as beer-can rip-tops when they are in fact clearly not can but stubbie tops (here the incongruities are of the international beer market, which is not everywhere exactly the same – locally significant classificatory distinctions may require more careful fieldwork). 'Paradise' starts as a second-person narrative description of a visit to the Museum of Mankind in London. The addressee 'You', I presume, could be Clifford's six-year-old son, who accompanies him, or it could also be the reader, for whom the significance of the various incongruous commodities of a PNG pig festival are explained. We are like a child before the critic's explication. The focus is on the 'strangeness of everyday things' (Clifford 1997: 154). A third photograph in the chapter, of Kulka Kon looking 'authentic', has Clifford on two occasions wondering what he would look like dressed in a Hawaiian shirt, as a taxi driver, a Christian – Clifford likes to play dress-ups with the natives (pp. 183, 187). There is yet another reference to the past of anthromonography as one of the 'natives' looks covertly at the camera in a staged shot, just as Clifford has already pointed out with regard to Malinowski's photograph of a Kula presentation in *Argonauts* (Clifford 1988: 21; 1990). Clifford's review of this exhibition explores a wide range of themes: PNG design; art, which includes beer advertisements, of a particular PNG style; reports on exhibition catalogue cover controversies (who chose to crop Clifford's cover? who controls the text?); inclusions and exclusions; debt and obligation; echoes of the past and experimental innovations. It was also a relief to get to this Museum of Mankind exhibit after a gruelling visit, with son trailing behind, poor kid, to the Guinness Book of World Records Trocadero show at Piccadilly (we do not get the younger Clifford's views on either show). But we also do not know if there is any sense in which Clifford feels drawn into the obligations and debt alliance with the Wahgi people which he discusses in the context of exhibition curator O'Hanlon's collecting (Clifford 1997: 170). Although their presence seems to be ever more elided in the abstracting processes of exhibition and then in exhibition review, the Wahgi were the ones who enabled O'Hanlon to put together the exhibition and they consciously involved him in ongoing obligations, which Clifford details. Being able to fill a book – at least a chapter – with images and discussion of the exhibit must, in these terms, indebt Clifford to the Wahgi too, yet we do not find out how such 'relations of collecting', all 'exchanged and appropriated in continued local/global circuits' (p. 171), obligate him, nor how his routes-review returns anything to the Wahgi themselves. Pointing out one's complicity in these relations of collecting and appropriation does not begin to undo them.

We have long known that what appeals to Clifford is the incongruous and the hybrid. He wants to 'quibble' with the terms used by those who would suggest that souveniring the incongruous and celebrating the syncretic initiates a new round of intellectual imperialism (Clifford 1997: 180, citing Shaw and Stewart's use of 'hegemony'). He paraphrases Marx, without acknowledgement, when discussing the ways that people from PNG 'make their own history, though not in conditions of their own choosing' (p. 161; the quote can be found in Marx 1968: 96) and he celebrates the hybrid in the face of those who would think it 'axiomatic' that culture is diminished 'in direct proportion to the increase of Coke and Christianity' (p. 161). Though it is not simply these two scourges of humanity that should be marked, surely it is necessary to rethink easy incongruity-hunting since the conditions of making history are now everywhere the context of an international capitalism that, as Clifford notes again, thrives on just such hybridity and cultural differences. For my part, it is not quite enough to suggest that the notion of some sort of 'anthropological hegemony' conjures up 'disempowered intellectuals – privileged no doubt, but hardly in a position to enforce their definitions' (p. 182). In a review of a definition-setting exhibition in London or in an anthropological text that circulates the world via bookshop, conference and course guide, this is blatant mystification. It is not the case that, since 'the Trobrianders are free to read Malinowski's accounts of their culture as parodies' as Clifford claims in *Predicament*, this somehow unravels any of the authority or privilege of either ethnographer or critic. Neither James Bosu nor the Trobrianders publish their diaries for global circulation via Harvard University Press, nor do they curate exhibitions in the old imperial capital. (I am resisting the temptation to diarise myself, but as I am writing this in Heidelberg, what should be made of the complete Masewa canoe from Kiriwana [1988 erworben] that can be glimpsed through the window of the Völkerkundmuseum, Palais Weimar, closed for the summer?)

There is more that could be said on the incongruous bits and pieces Clifford collects, especially so in the context of his museum studies. I would also want to question why trinket collection has taken the place of more systematic analyses. His text is a phantasmogoric, but ultimately limited, cabinet of curiosities, relics and snippets. Indeed, considerations of Clifford's much favoured collecting tropes, collage and pastiche, often seem to side-step the political. Just as travel, according to hooks and Kaplan, is of use to the well-placed and comfortable, might it also be so that collage, and the closely related, perhaps more calculated, montage has certain ideological effects (see McQuire 1995, 1997; D. F. Miller 1992)?

In a post-Clifford anthropological universe everything is in danger of becoming collage. Even Malinowski was a surrealist in Clifford's estimation. Wrenching details of Trobriand trade behaviour and identifying these with canoe magic and myth, then comparing kula valuables with the English crown jewels, is an example of 'the surrealist moment in ethnography' where the 'possibility of comparison exists in unmediated tension with sheer incongruity' (Clifford 1988: 146). Surrealist procedures 'are always present in ethnography' for Clifford, although Leiris's *L'Afrique fantôme* is the only pure example (p. 146). The ethnographic surrealist attitude has other Trobriand avatars, however; one Clifford singles out as prime illustration is Leach and Kildea's film *Trobriand Cricket*, where a gentleman's game brought by missionaries at the time of Malinowski – indeed he refers to it in *Coral Gardens* (Malinowski 1935: 211–13) – is turned into 'ludic warfare' by the Trobrianders with the inventive cultural skill of a Picasso (Clifford 1988: 148).

Writing in *Routes* of *The Predicament of Culture*, Clifford describes the use of collage 'as a way of making space for heterogeneity, for historical and political, not simply aesthetic juxtaposition' (Clifford 1997: 3). Yet the question is how useful are even 'historical and political' juxtapositions without thinking politically about what to do with them? And what does this mean in anthropology? Is such collage meant more adequately to represent the world? If so, what distinguishes this from the political and historical, and somewhat random sampling techniques, I can achieve with dextrous use of my remote control while watching the CNN and BBC satellite news feeds? Remote control? Not much control, say some. Another kind of politics awaits.

## Part 5

The work required for another kind of politics of anthropology and travel would not be easy, of course. But I believe it can be found in reconfiguring Clifford's version of diaspora taken up from the work of Gilroy (1993) and Brah (1996). Clearly, the circulation of culture and commodities along diasporic lines requires an analysis capable of dealing in luxury, violence, modes of communication and telematic advance. Clifford sees the need for study of these things, but does not need the rigour of a Marxist frame to implement such studies – 'unlike Marx' he does not need to work through the 'necessary evil' (Clifford 1997: 10) of capitalism, and so the context of his telematic mantra remains an unexplored tension. He repeatedly recites, on almost every page of the diaspora essay, the importance of 'technologies of transport; communication, and labour migration'; 'Airplanes, telephones, tape cassettes, camcorders'; 'business circuits and travel trajectories'; 'a discourse that is travelling or hybridising in new global conditions ... increased immigration, global communications, and transport'; 'articulation of travels, homes, memories, and transnational connections'; 'changing conditions of mass communication, globalization, post- and neo-colonialism, these circuits'; 'given transport and communications technologies ... television ... telephone circuits'. Then specifically reading Gilroy: 'Gilroy is preoccupied with ships, phonograph records, sound systems, and all technologies that cross' and so on right up to the very last line of the chapter where 'global technologies' (pp. 244–78) have still not been unpacked beyond this listing and yet we are left in a 'fraught existence'. The question to be asked is whether or not we are in a position more adequately to describe some of these processes, to add any detail to the list, to evaluate them and the ways that people are imbricated with these crossing technologies. The telematic mantra of information flow, new media, travelling culture and the internet is construed as a metonymic code which synecdochically signals both progress and change, but nothing is offered once it is named. Theorists of telematics repeatedly tell us that an intensification, abstraction and a speeding up of capitalism, financial flows, media and so on, are the defining characteristics of the current period, but what is to be done?

Where Avtar Brah attempts to get more serious is when faced with Clifford's point that it is hard to avoid a slippage between the term diaspora as theory concept, diasporic 'discourses', and distinct historical experiences of diaspora. She proposes that because these terms invite a kind of theorising that is 'embedded' in particular histories, 'this embeddedness is precisely why it becomes necessary to mark out the conceptual terrain that these words [diaspora, borders] construct and traverse if they are to serve as theoretical tools' (Brah 1996: 179). Brah sets out to 'explore the analytical purchase of these terms' in her book *Cartographies of Diaspora*, using 'historically contingent "genealogies" in the Foucauldian sense' to see diaspora as an 'ensemble of investigative technologies ... historical trajectories ... critique of discourses of fixed origins ... [and thus to analyse the] ... problematic of the "indigene" subject position and its precarious relationship to "nativist" discourses' (p. 180). Also invoking Deleuze and Guattari, for all the problems of their work in terms of romantic primitivism and deliriously excessive metaphorising, to address the strengths and limitations of the theme of borders as a political construct and analytical category, and of location, displacement and dislocation, Brah is able to emphasise the power relations within institutions and practices and provide 'a conceptual grid for historical analyses of contemporary trans/national movements of people, information, cultures, commodities and capital' (p. 181). A political programme offering more than 'lucid uncertainty' would not be incompatible with Deleuze and Guattari, especially where their work specifically addresses questions of capitalist transition. The possibility of adding specificity to 'how the materiality of economic, political and signifying practices is experienced' (p. 197) is entailed in such an approach, and the ways 'particular fields of power articulate in the construction of hierarchies of domination and subordination in a given context' (p. 198) can then be revealed. This is not the place to make a further evaluation of Brah's success or failure in the attempt, but it is possible to point to detailed and specific studies that have been inspired in part by her analytical orientation (of course I think it's in Sharma, Hutnyk and Sharma 1996 and Kaur and Hutnyk 1998). An interesting development relates to Clifford's note that 'transnational connections linking diasporas need not be articulated primarily through a real or symbolic homeland' (Clifford 1997: 249). This point made by both Brah and Gilroy on various occasions has been most usefully extended and detailed in the work of Raminder Kaur and Virinder Kalra (Kaur and Kalra 1996). The extension of the citation to the many others working in this field is a further obligation (for some recent examples I would also cite especially: Housee and Sharma 1998; Hesse 1998; Sayyid 1997).

## Part 6

What we can take from Clifford is his examination of how the polyphonic heteroglossia of Malinowski's experience in the Trobriands was rendered into text as a coherent, worked up, sifted and arranged, coordinated and orchestrated narrative. Whether Elsie had a greater or lesser hand in this (the *Argonauts* is inscribed 'to my collaborator'), whether Conrad was the deity hovering behind the project, and whether the *Diary* and the letters reveal some more primordial truth are not the point. What is revealed is the process of making narrative out of events: editing, arranging, conjuring. The travel metaphor here does the trick, in large part, for Malinowski. It also does so for Clifford, indeed, organising not just one text, but increasingly his entire oeuvre. This has implications for understanding travel, and tourism, since travel stories – whether told after the trip, or prepackaged in the brochure as a promise, or narrated by the guide as a product – are the stuff of contemporary travel economics. So, it is important to ask why travel theory emerges now, why Clifford in the 1990s, and so on, and rather than suggesting that Malinowski and Clifford are the same just because both write travel diaries, I think it is useful to point to the structural conditions of their travelling production. Such a reading would begin with the importance of the 1914–17 imperialist war for the practice of long-term fieldwork and the political conditions that have now forced a rethinking of fieldwork. In between these moments came the emergence of anti-colonial movements and non-aligned states, who, among other things, developed a shared suspicion of anthropologists. The 'fieldwork' discussion may seem to have been interrupted, but it was not displaced by the success, and failure, of the anti-colonial movements, of the Soviet experiment, and the ongoing permutations of the Chinese revolution and its subsequent adventures in Naxalites in India, Khmer Rouge in Cambodia, Shining Path and Tupac Amaru in South America and so on (I would concur with Gayatri Spivak's dismissal of post-colonialism as a 'bitter joke' [see Hutynk 1996: 36]). The difference between advocates of fieldwork now and then seem not so great when considered in terms of the necessity of 'safe passage' and the 'pax Europeana' (Stagl 1996: 262). Both Malinowski and Clifford (sensibly) seek out that safe site. It cannot be a simple co-incidence which aligns the range of interests, concepts, modes of analysis ('ethnographic' audience research for example) and criteria of relevance of travelling theory with processes of transnational restructuring. And though it is not yet clear that Malinowski's analysis of the kula really does line up so conveniently with the coordinates of post-First World War social and political dynamics, to begin to analyse travel politically with these pos-sibilities in mind might entail an opening for critical anthropology. The texts of Malinowski (and those of Clifford, complacent yet possessing a certain grandeur) may not have been intended as allegories of the political, but by being available to the reading requirements of different times they become so.

In the end, what is there to carry away from Clifford's travel stories? I would not say I have no problems with travel – as much that it might seem very worldly, and even at times humble, to gloss anthropology as travel, such a characterisation does not satisfy. This is not because anthropology should be defended as something better than travel (I recall a certain Melbourne anthropologist at one seminar holding up his passport stamped with an Indonesian 'Research Visa' to prove that he was different to a tourist – to which someone quipped, 'Where did you get it, CIA?'). Can anthropology become something better than it has been? The task of confronting, understanding and intervening in the violence and exploitation that so often (past and present) accompanies human movement requires much more than elaborate brochures. The paradigm offered by the travel guide, with scenic views, staged authenticity (however sustaining) and carved souvenirs is insufficient for a writing which would respond to the troubles and tribulations of the various movements we witness. Human dwelling together has often also meant moving past each other without comprehension, or worse, as Malinowski did also notice (but often failed to discuss), with violent and deadly repercussions. Without a critical perspective grounded in a practical politics dedicated to changing such troubles, and transforming the conditions of inequality, exploitation and oppression from which they arise, anthropology (multi-site or bounded), travel (alternative or mainstream) and 'the history of ethnography' (ortho-dox or Cliffordian) remains only so much sight-seeing. How long can we keep on saying, 'Je haïs les voyages et les explorations'?

## Note

Close reading by Peter Phipps and conversations with John Gledhill helped improve this text. The usual disclaimers apply, particularly to Clifford's own comments on an earlier draft – all errors which remain are of course my irresponsibility. I also owe John Gledhill thanks for many discussions.

A more detailed reading of Clifford's misuse of Marx can be found in a longer version of the present chapter, 'Clifford's Ethnographica', *Critique of Anthropology* 18: 4 (1998), 339–78.

# Lagging Behind: Bhabha, Post-colonial Theory and the Future

John Phillips

Does theory travel? The critique of western metaphysics that characterises much of what is now recognised as post-structuralist or postmodernist discourse is also inextricably related to work that develops as a self-conscious travelling theory, and is concerned with the phenomena of post-coloniality. This intellectual idiom both theorises the experience and representation of travel from perspectives distinct from that of the imperial and metropolitan centre, and may itself be read as a form of travelogue articulating the historical and geographical displacement undergone by the populations of the colonial periphery.

To what extent is the post-colonial critic's adoption of the West's self-critique a repetition of the colonising gesture itself? Homi K. Bhabha, arguably the most influential theorist of cultural hybridity in the wake of globalisation, and so of the impact of accelerated movement in the post-modern world, claims that contemporary critical discourse must continue to be grounded in the colonial struggle. This chapter examines how far Bhabha's project can be maintained on his own terms. In displacing western discourse and resituating it on the shifting frontiers of world history, Bhabha appears to be attempting the impossible. By taking theory on a trip he must simultaneously maintain a certain rationality while under-mining it at its very source. Is this impossible journey necessary? In this article I affirm that it is.

## Travel Writing and Post-colonial Theory

Since Edward Said's influential *Orientalism* established that European expansionism is as much a matter of discourse and hegemony as of technological and economic domination, critics have vigorously exploited the opportunities that his thesis makes available for politically-oriented scholarship. Literary criticism especially has been able to analyse the ways in which texts explicitly and implicitly negotiate the movement between political discourse and aesthetic discourse. There are two dimensions intrinsic to post-colonial theory. The first, as a colonial discourse analysis, examines European culture and literature for how the West produces representations of its others, against which and through which it defines itself. The second examines the ways in which the contradictions and inconsistencies of colonial discourse produce a locus of instability from which the central epistemological, ontological and legislative terms of the West can be challenged. In this sense, the logic of post-colonialism and, as we shall see, Bhabha's own theoretically abstruse discourse, can be regarded as extrapolations of the geographical and ethnic boundaries across which travellers of all kinds step.

While European travel and exploration writing can reveal how colonialism encodes and legitimates its social and political strategies through discourse, travel also provides significant material for the development of post-colonial theory in the figure of the migrant and through hybrid discourses produced in diaspora. Broadly, if schematically, travel writing in the first case challenges but ultimately supports notions of stable identity and in the second threatens them irremediably. There are thus two important points to be made at the outset regarding the relation between post-colonial theory and travel. The first concerns identity and the second concerns destination.

The travel narrative concerns situations in which the stability of the self is often challenged. 'People in motion', comments John Seelye (1977), 'are inherently interesting' (p. 283). The travel narrative can thus represent through the motif of the person in trouble the whole dialectic of identity, in which the stable self tested by unpredictable contingencies must respond in consistent and enlightened ways, often achieving considerable personal enrichment on the way. The subject of travel narrative must integrate new experiences and radical geographical and cultural differences within a stable cultural frame, whether this is the theological context of the eighteenth-century puritan in a disorienting and savage new world or the context of nineteenth-century heroic individualism, the first-person narrator commanding an aesthetic control over strange landscapes as a kind of corollary to the coloniser's economic plunder.

The dialectic of identity and difference, of stable subjectivity against capricious contingency, as G. W. F. Hegel's great *Logic* famously documents, can cope with as much trouble as it finds – the more the better – for within this logic difference will always be (and from the beginning will always have been) accounted for by the identity that it helps to shape and colour. Difference in this dialectic is, in the words of the *Logic*, 'the essential moment of identity itself', it is that through which identity 'determines itself and is distinguished from difference' (Hegel 1975: 417). The logic of identity and difference can be set alongside statements that easily justify Hegel's reputation as being profoundly eurocentric (like most western thinkers of the time). In *The Philosophy of History*, most obviously, Hegel gives an account of the four successive stages of world historical develop-ment that imposes an '*a priori* structure of history' on to an empirical reality by identifying the earliest stages with their lingering geographical and cultural existence in 'the Oriental World'. The Orientals are, in distinction to the Modern Christians, 'not yet self-sufficient' (pp. 352–3). The connection between logic and history in Hegel relies on the *Concept* [*Begriff*], which unfolds itself dialectically in so far as the contradictions of its earlier stages are each resolved (and cancelled out) in successive ones – i.e. history is the progress of a spirit that defines itself increasingly through the negation of its others. This logic, however, depends on the susceptibility to negation of all the fragmented and particular aspects of difference itself.

Post-colonial theory on the other hand is interested in a kind of difference, a notion of difference if that is possible, that is not negatable in dialectic, that is not reducible to an identity for whom difference is simply a word attached to its empirical others – the savage, the oriental, the African – which it thus economically, hegemonically and above all conceptually controls. Very generally, the figure of the exile – the unstable subject of numerous historical cases of exodus, diaspora, migration and decolonisation – represents a subject that belongs to no dialectic, that eludes the logic of identity. It is a subject for whom the origin (or home) is from the beginning a displacement and cannot thus be fixed. The figure of the migrant, nomadic in essence, begins in travel, or with a lost beginning, an essentially irreversible trajectory, and has nowhere to return, which brings us to the question of destination.

Neither the identity nor the destination of the post-colonial traveller exists in advance of the diverse narratives of displacement, disorientation and alienation that emerge in the wake of European expansion. This has to do with the false or failed dialectic of colonialism in which territorial annexation and economic exploitation are justified by the sense that im-perialism is basically a mission of civilisation. The inevitable consequences of colonisation on the colonised, including the advantages of modernisation – access to the coloniser's language, culture and advanced systems of education, advanced technics, massively increased trade options, as well as a whole legislative network based on institutions of government, law and policing – also involve the production of a colonised subject in terms of retarded political, economic and social development, habits of dependency and, crucially, lack of self-confidence or at the very least a confused and deracinated cultural identity. But in the hands of post-colonial theory the rootless colonial or decolonised subject becomes a challenge to the fundamental assumptions behind western notions of stable identity, and so to the future of modernity in the figure of the belated subject of colonialism. For post-colonialism, the very notion of home is undecidable, at best an opening to an uncertain future. This undecidability in the face of an incalculable future infects the western narrative of progress with a sense that it is in fact going nowhere.

## European Hallucination

While the earliest documents in an increasingly accepted canon of post-colonial theory concern colonised cultures and their resistance to colonialism (for example Fanon 1961), the field seems really to have taken off with Said's *Orientalism*, which has encouraged a range of practices concerned with theorising and criticising the West. The term 'Orientalism' describes the European invention of the concept Orient, which constitutes, over two millennia and in various forms, Europe's image of the other and through this image a means of defining itself.

Said makes a controversial though fairly limited use of Michel Foucault's theories of discourse as a way of describing the European construction of the Orient as other, and as a way of explaining how this construction enabled the West to dominate and ultimately colonise the Orient, reproducing it according to its discursive representation. Orientalism is thus a mode of discourse with a range of supporting institutions, a widely disseminated vocabulary, specialist forms of scholarship, exotic imagery, the growth of doctrinal literature and colonial bureaucracies and styles. Said isolates three conventionally accepted senses of the term which convey together how widespread Orientalism has been. The first refers to a range of academic disciplines (originally philological) which study the Orient, the second to a broadly generalisable habit of thought which is based on an attempt rigorously to distinguish between the Orient and the Occident, and the third, (probably) starting from the late eighteenth century, a whole network of interests bearing on the Orient and manifested in the corporate institutions set up to deal with it in practical, economic, legislative and cultural ways.

The point of Said's use of discourse theory is to show how all reference to the Orient is discursively constructed, whether the reference is positive or negative, whether idealised in opposition to aspects of the West (its decadent or prosaic aspects, for instance), whether denigrated as barbaric against the civilised progress of western culture and law, whether eroticised or execrated (the possibilities are strictly innumerable). Thus the literary instance cannot escape the delimited field that is discourse. (In a local and historical sense, Dennis Porter's insistence [1993] on the counter-hegemonic possibilities of travel writing is genuinely engaging; but fails to accept that a writer such as T. E. Lawrence effects this through perpetuating a profoundly ethnocentric interpretation of the world, in this case, manifesting a peculiarly British tradition of arabophile idealisation [cf. Pratt (1992) on the sub-genre of late nineteenth-century source-of-the-Nile exploration writings].)

So Said's failure to account for what Homi Bhabha to some effect identifies as the ambivalence of colonial discourse has less to do with the relative autonomy of aesthetic production or counter-hegemonic activities of the signifier than with a more fundamental aporia of western thought. Robert Young, in his *White Mythologies*, points out that what Said's analysis neglects 'is the extent to which Orientalism did not just misrepresent the Orient, but also articulated an internal dislocation in Western culture, a culture which consistently fantasises itself as constituting some kind of integral totality, at the same time as deploring its own impending dissolution'. It is this 'internal dislocation' that is described by Jacques Derrida in his seminal *Of Grammatology*, which ten years before *Orientalism* outlines the character and ground of the western fantasy of the East. *Of Grammatology* contains an analysis of western ethnocentrism which is possibly the earliest example of the initiative, represented forcefully by Said and others, to attempt to deal effectively with this cultural pathology.

Derrida (1976) links his analysis of the ethnocentrism that has always controlled the concepts of writing and of science in the history of metaphysics to the temporal dimension of the future, which, he says, 'can only be anticipated in the form of an absolute danger' (p. 5). It is what is intrinsically incalculable about the future that throws the whole structure of temporality (in metaphysics time is always oddly structural) out of 'synch' (as it were). It renders experience (and all knowledge and theory) intrinsically incomplete yet open to infinite and randomly determined contingencies called, for convenience, 'the future'. This disorienting temporal dimension opens all writing, all knowledge, science and technics to the monstrosity of its other in absolute alterity. That is, the future is not simply the dimension in which knowledge might ultimately be complete (the utopian aspect of modernity); rather, it is, as an integral component to experience per se, that which cannot ever be known. Knowledge is thus essentially incomplete. Modernity tends to respond to the experience of incompleteness with a characteristic ethnocentrism. For instance, Descartes, Leibniz and others saw Chinese writing as the answer to the problem of a universal language by which philosophy might complete itself. 'The concept of a Chinese writing', writes Derrida, 'functions as a sort of

European hallucination,' an occultation that, 'far from proceeding from
ethnocentric scorn, takes the form of an hyperbolical admiration' (p. 80).
Which ties us back into Porter's misrecognition of Lawrence's fantasy in
*The Seven Pillars*. The concept of the sign and the concept of writing are
what bring to light the central aporia of western thought, the inability to
overcome the difference between what is empirical (therefore lacking) and
what is transcendental (a mysterious beyond). The attempt to reduce this
difference is the effort to maintain and fulfil an interior, the sense of a
complete identity, and can thus be understood as an attempt to domesticate
the alterity of the other, whose appearance is strictly and necessarily always
to come in a monstrous, incalculable future.

One might be tempted to develop this as a generic model for the internal
dynamic of travel writing; I shall, however, now go on to examine Bhabha's
attempts to counter the totalising discourse of colonialism by locating an
irreducible contingency beneath the privileged concepts of western teleological thought.

## The Arrival of the Post

> The supplementary strategy suggests that adding 'to' need not 'add up'
> but may disturb the calculation. (Bhabha 1994: 155)

The notion of contingency troubles the whole field of the calculable in
modern western thought, opening it up to the fragility of its own legislated
limits. If its essential impulse is the will to calculability, its achievement is
therefore made at the cost of relegating the contingent, in so far as it is
not calculable, to a threatening outside. The logic is exemplified in the
complex narratives of colonial history and post-colonial theory. Bhabha
plays on the fact that contingency has two senses, spatial and temporal. It
is here particularly that the theoretical dominance of the West can be
shaken. The various 'ends' of metaphysics in Friedrich Nietzsche, Martin
Heidegger, as well as Sigmund Freud and others, are often echoed in post-
colonial theory to an extent that cannot fail if not to disqualify then to
lessen the persuasive force of the various discourses of emancipation and
revolution, which include traditional Marxist theories of class conflict,
ideology and political economy as well as modern post-Enlightenment
narratives of progress, liberation and humanity.

To these potentially totalising narratives and against the disgruntled
polemic of his critics, Bhabha can oppose the persistently disruptive 'third
locus', in which the spatial contingency of national and racial borders is
combined with what he describes as the temporal contingency of the undecidable. Bhabha (1994) claims that an agency, or 'the activity of the

contingent', is made possible when 'the spatial dimension of contiguity is reiterated in the temporality of the indeterminate' (p. 186). 'The temporality of the indeterminate' refers to the inexplicable contingency of unpredictable events. A spatial contingency, 'contiguity, metonymy, touching spatial boundaries at a tangent', is repeated in a temporal contingency, 'the temporality of the indeterminate and the undecidable' that empties social symbolisation of its authority (pp. 186–90). In this formulation resides the concept of 'time-lag'. On an empirical level, the time-lag affects global travel in so far as the movement across spatial boundaries challenges the stability of subjective identity (the significant factors of which may be at any one time personal, national, ideological, spiritual, cultural, fantasmatic and historical); on a more conceptual level, the temporal contingency, in which the terms of one's understanding as represented by cultural signs are opened to the future contingencies of unheard-of addressees, troubles the grounds of understanding itself. Signs have meanings that are cultural and specific because of the indeterminacy that opens them in repetition to the future (the possibility, therefore, not only of travel but of translation). A sign is cultural and specific only because it must always be able to appear in different specific cultural contexts and each time signify differently.

In its most basic sense, the post-colonial implies both historical discontinuity and geographical displacement, that can be analysed in traditional ways. As Bhabha states in his 'Commitment to Theory', one can use the language of political economy to 'represent the relations of exploitation and domination in the discursive division between the First and Third world, the North and the South'; and it is possible to chart the distinctions 'between different national situations and the disparate political causes and collective histories of cultural exile' (pp. 20–1). But to the finite sense of the 'post' in which multiplicitous temporal and spatial displacements can be located historically, there must be added the senses of the term 'post' at work in post-structuralism and postmodernism, which imply a 'coming after' or secondariness that disqualifies the originality of that which 'came before', a secondariness that precedes and conditions the experience of 'being first'.

Thus, post-coloniality suggests that the experience of cultural identity involves a situatedness that is always threatened by exteriority, alterity and difference as the very conditions of existence for any cultural sign at all. The temporal contingency that disturbs all attempts to grasp and structure any experience of the present turns out to be the very condition of all experiences of the present whatsoever. So although Bhabha gives the time-lag this historical necessity, the post clearly also designates a priori difference as condition for the emergence of the multiple empirical differences in any situations, causes and histories, a difference that is neither sensible nor intelligible and is thus prior to and independent of any subordination of one identity to another. The post thus refers to the very conditions of colonial history, to all the histories of colonisation, its origins, its emergences and its declines as well as its relations to forms of imperialism and neo-imperialism. The post refers to the very historicity of colonialism.

This is at least implied when Bhabha describes the 'shifting margins of cultural displacement' as 'the paradigmatic place of departure' (p. 21). Travel has 'always already' begun, having no 'proper' place of departure. A beginning in the shifting margins is at once an affirmation of a priori difference as opposed to essence and, at the same time, a refusal to submerge particular cultural situations under general theoretical paradigms; but it does suggest a generalisation. Anne McClintock (1994) has forcefully disputed the tendency to regard the post-colonial as a singular totality which may 'license too readily a panoptic tendency to view the globe within generic abstractions voided of political nuance' (p. 396). Bhabha's work may be seen as an attempt to mobilise a *necessarily* paradoxical generalisation. Theory in some sense is indispensable for in its absence one is abandoned to the multiplicitous and otherwise ungrounded realm of contingent being. As in the case of government, in the absence of some kind of unifying bond, contradiction and ambivalence rule over subjects who, divided in themselves, are also in irreducible conflict among themselves, interests seldom meet and antagonism and dissent characterise struggles that are inevitable yet absolutely unpredictable. Hegel, as the great spokesman for western metaphysics, gives an account of civil society that shows how the power of universality is required to hold contingent particulars in check. He writes:

> Particularity by itself, given free rein in every direction to satisfy its needs, accidental caprices, and subjective desires, destroys itself and its substantive concept in this process of gratification. At the same time, the satisfaction of need, necessary and accidental alike, is accidental because it breeds new desires without end, is in thoroughgoing dependence on caprice and external accident, and is held in check by the power of universality. (Hegel 1967: 123)

Post-colonial theory must on the one hand act on elements that defeat the logic of the West in its attempt to hold on to the power of universality; but at the same time it must avoid falling into the self-destructive contingency that is its negative. To avoid transcendence is to be caught in indefinite empirical relativity; hence the commitment to *theory*.

## Sentences Decidable and Undecidable

There are two mutually contradictory traits in Bhabha's work. The first involves the application of recognisably post-structuralist axioms. Some of these are borrowed from psychoanalysis, which serves as a fund of suggestive schemata for describing ambivalent constructions of the self–other relation as well as the unconscious structure of the psychoanalytic subject. They also include arguments about the locus of enunciation in discursive formations. But invariably and with increasing confidence they are characterised by an insistent invocation of the incalculable, the staging of undecidability and indeterminacy folded into the finite and contingent margins of the cultural text itself. The axioms have correlatives in a range of found examples: the fragments, sentences, stanzas, remarks and extracts of missionaries, philosophers, poets, friends and academics; read by chance on a train, suggested at a conference, overheard in the IDS bar, or plucked ruthlessly out of context, a marginally suggestive sentence becomes axiomatic once freed of the less promising thesis to which it once ambivalently owed its service (see, for example, Bhabha 1994: 269). This travelogue of moments is theory on the move, made up of the fragmented and contingently anecdotal manifestations of the shifting logic of the time-lag. The travelogue requires careful analysis. It is Bhabha's theory in performance. But this is a performance that cannot be separated from the axiomatics it is supposed to exemplify, for it is the 'performative', in a special sense, that is for Bhabha the a priori condition of theory per se. And the performative a priori that grounds Bhabha's work suggests that history as such is for him a question a priori of performance.

Terms of cultural engagement, whether antagonistic or affiliative, are produced performatively. The representation of difference must not be hastily read as the reflection of *pre-given* ethnic or cultural traits set in the fixed tablet of tradition. Here a priori difference is explicitly connected to the concept of performativity, which again involves Bhabha's adoption of a radicalisation of that term in post-structuralist theory. In linguistics a *performative* utterance is one that allows the accomplishment of something through speech itself, e.g. warning or promising, both of which are speech acts that have some effect on the situation and the addressee (see Austin 1984). By comparing this with an assertoric sentence, or *constative* utterance, which classically is considered as a true or false description of facts, language philosophy is led to consider an act of communication as being produced in the total situation of utterance. It thus becomes possible to say that any speaker, in uttering a sentence, has produced an illocutionary act (performed an act rather than simply uttered a true or false sentence). In so doing it follows that such a speaker has also performed a perlocutory act in so far as it will have had some effect on its addressee(s). But one can 'perform' a speech act in two senses. In the linguistic sense a performative act brings about some state of affairs by simply being uttered (as with a promise). But such acts can also be performed in the dramatic sense – i.e.

one can act out the performative in a performance (in theatre). Jacques Derrida's controversial reading of J. L. Austin shows that one can general-ise this acting out as citationality or iterability (the repeatability of all statements) and he shows that this is the condition for *all* types of utterance. The possibility of disengagement and citational graft, which demonstrably characterises all iterable marks, is the very condition of experience, including the limited experience of intentional communication. This, of course, is not (as Austin, for instance, must assume) an irritation or impropriety that accidentally attaches itself to proper usage. Rather, one can easily see that without it any future utterance, and crucially any future addressee, would be impossible. The future addressee is absolute alterity itself, then, for no such existent is possible – no addressee can 'finish' a statement, owing to its in principle infinite iterability.

So when Bhabha writes of the performative production of the terms of cultural engagement he is describing cultural engagements as situations made possible by the fact that every (linguistic or non-linguistic) sign functions as such because it can be cited (e.g. in a dramatic or poetic performance). No context can exhaust a sign, and its ability to generate a potential infinity of new meanings. And that condition of possibility applies both to performative utterances in the strict sense and all other utterances as well. Bhabha's notion of performativity is thus intended to exploit this lack or gap in conscious intention, to produce an agency that exploits the iterability or (which is the same thing) the openness to-the-other of cultural signs, their openness to a future addressee who is strictly and permanently unheard of. Bhabha, as we have already seen, exploits those instances that disrupt things. In exploiting the accidental otherness of the boundary, frontier, contact zone, or whatever, Bhabha is committed to this deconstruc-tion that affirms a ground in iterability, and that is nothing less than an opening to the absolute alterity of the other. What this means is that 'the other', as that which makes possible the citationality of cultural signs, can be neither named nor known, it is absolutely other. This is the only possible measure of a contingency that cannot be subordinated, as a property, to the necessity of the knowable. So it is clearly not enough simply to affirm the accidental other of colonial discourse. Any 'resistant' affirmation must challenge the system that constructs the metropolis–periphery as, say, necessary–accidental. A structure that names its other maintains the ethno-centric desire that post-colonial theory sets out to overturn.

The second trait that I want to draw attention to in Bhabha's work involves the attempt to historicise the axioms drawn from post-structuralism. Here the performative is from time to time apparently eclipsed by the constative, as if the act of pointing, or turning one's gaze, was not itself a performance but a description, an assertoric sentence, a statement describing a historical performance. Here we can see that Bhabha is attempting two rather different operations in the same discourse – and this could account for the notorious difficulty of his style. Bhabha wants *to say* that post-structuralism is a historical consequence of colonialism, that 'colonial textuality' anticipates 'many of the problematics of signification and judgement that have become current in contemporary theory' (Bhabha 1994: 173). He wants *to say* that 'cultural contingency and textual indeterminacy' are first of all 'forces of social discourse', consequences of 'the attempt to produce an enlightened colonial or post-colonial subject' (p. 173). So, on one hand, Bhabha's fragmented polylogues and disjunct travelogues attempt to exemplify the inevitable indeterminacy that colonial discourse must both rely upon and deny. But, on the other hand, he wants to show that post-structuralism, and by extension postmodernism too, are also exemplifications of a disruptive post-colonial discourse that *they* fail to acknowledge. It is on the second point that Bhabha tends to drop the deliberate 'performativity' of his own discourse. In the radical, post-structuralist sense of performativity, any 'proper' place is denied at 'the origin'. But it seems that Bhabha wants an origin, and a proper place, for this wayward discourse of indeterminacy. It now must be located, placed, brought to face its other, in what Bhabha calls a 'lagging' so that a changing vocabulary (describing the shift from modernity to postmodernism) is anchored in historical embodiments of the kind of displacements it describes:

> From the post-colonial perspective we can only assume a disjunctive and displaced relation to [those] 'postmodern' writers who, in pushing the paradoxes of modernity to its limits, reveal the margins of the West, we cannot accept them until we subject them to a *lagging*, both in the temporal sense of post-colonial agency ... and in the obscurer sense in which, in the early days of settler colonisation, to be lagged was to be transported to the colonies for penal servitude! (Bhabha 1994: 247)

On the one hand, the time-lag specifies that form of belatedness in which the standard temporality of modernity – technological, cultural, juridical modernisation considered as human progress – is interrupted by the historical performativity of marginalised, displaced and diasporic peoples, belatedly repeating the authorised figure of the 'human' in an unintentional satire (pp. 236–47). The insertion of 'another locus of intervention and inscription' can be made in that interruption, which breaks the frame around the figure of the white man as universal and thus disorders the progressive 'Hegelian-Marxist schema' in which the black man is a minor term in the dialectic. In the time-lag the minor term uncannily doubles the major term as a kind of non-negatable other that

stands in the way of sublimation. It is unauthorised, a 'hybrid, inappropriate enunciative site', a 'middle way' that opens up between the
representation of subjectivity in social symbols, on the one hand, and the
repeatability of the sign deprived of subjectivity, on the other (p. 242).

On the other hand, postmodern discourses tend to adopt the rhetoric
of semiotic difference, infinite deferral, emptiness and eccentricity without
reference to the hegemonic structures of power in which they are historically performed: 'the mimetic contents of a discourse will conceal the fact
that the hegemonic structures of power are maintained in a position of
authority through a *shift in vocabulary* in the position of authority' (p. 242).
The 'mimetic contents' can refer only to that aspect of discourse that
traditionally is regarded as improper – the empty repetitions of cultural
signs divorced from their essential meanings – and thus to what in the
post-structuralist discourse that Bhabha employs constitutes the very possibility of discourse itself, the repeatability of the performative utterance.
So post-structuralism falls prey to what it claims all discourses depend
upon. If it is this that allows colonialism to remain intact long after the
discrediting of western metaphysics, then how can colonialism be resisted?
The structures of power between colonial subjects, between coloniser and
colonised, remain in place so long as the discourse capable of questioning
such structures fails to recognise the historical grounding from which it
emerges. It is no good just deconstructing western philosophy and political
economy, Bhabha seems to want to say, you've got to look at the historical
grounds that fissured it first, in its form as colonial discourse. The origin
of deconstruction is the post-colonial counter-discourse.

Bhabha attempts to mediate between the closures of metaphysics and
the indeterminacy of postmodernism by positing what he calls 'contingent
closure': 'Agency requires a grounding, but it does not require a totalisation
of those grounds. It requires movement and manoeuvre, but it does not
require a temporality of continuity and accumulation. It requires direction
and contingent closure but no teleology and holism' (p. 185). Contingent
closure is thus a step into the time-lag between the universalising discourses
of modernity, in which the black man signifies the past of the white man's
future, and postmodernism's 'endless slippage of the signifier', which in
celebration of fragmentation appropriates the third world as a sign of its
'new historicity', or its loss of history – just another repetition of the
West's attempt to complete itself (p. 239).

Bhabha thus begins not with an origin as such but with the basic 'there
is' of the post-colonial 'counter' which embodies the principle of contradiction – a kind of Hegelianism in reverse. Subaltern history is not one
example among others of the transgressive potential of the marginal, it is
the 'limit-text' of western culture itself.

When Bhabha first published his paper 'The Other Question' (1986), he included the following observations: 'It is there, in the colonial margin, that the culture of the West reveals its *"différance,"* its limit-text, as its practice of authority displays an ambivalence that is one of the most significant discursive and psychical strategies of discriminatory power – whether racist or sexist, peripheral or metropolitan' (p. 148).

Just as the post, the a priori incalculable difference itself, conditions the doubled discourse of colonialism, so the post-colonial, the colonial margin itself, conditions the doubled discourse of post-structuralism. Bhabha uses post-structuralism for its vocabulary, its formulations, its schemata and its axioms, while at the same time subjecting them to the very ambivalence that they describe yet fail to name properly. Logically speaking, Bhabha is providing proofs for post-structuralist sentences as if they had no such proofs, as if they lacked a truth value (under the term politics) that historicisation could provide. Consistency, provability and truth are the profound concepts that silently and unintentionally underlie Bhabha's own discourse on theory, history and politics. But by grounding post-structuralism in a historical catachresis, has Bhabha displaced the system in which the opposition between proper and improper is maintained? In what way does this reversal escape being a repetition of the metaphysical drive for closure – the completion of an empty post-structuralism via the addition of post-colonial history in the transcending concept of the time-lag? In what way is this pattern of thought anything other than Hegelian through and through?

### 'Bhabha'

The extent of the problem may be glimpsed when Bhabha 'gives way' to the polyphony of migrant voices, 'the *vox populi* ... wandering peoples who will not be contained within the *Heim* of the national culture and its unisonant discourse, but are themselves the marks of a shifting boundary that alienates the frontiers of the modern nation' (Bhabha 1994: 164). Simultaneously 'giving way' to and naming the shifting boundary, giving up to the incalculable while performing a calculation, Bhabha's reading takes on a tone that echoes Nietzsche's strategies to unsettle the modern *episteme*. 'They are Marx's reserve army of migrant labour who by speaking the foreignness of language split the patriotic voice of unisonance and became Nietzsche's mobile army of metaphors, metonyms and anthropomorphisms' (p. 164). From Marx to Nietzsche: Bhabha evokes a profound translation. The shifting boundary is transformed from a 'minor term' in political economy to the abyssal grounds of western discourses on truth, for the almost throwaway reference performs its own 'lagging' in this ironic repetition of a favourite quotation. Now named, the shifting boundary, the time-lag as truth beyond truth, is the limit itself (the *horos* of the Greek horizon and the *Begriff* of the German concept). The extent to which Bhabha's project can be considered scientific lies precisely here, where the aspiration to form a determinate concept can be opposed to modes of thought that enthusiastically embrace the indeterminate to proclaim that there is no truth, but only perspectives within a finite multiplicity. Hegel (once again) expresses the issue clearly in the 'preface' to *The Phenomenology of Spirit*: 'Whoever seeks to shroud the worldly multiplicity of his existence and of thought in a fog to attain the indeterminate enjoyment of his indeterminate divinity ... views the determinate [Horos] contemptuously, and deliberately keeps his distance from the Concept [Begriff] and from necessity, associating them with reflection that makes its home in the finite' (Bhabha 1977: 5–6). Although Bhabha also sees the infinite and the de-terminate limit as inextricable, this does not necessarily commit him to Hegelianism, but it does illustrate that what Bhabha is trying to formulate as 'time-lag' is a determinate concept in the philosophical sense and cannot be reduced to the 'bad' infinity of metaphysics. The time-lag designates not the existence of finite things but the limit that makes them possible.

As this is a matter of agency, Bhabha seldom misses the chance to exploit his own location on 'the shifting margins of cultural displacement'. He begins his introduction to the sixth ICA Document on *Identity*, from 1987, with the following typically cataphonic sentence:

> It is one of the ironic signs of our times that the Introduction to *The Real Me? Postmodernism and the Question of Identity* should be written by an Anglicized post-colonial migrant who happens to be a slightly Frenchified literary critic. For in that hybidity of histories and cultures you have the spectacle of the simulacral: the corrosive craft of colonial mimicry exposing the limits and borders of the sustaining subject of Western mimesis. (Bhabha 1987: 5)

The post-colonial writer is grounded on the paradigm of travel, an iden-tity produced disjunctively, out of fragments, in travel. But the playfulness of Bhabha's writing belies the power of the claims that this short passage represents, even as it performs the irony that is certainly intended here. For the post-colonial precisely anchors the postmodern in a finitistic 'spectacle' (this post-colonial migrant here) that grounds the eternal *abgrund* of the postmodern simulacrum on the shifting margins of identity itself.

Any attempt on my part to frame the problem of identity leads in-variably to my being caught athwart the frame, at once inside and outside. And if the 'frame within the frame', *mise en abyme*, is one of the central tropes of postmodern culture, then such double inscription also provides the *mise-en-scène* of the post-colonial writer writing on postmodern 'identity', performing a certain problem of identification between nations and cultures, between foreign and floating signs (Bhabha 1987: 5).

Bhabha's identity is strictly a matter of performance here, the idiomatic mask of hybrid histories and cultures beneath which no face is hidden. The post-colonial hybrid is the proof of the postmodern axiom of identity: 'What is transformed in the postmodern perspective, is not simply the "image" of the person, but an interrogation of the discursive and disciplinary place from which questions of identity are strategically and institutionally posed' (p. 5). Bhabha is at once finite particular ('this post-colonial migrant here') and at the same time he represents the repeatability of the particular in its performative mode, generalising particularity, posing questions from the particular perspective. (Fanon's proper name is also privileged in this respect: 'Despite its very specific location … I claim a generality for Fanon's argument because he talks not simply of the historicity of the black man, as much as he writes in "the fact of blackness" about the temporality of modernity within which the figure of the "human" comes to be authorised' [Bhabha 1994: 236].)

In this passage, then, Bhabha performs a movement from the specific to the general – from this post-colonial migrant here to postmodern identity – a passage in which the finite includes the infinite. This is possible, according to Bhabha, because the conceptual is always metaphorical. Bhabha's generalisation of his own performance makes his finite existence a metaphor for postmodernist identity as such: 'The move from the specific to the general, from the material to the metaphoric, is not a smooth passage of transition and transcendence. The "Middle Passage" of contemporary culture, as with slavery itself, is a process of displacement and disjunction that does not totalise experience' (p. 5). By 'metaphor', he means an example that stands in place of a concept that has no real generality (as Plato's sun stood for a truth that was otherwise radically absent). Bhabha 'stands for' identity only in so far as it is 'performance', or *standing-for*, that is generalised; that is, identity is always a contingent adoption of roles. This 'middle passage' as a metaphor of forced 'travel' anchors the postmodern in the post-colonial. (This is a perhaps heady metaphor, for between 1502 and 1865 the middle passage was used to ship roughly 10 million Africans to the Americas, approximately 20 per cent of whom died on the way, and another 30 per cent within three years of arrival.) The process of displacement and disjunction is generalisable metaphorically, rather than transcendentally, in a performative utterance, as if the sense of a Bhabha sentence was always 'I hereby generalise my particular hybrid identity' and its reference was the shifting here and now of the utterance already severed from its moment, its illocutionary force ungrounding its context, its perlocutory force undoing the identity of its addressee. This, then, is post-colonial travel writing. Particulars achieve generalisation, contingency becomes necessity, but only in metaphor, in the complex mapping whereby specific realities – always discursive systems – can be articulated otherwise.

## The Liar

As we have seen, Bhabha's attempt to go beyond, or to step outside, the assertoric or constative sentences of modernity involves him in a complex metaphorical/performative web of discourse that, strictly speaking, is not grounded (hence the identification with postmodernism). Yet in attempting to ground postmodernism in the social forces of colonial history and post-colonialism he has been forced to develop a conceptual framework that both ungrounds and grounds at the same time. The privileged concept here is the time-lag, which checks 'the endless circulation of significations', in so far as it is this that anchors the endless significations of postmodernist discourse. So the post-colonial provides a grounding concept for a chain of signifiers that is otherwise without one. It designates an immaterial element that is absolutely exterior to the finite multiplicity of endlessly sliding signifiers. It thus resides in the place of the unattainable, it is the last word, the full stop, the end of the question mark. As Bhabha (1994) says: 'Time-lag is not a circulation of nullity, the endless slippage of the signifier or the theoretical anarchy of apona. It is a concept that does not collude with current fashions for claiming the heterogeneity of ever-increasing "causes," multiplicities, of subject positions, endless supplies of subversive "specificities," "localities," "territories"' (p. 245).

Time-lag is a limit, a concept, 'a signifying "cut" or temporal break' (p. 245). Thus it serves as a singularity, a contingent closure, an excess, a disturbing alterity, an anchor, a *point de capiton* (the Lacanian term for the nodal point which 'quilts' floating signifiers into a unified field: see Zizek 1989: 87). Time-lag is neither a zero nor a one, 'it is the problem of the not-one, the minus in the origin and repetition of cultural signs in a doubling that will not be sublated into a similitude' (p. 245). And it checks the endless circulation of significations, 'it halts the endless signification of difference' (p. 245), which in Hegelian terms would immediately signify identity. It is both an infinite identity that remains extrinsic, and a finite concept that refers to itself. Its other name is Bhabha, a subject of enunciation who must speak the truth from outside the sentence itself.

Unlikely as it may seem, Bhabha's abandonment of the sentence has support in developments based on the discovery by Kurt Godel of the existence of undecidable sentences in formal systems containing arithmetic (see Godel 1967; and also the admirably clear exposition in Nagel and

Newman 1965). This starkly logical problem emerges out of Epimenides's celebrated paradox of 'The Liar' in which a person says during a given period that each sentence he makes is false. Godel's explanation claims that to be precise about this, the person would need to specify a language (A), saying 'every sentence I make today in A is false'. But because 'false sentence in X' cannot be expressed in A, the sentence would have to be expressed in a different language. By virtue of this paradox of the un-decidable sentence, it is possible to show that the concept of a true sentence is not viable within the bounds of a given language. (See Davis 1965 for Godel's remarks on 'The Liar'; also von Neumann 1966, and Feferman 1991; and Tarski 1956: 274 ff, for systematic discussions of the concept of truth relating to sentences of a language.) Undecidability thus serves a prohibitive function with regard to truth, which is involved only in so far as it is excluded from the utterance while simultaneously declaring it false. Truth in the sentence is disqualified in the enunciation or performance of the sentence, which is itself declared false by the truth it excludes. Truth can be located only outside the sentence. It is this *formal* problematic that bears directly on what Bhabha calls the post-colonial project that, as we have seen, must rename the (infinite) postmodern from the perspective of the (finite) post-colonial. It is from this point of potential transcendence that Bhabha produces his theory.

## Fog, Seg, Lag

Bhabha's concept of time-lag, by resisting the logical reduction to sentential structure that would make it calculable, achieves a status that not even he appears to have intended. As a result his discourse contains a residual idealism, a kind of unintentional Neo-Platonism. Like an un-authorised proper name, it refers to itself at the moment of its construction and thus begins again an infinite journey within a finite domain, the paradigm of post-colonial travel. However, the nature of its singularity, which makes it absolute, is such that it cannot exist without a con-text, which it transforms and immediately transcends. And that makes it fragmentary. It is the unrepresentable concept of the Other in its absolute alterity and thus must always start again from somewhere else. Bhabha too is subject to the lag.

So the time-lag functions for Bhabha as a kind of unattainable ideality that at each moment offers the space for transformation, the traces of which are found only in the ruins of some master discourse. At the same time it designates the conditions of cultural engagement itself without attempting to grasp that engagement in calculable functions or numbers. Numbers always and everywhere name limitations, reduce to calculable

units; even infinite sets and transfinite numbers name limits within the
infinite: unlimited limits suggest an infinity within infinity, a monstrous
chaos for calculability. But there is no number for limitation itself and, as
we have seen, the post-colonial time-lag names that limit out of which
limited beings emerge in their finite multiplicity. It is the 'last word' – the
lag word from the archaic children's chant (in the colloquial 'fog, seg, lag';
first, second, last; one, two, three)  – echoed obliquely in the streets of
Kingston, Jamaica:

> One, two, tree,
> All de same;
> Black, white, brown,
> All de same.,
> All de same.

> One, two, etc.  (P. Burnett 1986: 5)

Robert Renny, who recorded this, notes that it 'was, in the year 1799,
frequently sung in the streets of Kingston', repeating in the lag a satire on
the discourses of enlightenment eight years before the abolition of slavery
yet another twenty-seven before emancipation. The lag is not a number. It
is 'not simply added' (Bhabha 1994a: 155). Bhabha borrows the Derridean
'supplementary strategy' to show how his mathematics is formally beyond
the *mathematica* of the Greeks, but resides in an *other math* outside the
sentence (p. 184):

The supplementary strategy interrupts the successive seriality of the narrative of plurals and pluralism by radically changing their mode of articulation. In the metaphor of the national community as the 'many in one,' the
*one* is now both the tendency to totalise the social in a homogeneous empty
time, and the repetition of that minus in the origin, the less-than-one that
intervenes with a metonymic, iterative temporality. (p. 155)

Fog, seg, lag. Lag is the last word, the adding to but not adding up. The
transition from fog to seg is disturbed by the addition of the lag which
makes up for the lack of origin in the fog and which generalises the
secondariness of the seg. The seg is the discourse of modernity, fixing its
stars in an infinite firmament, of which the fog is the absent origin. The
lag is the infinite projection of unborn stars, the impossible ideality where
the buck stops for postmodernism, the last word, not yet spoken: Bhabha.

It may yet be possible to imagine a post-colonial writing that acknowledges the ethical demand of the other's alterity, a writing that opens itself
both to the home and to the other, the home as other, writing perhaps that
anticipates the other's arrival without naming the other in advance, an
other-travel-writing, writing of travel to come. But not yet.

# Part II

## Prefigurations of Empire

# The Discourse of Cannibalism in Early Modern Travel Writing

Ted Motohashi

[T]here is nothing more consistent than a racist humanism since the European has only been able to become a man through creating slaves and monsters. Jean-Paul Sartre (1967: 22)

## 1. Discovery and Invention

On 18 August 1492, exactly fifteen days after Columbus had departed the port of Palos for the 'golden island of Cipangul', *Gramatica Castellana* by Antonio de Nebrija was published in Salamanca. In his introduction dedicated to the Queen Isabella of Castile, Nebrija wrote: 'My Illustrious Queen. Whenever I ponder over the tokens of the past that have been preserved in writing, I am forced to the very same conclusion. Language has always been the consort of empire, and forever shall remain its mate. Together they come into being, together they grow and flower, and together they decline' (Illich 1981: 34).

According to Nebrija, the national language is a perfect instrument for conquering Others within the country and without. Those transgressive subjects were to be deprived of their agency by such 'language of empire', the language of Self as imagined by Nebrija as a tool of empowering Spanish expansionism. And it is through that language that Columbus 'discovered' Others at the genesis of modern European imperialism.

Instead of 'discovering' the subjectivity of the native people, the Europeans 'invented' the 'Indians', thus initiating the history of the American continent as 'the promised land' (O'Gorman 1961). In fact, it was a succession of atrocities of genocide, displacement and destruction. This essay is an attempt to examine the surcharged cultural signification of the 'Canibal', in which the act of disavowal of fantasised others involves an ambivalent practice of affirmation and denial. It will analyse the evolution from an initial dialogism inherent in the term, invented by Columbus in 1492, into a colonising dynamic which justifies the oppression and extermination of native populations, but also reveals a division within the very desire to control by imputing to the other its own instinctual forces.

## 2. Naming and Reciprocity

One of the misfortunes Columbus had when he believed he was in 'Inde', a peripheral zone of the kingdom of Cathay, was that his translator, one Torres, could speak only Hebrew, Cardian and Arabic. Observe the entry on 23 November 1492 in his *Journal* of the first voyage:

> and beyond this cape there stretched out another land or cape, which also trended to the east, which those Indians whom he had with him called 'Bohio.' They said that this land was very extensive and that in it were people who had one eye in the forehead, and others whom they called 'Canibals.' Of these last, they showed great fear, and when they saw that this course was being taken, they were speechless, he says, because these people ate them and because they are very warlike. The admiral says that he well believes that there is something in this, but that since they were well armed, they must be an intelligent people, and he believed that they may have captured some men and that, because they did not return to their own land, they would say that they were eaten. They believed the same of the Christians and of the admiral, when some first saw them. (Colombus 1968: 68–9)

This entry is significant not only because it provides the first appearance of the word 'Canibals' ('*Canibales*' in original Spanish) but also because we here glimpse, along with Columbus's doubt about the Indians' claim about the man-eaters, a kind of dialogical reciprocity in the discourse of cannibalism: the first encounter with an alien race, European or Indian, will produce fear and suspicion on both parts that strangers might eat man's flesh. The encounter between different cultures hinges on the reciprocal (though not symmetrical) nature of cannibalistic discourse.

The diary account immediately poses questions: how well Columbus understood what the Indians said to him; how accurately Las Casas, transcriber of the present record, conveys the contents of the original diary (now lost); the degree of authenticity of the Indians' testimony and the sincerity of their intention in telling such fantastic stories to the newcomers. Among these questions, most important to our present concerns is the one related to a signifying process manifested in Columbus's acts of naming which, as Zizek (1989) puts it, 'retroactively constitutes its reference. Naming is necessary but it is, so to speak, necessary afterwards, once we are already "in it"' (p. 95).

In the above account, there appear two local names: 'Bohio' and 'Canibals'. Yet from this day on, the former, 'Bohio' (meaning a 'hut' in

Arawakan), is marginalised, while the latter is foregrounded as a normative term – whatever its meaning is in the original Arawakan terminology (it has been suggested that the Arawak word 'carib' meant either 'manioc eater' or 'valiant warrior' [Boucher 1992: 139n]) – to signify the practice of man-eating; not only will the adjacent area be called 'the islands of Canibals' but its inhabitants will be named 'Caribes'. The process of marginalising 'Bohio' and centralising 'Canibals' is, however, accompanied by dialogic recognition of the reciprocity of the sign, as well as by suspicion about the real existence of man-eaters. (Scepticism about the reality of cannibalism, because of lack of reliable evidence of its practice between 1492 and 1611, is expressed, among others, by Arens 1979; Pagden 1982; Boucher 1992; believers in Aztec human-eatings and the nineteenth-century cannibalism in the Pacific include Sahlins 1978: 45–53; 1979: 45–7; 1983: 72–93; Sanday, 1986.)

Fantasy about man-eating is probably as old and widespread as human history and community. When encountering an alien people whose appearances and customs are distinctively different from one's own, both fascination towards and repugnance against man-eating are released as a practice and discourse. It is quite likely that during those first encounters between the Spaniards and the native islanders, the incoming strangers inquired, at every possible opportunity, sometimes with apparent threat, about the properties and the lives of the islanders, about man-eating, amazonian females, monsters, gold, and other fantasies familiar to the Europeans through a long history of the exotic tales about Others, which were quite beyond the natives' understanding. (On Cook's encounter with the Polynesian 'practice' of cannibalism, see Obeyesekere 1992: 630–54.)

Columbus, as Ivan Illich reminds us, 'wrote in two languages [Latin and Spanish] he did not speak, and spoke several [including Genovese and Portuguese]. None of this seems to have been problematic to his con-temporaries. However, it is also true that none of these was a language in the eyes of Nebrija' (Illich 1981: 39). It is a paradox that 'Canibals', a vernacular word orally apprehended by Columbus, became one of the most powerful terms in the written literature of conquest. For the 'Canibals' sign to be circulated as a normative representation of the transgressive Other, it was necessary to conceal the initial dialogism of its inception. As the sign articulated its power over its referent, the referent itself – the body of the man-eater and the practice of man-eating itself, whether the practice was actual or not – was marginalised. The dialogism detected in Columbus's *Journal* is reiterated in Sebastian Munster's account of Columbus's voyage included in *Cosmographie*, which was translated into English by Richard Eden in 1553. This provides one of the first English references to the 'canibals' in America, which was rapidly displacing the Greek term 'anthropophagi'. Here, the word 'Canibales' is introduced by the author in his section title, 'Of the people called Canibales or Anthropophagi, which are accustomed to eate mans fleshe', still accompanied by 'Anthropophagi'. Then the text reads:

> Whereas the people of the forenamed Ilanders [the two islands Columbus called Johanna and Hispana], fled at the sight of our menne, the cause thereof was, that they suspected them to haue been *Canibals*, that cruel and fearse people which eate mans fleshe, which nacion our men had ouerpassed, leauing them on the southsyde. But after they had knowledge of the contrary, they made greuous complaynt to our men, of the beastly and fearse maners of these *Canibals*, which were no lesse cruel agaynst them, then the Tyger or the Lyon agaynste tame beastes. (Arber 1885: 29)

This is a typical instance of exclusion of the third term. As the Spanish visitors 'proved' to be far from cannibalistic invaders, benevolent agents shielding the islanders from the cruel 'Canibals', the 'Canibals' themselves were banished beyond the boundary as invisible Others, who, as the excluded third term, kept the binarism between the kind and strong Spaniard and the gentle and obedient Arawak. The reciprocity within the naming process is here turned into unilaterality. The binary opposition between Us and Them was complete with 'Canibals' as a consciously employed sign of differentiation. This sign – now devoid of the reciprocity – could now be arbitrarily applied.

The so-called 'First Three English Books on America', a large part of which comprises chronicles of Spanish conquest translated by Richard Eden, are suffused with the word 'Canibales'. The 'ferocious and daringly cruel' tribe was rapidly gaining recognition among readers in Europe, and the Classical/African term 'anthropophagi' was increasingly displaced by Modern/American 'Canibales' or 'Caribes'.

The cruel savagery of the 'canibales' was at the centre of the European imagination which tried to justify the violent colonial enterprise. Peter Martyr's 'Preface' to his 'Decades', also translated by Eden in 1555, perhaps represents this sentiment. According to Martyr, the bondage of the native people to the Spanish is: 'suche as is much rather to be desired then theyr former libertie which was to the cruell Canibales rather a horrible licenciousnesse then a libertie, and to the innocent so terrible a bondage, that in the myddest of theyr ferefull idlenesse, they were euer in daunger to be a prey to those manhuntynge wooloues' (Arber 1885: 50).

According to this logic, the European conquest was mutually beneficial, even more so to the natives who were given a true 'libertie' free from 'cruell' and 'licencious Canibales'. This kind of reasoning led to the binary distinction between the 'gentle Arawaks' and 'cruell Canibales'. A key to the crucial discursive distinction between 'anthropophagi' and 'Canibales' lies in this binarism, and in order to examine this claim let us look at some classic examples of 'anthropophagi'.

The term 'anthropophagi' used since Homer and Herodotus signified those who lived beyond the Black Sea, beyond the limit of civilised human habitation from the Greek point of view; it referred to those ultimate Others residing beyond rational understanding. In Herodotus: 'The Andro-phagi ("Man-eaters") have the most savage customs of all men; they pay no regard to justice, nor make use of any established law. They are nomads, and wear a dress like the Scythians; they speak a peculiar language; and of these nations, are the only people that eat human flesh' (Herodotus 1992: 270).

Here we can detect a few themes which will later declare themselves in Columbus's account of the native Americans. They are the claims that there are connections between the peculiarity of language and that of custom – having no sense of justice or law, nomadism, dressing like the Scythians who, as far as the Greeks were concerned, comprised the nation of marginality between the civilised and the barbaric. However, this account by no means suggests any possible encounter between the two. In order for the man-eaters to be 'discovered', the word 'Canibales' had first to be discerned and recorded in the language of empire. When Columbus heard the word 'Canibales' for the first time on 23 November 1492, having acquired a surprising amount of information for a man who had been in this region for less than six weeks without any previous knowledge of its languages, he still seemed to have some doubt about the authenticity of the information. But after three months' experience with the native people, Columbus was able to 'identify' positively the man-eating 'caribes' whom he met on the northern coast of Hispaniola, because they looked so different from ('uglier' than) the other natives. In his *Journal*, Columbus described on 13 January 1493 how he encountered one of the 'Caribs' for the first time:

> He sent the boat to land at a beautiful beach, in order that they might take *ajes* to eat, and they found some men with bows and arrows, with whom they paused to talk, and they bought two bows and many arrows, and asked one of them to go to speak with the admiral in the caravel, and he came. The admiral says that he was more ugly in appearance than any whom he had seen. He had his face all stained with charcoal, although in all other parts they are accustomed to paint themselves with various colours; he wore all his hair very long and drawn back and tied behind, and then gathered in meshes of parrots' feathers, and he was as naked as the others. The admiral judged that he must be one of the Caribs who eat men and that the gulf,

which he had seen yesterday, divided the land and that it must be an island
by itself. ... The admiral says further that in the islands which he had passed
they were in great terror of Carib: in some islands they call it "Caniba' but
in Espanola 'Carib'; and they must be a daring people, since they go through
all the islands and eat the people they can take. (Columbus 1968: 146–7)

This was the day when the hitherto mythical 'canibales' were personified
into the 'Caribs', hence establishing not only the mythical tale of the
'island of canibales' which fascinated so many voyagers/writers after
Columbus, but the Carib/Arawak binarism. A linguistic history of these
'modern' terms referring to man-eating can be summarised as follows: first
'canibales', which Columbus heard on 23 November 1492, was introduced
into Spanish and the other European languages, referring to a group of
existing tribes called the Caribs, as Columbus later heard from those who
feared them. The implication of man-eating was the linchpin of the two
identical words. Gradually, there was established a distinction between
'cannibal' (man-eater) and 'Carib' (native of the Antilles). Much later,
'cannibalism', the general term referring to the custom, was introduced
(OED's first entry is dated 1796), completing the distinction between the
behaviour and the people. Each term was, as it were, separated by the
'gulf' dividing the two regions respectively inhabited by them, thus providing justification for genocide of the indigenous people.

Apart from Columbus's observation that the man had 'many arrows' –
the feature that might match one of the characteristics of the 'canibals'
reported by the natives on 23 November – his judgement depended solely
on the man's external appearances: socio-cultural traits of dressing codes
and facial decorations. What is more disturbingly predictable is that, as
Columbus himself admitted ('he was as naked as the others'), there was no
way of telling *ipso facto* the difference between the 'gentle Arawak' and the
'cruel Carib' from their overall extrinsic features. The only way to distinguish between the two was their intrinsic characters: the one was *by
nature* gentle and servile, hence cooperative to the Spanish, attentive to
Christian dogmas and fearful of and victim to the 'canibales'; the other
was the opposite, simply because they possessed and were ready to use
their 'weapons'. As Columbus (1968) confidently stated in the same entry,
when he learned that the 'Caribs' had unsuccessfully assaulted the Spanish:
'they would be afraid of the Christians, *for without doubt*, he says, the
people there are, as he says, evil-doers, and he believed that they were
those from Carib and that they eat men' (p. 148). Columbus's Christian
identity, as it frequently did during the course of his voyage, came to
provide a rational explanation to the internal nature of the 'Carib'.

Judging from the above passage, there are two main reasons for

Columbus's judgement of the man as a 'Carib'. One is his ugly appearance (stained face, long hair, naked body), the other is his ability to fight and resist (weapon, fortitude, independent aptitude which enables him to come alone among the Europeans). At the root of his 'judgement', however, lies Columbus's reasoning that for him whose quest was so far unfruitful, 'gold' and 'Canibals' became gradually interchangeable as objects of desire.

This is suggested by the fact of Columbus's persistent questioning the man about the existence of gold. In his mind, as prospects of gold were unpromising, slaves came to be foregrounded as gifts to be brought back and presented to the Spanish monarchs. From this day on, he tried to capture as many 'Caribs' as possible. As far as the coloniser was concerned, the term 'Carib' could be conveniently applied to those who possessed weapons and dared to resist: these were all signified as 'Carib/Canibals', hence their slavery legitimated. Columbus after all did not meet the 'real' man-eaters; instead, he 'invented' the 'Caribs'. If we want to talk about the 'discovery' in real terms, it was the natives of the 'Caribbean' islands who discovered Columbus and his men as ferocious and greedy murderers.

Furthermore, the actual identity of the fierce tribe did not matter here. It was sufficient to suppose that they were fearless and consequently likely to pose an obstacle to European colonisation; as the diary continued: 'and he says that if they were not Caribs, at least they must be *neighbours of them and have the same customs*, and they are a fearless people, not like the others of the other islands, who are cowardly beyond reason and without weapons' (pp. 148–9; my emphasis). In fact, this neighbourhood could limitlessly expand as the Europeans wished to set new boundaries between the 'fearless' and the 'cowardly': the 'customs' were 'discovered' wherever they were 'a daring people' with weapons in their hand. Founded here is a discursive power base supported by this flexible sign system of the 'Carib/canibales', which is linked to the most horrific violence upon human beings for the last 500 years wherever the force of European colonialism has left its marks.

After several years of Spanish settlement in the islands, it became no longer possible to know what that fatal word 'canibales' really *meant* in the native language, because the 'Caribs' were all annihilated by direct conflicts against the Spanish, by diseases, or by slave labour. Nevertheless, as the *Oxford English Dictionary* exemplifies (in defining 'Carib' as 'cannibal' and 'cannibal' as 'Carib' without mentioning why it is so in the first place), the tautological dilemma that has caught the Carib/cannibal since Columbus identified the two as synonymous. Bearing in mind this tautology and in view of the subsequent history of brutal colonisation, it would be of only limited epistemological interest to ask whether the natives of the Antilles did *in fact* eat human flesh or not; for even if the natives did exercise cannibalism as a social form of religious ritual, would it have justified annihilation of a tribe? An answer to this question is supplied by Michel de Montaigne, who, seeing the Tupinamba Indians in Rouen in 1562, recorded their words when they were asked if there were any thing by which they were impressed among the Europeans. The Tupis answered, according to Montaigne:

> They had perceived there were men amongst us full gorged with all sortes of commodities [gorgez de toutes sortes de commoditez], and others which hunger-starved, and bare with need and povertie, begged at their gates: and found it strange, these moyties so needy could endure such an injustice, and that they tooke not the others by the throate, or set fire on their houses. (Montaigne 1886: 98)

What Montaigne provides, through the mouths of the native people of the lands which were about to be colonised by Europe, is a rhetorical question: which is the real 'cannibal', Europe or its Other?

### 3. The Morality and Logic of English Colonisation

The colonisers who tried to construct their identities according to such paradigms as white, Christian, civilised, rational, sexually controlled, termed those who transgressed their norms as 'savage', impugning 'abnormalities' to the native population. Yet in describing the Other's transgressive behaviour, the colonisers in fact expressed their own fantasised desires (and actual behaviour): treachery, rape, murder, misogyny, sexual deviance – they themselves were hybrid, transgressing entities. 'Canibals' could be assigned not only to the Indians but also to the Europeans. If the native Arawakans had known the name of the alien visitor to their land in 1492, the ferocious man-eaters could have been called 'Columbals'. One of the most effective strategies to designate Self as pure and as remote from hybridity as possible was to produce an alien race close to its own European origin, and to emphasise differences between the two – say, between the Spaniards and the English. This is the moralised logic behind the English colonising ideology as a latecomer to the expansionist venture.

These reasonings can be abundantly detected in accounts of expeditions by English captains such as Drake or Ralegh. Their main objective was to accelerate the English colonial interests which lagged far behind those of the Spanish. If we may call Jamestown in Virginia the first permanent English settlement in America, its establishment in 1607 (as was the case with the French who built their Quebec colony in 1608) was more than 100 years behind the Spanish pioneering precedent. The historical backwardness of the English in their colonial venture forced them to engage in piracy on a national scale, and to try to justify this pillage of Spanish gold under the auspices of the idealised Queen Elizabeth who, contrary to the evil Catholic King of Spain, truly cared for the well-being of the native population. This need for differentiation has again transformed the 'Canibal' topos as a commonplace theme into the 'Canibal' trope.

Early English intervention in America was more piratical than commercial. Drake (in)famously hijacked so many Spanish bullion ships as severely to damage the now mighty empire in the Spanish Main. His main enemy was not the Indians *per se* but the Spanish and the Indians associated with them. To outmanoeuvre them, Drake even claimed to be affiliated with 'Symerons', who, he explained, were 'A black people, which about 80 yeares past, fledd from the *Spaniards* their Masters, by reason of their cruelty, and are since growne to a nation, vnder two Kings of their owne: the one inhabiteth to the west, th'other to the East of the way from *Nombre de Dios to Panama*'. The accounts of his guerrilla tactics against the Spaniards are sometimes exhilarating as well as sinister in their nationalistic representation of pirate as a genuine emancipator:

> Our Captaine willing to vse those Negroes well (not hurting himselfe) set them ashore vpon the maine, that they might perhaps ioyne themselues to their contrymen *the Symerons*, and gaine their liberty if they would, or if they would not, yet by reason of the length and troublesomenes of the way by land to *Nombre de Dios*, hee might preuent any notice of his comming, which they should be able to giue. For hee was loath to put the towne to too much charge (which hee knew they would willingly bestowe) in prouiding before hand, for his entertainment, and therefore hee hastned his going thither, with as much speed and secrecy as posibly hee could. (Nichols 1626: 8–9)

To confound the Spanish, Drake no doubt would have ventured on fighting alongside of the 'cannibale'; yet it was not 'their liberty' but a tactical gain that Drake aspired to. It suffices here to remind ourselves that the first English Atlantic slave voyage by John Hawkins – it was reported that he kidnapped 300 Africans in Sierra Leone, 'partly by the sworde, and partly by other meanes', and sold them in Hispaniola, which brought 'prosperous successe and much gaine to himself and the aforesayde adventurers' (Hakluyt 1925–28, vol. 7: 6) – was carried out ten years before in 1562, which initiated the English maritime boom in the West African slave trade (although, of course, the Africans themselves and the Arab traders there had been practising slavery for centuries).

If the Spanish colonists built cities and from there governed the countryside by manipulating the native labour-force, the English were first and foremost frontiersmen cultivating the lands. It was vital for them to

settle down as quickly and efficiently as possible to acquire arable lands for
their own food production, although the early colonists were notably bad
at this, and almost wholly dependent on the goodwill of the local Indians.
Once the logistical problems of survival were settled, they started harvest-
ing crops, first sugar then tobacco with varying degrees of success (see
Mintz 1985; Kulikoff 1986). Richard Hakluyt the elder (of Middle Temple)
represented this view when he stressed the need for colonists' agricultural
production and maintenance of the settlements as a prelude to trade: 'The
soile and climate first is to be considered, and you are with Argus eies to
see what commoditie by industrie of man you are able to make it to yeeld,
that England doth want or doth desire' (Hakluyt 1935: II 333).

In order to attain the three ends of the Virginia enterprise – 'To plant
Christian religion', 'To trafficke', and 'To conquer' (vol. II, p. 332) –
Hakluyt recommends 'a gentle course', which should distinguish the
English from the precursor Spaniard:

> we become not hatefull unto them, as the Spaniard is in Italie and in the
> West Indies, and elsewhere, by their maner of usage: for a gentle course
> without crueltie and tyrannie best answereth the profession of a Christian,
> best planteth Christian religion; maketh our seating most void of blood,
> most profitable in trade of merchandise, most firme and stable, and least
> subiect to remoove by practise of enemies. (vol. II, p. 334)

The most important aspect of the conquest was, according to Hakluyt,
to expel the native people from their lands with minimum force, preferably
without recourse to violence despite the fact that the Europeans in general
depended on the Indians for subsistence. These pragmatic considerations
had no room for such indulgence in philosophical argument about the
Indians' humanity as the one between Bartholème de Las Casas and J. G.
Sepalveda from 1550 to 1551 in Valladolid. For the English, it was the
'cannibal', rather than Christianity, that came to avail itself of the task.
'Cannibal' was utilised as a sign of differentiation between the rival colonists, as the following passage from Walter Ralegh's *The Discovery of the
Large, Rich and Beautiful Empire of Guiana* shows:

> Among manie other trades those *Spaniards* vsed in *Canoas* to passe to the
> riuers of *Barema*, *Pawroma*, *and Dissequebe*, which are on the south side of
> the mouth of *Orenoque*, and there buie women and children from the
> *Canibals* which are of that barbarous nature, as they will for 3 or 4 hatchets
> sell the sonnes and daughters of their owne brethren and sisters, and for
> somewhat more euen their own daughters: heerof the Spaniards make great
> profit, for buying a maid of 12 or 13 yeeres for three or fower hatchets, they
> sell them againe at *Marguerita* in the west Indies for 50 and 100 pesoes,
> which is so many crownes. (Ralegh 1596: 33–4)

Here the 'Cannibals' are indeed naturalised as 'barbarous', but their barbarity is interpreted as a crude commercial greed (not unlike that of the indigenous black African slave traders), rather than as a natural blood-thirstiness: their nature can only give an *explanation* for their behaviour which is more important to Ralegh. The 'Cannibals' are to blame because they forsake their family ties for the material profit gained from the mercantile network constructed by the capitalistic Spanish. What makes the 'Cannibals' truly barbarous is not their intrinsic cultural features but their participation in the intruding European economy initiated by those Spaniards. The binary opposition is squarely set between the bad Spanish and the good English (who will never encourage the 'Cannibals' into this kind of inhuman barter), with the 'Cannibals' as the third term at once sustaining the binarism and excluded from both of the terms as the culturally alien, the inhumanly callous and the economically instrumental-ised. Here the final target of discrimination is the Spaniards, and the 'cannibal' sign is employed as a symbol of the shrewd yet manipulated tribe. In fact for Ralegh, these 'cannibals' need not represent man-eaters at all: it is enough to verify that they are inhuman and evil enough to be associated with the Spaniards – chief rival in his colonialist enterprise. Ralegh attempts to establish a clear moral distinction between 'us' (the English) and 'them' (the Spaniards). Here the same rhetorical strategy is employed with more complexity in which the distinction is underlined in economic and sexual terms. The imaginary tour-de-force of this passage deserves a long quotation:

> *This Arawacan* Pilot with the rest, feared that we would haue eaten them, or otherwise haue put them to some cruell death, for the Spaniards to the end that none of the people in the passage towards *Guiana* or in *Guiana* it selfe might come to speech with vs, perswaded all the nations, that we were men eaters, and *Canibals*: but the poore men and women had seen vs, and that we gaue them meate, and to euerie one some thing or other, which was rare and strange to them, they began to conceiue the deceit and purpose of the *Spaniards*, who indeed (as they confessed) tooke from them both their wiues, and daughters daily, and vsed them for the satisfying of their owne lusts, especially such as they tooke in this maner by strength. But I protest before the maiestie of the liuing God, that I neither know nor beleeue, that any of our companie one or other, by violence or otherwise, euer knew any of their women, and yet we saw many hundreds, and had many in our power, and of those very yoong, and excellently fauored which came among vs without deceit, starke naked. (Ralegh 1596: 51–2)

As in Columbus's testimony on 23 November 1492, the discourse of cannibalism here elicits a certain reciprocity which is manipulated to demonise that false originator: it is the Spaniards who are now excluded as the third term, because they have transgressed the 'universal' – European and Indian – code of human ethics. With the exclusion of these 'white devils', a commonwealth based on an imaginary reciprocal accord and well-being is established between the Arawakans and the English. Alongside the innocent purity of the Arawakan women, and the obedient gullibility of the Arawakan men, the English, endowed with gentlemanly sexual restraint and generosity guaranteed by the saintly authority of Queen Elizabeth, whom the Arawakans 'admire' and 'whose commandment' Ralegh here (1596) claims to carry out in treating them well (p. 52), can build an ideal land of mutual wealth and ethical understanding. What is definitively lacking in this republic is the ferocious man-eaters themselves who have a disturbing capacity to resist and subvert such a programme.

Ralegh mentions that the 'Cannibal' sign is employed by the Spaniards against the English within the Spanish plot to prevent the natives from doing business with the English. In this kind of tit-for-tat linguistic game within the European factions to gain the natives' approval and to justify their colonialist activities on the grounds that they exercised them for saving them from evil (be it that of the 'Cannibals' or the 'Spaniards'), it is the 'cannibals' themselves who are eternally marginalised, uprooted and depersonalised. If any reciprocity exists in Ralegh's imaginary 'empire' (a glittering commonwealth not unlike the fool's gold his men were reported to have brought back from there), it is between the 'poor men and women' and the subjects of 'her Majesty' (with the Spanish as the discriminated third term). In this nation there is simply no place for the 'cannibals', who are now not only displaced but also discursively nullified. If the 'Cannibals' can be applied to one set of European nationals by another, the sign merely functions as a means of demonisation without ambivalence inherent at its inception. First the Spaniards employed, it is reported, the 'cannibal' sign as a common indicator of cruelty; then the English more subtly manipulate the 'cannibal' discourse by at once distancing themselves from the 'Cannibals' and from the Spanish.

Instead of recognising a subversive ability to devour human flesh and resist the colonising forces, Ralegh here creates the notion of the Other (now indiscriminately inclusive of the 'Cannibals' and the 'Arawaks' alike) as a vacant signifier devoid of cultural specificities outside of their assigned role as a boundary marker fabricated by the dominant culture. In this process, the 'cannibals' are absolutely marginalised as a mere sign of 'the Other's Other', while as an imaginary substance another 'Other's Other' – the native female – is foregrounded. It is not difficult to question the validity of Ralegh's claim here. How on earth was it possible for the Arawaks to distinguish between the English and the Spanish and begin 'to conceive the deceit'? *Any* European would have given 'something or other' to the natives to court their favour. It seems a far cry from giving them trifles to sexually respecting their women. The sexual language forcefully yet somewhat uneasily takes over the 'cannibal' discourse only to be replaced by a desexualised rhetoric sanctifying 'her Majesty' (see Montrose 1991).

For Ralegh, the 'Cannibals'-sign serves two distinct ideological purposes. One is to confirm the *absolute* (which was in fact relative – a matter of degree) difference between the English and the Spaniards. The other is to create an illusion of congruence between the natives and the English, both of whom revere and idealise the chaste, the daughterly and the motherly, valorising the unlikely pair of the wives of the native men and the Queen Elizabeth who now stands in God's place. Here it is implicitly assumed that the Arawakan women 'belong' to their men (as the Other's Other) waiting and willing to be conquered with their sheer nakedness by the English, as the English company of men are subject to their captain Ralegh and ultimately to the Queen (from Ralegh's point of view, then, the English soldiers are part of a collective enterprise whose sexual and monetary desire are felt to be hard to cope with). At the crossroads of racial, gender, class and religious difference, one difference – between the English and the Spanish – is formalised by Ralegh's rhetorical force employing the 'Cannibals'-sign, while the other differences – between the Arawak and the English, between the soldiers and the captain – are suppressed. As a result, the original Columbian binarism between the good 'Arawak' and the bad 'Carib' (who is now so marginalised that it is almost impossible to find any trace of him) is reinforced. If any notion of reciprocity exists in Ralegh's account, it is quite misleading, because the natives, whether 'Arawak' or 'Carib', are deprived both of a voice expressing their suspicion of the conquering Europeans, and of the ability to reappropriate the cannibal power to resist. In the quintessential figure of the sexually desired and desiring woman, the natives are there to be unilaterally seen by the colonialist gaze as a non-agency. In this neatly divided scheme of differentiation, it is the 'cannibals' who are discursively expelled, leaving no trace of dialogical relationship between the eating and the eaten.

It can be generally observed in the texts produced by the English, relative newcomers in the colonialist enterprise, that the 'cannibal' sign was dissociated from its (imaginary) intrinsic feature, man-eating. We could perhaps argue that a long-term English strategy to keep 'friendship' with the native population included a linguistic scheme which dismantles the original equation: the 'cannibal/Carib' = man-eaters = the native of the Antilles. On the one hand, it reinforced the Arawak/Carib binarism; on the other hand, however, as the 'cannibal' sign is deprived of its referent, the text is suffused with the contented members of the illusory 'empire':

the 'large' and bountiful Queen, the 'rich' and gentle Englishmen, the 'beautiful' and innocent maids of Guiana. There is no room for the 'cannibals' in this kind of con/text.

## 4. The Irish and the Discourse of Cannibalism

There is a long tradition of discrediting the Irish through cannibalistic discourses. Elizabethan writer William Harrison in *The Description of Britain* mentions:

> These Scots were reputed for the most *Scithian-like* and barbarous nation ... For both Diodorus ... & Strabo ... do seem to speake of a parceil of the Irish nation that should inhabit Britain in their time, which were giuen to the eating of man's flesh, and therefore called *Anthropophagi* ...
>
> Those Scots ... who vsed to feed on the buttocks of boies and women's paps, as delicate dishes. (1587)

It is notable that Harrison, in degrading the Irish and the Scots, here still employs the pre-Columbian paradigm of Scythian Anthropophagi.

Again we can see two models to depict Irish 'barbarity' through the employment of cannibal discourse. One is the pre-Columbian paradigm which does not employ the 'Canibal' sign. Edmund Spenser was one of the foremost and earliest users of this type of cannibalistic discourse for the purpose of legitimising English colonisation of Ireland. He described the starving Irish in graphic terms, as if they were totally unable to fight against their misery: 'they did eat of the dead carrions, happy were they could find them, yea and one another soon after in so much as the very carcasses they spared not to scrape out of their graves' (Spenser 1790: 104).

Fynes Moryson in his *Itinerary* (1617) also recorded that during the famine of 1590s, some of his acquaintances saw 'a most horrible spectacle of three children ... all eating and gnawing with their teeth at the entrails of their dead mother' (cited Maxwell 1923: 198–9). Later, Thomas Waring, in his dedicatory letter to Oliver Cromwell in *An Answer To certain seditious and Jesuitical Queres* (1651), regards the Irish more specifically as:

> The present seed of the ancient *Scythians*, and other barbarous Easterlings (the now *Irish*), assisted with som collapsed and degenerate *English* Papists, striking at the verie root of the tree of *Protestanism*, do not content themselvs with their barbarous torturing, and murdering of vast numbers of our Religion, and blood, everie daies fierie malice (as I may saie) producing a new waie of the most innocent people in coolness of blood, wherein they glutted themselvs. (Waring 1651: A3r)

Perhaps we can detect an exchange of tropes: while 'Scythian' nomadism was exported from Europe to America, the 'Cannibal' savagery was imported from America to Europe. The former 'Scythian' paradigm can be illustrated by the long history of the white extirpation of the native Americans. One of its earliest examples is given by a Jesuit missionary who described the 'nomadic' pattern of some of the Indians living in Northern Virginia: 'Thus four thousand Indians at most roam through, rather than occupy, these vast stretches of inland territory and sea-shore. For they are a nomadic people, living in the forests and scattered over wide spaces as is natural for those who live by hunting and fishing only' (Biard 1896–1901: II 72–3). This kind of description, which may have been truthfully applied to a certain tribe, was soon universalised to signify the 'generally nomadic' condition of the Indians according to the coloniser's greed for their lands.

The latter 'Cannibal' pattern is realised in a specific relationship between the American 'Cannibals' and their Irish counterparts. Perhaps the most telling parallel was provided by the editor of another pro-Commonwealth newspaper, the *Metropolitan Nuncio*, who described the Irish rebel leader Owen Roe O'Neill as:

a most accursed murderer of Innocents, an unparalel'd monster whose body and soul are of a scarlet dye with the bloud of poor English Protestants, and the only ringleader of those purple Charybes and bloud-quaffing cannibals ever since the first of that inhumane Rebellion, who in two moneths space did murder and massacre above one hundred and forty thousand souls ... (1649: A3r)

After the 1649 massacres at Drogheda and Wexford by Oliver Cromwell's troops, which marked a decisive stage in the English colonisation of Ireland, the editor of a pro-Commonwealth newspaper, the *Moderate Intelligencer*, compared unfavorably the Irish with the Indians:

An Indian will be taken with anything that is neat, handsome or usefull, if given, return thanks for it, if not so, purchase it if he can; if the Irish be more bruitish then the Indians, why may not it be reasonable to tame such wilde beasts had they never been in any kinde so cruell and bloody to the English, who by inhabiting among them (besides the good example they had from them) raised their revenue from 20 *Shil.* to 10 *lib.* and took nothing from them. (1649: 10H2r-v)

With rare exceptions such as the Leveller, William Walwyn, the 'Cannibal' sign was utilised as proof of Irish inferiority and degradation. It was exemplified by Sir John Davies, the Attorney General of Ireland, who wrote in 1612 of the Irish customs which he considered vile: 'Wherein they were little better than cannibals, who do hunt one another; and he that hath most strength and swiftness, doth eat and devour all his fellows' (Davies 1786: 135). According to Davies, most to be blamed were 'the stronger' soldiers of Ireland, who consumed and devastated the husbandry of 'the weaker' ordinary people of the land, but his comprehensive indictment of the *whole* Irish people as a 'barbarous' nation is empowered by the indiscriminate use of the 'cannibal' sign. This observation leads Davies to a conclusion that 'the mere Irish were not only accounted aliens, but enemies; and altogether out of the protection of the law', and that their land was 'waste ... the people idle' (pp. 83, 141). In the context of English colonial expansion, it is important to note that the 'nomadism' was employed to justify the colonisation of the Irish, who were regarded, like the Scythians, as 'nomads' having no claim to the land.

However, these colonial discourses which attempt to marginalise others through the employment of 'cannibal' discourse were seriously challenged by another Irish writer. Jonathan Swift's extraordinary satire voicing protest against Irish misery and displacement gets its rhetorical energy from the transgressive act of man-eating itself, and merits a lengthy quotation:

> I have been assured by a very knowing American of my acquaintance in London, that a young healthy child, well nursed, is at a year old a most delicious, nourishing, and wholesome food, whether *stewed, roasted, baked, or boiled*, and I make no doubt that it will equally serve in a *fricassee*, or a *ragout* ... That the remaining hundred thousand may at a year old be offered in sale to the *persons of quality and fortune*, through the kingdom, always advising the mother to let them suck plentifully of the last month, so as to render them plump and fat for a good table. A child will make two dishes at an entertainment for friends, and when the family dines alone the fore or hind quarter will make a reasonable dish, and seasoned with a little pepper or salt will be very good boiled on the fourth day, especially *in winter*. (Swift 1984: 493–4)

Relying upon the whole tradition of the discourse of cannibalism reintroduced, as it were, from the American soil (from which Swift derives an authority for his discourse), this text questions the whole colonialist strategy such as Spenser's or Davies's, by insinuating that it is those 'ladies and gentlemen' who became fat by eating the Irish babies that should be called 'Cannibals'. What Swift does here, through an abashed acceptance of the horrid custom rather than a protest against it, is to expose the mechanisms of power and domination: what is happening and will go on happening on Irish soil is described to devastating effect through the 'cannibalistic' metaphor which no possible stance of opposition can match.

In this panoramic exposition of middle-class avarice, the discourse of cannibalism rediscovers its reciprocity in a most disturbing fashion.

## 5. Conclusion

What was 'discovered' by Columbus was, rather than the Indians or America, the 'canibales'-sign which was opportunistically applied to its referents according to the colonisers' needs. To reveal their opportunism, we could scarcely do better than to go back to Montaigne again for what cannibalism means. According to Montaigne, man-eating is:

> not, as some imagine, to nourish themselves with it (as anciently the Scithians wont to doe), but to represent an extreame and inexpiable revenge ... I am not sorie we note the barbarous horror of such an action, but grieved, that prying so narrowly into their faults we are so blinded in ours. I thinke there is more barbarisms in eating men alive, then to feed upon them being dead; to mangle by tortures and torments a body full of lively sense, to roast him in peeces, to make dogges and swine to gnaw and teare him in mamockes (as wee have not only read, but seene very lately, yea and in our owne memorie, not amongst ancient enemies, but our neighbours and fellow-citizens; and which is worse, under pretence of pietie and religion) than to roast him and eat him after he is dead. (Montaigne 1886: 96)

Montaigne's argument that accords the cannibalistic discourse symmetrical mutuality was all too rare. What one can do, however, is to return to Columbus in 1492, where we started, and uncover duplicity in the deceptive reciprocity in the Columbian paradigm shift from 'anthropophagi' to 'cannibal', in order to recover the *same* substance hidden behind these signs. Those distinctions between the two terms, 'anthropophagi' and 'cannibal', however elaborate, are but linguistic differences – products X of the magical representations by European languages: hence what looks surreal and grotesque in the discourse of cannibalism may in fact be regarded as fundamental to the workings of the discourse of European colonialism.

# Writing up the Log: The Legacy of Hakluyt

## T. J. Cribb

'The history of Hakluyt's career is in large part the intellectual history of the beginnings of the British Empire' (Parks 1928: 2). I believe this resounding claim by the first biographer of the Elizabethan geographer still stands, though how that intellectual history should best be described is open to debate. In joining the debate I shall first attempt to use old and new readings of Hakluyt as an approach to specifying the editorial method of his compilation of voyage narratives, with their simultaneous exhortation to future mercantile expansion and consolidation of a newly emergent sense of national identity (see Helgerson 1992). In the course of this I hope to show that his method participates in an emergent episteme which has both scientific and imperial aspects and which has been neglected in standard accounts of the rise of realist narrative. Lastly, I shall turn to *The Guyana Quartet* by Wilson Harris for a practice of writing which is fully conscious of the imperialising power of the narrative episteme of the traditional novel and which seeks to break it.

The old way of reading Hakluyt was set up by Froude in his article 'England's forgotten Worthies', in the *Westminster Review* of July 1852. This was nominally a review of the first three publications by the newly formed Hakluyt Society: *The Observations of Sir Richard Hawkins, Knt.*, edited by R. H. Major, *The Discoverie of the Empire of Guiana* by Sir Walter Ralegh, edited by Sir Robert Schomburgk, and *Narratives of Early Voyages undertaken for the Discovery of a Passage to Cathaia and India by the North-west*, edited by Thomas Rundall. (Froude carelessly ascribed the editing of Hawkins to the Keeper of Maps at the British Museum, R. H. Major, whereas the volume was in fact edited by Captain Bethune.) I shall return to the first two of these later. Froude did not like the editing, save for Schomburgk's, and his objections derive from the way he read Hakluyt, to whom he devotes the bulk of his 'review'. What he wanted was a 'people's edition' in accordance with his reading of Hakluyt as 'the Prose Epic of the modern English nation'. For Froude, prose implies class, in an explicit contrast with earlier societies. These English epics are 'Not mythic, like the Iliads and Eddas, but plain broad narratives of substantial facts ... What the old epics were to the royally or nobly born, this modern epic is to the common people.' Over-riding the varieties of rank among Hakluyt's many authors, Froude insists on a populist unity and virtual anonymity of authorship, like the Romantic notion of gothic architecture as built by 'the people', a product of nature, not of art. The Carlylean phraseology with which he colours his writing betrays the ultimately German Romantic origins of his portrayal of a spirit of the times which sweeps through all men, using them as mere instruments of destiny. Hence his emphasis on martyrdom, as Hakluyt's simultaneously noble and common heroes bear witness to England's manifest destiny. Froude is Hegel waving the British flag; no wonder that during the heyday of empire this became the accepted way to read Hakluyt.

The new way of reading goes to the other extreme and is well exemplified by the subtleties of Mary Fuller's *Voyages in Print* (1995). According to the lights of this New Historicist analysis, the writings of Hakluyt and his predecessors are revealed not as natural but as highly artificial constructs, in which 'if the history of these early decades is about any one thing it is about the ways in which the failure of voyages and colonies was recuperated by rhetoric' (p. 12). The grand narrative of empire is abridged and its thrust turned back so that, in the case of one of Hakluyt's voyages, Sir Humphrey Gilbert's: 'A corporate and national endeavour is converted into a spiritual and intensely personal one' (p. 42; cf. 'The most referential of forms [the list] turns back onto claims about the traveler himself', p. 54). Because this particular endeavour failed and the account recuperates it as martyrdom, Fuller takes this to license a general psychologisation of history, forgetting that a martyr bears witness to something greater than himself. Her analysis is at its subtlest on Ralegh's *Discoverie of the Empire of Guiana.* This is read as Ralegh's attempt to establish his moral and political trust-worthiness on the veracity of his geographical discoveries in the real world, where 'discovery' has its modern meaning; pitted against that meaning is the attempt by his prosecutors to dis-cover his true intentions, where evidence of the kind Raleigh adduces counts for nothing. The focus is on writing itself and on writing as a defensive self-fashioning, a manoeuvring for power to define the self, shoring up the fragilities of identity. This approach reaches its climactic conclusion in Hakluyt's exploitation of the two Elizabethan meanings of 'travel/travail' to subsume the actual travels of others into his own labour of compilation and writing.

Given the extremity of these differences between old and new readings, it is surprising that one can discern a certain convergence between Froude and Fuller on the ground of Hakluyt's editorial method. Fuller (1995) may conclude that Hakluyt fashions others into himself, but she devotes the greater proportion of her analysis to his image of his collection as a reassembled body which is not his own, a body which 'also looks something like a recomposed memory, precisely, the memory of a national(ist) history; Hakluyt's role in assembling the body is limited merely to editorial articulation' (p. 152). This intriguingly resembles Froude's notion that Hakluyt is the purest of editors, a transparent vessel for the spirit of the age.

Convergence from such different points of departure suggests that it is the editorial method which demands scrutiny, and on this Fuller has some penetrating remarks:

> His commitment was not to travel but to information ... This information contained its own replicatory mechanisms ... Even the most neutral transcriptions of bare facts, the degree zero, so to speak, of dates, headings, weather, and so on, reach beyond themselves to become instructions for repetition ... Hakluyt stimulated writing by soliciting narratives, and in so doing helped to create an on-going demand for such narratives. To this generative process his name has become attached. (Fuller 1995: 145, 148–9)

If this line of approach is followed through, one is led not towards the psychology of self-fashioning but towards the establishment of narrative structures. One is also brought back to a traditional account of Hakluyt's motives for writing, for it is these which determine the narrative structures. His motives were urgently practical. Fuller emphasises the degree to which the writings substitute for discoveries not actually made and for projects that failed. More historically apposite is the fact that England was a late arrival on the seas of exploration. When Penrose (1952) comes to the English material in his comprehensive survey of European travel in the Renaissance, he notes that its distinctive character derives from its lateness: 'In the case of the other nations, travel literature followed expansion: the great chronicles ... were published when Portuguese power was even beginning to decline ... Of the various types of travel literature, therefore, it may be said that England's alone was aimed explicitly at stimulating expansion' (pp. 312–13).

This is why Hakluyt adopts the method he does, which is not to abstract a narrative from his documents in the chronicle fashion, but to present the documents themselves, collated by time and location, so that a reader may *use* the information retailed for practical purposes. Precisely such information was suppressed from the continental chronicles, lest it present opportunities to rivals. Hakluyt's whole purpose is indeed to promote replication of his narratives in real life, and hence they carry the technical information and instructions enabling that to be done. It is this practical purpose that informs his method.

In his dedicatory epistles Hakluyt (1925–28) shows himself fully aware both of earlier procedures and of his own originality. With reference to precedents, he compares his compilation to a memory theatre as described by Sallust, with the images of the ancestors 'so arranged as to inspire the present generation to equivalent achievements' (vol. I, p. 39). As an earnest advocate of colonisation of the western world, he is of course conscious of Virgil's Aeneas and his Trojan piety as a model for the achievement of empire. He also alludes to Foxe's *Actes and Monuments*, with its martyro-logical interpretation of Protestant history, thus pre-empting Fuller's reading, though without her psychologisation (Hakluyt 1925–28: I 7, 37; VII 62). With reference to innovation, he uses documents by and frequently mentions John Dee, credited with coining the phrase 'the British Empire' (Penrose 1952: 175). Besides Dee, there are references to Mercator, Thevet (the French Cartographer Royal), William Gilbert, Hariot and other ad-vanced thinkers in the field at home and abroad (Hakluyt 1925–28: I 31, 32, 38 and passim).

On matters of substance, Hakluyt contrasts his narrative method polemically with the preceding models of knowledge he offers to displace, 'those wearie volumes bearing the titles of universall Cosmographie', now discredited by the discovery of whole continents not included in their symbolically tripartite division of the world (vol. I, p. 6). He goes to new sources and authorities for his material, not previous cosmographers but 'the chiefest Captaines at sea, the greatest Merchants, and the best Mariners of our nation' (vol. I, p. 2). Instead of digesting these sources into his own account, Hakluyt attributes 'every voyage to his Author, which both in person hath performed, and in writing hath left the same' (vol. 1, p. 6). This too is part of a programme that redefines truth not by tradition but by experience, not holistically but individually, each man his own author. Exceptions allowed, what matters is that the person writing shall have been there at the time: 'The Register and true accounts of all herein expressed hath beene approved by me John Sparke the younger, who went upon the same voyage, and wrote the same' (vol. VII, p. 53). The authenticity of the experience is further guaranteed by the style of writing, which is anti-literary in its eschewal of adornment: 'Expect onely a plaine truth, as from the pen of a souldier and Navigator', a trope repeated in numerous narratives (vol. VII, p. 200). This stylistic feature exactly illustrates Stephen Greenblatt's (1991) comments on Montaigne's 'Des Cannibales': 'Discursive authority in the early literature of travel then derives from a different source than it would in other forms of poesis – not from an appeal to higher wisdom or social superiority but from a miming, by the elite, of the simple, direct, unfigured language of perception Montaigne and others attribute to servants' (p. 147).

In all these respects, Hakluyt's selection of material is, to take an analogy from the history of cartography analysed by John Gillies in his valuable *Shakespeare and the Geography of Difference* (1994), biased towards the portolan chart as opposed to the monumentally symbolic mappa mundi. This is not to imply that the *Navigations* is a mere miscellany. As Hakluyt explains, his documents are organised on a double principle of time and place: the southern voyages first, since they happened first in time; then the northern and eastern voyages; lastly the western discoveries 'succeed naturallie in the third and last roome, forasmuch as in order and course those coastes, and quarters came last of all to our knowledge and experiences' (Hakluyt 1925–28: I 9). The plan of the whole reproduces the principle of authentic experience reported as it occurred in each part. Hakluyt confirms this principle in the second edition: 'By the helpe of Geographie and Chronologie (which I may call the Sunne and the Moone, the right eye and the left of all history) [I have] referred each particular relation to the due time and place' (vol. I, p. 9). Thus 'each particular' narrative is part of a larger narrative structure, and this structure is not derived from literary or symbolic principles but from what Hakluyt prefers to think of as the more authentic authority of the coherence of time and place. This, as we shall see, becomes an important element in the emerging episteme of science.

Hakluyt meets his new criteria for truth by reproducing the navigators' actual journals, in effect their ship's logs. The method for keeping a log is set out in his first volume by Sebastian Cabot in the seventh item of his instructions of 1553: 'The merchants, and other skilful persons in writing, shal daily write, describe and put in memorie the Navigation of every day and night, with the points, and observation of the lands, tides, elements, altitude of the sunne, course of the moon and starres' (vol. I, p. 233). Each ship sets out on its voyage of three months or more as a little scriptorium of mensuration, daily secreting its deposit of writing, all of it exactly tied to place and time. And the writing is obligatory, the narratives required of the masters or captains by law of contract.

In taking the decisions he did in selection and organisation of material, Hakluyt participated in the construction of a new episteme, the scientific. At this stage of construction, given England's belatedness on the international scene, Fuller is right to emphasise that the writing is as much a project as a record of achievement. This double aspect of the practical and the aspirational, the one intended to bring the other to fruition, fits with the European science of the day in its Paracelsan aspect. This still participated, like many of the maps Gillies describes, in symbolic systems descending from antiquity, but it also consciously proclaimed new principles. One of these was the value of knowledge acquired by doing –

experiential knowledge to be found not in books but among artisans, the kind of knowledge which makes Hakluyt value the reports of common sailors (Rossi 1970). It is the newly acquired prestige of this knowledge that allows the learned Bacon to contrast the way of the library with the way of the road in the advancement of learning; and by choosing for his frontispiece a ship sailing through the pillars of Hercules which had set limits to the ancient world, Bacon can thereby show that it is the New World which he sets towards (Franklin 1979). The origins of empiricism are not epistemological but practical.

This powerful prototype established, I now turn to its self-contradictions. The most interesting is the glaring exception, which Hakluyt himself points out, of printing the accounts of Essex and Howard's Cadiz expedition and of the defeat of the Spanish Armada in his first volume, supposedly exclusively devoted to northern expeditions, breaching both principles of time and place. He justifies this as follows: 'I have set [them] downe as a double epiphonema to conclude this my first volume withall … partly to satisfie the importunitie of some of my special friends, and partly, not longer to deprive the diligent Reader of two such woorthy and long-expected discourses' (Hakluyt 1925–28: I 35).

An epiphonema is an exclamatory outburst coming at the end of a work, glossed in *The Shepherd's Calendar* as containing in striking form 'the moral of the whole tale'. Hakluyt's deviation from the experiential into the literary betrays the principle at work which motivates the whole. For all their scrupulosity of serial observation, these voyages are of course thoroughly end-directed and seen from that point of view the careful coordinations of time and place are merely means to that end. The end is personal wealth and imperial power in this world, a departure from the medieval cosmography once again, for there was no human end in view implicitly shaping those compilations, no inner project of desire tensing them into the kind of historiography with which we have become familiar. Michel de Certeau (1988) makes a similar point about historiography: 'Since the sixteenth century … historiography has ceased to be the representation of providential time, that is, of a history decided by an inaccessible Subject who can be deciphered only in the signs that he gives of his wishes. Historiography takes the position of the subject of action – of the prince, whose objective is to make history' (p. 7).

The OED shows that the same paradigm shift governs the definition of the word 'discover', during this period. Until the sixteenth century it means to remove a covering, such as a hat or roof, and secondarily to remove the cover of something hidden, so that a discoverer might mean an informer. In both cases what is discovered is in principle already known. The earliest instances where it means to obtain sight or knowledge for the

first time of something previously unknown are in 1555 and 1585 and both
are from accounts of navigations; the third is from 1670 and concerns a
discovery in science. The first use of 'discoverer' in the modern sense is
in Hakluyt. Discovery now becomes a special activity, a project, animated
by an end in view (cf. Washburn 1962).

Similar considerations apply to an acquisition of meaning by the word
'observation' as in *The Observations of Sir Richard Hawkins, Knt.* The
original meaning is 'the action or practice of observing a law, covenant, set
day, or anything prescribed or fixed'. The quality of attention so demanded
allows the meaning then to be extended to include 'the action or an act of
observing scientifically; esp. the careful watching of a phenomenon in
regard to its cause and effect, or of phenomena in regard to their mutual
relations, these being observed as they occur in nature (and so opposed to
experiment)'. The first use in this sense is attributed to Willoughby
Cunningham's *Cosmographicall Glasse* of 1559, cited by Penrose as the first
of the scientific texts in which English mathematicians and scientists
attempted to enhance national skills in navigation compared with other
European powers. Cunningham is also cited as the first source for a special
use of the general scientific meaning, the taking of the altitude of the sun
(or other heavenly body) by means of an astronomical instrument, in order
to find the latitude or longitude. Scientific knowledge and its practical
motivation go hand in hand.

We thus have on the one hand an empirical serialism masking a driving
teleology, and on the other the promotion of individual experience as the
only verifiable source of truth and knowledge. The two combine and receive
their rationale from the systematic observations and recordings of the new
scientific method. Hence the familiar paradox that Europeans can speak of
discovering whole peoples, as if they were unknown to themselves. Hence
too a narrative paradigm deeply implicated in the project of empire.

This pattern for the narrating of voyages, once established by Hakluyt,
is replicated in his descendants. The principal agent of transmission in the
latter part of the seventeenth century is the Royal Society, some of whose
members, such as Sir Hans Sloane, play the same role of assembling
documentary resources, stimulating other collectors and translators and
acting as consultant to projects as Hakluyt had done in his day. One of the
early collections is published by Locke's friend, Awnsham Churchill, whose
introductory discourse later finds its way into editions of Locke's own
works. The motive for providing narratives on this model remains the same
as with Hakluyt: practical application. But about this time a second motive
begins to make itself felt: publishing for profit to entertain a market of
general readers. Thus at the same time that the folio collections of voyages
appear at regular intervals throughout the eighteenth century, Grub Street

is furnishing less scrupulously edited selections in monthly shilling numbers. This is the world of Defoe, who believed himself descended from Ralegh, and accordingly produced an edition of *The Discoverie of Guiana*. The same market is served by Smollett, who is very clear about the editorial criteria for his seven-volume *A Compendium of Authentic and Entertaining Voyages, digested in a chronological series*. He dismisses the faithful redactions as: 'So stuffed with dry descriptions of bearings and distances, tides and current, variations of the compass, leeway, wind and weather, sounding, anchoring, and other terms of navigation, that none but mere pilots or seafaring people can read them without disgust. Our aim has been to clear away this kind of rubbish' (Crone and Skelton 1946: 111).

While Smollett may jettison some of the detail which is the practical sinew of Hakluyt, he adheres to the narrative structure and the criterion of authenticity. These are now naturalised as pleasure, pleasure which can be endlessly replicated and consumed, without need for reflection. Actual history is on the way to being produced and consumed as a tale of adventure. And by editing the first-person narratives into the third person, as becomes normal during the century, the clear distinction between fiction and reality becomes blurred in a generalised effect of the real.

The same principles serve to describe the classic realist novel, as defined by Elizabeth Ermarth in *Realism and Consensus in the English Novel* (1983). Her categories are derived from Renaissance perspectival realism transferred to a new base line, time. They might equally be derived from the narrative of discovery and its ultimate source, the ship's log. The advantage of referring to the latter is that it supplies a missing link between the novel and actual history. Without such a link one is left with purely epistemological accounts in which the novel hoists itself into being by its own bootstraps, as in Ermarth and her distinguished predecessor, Ian Watt, admirably conceived and indeed illuminating as their studies are. On the other hand, studies like Martin Green's *Dreams of Adventure and Deeds of Empire* (1980) bring an historian's sense of what is happening in the world to bear on the history of the novel, but have little to say about the internal structures of the novels themselves.

In our present state of knowledge, it is comparatively easy to document the continuities of the episteme at the level of, say, scientific and literary institutions. Thus, moving into the nineteenth century, the Royal Geographic Society, founded in 1830, is one of a succession of specialist societies splitting off from the Royal Society as the fields of science proliferate and set themselves up as disciplines. It absorbs the remains of the Association for the Exploration of Interior Africa, set up by the scientists and travellers Sir Joseph Banks and Major Rennell, which had promoted a number of expeditions and publications, most famously Mungo

Park's. From the Royal Geographic Society is derived the Hakluyt Society in 1846, which borrowed its rule book from the Camden Society of 1837, thus indicating a turn towards history. However, Hakluyt's geography and chronology are still duly combined in the overlapping personnel of the two societies, notably Sir Clements Markham, first hon. sec. (1863–88), then president (1893–1905) of the RGS, while also president of the Hakluyt Society (Crone and Skelton 1946: 139–40, 156). It is Markham who notes that founding members were Charles Darwin and John Forster (who later recruited Dickens) and reminisces that Charles Kingsley used to sing the praises of Schomburgk's edition of Ralegh's *Discoverie of Guiana*, from which he derived much of the material for that most imperialist of novels, *Westward Ho!* Markham also reports that the society's fiftieth anniversary dinner for members was attended by George Nathaniel Curzon and Joseph Chamberlain (Markham 1896). To supply the readings of novels corresponding to these institutional changes and continuities, *hoc opus, hic labor est*.

As a foil to such a putative account, I shall now offer a reading of Wilson Harris's engagement with these powerful narrative patterns in *The Guyana Quartet*, especially the last of the four, *The Secret Ladder* (1963). The connections with the material I have been surveying are both large-scale and intimate, for the names of the crew in the first novel, *Palace of the Peacock*, are the real names of the crew members of Harris's own first three-month surveying expedition into the interior of Guyana in 1942. Moreover, one of the crew is called Schomburgh, according to Harris an actual descendant of one of the brothers Schomburgk who explored Guyana in the 1840s (for further discussion of the archival basis to Harris's characters see Cribb 1993). A translation of Richard Schomburgk's account of their explorations was published by Walter Roth in Georgetown in 1927, and his introduction compares it not only with Waterton's *Wanderings in South America* of 1825 but with *Robinson Crusoe*, neatly linking log and novel. For good measure, brother Robert Schomburgk edited, as we have seen from Froude's review, Ralegh's *Discoverie of Guiana*. Richard was an avid reader of Fenimore Cooper and stayed with Captain Marryat's mother when fitting out his expedition in London. He shows his consciousness of the narrative model he follows artlessly enough: 'According to the plan laid down for efficiently carrying out my work, I ought now to set down in chronological order all my experiences in the city proper.' He in fact departs from 'due time and place' only slightly and is perfectly capable of ending a chapter with the resoundingly anti-epiphonematic: 'On an average, the current of the River amounts to 2½ knots, while at the mouth, owing to the falling of the tide, it is often increased to 7 knots an hour, i.e. 11.9 feet per second' (Schomburgk 1922: I 20, 16).

The Schomburgk brothers were, of course, not conquistadors but representatives of the then recently founded Royal Geographic Society. As such, to borrow Mary Louise Pratt's classifications of travel narratives in *Imperial Eyes* (1992), the Schomburgks belong to the Linnaean, scientific phase that begins in the eighteenth century. Robert preserves the more severely scientific style, but in fact shares many of Richard's effusively expressed liberal sympathies with the plight of the recently liberated slaves; Richard eventually had to emigrate to Australia because of his support for the 1848 revolutions in Germany. They thus incorporate the models of both the sentimental traveller established by Mungo Park and the Romantic traveller pioneered by Humboldt.

These same variants on the basic pattern of discovery are exhibited by the last protagonist of Harris's *Guyana Quartet*, Russell Fenwick. He is a scientist and explorer engaged on a survey; he is a sentimentalist ill at ease with his position as captain of the crew; he is a liberal intent on winning over by rational persuasion and love the descendants of the slaves who obstruct his expedition. And he is open to the usual charges of hypocrisy brought against liberal reformers, because of his divided allegiance between humanism and science, his personal ambition as a brilliant young surveyor with a promising future linked to his country's imminent independence, and his economic motivation – to pay off his mother's mortgage. He is also infused with the poetic inspiration signalled by the name Donne in the first of the novels, for as he goes to check his river gauges at midnight he looks up at the stars and is 'filled with an almost mathematical ecstasy, the poetic frenzy and delirium of a god'. The language may seem overblown unless one recalls the Renaissance theory of heroic furies which pervades the art of the period from Michelangelo to Shakespeare. (Hakluyt himself refers to 'the Heroicall intents and attempts of our Princes' [vol. I, p. 39].)

However, it is primarily as a scientist that Fenwick conducts his expedition. The spatial and temporal coordinates of the narrative are carefully recorded, from the opening sentence: 'It was the month of September, noon on the Canje River', through the following days to the sixth: 'When he awoke it was just 9. The rain was drizzling.' But the instruments by which time and place are coordinated are no longer the compass, star and chronometer of the eighteenth-century explorer but the Dumpy level, staff and gauge of the nineteenth- and twentieth-century hydrographic surveyor. These are the instruments Fenwick is using on his second encounter with the aged leader of the slave descendants, Poseidon:

> A bench mark had already been planted on the bank of the creek; and this would ensure his setting the temporary pole on the same datum as the Skeldon gauge. Readings at both places would give some useful indication

of the river's mean slope at this phenomenally low stage, he mused, sketching in his notebook the rough dispositions of tide pole, bench mark and creek-mouth.

He had come fully prepared, and Bryant nailed the pole they had brought with them to the overhanging limb of a tree. Fenwick set up his spirit-level midway between the new gauge and the permanent bench mark.

'I wonder whether it'll be safe to leave this gauge here until tomorrow?' he thought, his eye glued to the inverting telescope of his level as he checked his reading on the bench mark. The staff suddenly pitched and vanished, and Fenwick's astonished sight beheld instead the accusing image of Poseidon, eyes inverted, brow pointing down. Fenwick shot up, and the old man straightened his bent back (upon which the sky revolved). He lifted a load of firewood from his shoulders and deposited it on the ground not far from Fenwick's feet. (Harris 1985: 393–4)

Fenwick sketches on the right page of his note- or Level Book, the left page being ruled to record his field readings and their reductions. The field readings are reduced in relation to the datum, which in most countries is Mean Sea Level. Fenwick carries a miniature version of the Sea Level datum with him in his instrument's Bubble Level, which works on the principle that the 'free surface of a still liquid, being at every point normal to the line of gravity, is a level surface' (Clark 1972: I 33; first published in 1923, revised 1939 with added material 'which, perhaps, is of greater importance to engineers or surveyors working abroad or in the Colonies', p. xii). His instrument can thus be set in the same plane as the Sea Level datum, though of course at some height above it. That height is established by standing a graduated pole on the surface of the ground or water whose height above Sea Level is to be ascertained, recording the reading on the pole where the horizontal hairline of the bubble-levelled telescope cuts it, and comparing that reading with one previously established, a bench mark, derived by succession from the ultimate zero reading of Mean Sea Level. When Fenwick combines his reduced readings with others measuring the velocity and volume of the current at different points along its course, he will be able to plot the river's stage discharge curve, as he does late at night on the third day. All thus depends on the first measurements established by triangulation at sea level. The same system governs the priorities of the Schomburgk brothers' expedition to settle a border dispute with Venezuela: 'It was essential for … further determinations that a definite point in the interior should now be fixed so that future observations could be connected up with it' (Schomburgk 1922: I 101–2).

A reading in the language of surveying is thus a point on a standard scale (or ladder) which correlates a selected object with a given fixed datum;

the method is essentially that adumbrated by Hakluyt. In this kind of reading meaning is as monologic as it is possible to be. Plurality and ambiguity are utterly excluded, for only one point can occupy that place at that time – or rather, that place and that time within that formal system. The unknown is produced by extrapolation from the known, but the known itself is ultimately an arbitrary datum. Like any mathematical language, the geometry of surveying is self-defining and self-sufficient and this property contributes to its appearance of unquestionable rightness when, as a language, it is used to describe the world. However, although this language carries no originary moment within itself and as such is ahistoric, it is certainly not the case that the development of scientific language and its rise to power is outside history. On the contrary, the adoption of the language is strongly motivated as a means to an end, though because of its formalism, as we have already seen in Hakluyt, the method is apt to mask its historical motives.

To return to Fenwick, he is checking his reading first by rotating the Dumpy Level in a horizontal plane between the bench mark and the graduated pole, second by checking the bubble level each time, and third by adjusting the telescope's focus to remove parallax. This is necessary because the eyepiece of his Dumpy Level is focused on the hairlines further up towards the end of the telescope; the image produced by the telescope lenses beyond the eyepiece and hairlines must therefore be made to fall in the same plane as the hairlines, and that is achieved by adjusting the telescope's focus.

It is this operation that Poseidon interrupts. Suddenly obtruded into the view-finder of science is an image which refuses to be surveyed, levelled and read on the scale of plane geometry, yet it is only by virtue of the instrument that the image is seen in its striking aspect. It is the nature of the Kepler telescope used for surveying that the image Fenwick sees is inverted, magnified and virtual – that is, it is a second image derived from a primary image within the system of lenses. The inversion dislocates because while it may be true that 'all surveyors soon become accustomed to seeing everything upside-down', unexpectedly to see a human face so inverted is disconcerting. The magnification contributes to the aggrandise-ment of Poseidon, flying downwards like some avenging god on a baroque ceiling. It also gives the image a startling proximity, even intimacy. There is a comical aspect too, as both figures mirror each other in an O'Grady symmetry: Fenwick stooped over his telescope concentrating on his work of cognitive control, Poseidon stooped under his load of wood, both straightening together. The overall effect is of estrangement, releasing reality from the lethargy of the objectively given, re-realising it as a strenuous intersection of different modes of perception – a sort of virtual image. Or one might say that it is an image that insists on retaining parallax – on making visible the overlap of one image by another, one language by another, one system of perception and values by another. This is the secret ladder, the human scale which is always multiple, and it is Harris's genius to have discovered it without the least hint of irrationality or Romantic obscurantism in the very act of scientific observation. To change the metaphor, not only is the world of things liberated from the petrifying fixity of the gorgon stare but Medusa's head is reunited with her body so that head and heart can resume their functional relations.

It is important not to privilege the mythic dimension of the books, for it is only one dimension among many, with no superior fixity or definition. It has somewhat the same status as Homeric parallels in *Ulysses*, serving to interfere with preconception, expand perception, but never settling into a system. Fenwick acknowledges that Poseidon is a god, but also that he is not to be worshipped in his current, or any actual, form. The explorer's log is superimposed on the Seven Days of Creation, as in *Palace of the Peacock*, but that is only another kind of calendar, and Harris is at pains to make his Creation an immaterial one. A frequent device in the book is the unfinished sentence or unvoiced speech. It is an unfinished creation, and that is essential to its nature. There are no epiphonema here.

Thus the narrative pattern Harris inherits from Hakluyt and history is subjected to a radical epistemological mutation. The compelling coordinates of time and place that inform the novel of adventure and discovery from Defoe to Conrad and Golding can still be discerned, but often with some difficulty, as the reader is forced to locate the same events simultaneously on quite different scales of perception and value. Hence the strenuousness of reading Harris, but hence too a sense of liberation that grows with every reading. Events are freed from fixed bearings within a single culture and its recent history, releasing a sort of gnostic comedy and sense of plenitude rarely found in narrative since the cosmographies Hakluyt's new method displaced. One is reminded of the parallels Umberto Eco draws between medieval and modernist poetics in *The Middle Ages of James Joyce*. *The Guyana Quartet* is thus framed by two stories of exploration, one Renaissance in style, the other post-eighteenth-century. It is fitting that the last novel in the *Quartet* should be the one in which the scientific paradigm adumbrated in the Renaissance both emerges into full self-consciousness and is dialectically transcended.

# From Classical to Imperial: Changing Visions of Turkey in the Eighteenth Century

Katherine S. H. Turner

Lady Mary Wortley Montagu's Turkish *Embassy Letters*, written between 1716 and 1718 but published (posthumously) only in 1763, remains one of the best known of eighteenth-century travelogues, and Montagu herself was one of the most celebrated woman writers of her time. Born in 1689, she was an indefatigable and accomplished letter writer, corresponding with leading literary figures such as Alexander Pope as well as an extensive network of family and friends. She also wrote essays and poems (both romantic and satirical), and a play (collected in Montagu 1977); her participation in a wide range of genres, including travel writing, indicates her ability to transcend gender-based literary categories. Fewer than twenty British women published travel narratives during the eighteenth century, and Montagu was a pioneer of this small but highly significant cluster of women, whose works provide a fascinating, often oblique, commentary on the cultural and political trends of their time.

The attractive vision of Turkey presented in the *Embassy Letters* typifies a particular version of English Enlightenment culture and aesthetics. Bernard Lewis sees in Montagu's account 'the new myth, still in its embryonic form, of the non-European as the embodiment of mystery and romance' (Lewis 1993: 83). In many ways, however, Montagu's *Letters* are uncharacteristic of the eighteenth century of which they are so often claimed to be paradigmatic. In 1789, Lady Elizabeth Craven, England's other great eighteenth-century woman traveller to Turkey, takes issue with many of Montagu's opinions in her own travelogue, *A Journey through the Crimea to Constantinople*, and pronounces indeed that Montagu 'never wrote a line of them' (Craven 1789: 105). In her later *Memoirs*, and in the enlarged edition of the *Journey*, published in 1814, Craven expands on this view, pronouncing that the *Embassy Letters* 'were most of them *male* compositions, pretending to female grace in the style, the facts mostly inventions' (Craven 1814: 289). There had in fact been a spurious 'fourth' volume of

Montagu's *Embassy Letters* published in 1767, perhaps written by John Cleland; but by the 1780s its spuriousness, and the authenticity of the 1763 volumes were not in doubt.

Montagu's highly favourable impressions of abroad, especially of Turkey, and especially of Turkish women, are Craven's chief targets. Craven found an unexpected ally in the person of Lady Bute, Montagu's daughter, who, having failed to suppress the publication of the *Embassy Letters* in 1763, was later delighted to find support for her disowning of her mother's vulgar publishing activities. Ladies Craven and Bute later corresponded about the authorship of the *Embassy Letters*, Lady Bute agreeing heartily that most of the Letters were 'composed by men', and suggesting that Horace Walpole 'and two other wits' had written them (Craven 1826: II 116).

No one else seems to have taken these assertions seriously; yet, questions of personal grievance and arrogance aside, this curious episode suggests how uncongenial Montagu's account became to at least some later eighteenth-century readers. It therefore provides a point of entry into a wider discussion of changes in eighteenth-century perceptions of travel writing, of women travel writers, and (not least) of Turkey itself. It is worth noting here that Craven's critical observations on Turkey, which to a large extent are a reactionary engagement with Montagu's, were taken seriously by the influential reviews (the *Monthly*, the *Critical* and the *Analytical*), although they slyly mocked her style and arrogance. Moreover, the *Monthly Review* commended her liberal reflections, 'which do honour to the writer, both as a lover of her own country, and as a citizen of the world' (*Monthly Review* 80 [1789], 209).

There are two main reasons for the generally positive reception of Craven's text in 1789. First, little else in the way of original travel writing on Turkey had been published since Montagu's text in 1763: James Porter's *Observations on the Religion, Law, Government, and Manners, of the Turks* (1768) was a compilation of travellers' accounts, and the focus of Richard Chandler's *Travels in Asia Minor* (1775) was largely archaeological. Second, a woman travel writer was still something of a novelty in her own right, no doubt because the genre's roots in masculine erudition and experience – at least until the closing decades of the century – remained powerfully deterrent (see Turner 1995: 168–246). The *Analytical Review*, anticipating its readers' interest in Craven's travelogue, notes that 'The letters of this sprightly female will naturally excite curiosity' (*Analytical Review* 3 [1789], 176). Craven's personal notoriety – her private life was nothing if not colourful – is also hinted at here.

The Turkish aspect of Craven's account seems to have been its main source of marketable interest. The title of the travelogue places Constantinople as the climax of her journey, and the running head throughout the volume is 'Lady Craven's Journey to Constantinople'. In fact, only about 70 of the 327 pages of Craven's *Journey* deal with Turkey, as critics were quick to point out (e.g. *Monthly Review* 80 [1789], 200–1; *Critical Review* 67 [1789], 281; *Gentleman's Magazine* 59 [1789], 237); and the revised title of the 1814 edition duly read *Letters from the Right Honorable Lady Craven, to His Serene Highness the Margrave of Anspach, during her Travels through France, Germany, and Russia in 1785 and 1786*. In 1789, though, Craven was no doubt exploiting public interest in Turkey: not only did the harem still exert a powerful pull on the British reader's imagination, but recent political developments made the Turkish focus of the *Journey* topical. The increasingly aggressive behaviour of Russia and Austria towards the declining Ottoman Empire was becoming an alarming threat to British trading interests in the Levant. Craven's account was published during the Russian and Austrian war against Turkey, 1787–92 (though her journey was made earlier, 1785–86). Britain had formed the Triple Alliance with the United Provinces and Prussia *against* Austria in 1788; and by 1789 all parties were eager for peace between Turkey and its aggressors, not least because the Triple Alliance were anxious to direct their energies against the tide of the French Revolutionary army (Shaw 1976: i 258–60). With the turmoil, indeed even disintegration of European affairs, following a decade on from the loss of America, it seems likely that Britain was anxious to preserve trading links with a safely weak but *intact* Ottoman Empire, which might indeed offer itself as an arena ripe for colonial domination; by British rather than Russian or Austrian interests.

What follows is a comparison of Montagu's and Craven's accounts, which will illuminate crucial changes in representations of gender and empire, as mediated through the eyes of the woman travel writer in Turkey. An account of the publishing histories of the travelogues will lead – through the issue of gender and propriety – into an analysis of the conflicting visions of Turkish women offered by Montagu and Craven. The latter part of the chapter will probe the changing concepts of cultural politics and history which the texts illuminate. In particular, Craven's repudiation of Montagu is a significant contribution to an emergent colonial discourse, displacing Montagu's classical, tolerant and largely ahistorical stance. Craven's text exemplifies what Homi K. Bhabha has defined as 'the objective of colonial discourse', which is to construe the colonised as a 'population of degenerate types on the basis of racial origin, in order to justify conquest and to establish systems of administration and instruction' (Bhabha 1986: 154).

The mere existence of their narratives testifies to the privileged status of Montagu and Craven. Their rank made possible nor only their access to European and Turkish high society – 'The Turks are very proud, and will not converse with a stranger they are not assured is considerable in his own country' (Montagu 1763: II 131–2) – but their very expeditions. Lady Mary, who travelled through Austria and Hungary to Constantinople, with 'thirty covered waggons for our baggage, and five coaches ... for my women' (vol. II, p. 110), points out that:

> The journey we have made from Belgrade hither, cannot possibly be passed by any out of a public character. The desert woods of Serbia, are the common refuge of thieves, who rob, fifty in a company, so that we had need of all our guards to secure us; and the villages are so poor, that only force could extort from them necessary provisions. (Montagu 1763: II 2)

Elsewhere, she describes her distress at the 'insolencies' of their escorts 'in the poor villages through which we passed' (vol. I, p. 152). Craven travelled with a smaller entourage but rather less sensitivity. Her *Journey* (1789) is peppered with name-dropping, and pervaded by a strong sense of her own importance, as in this passage: 'At Soumi I conversed with a brother of Prince Kourakin's and a Mr. Lanskoy, both officers quartered there; and to whom I was indebted for a lodging: they obliged a Jew to give me up a new little house he was upon the point of inhabiting' (p. 154).

The *Critical Review* concludes its account of Craven with the waspish pronouncement that the 'rest of the journey affords little subject of remark, except that whatever accommodations rank and beauty could demand, and despotic power could procure, Lady Craven enjoyed' (*Critical Review* 67 [1789], 286).

The circumstances under which Montagu's and Craven's texts were published testify to the critical significance not only of their rank, but also of their gender, and illuminate changing concepts of private and public identity. The *Embassy Letters* emerged into the literary world like the elegant ghost of their recently deceased author, appearing in 1763 in three small octavo volumes. The first of these contained a preface written in 1724 by Mary Astell, confessing herself

> malicious enough to desire, that the world should see, to how much better purpose the LADIES travel than their LORDS; and that, whilst it is surfeited with *Male-Travels*, all in the same tone, and stuff with the same trifles; a lady has the skill to strike out a new path, and to embellish a worn-out subject, with variety of fresh and elegant entertainment. (Montagu 1763: I viii)

Montagu is the eighteenth-century woman travel writer of whom it was most often and enthusiastically proclaimed that her gender qualified her to describe scenes 'not to be paralleled in the narrative of any *male* Traveller' (*Monthly Review* 28 [1763], 392): namely, the Turkish bath, the harem, and the lifestyles of aristocratic Turkish women. She was evidently proud of this privilege and of the distinction it guaranteed her within the corpus of travel literature; she concludes the letter describing the bath as follows: 'Adieu, Madam, I am sure I have now entertained you, with an account of such a sight as you never saw in your life, and what no book of travels could inform you of, as 'tis no less than death for a man to be found in one of these places' (Montagu 1763: I 164–5).

For all her contempt of authors who descended to the vulgar activity of publication (see for example Montagu 1965–67: III 37; 'it [is] not the busyness of a Man of Quality to turn Author'), Montagu was clearly anxious that the *Embassy Letters* eventually be published. She kept the manuscript with her wherever she travelled, and on her final journey home entrusted them to an English clergyman at Rotterdam, with instructions to publish them after her death. (See Halsband 1956: 278–9, 287–9, for an account of their journey into print.) It was her travel letters, rather than her poems or essays (some of which had been circulated in manuscript or even published anonymously during her lifetime), that Montagu was concerned to have preserved for posterity.

Astell's 'Preface' aside, the propriety of publishing is not an issue within Montagu's text, for all its prominence in her thought and activity elsewhere. Craven, however, engages vigorously with the issue. She seems to have had few qualms about the propriety of publishing; indeed, she somewhat showily published in a quarto volume illustrated with six engravings. Of the women travel writers who published in the eighteenth century, only Craven and Radcliffe (whose literary reputation was already well established) published in anything grander than octavo; and only Craven's book had plates. The *Gentleman's Magazine* is unimpressed, however, noting that 'What Lady C. here offers to the publick in a costly quarto might certainly have been very well compressed to the size of Lady Montague's Letters' (*Gentleman's Magazine*, 59 [1789], 237). The *Journey* is prefaced with a claim that Craven is publishing in order to satisfy friends' curiosity, and 'to show the world Where the real Lady Craven has been', her husband's mistress having for some years passed herself off as Lady Craven on *her* travels through France, Switzerland and England. The *Monthly Review* observes: 'the one great object in view, in publishing this correspondence, appears to be an effort to wipe away some unfavourable imputations at home, and to manifest the respect shewn to the writer abroad' (*Monthly Review* 80 [1789], 201).

The 'letters' which make up the *Journey* are written to the Margrave of Anspach, with whom Craven had developed 'a more than *sisterly* affection' on her travels in Europe following her scandalous separation from Lord Craven in 1781 (*Monthly Review* 53 [1789], 201). Unfortunately, his wife the Margravine was still alive, albeit in a sickly fashion, and it appears that Craven decided on a grand tour of exotic locations in order to remove the embarrassment to the Margrave created by her continued residence at Anspach, and to kill time until both the Margravine and Lord Craven had expired; he in fact held out until 1791, at which point she promptly married the Margrave. She and the Margrave then returned to England, but her long absence and widely publicised adultery had enabled Lord Craven to turn their children against her: all six refused to acknowledge her (J. Robinson 1990: 87). Moreover, she was no longer received at court, which must have been a serious blow to a woman of her pretensions. In 1814, Craven, now the Margravine of Anspach, reissued the *Journey* with minor alterations and additions. The new title blazons the name and rank of her correspondent, and celebrates their relationship: *Letters from the Right Honorable Lady Craven, to His Serene Highness the Margrave of Anspach* ... Their relationship and Craven's virtue are indignantly defended in several additional letters, and in the new preface, where we are informed that she 'constantly refused estates and titles' offered by foreign potentates lest she be called suddenly home by her husband and children:

> my husband had all his [sic; for 'my'] fine property in his own power, and therefore I could not consent to take any duties on me, when I felt, that my first duty, that of a mother, must make me forsake those duties my gratitude and pride might have made me take elsewhere – my duty as a mother lay in England. (Craven 1814: v)

The 1814 edition also inserts references to her marital problems with Lord Craven and her deepening friendship with the Margrave; he is presented as a saintly refuge from the callous Lord Craven, who had prevented their children from writing to her, and whose appalling behaviour is clearly intended to exonerate her from any accusations of unwifely conduct. Craven casts herself in the role of restless exile, happy neither at home nor abroad, whose journeying is less a violation than a proof of propriety. The changes made to the 1814 edition engage with the increasingly severe moral climate of the late eighteenth century and early nineteenth, and negotiate the difficult no-man's-land between public propriety and private affairs which the earlier *Journey* had, perhaps naively, opened up for public inspection.

Craven capitalises (in both editions) not only on her personal notoriety but also on the increasingly autobiographical scope of travel writing in the later eighteenth century. While Montagu's reasons for travel and her personal affairs are largely absent from the *Embassy Letters*, Craven's private dramas provide, quite publicly, a moral justification for her travels, as well as an almost novelistic source of semi-scandalous interest. This expanding narrative scope within travel writing could create problems for women travel writers, for whom the acts of publication and indeed travel might appear morally questionable, and for whom autobiographical frankness might be problematic. Craven's text and apologetic signals her awareness of these issues, but her aristocratic self-importance permits her to rise above bourgeois anxiety. When it comes, however, to describing Turkish women, Craven's moral sensibility is closer, as we shall see, to the middle-class propriety of the 1780s and 1790s than to any aristocratic largesse. Moreover, the emphasis she increasingly places on her submissive married relationship (Montagu, by contrast, barely mentions her husband, although she does briefly describe her experiences of childbirth in Turkey) can be related to an emergent imperial sensibility, within which visible domestic affection in the Christian institution of marriage testifies to the moral superiority of the coloniser. Craven and Montagu present strikingly different accounts of Turkish women. Montagu's approach is poetic and aesthetic, Craven's moral and economic. Robert Halsband has observed that while in the courts of western Europe Montagu mingled with princes and diplomats, at the Ottoman court her sex deprived her of this privilege (Halsband 1956: 71). Craven is similarly excluded, but with chagrin; at one point she resorts to spying on the Sultan through a telescope. This exclusion partly explains the absence of political and diplomatic material in both women's accounts and their focus instead on the status of Turkish women. Both writers commend the respect and apparent liberty granted to Turkish women, but Montagu's account of their grace and beauty is vigorously contradicted by Craven. Montagu describes the women of the harem with admiration:

> They have naturally the most beautiful complexions in the world, and Generally large black eyes. They generally shape their eye-brows, and both Greeks and Turks have the custom of putting round their eyes a black tincture, that, at distance, or by candle-light, adds very much to the blackness of them. I fancy many of our ladies would be overjoyed to know this secret; but 'tis too visible by day. (Montagu 1763: II 31–2)

Craven is less favourably impressed:

> I have no doubt but that nature intended some of these women to be very handsome, but white and red ill applied, their eye-brows hid under one or two black lines – teeth black by smocking, and an universal stoop in the shoulders, made them appear rather disgusting than handsome . . . The frequent use of hot-baths destroys the solids, and these women at nineteen look older than I am at this moment. (Craven 1789: 225–6)

'Nature' here is implicitly associated with British standards of beauty; Craven frequently equates it with western, and usually British, behaviour.

The *Critical Review* notes the prevalence of the adjective 'ugly' in her account (*Critical Review* 67 [1789], 282). More recently, Montagu has also been accused of forcing Turkish women into a western frame of reference, most notoriously in this famous description of the Turkish bath:

> They walked and moved with the same majestic grace, which Milton describes our General Mother with. There were many amongst them, as exactly proportioned as ever any goddess was drawn, by the pencil of a Guido or Titian, – And most of their skins shiningly white, only adorned by their beautiful hair, divided into many tresses, hanging on their shoulders, braided either with pearl or ribbon, perfectly representing the figures of the graces. (Montagu 1763: I 161–2)

Such aestheticising strategies, Isobel Grundy (1992) and Cynthia Lowenthal (1990) have argued, allow Montagu simultaneously to appreciate the exotic otherness of Turkish women and to evade the more problematic issues of freedom and happiness within the harsher realities of Turkish women's experience. Elizabeth Bohls (1995), however, has recently presented a more radical version of Montagu's aestheticising strategies, arguing that she presents herself, daringly, as an aesthetic subject (a privilege usually reserved for males) in order to neutralise orientalist stereotypes of women, and to re-present them as aesthetic rather than erotic objects: statues and paintings rather than the lascivious harpies of seventeenth- and eighteenth-century male-authored travels by the likes of Paul Rycaut and Aaron Hill.

Craven's strategy, by contrast, is simultaneously to de-aestheticise the oriental female, and to render her morally dubious once more. Where Montagu celebrates the steamy beauty of the Turkish bath, Craven (1789) is appalled by the baths at Athens, 'full of naked fat women; a disgusting sight' (p. 264). Craven's account of a 'Turkish' bath in fact occurs in Athens. This displacement testifies not only to Craven's tendency to lump together Greeks, Turks, Tartars and Cossacks as eastern and primitive, regardless of politics or national identity – and indeed to use the term 'Turk' as a term of abuse for any objectionable eastern individual – but also to the distance which Craven strenuously constructs between herself and the eastern other, especially in Turkey and its dominions, where the pernicious influence of Islam is stressed. The *Critical Review* observes that Craven is interested not only in 'the stupidity and indolence of the Turks', but also in 'the effects of their despotism on the conquered Greeks' (*Critical Review* 67 [1789], 285).

Craven's horror at the Turkish bath is similar to her 'disgusted' reaction to a Cossack belly dancer, 'who never lifted her feet off the ground but once in four minutes, and then only one foot at a time, and every part of her person danced except her feet' (Craven 1789: 173). A description in

Montagu's earlier account of a similar entertainment had, by contrast, employed the term 'proper' in an aesthetic sense devoid of moral implication, and envisaged a neutralising coalescence of art and eroticism which would cast the insensitive western prude as the villain of the piece:

> This dance was very different from what I had seen before. Nothing could be more artful, or more proper to raise *certain ideas*. The tunes so soft! – the motions so languishing! – Accompanied with pauses and dying eyes! half-falling back, and then recovering themselves in so artful a manner, that I am very positive, the coldest and most rigid prude upon earth, could not have looked upon them without thinking of something not to be spoke of. (Montagu 1763: II 89–90)

In the more proper climate of the 1780s, Montagu's aesthetic oriental women are re-becoming lascivious. Craven's reintroduction of moral judgement signals a germinating imperial ideology, as potent as had been previous moral assaults on Turkish sexuality (see Bohls 1995: 28–31 on the 'sexualised Orient' constructed by earlier male travel writers), but further bolstered, as we shall see, by a broader sense of Turkish cultural degeneracy. This new grounding permits Craven to claim what Norman Daniel (1966) has described as 'imperialism's perceived "moral right" to civilise any alien people which comes to replace the legal right that had characterised the Crusading impulse' (p. 67).

Craven treats with prurient disapproval what Montagu had appraised with amused tolerance in their respective accounts of Turkish women's 'liberty'. Both mention the freedoms offered by the anonymous garb of Turkish women, but Craven dwells repeatedly on its possibilities for intrigue and licentiousness, even imagining sexual assignations being conducted during services at Santa Sophia, by figures 'wrapped up like a mummy' (Craven 1789: 218). Montagu herself exploits the liberty which Turkish dress affords, wandering the streets of Constantinople 'every day, wrapped up in my *Feriae* and *Asmak*' (Montagu 1763: III 26). Craven would not countenance such assimilation:

> As to women, as many, if not more than men, are to be seen in the streets – but they look like walking mummies – A large loose robe of dark green cloth covers them from the neck to the ground, over that a large piece of muslin, which wraps the shoulders and the arms, another which goes over the head and eyes ... If I was to walk about the streets here I would certainly wear the same dress, for the Turkish women call others names, when they meet them with their faces uncovered – When I go out I have the Ambassador's sedan-chair, which is like mine in London, only gilt and varnished like a French coach, and six Turks carry it; as they fancy it impossible that

two or four men can carry one; two Janissaries walk before with high fur caps on – The Ambassadors here have all Janissaries as guards allowed them by the Porte – Thank Heaven I have but a little way to go in this pomp, and fearing every moment the Turks should fling me down they are so awkward. (Craven 1789: 205–6)

Montagu's experience of Turkey stands in opposition to the restrictive idea of gendered space which was becoming a fact of life in eighteenth-century England, and London especially (see Lew 1991: 445–6). The trappings of Turkish femininity offer unlimited access to public spaces (and Craven also notes that 'as many, if not more' women than men occupy the streets). Craven's text rewrites the concept of separate spheres so that space and activity are divided along racial lines. Her 'if I was to walk about the streets here' is purely rhetorical. The Englishwoman is resolutely opposed to the anonymity of Turkish feminine costume (perhaps here the developing discourse of English individuality and strong character is an influence). Consequently, her evident difference opens up perceptible hostility between the women of different races, which can only be contained, quite literally, within a sedan chair borne by Turkish males. And yet this too poses a threat, Craven 'fearing every moment the Turks should fling me down they are so awkward'. For her journey out of Turkey, Craven is given as an escort another threatening male, 'a Tchouadar, that is to say, a kind of upper servant, or rather creature of the Visir' (Craven 1789: 285). This 'yellow looking Turk' (p. 286) is a constant source of irritation to Craven, competing with her for the servants' attention and for the lion's share of the party's provisions. At one point she finds that he has used her kettle to make himself coffee:

If any travellers were to meet us, they would certainly take him for some *Grand Seigneur*, and that I am of his suite, by the care taken of him, and the perfect indifference all, but my two companions and my servants, show for my ease and convenience … I thought it right to point to two most excellent little English pistols I wear at my girdle, and assure him they would be well employed against any offence I met with. And when the interpreter had done I could not help calling him a stupid disagreeable Turk, in English, which he took for a compliment, and bowed his head a little. (Craven 1789: 291)

Turkish degeneracy and luxury here emerge as *sexual* savagery, barely containable through the brandishing of English pistols worn in a highly defensive position, 'at my girdle' (and through the futile yet cathartic effect of English insults). The 'moral right' of the English over the Turk is again asserted.

In 1763, the *Monthly Review* praises the *Embassy Letters* in gendered terms: 'There is no affectation of female *delicatesse*, there are no *prettynesses*, no *Ladyisms* in these natural, easy familiar Epistles' (*Monthly Review* 28 [1763], 385). Paradoxically, Montagu is celebrated as a writer because she is not typical of her gender, even though it is her gender which makes possible her most novel observations (her descriptions of the harem). In 1789, by contrast, the *Critical Review* notes archly that Craven saw objects 'in the true female view' (*Critical Review* 67 [1789], 282). If this is true, then Craven is doing so partly in response to the increasing cultural and ideological separation of male and female fields and abilities. Similarly, her highly restrictive notions of sexual propriety are very much of her time. If we recall Craven's aspersions on the authorship of Montagu's text, moreover, it becomes clear that narrowing concepts of female activity colour Craven's reading of Montagu's text to the extent that the *Embassy Letters*' tolerant view of Turkish manners evinces their spuriousness.

Montagu's broader cultural tolerance is if anything still more offensive to Craven than her views on women. Jill Campbell (1994) has described how Montagu imagines Turkish culture as 'outside history, as a place where past and present, the literary and the natural, coexist' (pp. 74–5). She relates this to the anthropological phenomenon observed by Johannes Fabian (in *Time and the Other*), by which western travellers deny the contemporaneity of different cultures, co-existing in the same historical moment, and instead imagine the alien cultures they encounter as inhabiting the distant past of their own culture's history or prehistory (p. 75).

A letter to Pope, written at Adrianople, shows Montagu adopting precisely this position:

> I read over your *Homer* here, with an infinite pleasure, and find several little passages explained, that I did not before entirely comprehend the beauty of: Many of the customs, and much of the dress then in fashion, being yet retained. I don't wonder to find more remains here, of an age so distant, than is to be found in any other country, the Turks not taking that pains to introduce their own manners, as has been generally practised by other nations, that imagine themselves more polite. (Montagu 1763: II 44)

This is to Pope, and about poetry, and is therefore consciously idealistic. This letter invokes a cultural continuity which dissolves national boundaries and represents difference as innocence from the ravages of civilisation: 'I never see half a dozen of old Bashaws (as I do very often) with their reverend beards, sitting basking in the sun, but I recollect good King *Priam* and his counsellors' (vol. II, p. 45). The *Embassy Letters* as a whole strives to articulate an innocence of history and politics, which are barely mentioned, and also of cultural judgement. Crucial to this project is the fragmentation of narrative identity which occurs within the *Embassy*

*Letters.* Montagu's text differs markedly from Craven's in being addressed (rather unusually, in eighteenth-century travel literature) to a wide range of correspondents (fifteen in all, twelve of whom are women), ranging from her depressed sister, Lady Mar, to the Abbe Conti, to Alexander Pope, and including assorted female friends. All of Craven's letters, by contrast, are addressed to the Margrave (which may partly account for their celebration of her virtues and of the esteem in which she is held throughout Europe, Russia and Turkey). This formal difference makes for a greater stylistic variety within the *Embassy Letters* than in Craven's *Journey.* Montagu uses different literary and conversational registers for different correspondents, and deploys a range of descriptive topics. She addresses one letter to the Princess of Wales, writing as ambassadress for Christendom as well as Britain: 'I have now, Madam, finished a journey that has not been undertaken by any Christian, since the time of the Greek Emperors; and I shall not regret all the fatigues I have suffered in it, if it gives me an opportunity of amusing your R. H. by an account of places utterly unknown amongst us' (vol. I, p. 151).

To Lady Mar, Montagu writes anecdotal, humorous accounts of social and sexual customs and visits to exotic notables like the Grand Vizier's 'lady' and the Sultana Hafiten. With assorted Ladies, she is chatty and occasionally risqué. All her detailed (and celebrated) accounts of Turkish women, in harem or public bath or private audience, are addressed to women.

With the Abbe Conti and with Pope, not surprisingly, Montagu is most scholarly and philosophical. To the Abbe she writes 'of manners and religion' (vol. II, p. 1), government and welfare, antiquities and architecture, commerce, military parades, and Islam. To Pope she addresses witty and sometimes flirtatious letters, writing about poetry and pastoral; she resolutely denies Pope the almost erotic satisfaction which her letters to women friends offer, in accounts of her Turkish costume and luxurious lifestyle. One detects a distinctively plaintive note to Pope's declaration: 'I long for nothing so much as your Oriental Self. I expect to see your Soul as much thinner dresed as your Body' (Pope 1956: I 494). Through this dazzling variety of subjects and styles, Montagu refracts her narrative identity into a prismatic multiplicity. The *Letters'* observing self becomes, quite literally, an embodiment of Enlightenment pluralism. Their multi-faceted narrator was no doubt an important factor in the enthusiastic reception of the *Critical Review* which itemises the narrator's separate attractions, declaring that the letters will display, 'as long as the English language endures, the sprightliness of her wit, the solidity of her judgement, the extent of her knowledge, the elegance of her taste, and the excellence of her *real* character' (*Critical Review* 15 [1763], 435).

The freedom of the *Embassy Letters* from opinion, judgement, or 'vulgar prejudice' (to use a frequent eighteenth-century criticism of travel writing) seems to have made them peculiarly attractive to the critical and reading public of the 1760s. Montagu must have seemed a true citizen of the world. The *Embassy Letters* were published in the year of the cessation of the Seven Years' War in Europe; the war had in some ways undermined the viability of Enlightened ideals and seen them compromised by political contingency and nationalistic feeling. Montagu's visions of a distant and not immediately threatening foreign world perhaps reassured the reading public that Enlightened tolerance was still, albeit remotely, alive and possible. Alternatively, the confidence-boosting territorial gains made at the Peace of Paris may have fostered a relaxed and culturally tolerant mood among the reading and critical public. Furthermore, remarks like 'Upon the whole, I look upon the Turkish women, as the only free people in the Empire' (Montagu 1763: II 35) must have offered a pleasurable alternative to the bitter resonances of 'liberty' in its domestic context in 1763. The *Embassy Letters* were published and reviewed in May of 1763; the anti-government *North Briton* edited by John Wilkes had published its incendiary issue 45 in April; and 'Wilkes and Liberty' was becoming a rallying cry.

For all the enlightened pluralism of the *Embassy Letters*, one might argue that there are letters in which Montagu's narrative persona is more emphatically English and where, correspondingly, things Turkish are presented in a more ambivalent light. The first is in a letter (her only) to the Princess of Wales, in which (as mentioned earlier) she writes as spokeswoman for Christendom. She describes her arrival in Turkish territory:

> The country from hence to Adrianople, is the finest in the world. Vines grow wild on all the hills, and the perpetual spring they enjoy, makes every thing gay and flourishing. But this climate, happy as it seems, can never be preferred to England, with all its frosts and snows, while we are blessed with an easy government, under a King, who makes his own happiness consist in the liberty of his people, and chooses rather to be looked upon, as their father than their master. (Montagu 1763: I 155)

This is a striking passage in Montagu's text; all the more so in that it sounds, almost parodically, like a great deal of other eighteenth-century travel writers who draw such comparisons so frequently as to make them at best a trope, at worst a cliché, of the genre. It is, however, hardly xenophobia; the same could *not* be said for a letter to Pope, describing Austro-Turkish atrocities in the battle for Belgrade, which contains a virulent diatribe against the Turks:

> You see here that I give you a very *handsome* return for your obliging letter. You entertain me with a most agreeable account of your amiable connexions

with men of letters and taste, and of the delicious moments you pass in
their society under the rural shade; and I exhibit to you in return, the
barbarous spectacle of Turks and Germans cutting one another's throats.
But what can you expect from such a country as this, from which the muses
have fled, from which letters seem eternally banished, and in which you see,
in private scenes, nothing pursued as happiness but the refinements of an
indolent voluptuousness, and where those who act upon the public theatre
live in uncertainty, suspicion, and terror. (Montagu 1767: 27–8)

This letter implicitly rejects the classical idealising of Turkey which
dominates most of the *Embassy Letters*, and declares indeed: 'I long much
to tread upon English ground, that I may see you and Mr. Congreve, who
render that ground *classick ground*' (Montagu 1767: 32). These passages
are almost worthy of Smollett's Smelfungus, and disrupt the tolerant
pluralism of the other letters. Or, I should say, *would* disrupt; although a
recent editor of Montagu (Clare Brant, Montagu 1992: 148–50) includes
this letter, it did not in fact appear in the 1763 edition of *Embassy Letters*.
It was first published in the spurious 'fourth volume', containing five fake
letters and some genuine material (an essay, a letter, some verse), which
appeared in 1767. Robert Halsband, in his definitive edition of Montagu's
letters, has documented the inauthenticity of most of the 1767 volume
(Montagu 1965–67: I xviii and I 371). Discredited by the time Craven was
writing, this literary imposture had nevertheless 'deceived even ... the
critics' in 1767, as the *Monthly Review* (70 [1784], 575) ruefully admits.
The 1767 volume is a fascinating hoax, and reveals the extent to which
Montagu's pluralistic tolerance is already nostalgic, indeed outdated, by
the later 1760s; or at least is co-existing somewhat uneasily with a more
xenophobic, politically defensive sensibility. Revealingly, Lady Bute was
convinced that the volume published in 1767 must be 'genuine' (Montagu
1965–67: I xviii). In the genuine volumes of the *Embassy Letters*, by
contrast, Turkish indolence is invested with a complex philosophical value,
embodying both classical (specifically, Elysian) tranquillity, and the possibility of a modern epicureanism:

I am almost of opinion they [the Turks] have a right notion of life. They
consume it in musick, gardens, wine and delicate eating, while we are tor-
menting our brains with some scheme of politicks, or studying some science
to which we can never attain ... Considering what short liv'd weak animals
men are, is there any study so beneficial as the study of present pleasure? I
dare not pursue this theme. (Montagu 1763: III 52–3)

Elsewhere, Montagu surrenders to the 'wicked suggestions of poetry',
and observes 'the warmth of the climate, naturally inspiring a laziness and

aversion to labour' (Montagu 1763: II 40–2). For Craven in the 1780s, however, indolence is anything but 'naturally' inspired: her 'nature' favours industry and (where such industry is not indigenous) colonisation. And her version of pastoral, as in this description of the valley of Baydar in Turkey, is decidedly imperial: 'a most enchanting and magnificent spot, intended by nature for some industrious and happy nation to enjoy in peace – A few Tartar villages lessen the wildness of the scene, but, in such a place, the meadow part should be covered with herds, and the mountainous with sheep' (Craven 1789: 190–1).

Craven's response to Turkish languor is one of prosaic disapproval: 'The quiet stupid Turk will sit a whole day by the side of the Canal, looking at flying kites or children's boats ... How the business of the nation goes on at all I cannot guess' (p. 207). Her visions of commercial imperialism are couched in the language of emancipation and vision:

> Can any rational being, dear Sir, see nature, without the least assistance from art, in all her grace and beauty, stretching out her liberal hand to industry, and not wish to do her justice? Yes, I confess, I wish to see a colony of honest English families here; establishing manufactures, such as England produces, and returning the produce of this country to ours – establishing a fair and free trade from hence, and teaching industry and honesty to the insidious but oppressed Greeks, in their islands – waking the indolent Turk from his gilded slumbers, and carrying fair Liberty in her swelling sails ... This is no visionary or poetical figure – it is the honest wish of one who considers all mankind as one family. (Craven 1789: 188–9)

This passage is especially commended by the *Monthly Review* for its 'liberal reflections, which do honour to the writer, both as a lover of her own country, and as a citizen of the world' (*Monthly Review* 80 [1789], 209). This judgement testifies to the ideological gulf not only between Montagu and Craven, but between the values of mid-century and those of later eighteenth-century culture, which looks forward to a new world of imperial expansion. The East is no longer merely an exotic playpen, but a land ripe for the type of colonial appropriation already well under way in India.

Although the reviews criticise Craven's arrogant style, her ideological stance is congenial, and she represents an important strand in travel literature (and much else) of the 1780s and 1790s. P. J. Marshall and Glyndwr Williams (1982: 67) have claimed that, despite continuing interest in the Near East, the growth of British influence in India was rapidly eclipsing Near Eastern concerns. Craven's account and its reception would suggest otherwise; or, indeed, might suggest that the Turkish experience was providing a paradigm for British attitudes towards India in the following century. As Norman Daniel puts it:

It was in Turkey that the imperial attitude developed most rapidly, and not in India, where empire was further advanced. The mood of the conquerors of Bengal was as humble culturally as it was active, even aggressive, in war and commerce. Warren Hastings was a great patron of the study of Persian culture. The serious-minded servants of the Company contributed learned notes and translations and adaptations of Persian verse to specialised periodicals. The forms of the Mogul Empire were carried on, and diplomacy in India still used the Persian language. The significant change in the European attitude came in relations with the Ottoman Empire, a change that soon affected India. (Daniel 1966: 71)

The years separating Montagu and Craven show quite graphically the disappearance, as far as Turkey is concerned, of such cultural interest and humility. Montagu transcribes Turkish poetry, pronounces herself 'pretty far gone in Oriental learning' (Montagu 1763: II 46–56), and is enormously impressed by Turkish cultural traditions. Craven displays no such interest, and represents the Turks as barbaric philistines. Admittedly, she has some justification for this view, given that the Turks are bombarding Athens during her journey; however, her concern is less with the destruction of the Parthenon per se, and more with the British failure to get in on the act: 'ruins, that would adorn a virtuoso's cabinet, are daily burnt into lime by the Turks; and pieces of exquisite workmanship stuck into a wall or fountain' (Craven 1789: 221). She is particularly chagrined when the Turks forbid any of her party to remove any fragments of sculpture: 'alas, Sir, I cannot even have a little finger or a toe' (p. 256).

The sense of Turkey as a degenerating culture which is expressed only in the *spurious* letter from Montagu to Pope dominates Craven's account, and chimes with contemporary opinion, which was coming to view the Turks not only as 'idle and effete under the influence of despotism, but as worse than savages' (Burke, speech on 29 March 1791; cited Marshall and Williams 1982: 165). Montagu combines a respect for Turkish cultural history with a poetic imagining of Turkish culture as existing *outside* history and indeed politics; Craven constructs an alternative history, within which Turkish culture is erased, and the Turks are instead configured as almost pre-historic in their barbaric indolence. Craven's travelogue looks forwards, not back, to the assimilation of the East into British imperial history. And the forceful narrative personality projected by Craven's text foreshadows the emergence of the moral centre which the colonial woman is to provide for the colonial project.

# Part III

# High Imperial: Taxonomy and Gender

# 'Stifling Pity in a Parent's Breast': Infanticide and Savagery in Late Eighteenth-century Travel Writing

Bridget Orr

The following Inquiry is intended to illustrate the natural history of mankind in several important articles. This is attempted, by pointing out the most obvious and common improvements, which gradually arise in the state of society, and by showing the influence of these upon the manners, the laws and the Government of a people.

With regard to the facts made use of in the following discourse, the reader, who is conversant with history, will readily perceive the difficulty of obtaining proper materials for speculations of this nature. Historians of reputation have commonly overlooked the transactions of early ages, as not deserving to be remembered; and even in the history of later and more cultivated periods, they have been more solicitous to give an exact account of battles, and public negociations, than of the interior police and government of a nation. Our information therefore, with regard to the state of mankind in the rude part of the world, is chiefly derived from the relations of travellers, whose character and situation in life, neither set them above the suspicion of being easily deceived, nor of endeavouring to misrepresent the facts which they have related. (Millar 1779: 14)

As John Millar, the eminent author of *The Origin of the Distinction of Ranks* acknowledged, the great synthetic accounts of the progress of civil society produced in the Scottish Enlightenment relied heavily on 'the relations of travellers'. The genre thus not only mediates direct encounter with other cultures; it also provides the basis for more ambitious philosophical extrapolation of 'the natural history of mankind'. The reliability of these source materials was, however, known to be questionable. Although there were early modern travel narratives and histories of exotic cultures by aristocrats, diplomats and missionaries which commanded considerable respect, and a separate tradition of plain-style testimony in the voyage narratives of merchants and seamen, these had to confront a long-established scepticism about travellers' tales ('the suspicion of being too easily deceived' and even of 'endeavouring to misrepresent the facts' [see Adams 1983]). De Buffon went so far as to doubt the very existence of customary cannibalism, infanticide and parricide among savages, arguing that reports of such incidents recorded isolated events rather than established practices, the effects of 'passion and caprice' rather than a 'determined standard of manners' (de Buffon 1812: III 412). Both Millar and Buffon emphasise the provisional and tendentious nature of their accounts, self-conscious about their status as Lévi-Straussian *bricoleurs avant la lettre*, suturing examples from other men's dubious reports into new forms of speculation. These good intentions notwithstanding, however, the philosophical use of voyage literature shows an unmistakable tendency to harden into certain regulatory operations of its own ('the interior police and government of a nation'). In this chapter I wish to argue that these are analogous to, even formally homologous with, the satiric and didactic attempts to govern female nature and behaviour legible in contemporary conduct books and misogynist verse which also drew on travel writing and, sometimes, on speculative history itself.

Recent accounts of 'Enlightenment' discourse are more certain than its originators of its truth-claims, as well as being convinced of its implication in oppressive class, gender and colonial relations. In her recent *Torrid Zones* (1995), Felicity Nussbaum attempts to rethink the way gender and maternity functioned in eighteenth-century imperial ideology. The control of reproduction, including the eighteenth-century perception of an epidemic of child murder, has become the focus of much recent research but little other than Nussbaum's work focuses on the connections between colonialism and the panic over, and the practice of, infanticide. My aim here is to re-examine the extensive and often ambiguous incorporation of travellers' accounts of infanticide as precisely, in Buffon's terms, a 'settled usage' in ancient, savage and oriental societies by philosophers such as Millar, Kames, Hume and Ferguson. Rather than providing a reliable marker of difference between civility and savagery, ancient barbarousness and modern British 'humanity', citations of the practice of infanticide often seem to provoke reflections on the frighteningly ubiquitous desire by women to escape what Luce Irigaray would call 'reduction to the maternal function' (Whitford 1989). Though generally convinced of the superiority of their own gender order, the Scottish *philosophes* often figure its perfect instantiation as a vanishing point, glimpsed in the very recent past or just visible in a reformed future. The imaginary figure of female virtue is haunted not just by her violent savage antithesis but by the actual practice of infanticide among Highland women; by a self-indulgent avoidance of maternal duty through the use of wet-nurses; and by the deluded cultural ambition of bluestockings. The most literal and lurid expressions of such anxieties form the focus of the ephemeral satire which recirculated the tropes of Pacific sexuality articulated in Hawkesworth's *Account of the Voyages ... in the Southern Hemisphere* (1773). The apparent opposition between the Enlightened discourse of an incipient human science and the Menippean expatiation of misogynist contempt collapses as the two sets of texts identify a violent depravity common to Tahitian and English women alike.

Feminist scholarship has begun to attend to the role the representation of the position of women played in the 'natural histories' of mankind, following Sylvana Tomaselli's (1985) claim that for a wide range of Enlightenment thinkers, the status of women determined the degree of any society's civility (p. 101). Felicity Nussbaum (1995) develops this argument by claiming that a strong cultural emphasis on the unprecedented liberty of eighteenth-century Englishwomen was, however, accompanied by a desire to compel their acceptance of an exclusively domestic and maternal role, and demonised figures of cannibal or infanticidal savage mothers which violated the idea of a naturally nurturant female nature proliferated along-side the celebration of the English matron (pp. 1-53). This identification of a drive to enforce English women of all classes to accept a maternal identity in the mid-eighteenth century is supported by other recent scholarship: Ruth Perry, for instance, argues in 'Colonizing the Breast' (1992) that the cult of maternity, drawing on the anatomical discovery of the specificity of the female reproductive system, emerged in the later eighteenth century to redefine women in maternal rather than sexual terms, as agents of reproduction. Other arguments set the date for such a redefinition earlier (see L. Brown 1982; Armstrong 1987; C. Gallagher 1992), with Catherine Belsey suggesting in *The Subject of Tragedy* (1985: 219) that the late seventeenth century is the period in which women are first installed as domestic and maternal subjects through the redefinition of the family which accompanied the defeat of English absolutism. Charles Gildon's (1698) prefatory remarks to his redaction of Euripides' *Medea* – surely the ur-text of maternal infanticide in the West – seem to support Belsey's contention. Justifying his softening of Medea's character, Gildon comments in his Preface to *Phaeton: or, the Fatal Divorce*:

> I saw a necessity on my first perusal of EURIPIDES of alt'ring the two chief Characters of the Play, in consideration of the different Temper and Sentiments of our several Audience. First I was Apprehensive, that *Medea*, as *Euripides* represents her, would shock *us*. When we hear of her tearing her Brother to pieces, and the murd'ring of her own Children, contrary to all the Dictates of *Humanity* and *Mother-hood*, we should have been too

impatient for her Punishment, to have expected the *happy Event* of her barbarous Revenge: nay, perhaps, not to have allow'd the Character within the Compass of Nature; or at least decreed it more unfit for the Stage, than the cruelties in *Nero*. Monsters in Nature not affording those just Lessons a Poet ought to teach his Hearers. (Gildon 1698: np)

In a process consonant with the cultural shift identified by Belsey, Gildon's *Phaeton* transforms the violent, vengeful, barbarian sorceress of Euripides and Seneca into a loving mother forced by male perfidy into destructive madness. Jason is also altered, reflecting Gildon's conviction that 'the Character ... of *JASON*, which however justifiable in the *Original*, I had some reason to fear would not be forgiven in my *Copy*. In the first Scene of my Fourth Act, on their meeting after his forsaking her, *Jason*, wou'd seem too harsh, rough, and Ungentleman-like, to a Lady on our Stage' (Preface). Revision of the characters banished female monstrosity and masculine barbarousness natural to the Ancients from a stage Gildon defended (*contra* Collier) as both polite and patriotic, exemplifying and inculcating the private and public virtue of the modern English nation. *Phaeton*'s action, focusing on the cost exacted by masculine ambition on domestic happiness, also demonstrates affective tragedy's refiguration of catastrophe as the invasion of the private by the public.

Writing well into this new system of 'interior police', the Enlightenment *bricoleurs* invoked classical literature along with the exemplary narratives provided by travellers, generally concurring with Gildon's judgement that the conduct displayed by the Greeks and Romans was disgusting by modern standards. In his *Sketches of the History of Man* (1773), Lord Kames (Henry Home) castigated Jason as unchivalrous and unmanly:

The manners of Jason, in the tragedy of Medea by Euripides, are woefully indelicate. With unparalleled ingratitude to his wife Medea, he, in her presence, makes love to the King of Corinth's daughter, and obtains her in marriage. Instead of shunning a person he had so deeply injured, he endeavours to excuse himself in a very sneaking manner, 'that he was an exile like herself, without support; and that his marriage would acquire powerful friends to their children.' Could he imagine that such frigid reasons would touch a woman of any spirit? (Home 1773: I 32)

The gradual idealisation of the modern British form of companionate marriage and a maternal female nature which is highlighted in the various eighteenth-century revisions of the *Medea* was not uncontested, however. Scriblerian and, later, more ephemeral satire continued to invoke the misogynist tropes of female concupiscence and immorality legible in the late seventeenth-century satires on women. Travel writing, which in its

various modes regularly focused on exotic differences from the contemporary British gender order, served as continual provocation to satiric
denunciations of female sexuality, both metropolitan and 'savage'. There
was a striking eruption of such attacks, including references to an
unrecuperated Medea, in the satires which followed the publication of
Hawkesworth's *Account of Voyages* to the Pacific.

To a man, the Scots instance infanticide as the effect of male custom
and male law, a violation of maternal instinct which reflects the depressed
position of women in classical, Asian and savage societies. According to
Kames in his 'Essay on the Progress of the Female Sex' in his *Sketches*:

> It was by slow degrees that the female emerged out of slavery, to possess the
> elevated station they are entitled to by nature. The practice of exposing
> infants, among the Greeks and many other nations, is an invincible proof of
> their depression, even after the custom ceased of purchasing them. It is
> wisely ordered by Providence, that the affection of a woman to her children
> commences with their birth: because, during infancy, all depends on her
> care. As, during that period, the father is of little use to his child, his
> affection is but slight, till the child begin to prattle and show some fondness
> for him. The exposing an infant, therefore, shows that the mother was little
> regarded: if she had been allowed a vote, the practice would never have
> obtained in any country. (Home 1773: II 258).

In his *Origin of the Distinction of Ranks*, John Millar discusses infanticide
as an index of the tyrannical nature of paternal power in the ancient
world, concurring with Hume's view that the exposure of children functioned as a means of population control:

> The exposition of infants, so common in a great part of the nations of
> antiquity, is a proof that the different heads of families were under no
> restraint or control in the management of their domestic concerns. This
> barbarous practice was probably introduced in those rude ages when the
> father was often incapable of maintaining his children, and from the in-
> fluence of old usage, was permitted to remain in later times, when the plea
> of necessity could no longer be urged in its vindication. (Millar 1779: 152)

In his essay 'On the Populousness of Ancient Nations' Hume argues:

> The common reason why any parent thrusts his daughters into nunneries is
> that he may not be overburdened by too numerous a family; but the ancients
> had a method more innocent, and more effectual to that purpose; to wit,
> exposing their children in early infancy. This practice was very common,
> and it is not spoken of by any author of those times with the horror it
> deserves. (Hume 1753: I 415)

And he comments later: 'China, the only country where this practice prevails at present, is the most populous country we know of, and every man is married before he is twenty. Surely such easy marriages would scarcely be general, had not men a prospect of so easy a method of getting rid of their children' (vol. I, p. 416). While Hume emphasises the material and sexual benefits men accrue through infanticide, Monboddo (Burnett 1773) sticks to population control: 'To prevent the too-great increase in population ... the ancient legislators used strange expedients, such as allowing the exposition of infants, and even the unnatural passion of men for one another' (vol. I, p. 255).

Hume's claim that China provided the only contemporary example of institutionalised infanticide ignored other references to the practice in societies considered to be 'savage' in contemporary voyage literature. Prior to the publication of Hawkesworth's versions of the Pacific voyages, accounts of South American 'savages' provided a significant number of examples of infanticide. In de Charlevois' *History of Paraguay* (1769), for example, it is claimed of the Abipone people:

> They seldom rear but one child of each sex, murdering the rest as fast as they come into the world, till the eldest are strong enough to walk alone. They justify this cruelty by saying, that, as they are almost constantly travelling from one place to another, it is impossible for them to take care of more infants than two at a time, one to be carried by the father, the other by the mother. (de Charlevois 1769: I 405)

In his 'Essay on the Female Sex', Kames also cites testimony provided by Lockman's compendium of Jesuit narratives as to the practice of infanticide in South America. Instead of an eyewitness account, however, he quotes a first-person confession:

> Father Joseph Guillama, in his account of a country in South America, bordering upon the great river Oroonoka, describes pathetically the miserable slavery of married women there; and mentions a practice, that would appear incredible to one unacquainted with that country, which is, that married women frequently destroy their female infants. A married woman, of virtuous character and good understanding, having been guilty of that crime, was reproached by our author in bitter terms. She heard him patiently with eyes fixed on the ground: and answered as follows: – ' I wish to God, Father, I wish to God that my mother had by my death prevented the manifold distresses I have endured, and have yet to endure as long as I live. Had she kindly stifled me at birth, I had not felt the pain of death, nor numberless other pains that life hath subjected me to. Consider, Father, our deplorable condition. We are dragged along with our infant at the breast, and another

in the basket. They return in the evening without any burden; we return with the burden of our children; and though tired with a long march, are not permitted to sleep, but must labour the whole night, in grinding maise to make chica for them. They get drunk, and in their drunkenness beat us, draw us by the hair of the head, and tread us underfoot. And what have we to comfort us for slavery that has no end? A young wife is brought in upon us, who is permitted to abuse us and our children because we are no longer regarded. Can human nature endure such tyranny? What kindness can we show our female children other than relieving them from such oppression, more bitter a thousand times than death? I say again, would to God my mother had put me under ground the moment I was born.' (Home 1773: II 288)

Guillama's native informant speaks in the accents of pathos; the brief but general sketch of gender relations in this nameless, vaguely located society embeds ethnographic detail (hunting and gathering, maize-grinding, marital arrangements) within a sentimental tale of domestic tyranny whose climax is female infanticide. Ventriloquising the confession allows Kames and the reader to share Guillama's position as intimate witnesses to the account, a witnessing which is simultaneously judgemental and pitying. Ethnographic 'evidence' is represented as a sentimental exchange in which European men stand in a relay of sympathetic auditors to an individual misery characterised as endemic, and clearly in need of reform; whether through conversion (by Guillama) or the civilising 'commerce' and settlement preferred by the British.

Millar also cites a South American instance of infanticidal violence, quoting directly from Byron:

The following account, given by Commander Byron, may serve in some measure to show the spirit with which the savages of South America are apt to govern the members of their family:

'Here,' says he, 'I must relate a little anecdote of our Christian Cacique. He and his wife had gone off, at some distance from the shore, in their canoe, when she dived for sea-eggs; but not meeting with great success, they returned a good deal out of humour. A little boy of theirs, whom they appeared to be doating fond of, watching his father's and mother's return, ran into the surf to meet them: the father handed a basket of sea-eggs to the child, which being too heavy for him to carry, he let it fall; upon which the father jumped out of the canoe, and catching the boy up in his arms, dashed him with the utmost violence against the stones. The poor little creature lay motionless and bleeding, and in that condition was taken up by the mother, but died soon after. She appeared inconsolable for some time; but the brute his father showed little concern about it.' (Millar 1779: 152)

Millar announces that the anecdote is intended to be exemplary of the nature (the 'spirit') of domestic governance among South Americans but the narrative is much more legible in Buffonian terms as a singular event rather than 'the fixed laws' of a nation (de Buffon 1812: III 314). As evidence, the story relies on an implied eyewitnessing by Byron, who was widely regarded as an unreliable narrator after he claimed to have seen the Patagonian giants when shipwrecked on Anson's 1767 expedition. But the spectator/narrator's position is in fact occluded, with the story's credibility turning on the inclusion of a few exotic details such as sea-eggs and an implicit reliance on familiar tropes of savagery. Thus the father's brutality is rendered plausible as the effect of an unrestrained passion which manifests itself intially as an excessive affection ('doating fond') and then turns into an equally excessive violence. The mother's inconsolable maternal grief testifies both to the universality of maternal feeling and the superior civility of the European men (Byron and Millar) who have twice memorialised her loss.

Adam Ferguson's *Essay on the History of Civil Society* (1767) provides a final example by contrasting the prudent sexual abstinence of North American Indian women with the suffering inflicted in Formosa:

> In warmer latitudes, by the different temperament, perhaps, which the climate bestows, and by a greater facility in procuring subsistence, the numbers of mankind increase, while the object is itself neglected; and the commerce of the sexes, without any concern for population, is made a subject of mere debauch. In some places we are told, it is even made the object of a barbarous policy, to defeat or to restrain the intentions of nature. In the island of Formosa, the males are prohibited to marry before the age of forty; and females, if pregnant before the age of thirty-five, have an abortion procured by order of the magistrate, who employs a violence that endangers the life of the mother, together with that of the child. (Ferguson 1767: 213)

The American examples of infanticide were used not just to provide evidence but to claim sympathy for the mistreated maternal objects of masculine savagery: sentimental rhetoric confirmed the Enlightened reader as benevolently civil. The Chinese instances, almost all drawn from Jesuit narratives, operated with a different logic. Child murder served as a lurid signifier of barbarity and scarcity in an otherwise formidably powerful and civilised state; notwithstanding Hume's emphasis on the masculine advantages gained by Chinese infanticide, missionary accounts of China often stress poverty as a cause: 'Yet, notwithstanding the great sobriety and industry of the Inhabitants of China, the prodigious number of them occasions a great deal of misery. There are some so poor, that for want of common necessaries for their children, they expose them in the streets, especially when the Mothers fall sick, or want milk to nourish them' (*New General Collection* 1747: IV 76).

Even more striking, however, is the emphasis on the provocation to maternal care outlined in these narratives, the appeal to a feminine reader. Despite the dearth of travelogues authored by women during the period, gender remains a paramount factor in the reception of the genre. John Lockman's 1743 translation of *The Travels of the Jesuits* includes a letter from a Father Premare to a Father Le Gobien in which the former suggested that affluent and devout Parisian women should be petitioned to provide funding for hospitals to rescue such abandoned infants:

> Among various Establishments wanting, and which would greatly advance the progress of the Christian Religion, by the Honour they must necessarily reflect upon it, there is one which myself, as well as several other Missionaries, have greatly at Heart. I mean the building, in five or six of the greatest Cities belonging to the chief Provinces of the Empire, a kind of Hospitals for bringing up those Foundlings whose Lives, as well as Souls, may have been saved. This would properly be a work worthy of the Piety of Ladies, to whom you subsequently ought to explain this Design. For these Hospitals would consist principally of Maidens; such being exposed, rather than the Males, by those Parents who have more Children than they can well maintain ... A considerable Number of pious Establishments are daily being founded in *Paris*, unless the Face of things be greatly changed, in this Particular, since I left that City. Now, could not a Lady of Quality do something like this, in favour of *Peking*, the Capital of *China*? (*Travels of the Jesuits* 1743: I 88-9)

Premare invokes the duty of care European women owe to Chinese female infants as, implicitly, an extension of their maternal solicitude. Whether by conversion or civil mission, these appeals to (civil) men and (maternal) women prefigure the invocation of infanticide as an important trope in British justifications of empire in India and in the Pacific.

Despite variations in reports of savage or exotic infanticide, then, there was a general consensus in the philosophical discourse which processed the voyage accounts, that the occidental eschewal of the practice was symptomatic of Europe's supersession of classical and oriental brutality. Equally pervasive was the assumption that mothers, whether savage or civilised, would resist the practice in that maternal feeling was understood as universal even while the British gender order was celebrated as peculiarly benign. Joseph Banks, writing one of the earliest accounts of infanticide in Tahiti in 1770, shared these assumptions. Describing the institution of the *arioi*, troupes of itinerant, aristocratic thespians, who were 'reputed like Comus in Milton to have entered into a resolution of enjoying free love in liberty without a possibility of being troubled or disturbed by its consequences', the normally imperturbable Banks expresses horror at the practice of smothering children begot at the moment of their birth. Unsurprisingly, he holds the men responsible:

> This custom, as it were natural to suppose, Owes as we were told its existence cheifly to the men. A Woman howsoever fond she may be of the name of Arreoy, and the liberty attending it before she conceives, generaly desires much to forfeit that title for the preservation of her child: in this she has not the slightest influence; if she cannot find a man who will own it, she must of course destroy it; and if she can, with him alone it lies whether or not it shall be preserv'd. (Banks 1963: I 315)

John Hawkesworth's rewriting of this passage, published in his widely read *Account of the Voyages* (1773), is informed by a pietistic revulsion alien to the philosophical Banks. The former's 'voice-of-Cook' opines:

> the poor infant is smothered the moment it is born, that it may be no incumbrance to the father, nor hinder the mother in the pleasures of her diabolical prostitution. It sometimes happens indeed, that the passion which prompts a woman to enter into this society, is surmounted by that instinctive affection which nature has given all creatures for the preservation of their well-being; but even in this case she is not permitted to spare the life of the child, except she can find a man who will patronise it as his child; but both the man and the woman, being deemed by this act to have appropriated each other, are ejected from the community, and forfeit all claims to the privileges and pleasures of *Arreoy*, for the future, the women from that time being distinguished by the term whannownow 'bearer of children' which is here a term of reproach; tho' none can be more honourable in the estimation of wisdom and humanity, of right reason, and every passion that distinguishes the man from the brute. (Hawkesworth 1773: II 208)

For Banks, the women 'generally' wished to keep their children, while for Hawkesworth, it is only 'sometimes'. In the latter's account, maternal love no longer figures as the ground of female nature; instead, the customary contempt for childbearing ascribed to Tahitians marks them out as scarcely human, violators of nature, wisdom, humanity and right reason (cf. Rennie 1995: 98).

Hawkesworth's account of Tahiti was the one which circulated and it provided the occasion for a widespread debate over the projects of natural historians, speculative or navigational, in which sexuality was a primary focus. Rejecting the philosophical ascription of infanticide to male custom, the welter of ephemeral verses published in response to Hawkesworth's

*Account* which included *Otaheite* (1774); *Seventeen Hundred and Seventy-Seven* (1777); *An Historic Epistle from Amiah to the Queen of Otaheite* (1775) and the *Poetical Epistle, Moral and Philosophical, from an Officer at Otaheite to Lady Gr[os]v[e]n[o]r* (1775) all call up the unrecuperated figure of 'savage infanticidal maternity': 'even in Arcadia there is Medea', as Rennie (1995) observes (p. 107). In the first example, *Otaheite*, published anonymously in 1774, the recent voyages of discovery are celebrated as triumphs of science and pedagogy, figuring the British as 'Teachers of Mankind' who will turn the Tahitians from a savagery chiefly characterised by maternal infanticide:

> Can cruel Passions these calm Seas infest,
> And stifle Pity in a Parent's Breast?
> Does here MEDEA draw the vengeful Blade,
> And stain with filial Gore the blushing Shade;
> Here, where Arcadia should its Scenes unfold,
> And past'ral Love revive an Age of Gold!
> Ah! See in vain the little Suppliant plead
> With silent Eloquence to check the Deed:
> He smiles unconscious on th' uplift'd Knife,
> And courts the Hand that's arm'd against his Life.
> Nor his last sighs the Mother's Bosom move;
> She dooms his Death, her Sacrifice to Love:
> Impatient hastes her am'rous Vows to plight,
> And seals with Infant Blood the barb'rous Rite.
> Reclin'd upon her Lover's panting Breast,
> See in his Arms the beauteous Mur'dress prest!
> No keen Remorse the Wanton Trance destroys,
> No thrilling Terrors damp their guilty Joys
> Nor Ties of social Life their Crimes reclaim,
> Nor rigid Justice awes, nor virtuous Fame.

In contrast to Banks's emphasis on the mother's reluctance to sacrifice her child, *Otaheite* stresses her shameless eagerness to dispose of the impediment to her voluptuous abandonment. The poem uses maternal infanticide as the chief means of contesting the already widespread figuration of Tahitian culture as Arcadian, suggesting instead that the failure of maternal love is symptomatic of an irreligious ('No keen Remorse'), uncivil ('Nor Ties of social Life') and lawless savagery ('Nor rigid Justice'). The trope resurfaces in Anna Seward's famous *Elegy on the Death of Captain Cook* (1780):

> Nor has he wander'd, has he bled in vain!

His lips persuasive charm th'uncultur'd youth,
Teach Wisdom's lore, and point the path of Truth.
See! Chasten'd love in softer glances show
See! With new fires parental duty glows.

She glossed the passage thus: 'Captain Cook observes in his second voyage, that the women of Otaheite were grown more modest and that the barbarous practice of destroying their children was lessened.'

Many of the satires produced in response to Hawkesworth's publication were, however, much more sceptical about the assumption that a huge gulf divided the savage mother from the refined English matron, and sceptical in consequence about the moral rectitude of British exploration and commerce with 'Indians'. The addressee of the *Epistle to Lady Gr[os]v[e]n[o]r* was herself sexually notorious and the poem climaxes in a deliberate blurring of an infanticidal Tahiti and a civil England. The poem's account of Tahitian *mores* closes with an evocation of child-murder which segues into an attack on bluestockings or, to quote Hume, 'the fair sex' in their role as the 'sovereigns of the empire of conversation':

Can the fond mother act Medea's part?
Can she expose the darling of her heart?
Without a tear, her infant cherub, doom,
And stab the smiling off-spring of her womb?
O dire effect of passions unrestrain'd,
O dire effect of Nature's laws profan'd.
From such black scenes the Muse indignant turns,
Where lust depraved, the maddened female burns.
Far different scenes in Britain's isle I see,
Where shines conspicuous the fam'd *Coterie*. (275-84)

The apparent 'difference' in the scenes is collapsed, however, as the 'Coterie's' 'social orgies' (or salons) are revealed to be as depraved as the Tahitians': 'So the stale Countess by a strange embrace/Yields to her Lord an unresembling race' (291-2).

The satirists' citation of Medea invokes the ancient figure of barbaric female violence to refute the increasingly widely-held assumption – codified by the Scots – that women everywhere are not only maternally benevolent but that their social position reflects a culture's progress towards civility. Given the extent to which an orthodox Christian scepticism – that of Samuel Johnson as much as Hawkesworth – continued to shape opinion about local and exotic gender orders and polities, that is hardly surprising. Interestingly, if less predictably, however, the satiric attacks on bluestockings castigated as vicious, sound in the end not unlike the misogynistic suspicion of female 'voluptuousness' articulated by the philosophical Kames. In modern states marked by opulence, he remarks, 'Women … regarding nothing but sensual enjoyment, become so careless of their infants, as even, without blushing, to employ mercenary nurses' (Home 1776: I 205). Despite his insistence on the 'equality' of the sexes, Kames was adamant that women were by nature not designed for sculpture or letters but for child-rearing.

> With regard to the outlines, whether of internal disposition or of external figure, men and women are the same. Nature however, intending them for mates, has given them dispositions different, but concordant, so as to produce together delicious harmony. The man, more robust, is fitted for severe labour and for field-exercises: the woman, more delicate, is fitted for sedentary occupations; and particularly for nursing children. The difference is remarkable in the mind, no less than in the body. A boy is always running about; delights in a top or a ball, and rides upon a stick as a horse. A girl has less inclination to move: her first amusement is a baby; which she delights to dress and undress. I have seen oftener than once a female child under six getting an infant in its arms, caressing it, singing and walking about, staggering under the weight. A boy never thinks about such matters. (Home 1776: II 270)

Kames's belief in women's maternal instinct is shared by Millar (1779), for whom women are 'Loaded by nature with the first and most immediate concern in rearing and maintaining the children' (p. 109), and, like Kames, Millar simultaneously celebrates the improved condition of women which accompanied his own culture's attainment of refinement while deploring a tendency to decadence most visible in the decline of female virtue. He praises the domestic women of a recent age: 'Accustomed to live in retirement, and to keep company with their nearest relations and friends, they are inspired with all that modesty and diffidence which is natural to persons unacquainted with promiscuous conversation; and their affections are neither disappointed by pleasure, nor corrupted by the vicious customs of the world' (p. 110). But he notes that such modest virtue seems to breed its own corruption as:

> Women of condition come to be more universally admired and counted upon account of the agreeable qualities which they possess, and upon account of the amusement which their conversation affords. They are encouraged to quit that retirement which was formerly esteemed so suitable to their character, to enlarge the sphere of their aquaintance, and to appear in mixed company, and a public meeting of pleasure. They lay aside the spindle and the distaff, and engage in other employments more agreeable to the fashion. (Millar 1779: 121)

This contradictory impulse to celebrate and condemn contemporary British womanhood and the civilising process of which their maternal virtue is so crucial an index, is nowhere more apparent than in Kames's etiology of infanticide in the barbarous Celtic fringe of England:

> We scarce ever hear of adultery among savages: though among them in-continence before marriage is not uncommon. In Wales, even at present, and in the Highlands of Scotland, it is scarce a disgrace for a young woman to have a bastard. In the country last-mentioned, the first instance of a bastard-child being destroyed by its mother through shame is a late one. The virtue of chastity appears to be there gaining ground; as the only temptation a woman can have to destroy her child is to conceal her frailty. (Home 1776: II 281).

In fact, of course, for many women not just reputation but social and economic survival depended on their ability to dispose of an illegitimate child. Legal historians Peter Hoffer and N. E. N. Hull (1981) have argued that the precipitous decline in indictments for child-murder in the late eighteenth century can be understood in terms of a widespread acceptance of the universality of maternal instinct – as juries found the crime more monstrous, so too a higher standard of proof was required for conviction (p. 109). This cultural investment in maternity is not only manifest in the speculative historians' contradictory invocations of lurid instances of the infanticide in ancient, oriental and savage societies, which allow them to emphasise the civil difference of their own gender order, but is equally apparent in their denunciations of contemporary female luxury.

During the 1770s, the authors of conduct books, tying the reform of female manners not just to modesty but to maternity, also begin to include comparisons between the unhappy condition of women in 'barbarous' countries and the fortunate circumstances of British womanhood. Writers such as Hester Chapone and the Rev. James Fordyce followed Hume in emphasising that voyages and travels were proper subjects and texts for young women's instruction. Thus Fordyce exhorts, in a sermon on 'Female Virtue, With Intellectual Accomplishments':

> On both accounts we would also recommend books of Voyages and Travels; a favorite study of the celebrated Mr Locke. How amusing to curiosity! How enlarging to our prospect of mankind! How conducive to cure the contracted prepossessions of national pride, and withal to inspire gratitude for the peculiar blessings bestowed upon our country; to excite our pity towards the many millions of human beings left by mysterious heaven in ignorance and barbarism. (Fordyce 1809: 139)

In the next sermon, Fordyce emphasises that voyage literature, unlike

'bad books' which inflame and corrupt the imagination, can help correct
the passions and govern female practice: 'To instance but in one subject
more; she must be wholly given up to trifles that can pursue them with the
same fondness, after having her imagination raised, and all her faculties
expanded by those wonderful representations of the works of God, which
are contained in many books of Philosophy and History, Voyages and
Travels' (p. 143). Fordyce's *Sermons*, like Mrs Chapone's, are directed not
at women in general but most specifically at 'young creatures of your sex',
whom he describes as 'the most distinguishing glory of Britain; the fairest
flowers ... in all the garland of British humanity' (p. 159). Disavowing any
missionary interests in 'infidel' women, Fordyce represents such females as
hopelessly debauched: 'To attempt the conviction of female infidels falls
not within my present design. Indeed, I fear it would be a hopeless
undertaking. The preposterous vanity, together with the hopeless profligacy,
by which they have been warped into scepticism, would in all likeliehood
baffle any endeavours of mine' (p. 65).

Fordyce is as eager as Kames and Millar to emphasise the superiority
of British women over the virtuous pagans of the Roman republic:

> The virtues of a Roman Matron, in the better times of that republic, appear
> on some accounts to have been greatly respectable. They were such as might
> be looked for, from her education amongst a people whose ideas of prowess,
> patriotism and glory, ran high ... But not to insist on national pride, and
> ungenerous prepossessions, on which those ideas were founded; it is manifest
> to me, that whatever force or grandeur of the female mind might in other
> views derive from them, such advantage was overbalanced by the loss and
> diminution of that gentleness and softness, which ever were, and ever will
> be, the sovereign charm of the female character. Nor do I wish the women
> of Great Britain, who profess a system so much more just, amiable and
> happy, to adopt for the regulation of their temper any standard different
> from that in my text. (Fordyce 1809: 118)

Fordyce's text is itself an instrument in what Millar called (following
French usage), the 'internal police' of the British nation, as it divides
British women from their pagan predecessors and infidel contemporaries
in order to emphasise the patriotic as well as private nature of their duty
to modesty and maternity.

In her own *Letters on the Improvement of the Mind* (1773), Hester
Chapone also emphasises the special virtues of history and geography, both
in warding off the charms of 'fictitious stories that so inflame the mind'
(pp. 114-15) and in educating women in an understanding of their position
as participants in imperial culture. Study of ancient history is advised so
that the 'parallel' between 'the character of your own countrymen' and that

of the Romans may be observed (p. 129); the British conquests in both the Eastern and Western Indies are compared, and the recent voyages to the Pacific are invoked with enthusiasm. The reading lists, as well as the actual narrative embodied in the text, recapitulate the story of the progress of civil society towards its triumphant apotheosis in contemporary Britain. Lacking Fordyce's gallant flourishes, Chapone is equally emphatic that women's cultivation is a duty owed to 'that empire of which you are a subject' (p. 138). And her enthusiasm for the records of 'the amazing progress of navigation and commerce' (p. 132) helps explain the virulence of the public response to Hawkesworth's *Account*. His tales of Tahitian abandon were precisely the kind of corrupting texts, stimulating to the imagination and the passions, against which Voyages and Travels were favourably compared by the writers of conduct books.

The late eighteenth-century discourses of speculative history, ephemeral satire and conduct literature are not often connected, despite their common concern, even obsession, with the condition of contemporary women. In addition to this theme, however, these texts shared a common archive: the huge and expanding literature of voyages and travels on which they all drew in their attempts to explain, deplore and regulate female nature and conduct. Reading across these disparate philosophical, didactic and obscene texts, and the 'unreliable' accounts of foreign and exotic peoples which they recirculate, a certain cultural consensus emerges. Even in the increasingly materialist accounts of human history provided by the Scots, for women, biology is becoming Providence. Against the various perversions and degradations inflicted on women by ancient, infidel oriental and savage societies, Britain's liberal treatment of 'the Sex' has produced the nation's 'fairest flowers', women who enjoy unparalleled dignity, ease and respect as softer, sensible incarnations of Roman matronage. According to this logic, attempts to avoid maternity, whether through the voluntary celibacy of the metropolitan bluestocking, the employment of wet-nurses by the monied, or the infanticide of shamed servants and *arioi*, all stand as violations of the universal law of female nature.

# Gender and Genre in Nineteenth-century Travel Writing: Leonie d'Aunet and Xavier Marmier

Wendy S. Mercer

In the context of empire, traditional studies of travel writing tended to focus on and implicitly glorify the role of the 'heroic' explorer, whereas in the post-colonial era, more recent work has followed Said (1979; 1993) in concentrating almost exclusively on its function as a mode of subjugation paving the way for exploitation. In feminist criticism, the relationship between gender and imperialism (and, by extension, travel writing) has most frequently been characterised as an analogy in which the oppression of women in patriarchal societies is compared to the exploitation of peoples in colonised countries; it is therefore argued that women will identify more closely with other oppressed groups of people (French 1985; Steinem 1995). The implicit binarism in which man = coloniser and woman = colonised has been sharply criticised for failing to take account of woman in her role as coloniser (e.g. Chaudhuri and Strobel 1992; Donaldson 1993), and for neglecting the heterogeneity of female perspectives (and therefore feminisms), particularly in a third-world context (notably Spivak 1990; 1996). Nevertheless, gender is still generally taken (albeit often strategically) as the decisive factor in the formation of identity, thereby veiling the fact that other elements (e.g. race, social class, age, education) may well be predominant in any given situation. Such thinking also fails to engage with the possibility of either complicity with or rebellion against prevailing social forces, and neglects both the fluid equivocations of gender identity and the residual importance of corporeal specificity, all of which may influence strategies of authorial self-representation.

The body lies very much at the centre of the theories of language put forward by (predominantly French) feminists, which can also be read as relevant to the production of travel writing in the context of imperialism. Drawing on re-readings of Freud by Lacan and others, these theories seek to characterise differences in 'masculine' and 'feminine' discourse by a theory of identity according to which the masculine subject is constructed in terms of distance from the m/other. Because his own autonomy depends on distance, the 'masculine' subject may need to subjugate that which is 'other' in order to maintain that distance. If travel and exploration are seen in this light, then imperialism and colonisation are consequences of the 'masculine' (i.e. man = coloniser). Feminists have argued that the pretended objectivity of scientific discourse, its deliberate distance from the object of study, and the conspicuous absence of the bodily specificity of the author are based on the assumption that the specificity of the (male) author is the standard or 'norm' against which all 'others' may be measured – and found wanting.

The 'feminine' subject, on the other hand, will construct her identity through 'same-ness', or through her relationships with 'others', because she has not experienced the same need for distance from the m/other. She will therefore not have the same need to subjugate; this potential bond with the 'other' is enhanced by the capacity for child-bearing and nurture. Where travel writing by women exists, we would therefore expect to find a different 'feminine' set of values appearing in the text: the boundaries between subject and surroundings would be less clear, 'objective' analysis would give way to involvement, mind to body. There would be a refusal to prioritise and judge or to measure and order; this would constitute an example of what Hélène Cixous terms 'écriture féminine'.

It would consequently be useful to read two accounts of exactly the same voyage, one by a man and the other by a woman, in order to gauge the extent to which gender difference alters the generic conventions of travel writing. This is, unusually, possible in the case of Xavier Marmier and Léonie d'Aunet, each of whom wrote about the historic 1839 expedition on board the corvette *La Recherche* to 'Recherche Bay' at Spitzbergen and the subsequent journey overland through Lapland by the 'Commission du Nord' (this voyage formed part of a series of prestigious scientific expeditions under the command of Paul Gaimard to destinations in the northern seas). Although both Spitzbergen and Lapland are constituent parts of modern-day Europe, it is justifiable to consider these accounts in the imperialist/colonialist context on several grounds. Spitzbergen had been the subject of territorial disputes over whaling rights in the seventeenth century between the English, Dutch, French and Danish, although by the nineteenth century the whale population had dwindled and was no longer considered to be of great value; this may have been one of the reasons why Spitzbergen had remained largely undocumented. Lapland had been even more recently carved up: annexed to Sweden in the sixteenth century, it had then been divided between Sweden, Denmark and Russia (1595 and 1613). The borders as recognised today had been drawn up in 1751 (between Finland and Norway); in 1809 (between Finland and Russia);

and as recently as 1826 (i.e. some thirteen years before the expedition) between Norway and Russia. The Laplanders (a distinct race) could then at this time arguably be viewed as a colonised people. Moreover, it has frequently been noted (see, for example, Pratt 1992: 10) that travel books about even the better-known regions of Europe frequently display characteristics and strategies often associated with imperialist expansion; the reading of the two texts in question here shows this to be the case.

Marmier, the official reporter of the expedition, was the epitome of the (male) traveller-as-celebrity, whereas d'Aunet was only grudgingly permitted to travel, as a concession to her partner. Although neither was from a particularly privileged background, both had become accepted as members of the well-to-do middle classes, although whereas d'Aunet was a professed liberal, Marmier was a right-wing Catholic and monarchist. In their accounts of the expedition, both engage in a certain degree of colonialist rhetoric. However, this is neither consistent nor gender-specific, and there is evidence of resistance on the part of each to certain aspects of imperialist ideology. D'Aunet's text shows a number of characteristics associated with 'écriture féminine': a refusal to engage in scientific discourse, the inclusion of domestic detail, and a great deal of 'writing of the body'. However, both texts also display characteristics of what might be termed 'masculine' discourse, and Marmier's writing about Lapp 'others' is undeniably more 'feminine' (to use this terminology) than d'Aunet's. However, Cixous herself acknowledges that 'masculine' and 'feminine' are no more than markers (in *Extreme Fidelity*; translation in Sellers 1994: 136–7), and suggests that we all perpetually fluctuate between different gender roles. Clearly it is necessary to identify the *variety* of forces that come into play at any one time to determine the position of a given individual. Even where sexuality may be seen to be decisive, it is important to remember Foucault's argument that sex is not so much a monolithic natural phenomenon as a (perhaps monolithic) cultural construct: even the body must be understood in its socio-historical context.

The expedition took place at a time of unprecedented bourgeois capitalist expansion in France following Louis-Philippe's ascent to the throne. The decade also saw the growing presence of France in Algeria, and scientific exploration was not always as benign as it claimed: as Evans (1993) observes, 'today's personal triumph was tomorrow's imperial supply route' (p. 8). In this context, it is interesting to read the comments of Marbeau (1834), published just five years before the expedition: 'To govern a social body, you must know it; in order to know it, it is necessary to study it as a whole, and as constituent parts, to know the role each part plays in the overall picture; know its origins, its history, its population, its territory, its customs, its spirit, its strength and its riches' (pp. 43–4).

People and land were increasingly seen in terms of utility and profit, as dominant ideologies sought to assert and maintain their status. As Eagleton (1991) argues: 'A dominant power may legitimate itself by promoting beliefs and values congenial to it; naturalising and universalising such beliefs so as to render them self-evident and apparently inevitable; denigrating ideas which might challenge it; excluding rival forms of thought, perhaps by some unspoken but systematic logic; and obscuring social reality in ways convenient to it' (p. 6).

Clearly, these strategies are based on notions of 'sameness' and 'otherness'; although in any given society the number of possible alterities (which can of course intersect and overlap) must be almost infinite, there are certain dominant symbolisms of alterity. In 1830s France it is possible to identify certain major groups of 'others' who had to be kept in their places, in a role of subservient productivity. The working classes, despite their role in the revolution which brought Louis-Philippe to power, were in practice still denied the right to vote; others whose subservient productivity had to be maintained included 'foreigners' and women.

Vital to the new burst of capitalist activity was a work-force. This necessitated maintenance of the birthrate, and around this time socially inculcated sex-specific gender roles grew even farther apart:

> Society must protect marriage and the family, so it must punish any attack on marriage and the family. Marriage is the natural state of the citizen; celibacy is an offence against nature and morality. Voluntary celibacy is the epitome of egoism. Every society needs a head. Why is the husband always the head? Because nature created him stronger, more active, more able; he is obviously the stronger half of the conjugal 'I'. The wife, gentle, timid, patient, condemned to pregnancy, burdened with feeding her children, shares the destiny of the protector who has chosen her ... When nature changes, these roles will change. (Marbeau 1834: 22)

The female body was represented as 'saturated with sexuality' (Foucault 1981: 104) or, in the words of Bland (1981) 'with the wild workings of her reproductive system'. Thus, according to Rose (1993), 'women gave birth to future workers, women's role in the home sustained and satisfied children and adults, and thus maintained the capitalist system ideologically, and materially women fed and clothed the labour force' (p. 54). This system was based on an exaggeration of biological sexual difference and drew similarly on biological justifications for its exploitation of foreign peoples. Clearly, the body was the focal point of oppression of this period. The very circumstances of d'Aunet's participation in the expedition illustrate both all these constraints and her alternating resistance to and complicity with them.

In 1839 Léonie d'Aunet was living with the painter François Biard, whom Gaimard hoped to enlist as an official artist on the forthcoming expedition to Spitzbergen. He approached d'Aunet to put the proposition to Biard on his behalf; she agreed to persuade Biard on condition that she too be allowed to join the expedition. This was a problematic proposition in that it went against all expectations of 'female' behaviour: women were strictly prohibited on board any vessel of the French navy. Eventually, an unprecedented compromise was reached. It was agreed that she might join the ship at Hammerfest, the most northerly point of civilisation, to which Biard and she would make their way overland

Despite the official permission for her participation, d'Aunet still had to deal with the crew's resentment of her intrusion:

> 'And what an idea, to bring a woman along! Is it a pleasure trip for women, a voyage like this?'
>
> 'Ah! That's true' said another, 'and if we get stuck in those lovely crystals, just like you were saying, you can be sure that she'll be the first to go.' …
>
> 'And then what sort of woman is she, anyway?' asked a helmsman in a rather contemptuous way. 'A small, pallid, skinny woman … a woman you could break over your knee and put the pieces in your pocket … with about as much resistance to the cold as a budgie from Senegal. If ever we are frozen in, she'll die at the first spell of cold, that's for sure.' (d'Aunet 1854: 180–1)

This discourse is significant in that it shows an attempt to restore the 'official' order in terms of denigration and oblique threats of physical harm. But in the narrative, this form of misogyny does not function in one direction only: d'Aunet exploits it to appropriate the captain's cabin and to obtain extra reindeer skins and eiderdowns with which she cocoons herself in what she describes as a 'nest rather than a bedroom' (p. 186). This could be seen either as subversion by exploitation or as 'pay-off' by the dominant system. Further gender-specific physical limitations become evident in the course of d'Aunet's text, and it is interesting to see when, and on what terms, d'Aunet accepts or reacts against these constraints.

Among the myriad ways in which the artificial gap between the sexes was widened was the dress code, which limited women's physical mobility. Prior to embarkation on *La Recherche*, d'Aunet is overtaken by a rainstorm during a walk along the river near Leerfoss, in Norway:

> The path, churned up and slippery, became impassable. I fell into the mud, and couldn't get out again; my clothes, which were soaking wet, increased my difficulties; my dress, an old velvet dress, which I had put on because of the cold, became so swamped with water that I could no longer bear its

weight, and it prevented me from moving my legs ... the relentless rain
froze me, and the moment came when I gave up trying ... I sat down in the
mud and wept with rage. Fortunately, my coachman had had the good sense
to go along the main road to meet me ... he discovered me in a state of
distress; I was wrapped up in a coat; I took the arm of a robust peasant
(paysan). (d'Aunet 1854: 103–4)

The episode must be read, at least partially, in terms of social construction. Although d'Aunet may be defying the conventions of her social
gender role by her presence in that place at that time and by walking, her
simultaneous failure to revolt by adhering to those conventions by dressing
in a long velvet dress makes the conditions for the first revolt thoroughly
impractical. The open admission of her failure (sitting down in the mud
and weeping) signals the temporary restoration of the old patriarchal order.
The remainder of the episode emphasises her resignation to powerlessness
and passivity, as if she had abdicated all responsibility for herself ('I was
wrapped up in a coat'). The only active agents of the latter part of the
extract are masculine: the 'coachman', the 'robust peasant'. It is of course
significant that she can be rescued only after submitting to the old order.
This extract highlights the advantages to be derived from acquiescence in
the system, yet there is also a point to be made about social privilege.
When d'Aunet sits down in the mud and bursts into tears, she is, to some
extent at least, relying on the fact that 'her' coachman is somewhere about,
and will presumably come and rescue her at some stage. Her attempt at
asserting her independence is, then, based on a largely false premise.
Finally, the very fact of her admitting in the printed narrative that she sat
down and wept is significant. The prioritisation of emotion is considered
to be a feature of 'écriture féminine'; here it can be seen, at least in part,
as a consequence of social rules, enabling d'Aunet symbolically to represent
her desire for re-entry into the old order. By sitting down and weeping,
she is behaving as women 'should' in nineteenth-century terms and
acknowledging the 'folly' of her rebellion; she may thus be again granted
male protection.

There are several occasions when d'Aunet not only accepts, but even
invokes gender stereotyping when this is to her advantage. When it becomes
impossible for the horses to carry the luggage any longer on the journey
through Lapland, for example, the men share out the load (p. 231), and
she becomes positively indignant because she is left to manage as best she
can on her own (p. 251).

On the matter of clothes, however, she finally decides to resist the social
pressures. In the course of the expedition, she abandons her female attire,
and sports

a pair of men's trousers and a muslin shirt in coarse blue cloth as a smock, a large scarf of red wool, a belt of black leather; felt-lined boots and a sailor's cap completed this outfit, which will not be imitated. I need not add that under all this, I was tightly encased in flannel. When I went up onto the deck, I added to this mountain of woollens a sailor's jacket with a hood, which turned me into a very shapeless bundle. I had also cut my hair, which had become impossible to untangle. (d'Aunet 1854: 184–5)

Such a description is rare in the texts of male writers, since their attire is regarded as the 'norm'. D'Aunet is articulating a circumstance which is exceptional for her, because of socially constructed gender difference. In this regard, it is significant that a number of women travellers assumed male attire (see, for example, Isabelle Eberhardt in Algeria [Kobak, 1988; Clifford, 1997]). This strategy is enabling in practical terms (physical freedom of movement), in social terms (overcoming rules and exclusions based on gender) and in psychological terms (overcoming the way in which female identity in western societies is closely bound to being the passive object of the masculine gaze), permitting her to observe with greater freedom.

References to physical appearance which might be termed as 'trivial' or 'feminine' can also be understood in terms of social (gender) status. In Norway, d'Aunet is alarmed to find that, in addition to fatigue, she is also suffering from 'sunburn on my face; this treacherous Northern sun, which has no heat, tans one horribly' (p. 59). This comment must be read in conjunction with an earlier part of the text, where a gender-specific argument is put to d'Aunet against participation in the expedition. The announcement to her friends of her decision to accompany Biard is met with a chorus of disapproval: '"What madness!" I was told. "You will come back ugly." "Why?" "Those are terrible regions, you are too young and delicate to make such a journey; wait a while, at least"' (p. 3). No such anxieties for Marmier; certainly, none is recorded. But to a woman in nineteenth-century France, these worries were not as trivial as they might appear today. The ways in which a single woman might hope to earn a living were severely limited, so for a middle-class woman, the most realistic alternative was marriage – and in the marriage market, women were judged above all on their appearance, wealth and home-making talents, none of which would be enhanced by d'Aunet's participation in the expedition.

If d'Aunet's participation symbolises a resistance to social pressures and a possible prejudice to her material future, the same can be said of Marmier's decision to join the expedition, since unlike most nineteenth-century travellers, he had no private income and worked for a living. Having gained a reputation from his studies of German literature and culture and his subsequent work on previous expeditions with the Commission, he had been appointed professor of foreign literature at the University of Rennes in 1838. When *La Recherche* set off on its second attempt to reach Spitzbergen, he had to choose between his university post with its regular income and the chance to join the expedition: he resigned from his university post.

Yet despite the comparable risks taken by d'Aunet and Marmier to participate, an important distinction still remains in terms of gender identity. Whereas d'Aunet's participation generally tends to diminish her 'femininity' in contemporaneous social terms, Marmier's enhances his male gender role.

The 'virility' associated with exploration in the period emerges from a comparison of passages where d'Aunet's passivity is juxtaposed with Marmier's active 'masculine' and often imperialist discourse (natural phenomena in Marmier's text tend to be seen as objects to be 'conquered'). These juxtapositions tend on one level therefore to privilege the man = coloniser hypothesis, although this has to be considered in the context of the frustration articulated by d'Aunet at her enforced passivity on these occasions.

One illustrative example is the narration by both authors of an expedition by rowing boat attempting to reach the great ice barrier beyond Hakluyt, the most northerly point of Spitzbergen. D'Aunet is excluded on the grounds of gender:

> They didn't want me to join in ... I envied the lot of those who were going to get several leagues closer to the pole; they might even approach the great ice barrier, the goal of all our ambitions. I tried to talk myself out of my disappointment. I finished by admitting that I had reached a sufficiently elevated degree of latitude, and told myself that I should not begrudge those poor men, whose pride had only demanded that they go twelve or fifteen leagues further than me. (d'Aunet 1854: 202)

D'Aunet's bitterness at her assigned gender role of passivity contrasts strongly with the heady bravado of Marmier's rhetoric (which is interestingly reminiscent in many respects of Walton's euphoric pursuit in *Frankenstein* [Shelley 1818]):

> We wanted to leave behind us the last shore where our vessel was anchored, to undertake a bold exploration beyond the extreme limits of the globe, to row to the edge of the eternal barrier which surrounds the pole, and try to penetrate it. But the sky was covered by a thick veil of mist. From time to time snow fell, as it does in our country in the middle of winter, and the caution of the helmsman calmed the vigour of our oars. 'You won't even get as far as that barrier ... if you try to reach it, you could be overtaken by a

thick mist; you would lose your bearings and could find yourselves trapped there, then crushed by the ice.' (Marmier 1844–47: II 351)

The venture is glorified by the use of epithets such as 'extreme', 'eternal', 'bold'; and is recounted in terms of active male domination ('exploration', 'vigour', 'penetration'). The warnings of the helmsman are referred to in terms reminiscent of an over-protective mother or nanny, fussing unnecessarily.

The conflation of male heterosexual gender identity and colonisation becomes more explicit in Marmier's text in his comments on the Swedish mining industry. He reports favourably on the mineworks at Kaafiord, which he sees as an English colony in microcosm, bringing prosperity to the local work-force. He applauds the enterprise which has successfully exploited the hitherto untapped resources of the country:

> This noble country of Sweden is, like the people who inhabit it, cold on the surface, but rich inside. Happy is the country where the nature of the people and that of the earth do not at first sight reveal their full beauty, but save their secret treasures as a precious reward for the friend who asks, for the confident gaze which penetrates. (Marmier 1844–47: II 87)

The rather arrogant conflation of nature and the feminine, seen in terms of the desire of the potential coloniser, suggests that the minerals of the earth in Sweden, like the women, are there for the taking. The eroticisation of landscape is a recognised motif in the history of travel writing (see, for example, Rose 1993) and is a logical consequence of the association of exploration and discovery with heterosexual virility in the context of a capitalist patriarchy. Nor is it merely a matter of the (male) explorer/coloniser taming (female) nature; there is also evidence of male rivalry in the conquest. At the Eyanpaïkka Falls, the parties are advised to leave the boats in the hands of an experienced local helmsman, and to disembark and follow on dry land. Marmier notes:

> There used to be four helmsmen here: two of them died as a result of the arduous nature of their work, and the third one drowned last year … The inhabitants of Munoioniska had not failed to tell us about the numerous accidents which had happened at this waterfall; but this just made M Gaimard and me more determined to go down. In addition to this, we were told that a few days previously, two English travellers had recoiled in horror when they saw the falls, and had hastily chosen the path on dry land … But we … decided to do it a second time. (Marmier 1844–47: II 21)

The Englishmen abroad are seen as representatives of a rival (imperialist) power and the French feel impelled to show their supremacy. Significantly, d'Aunet is ordered out of the boat to make her way on dry land ('I obeyed, but with the greatest reluctance' [d'Aunet 1854: 290]). Again, she obviously wishes to participate in the 'heroic' challenge to nature undertaken by her male counterparts. She is prevented not by some psychological reluctance on her part, but by the gender identity which is enforced upon her.

The prioritisation of material for inclusion is an interesting one. Marmier's (much longer) text (1844–47) is based on a great deal of 'homework': in preparation for the journey, he had learned Danish, Swedish and Norwegian, as well as the rudiments of the Laplanders' language, on which he includes a short chapter (vol. II, p. x). D'Aunet does not pretend to such 'comprehensive' knowledge; indeed, such aspirations are rejected at certain points in the text. She refuses, for example, to 'rack [her] brains taking sides for or against the different opinions' on the question of the ethnic origins of the Finns, which she considers to be 'seriously puerile'; she is 'just as happy to go along with the idea of Genesis, and suppose that the Finns, like us, are descendants of Japhet, the son of Noah' (d'Aunet 1854: 304).

Marmier's text offers greater detail not only in terms of 'background' information (historical data, linguistic analysis, surveys of literature, population figures and so on) but also in the precise manner in which dates and other phenomena are recorded. An easily comparable extract describes the first few days on board *La Recherche* after leaving Hammerfest. Marmier writes:

> On the 17 July we left Hammerfest with a southerly wind which seemed as if it would carry us rapidly to Spitzbergen. 'La Recherche' was cruising at eight knots full sail ... On 18, we had arrived approximately at the latitude of Bear Island. The underwater temperature had suddenly dropped by three degrees, which led us to believe that there was ice in the vicinity ... We were at 74° 30' latitude. On the 19, we hoped to arrive at Bear Island, the access to which was not blocked, as last year, by a thick ring of floating ice ... We didn't catch sight of it until the following day, and on the 21, at mid-day, we anchored about three miles off the coast. (Marmier 1844–47: II 332–3)

All details are recorded with precision and authority. Specific dates, times, wind-direction, nautical speed, geographical position, sea temperature and position at anchor are all recorded without qualification (even when suppositions are made, the grounds for them are recorded in good scientific fashion). This might thus be termed a 'masculine' piece of scientific writing. Authority is derived from objectivity; no trace is to be found of the specificity of the writer. The distance of the authorial voice is emphasised in French by the use of the pronominal 'on' ('one'; this is

awkward to convey in English and I have translated it as 'we'). Both the
tone and the elements selected for inclusion in d'Aunet's version of this
same period are different:

> We had left Hammerfest on 17 July, and I can't really give you an account
> of my impressions of the first few days: it would be too monotonous, because
> I saw fit to suffer from a severe bout of seasickness; I heard someone round
> about saying that the wind was full south, and that we were going very well;
> but that was a feeble compensation for the sorry state to which the pitching
> and rolling of the boat reduced me. I grew accustomed to it, however, and
> on the fourth day I felt strong enough to go up onto the deck and see what
> the sea looks at 74° of latitude, where we found ourselves on 20 July ...
> Whilst we were suffering these gusts of wind and this tiresome lurching, we
> were looking for Cherry Island. It appeared on 21 in the morning. (d'Aunet
> 1854: 159–60)

Much less dating detail is given here, and no figures are given for
windspeed, sea temperature and so on. Even the information about the
wind direction is consciously divested of its authority ('I heard someone
round about say ... '). The impersonal, 'disembodied' voice of Marmier's
statement is counterbalanced by d'Aunet's emphasis on physical sensation
which for her takes precedence over scientific data. It is significant that
when she does offer scientific data, they are often shown to be inaccurate.
Thus at this stage in the text (p. 165, in apparent contradiction to p. 159)
for example, she states that 'On many maps, Cherry is indicated as lying
at latitude of 74° 30' North, whereas its correctly determined position is
in fact 76° 30' North, an error of fifty leagues.' Marmier correctly gives
the latitude (without comment) as 74° 30'.

Some feminists would see in the 'masculine' impulsion to measure,
quantify and explain a means of subjugation, whereas d'Aunet's writing of
her body would suggest 'écriture féminine'. But even if we accept the
relationship between knowledge and subjugation, is the desire for knowledge necessarily 'masculine' in essence? Although in practice, those who
have measured, recorded and discovered have for the most part been men
(as indeed have been the exploiters and colonisers), this is surely to some
extent because of the secondary, passive role traditionally ascribed to
women. In the example cited above, a number of social factors are relevant.
As the official recorder of the expedition, Marmier was bound to record
as much detail as accurately as possible; d'Aunet, travelling virtually as a
tourist, had no such duty. Furthermore, age and previous experience cannot
be overlooked: Marmier was a seasoned traveller who had been attached
to several expeditions, whereas d'Aunet was only nineteen years old and
had never been on an expedition before. D'Aunet's education and her lack

of experience are surely also relevant: she had been educated in a convent, an education which, she later argues (notably in *Un mariage en province*, 1856), leaves a woman wholly unprepared for life in the outside world. Education for women (when and where available) was largely limited to the acquisition of social accomplishments such as music, painting, embroidery and the like – designed to perpetuate further the role of woman as a desirable object to be chosen by a future husband rather than to fulfil her intellectual potential or prepare her for an active role in society.

In contrast, there are a number of details included in her account which reflect the preoccupations of the sphere to which she is permitted access in her everyday life. In recording the banquet on board ship, for example, she notes that 'the cook, in order to get his jellies to set, only had to leave them outside on the deck for a few moments' (p. 169). And a further contrast to the predominantly scientific and objective discourse of Marmier's text is her recollection of the game played to keep warm at Spitzbergen (a detail apparently not considered proper for inclusion by Marmier):

> The idea was to climb about two or three hundred feet up the almost sheer face of one of the mountains ... Once you reached a plateau, you would sit on the slope and allow yourself to slide down to the bottom, steering yourself as best you could ... At first, I kept losing my balance, and I rolled like a solid mass, sometimes on my head, sometimes on my side, sending up clouds of snow in my efforts to hang on, laughing heartily at my clumsiness, and making all the others laugh as well. (d'Aunet 1854: 185–6).

D'Aunet is not only having great fun, but is able to laugh at herself, inviting the reader to do likewise. While some feminists might make much of the emphasis on physical pleasure, I would argue that d'Aunet is simply writing as a tourist. Mass tourism did not exist in those days (although Thomas Cook started to organise tourist parties to the Northern Cape as early as 1875 [Robinson 1995: 66]), but for d'Aunet the expedition is essentially a holiday (her travelogue takes the form of letters to her brother).

The sphere of childcare was obviously perceived as a gender-specific one, and although both Marmier and d'Aunet describe in detail the cribs used by Laplanders, d'Aunet uses much more effusive tones: 'In the midst of all this ugliness, one item full of charm offers itself to the traveller's gaze. That item is the crib for small infants; all the luxury, all the poetry of the poor Laplander is expressed in it; maternal tenderness blends with elegance; the heart filled with love has created something gracious' (pp. 141–2). This extract reveals, however, a curious mixture of rhetoric. Despite the effusion concerning the crib, there is a clear distance here between d'Aunet as subject and the Laplanders, the latter being constructed in ethnocentric terms as 'poor' and 'ugly' objects of the 'traveller's [i.e. d'Aunet's] gaze'. The use of the reflexive 'offers itself' also implies subjugation to the gaze. As Coward (1985) contends, 'the ability to scrutinise is premised on power. Indeed the look confers power' (p. 75). Here, d'Aunet constructs herself very much as the imperialist subject, this being the predominant motif in her dealings with the Laplanders and, less markedly, with other Scandinavians.

To a certain extent, her contact with the people is limited because she has no knowledge of their languages. When she does have dealings with them (usually when she wants something from them) she speaks through an interpreter. Her distance from them is emphasised by the fact that those interpreting are always referred to as 'my men' or 'my servant'; there is an obvious social hierarchy at play in her discourse, with herself at the top, 'her servants' somewhere in the middle, and the local people at the bottom.

The ethnocentrism of d'Aunet's discourse concerning the Laplanders is blatant: 'The Laplanders of Kautokeino leave a different impression from those at Hammerfest: they are the same people, but the two faces of the savage: at Hammerfest, the savage on holiday is drunken, vacant, hideous; at Kautokeino, in his family life, he is quiet, lazy and narrow-minded. Outside the home, he is disgusting; at home, he is pitiful' (p. 267). Here we have a classic example of the rhetoric of the oppressor, be (s)he colonialist or capitalist. The distancing of self from object and the evocation of supposed vices (drunkenness, idleness) are frequently used to justify exploitation (see Pratt 1992: 45).

In the course of the text, d'Aunet subjects the Laplanders, and particularly the women, to a process of dehumanisation and bestialisation (which is perhaps also in part an indirect expression of anxiety for her own physical attractiveness). From being devoid of 'normal' sexual characteristics (p. 148), they are characterised as 'ugly' (p. 147), 'horrible' (p. 259), 'repulsive' (p. 147), 'monsters' (p. 259), 'ogre's daughters' (p. 147), 'large grey bears walking on their hind legs' (p. 140) and 'monkeys' (p. 259). The presence and subservience of these (sub-)people are always taken for granted. Thus when d'Aunet chances upon a Laplanders' tent occupied by only two women, she sees their home only as a site to gratify her desire to wash. Ignoring the inhabitants, she acts '*as in a conquered land*' (p. 236, my emphasis), commandeers the tent, and proceeds to undress, causing the women to rush out in alarm. Humour is derived from the narration of the incident at the expense of the two women; their reaction is ridiculed on the assumption that their presumed inferiority precludes any necessity for respect.

D'Aunet also supposes that anything belonging to the Laplanders is available, if not for the taking then for sale. Her desire for a haunch of venison as a luxurious alternative to the monotonous but adequate diet supplied is implicitly more important than the survival of the Lapp who refuses to sell his reindeer (pp. 247–8). Similar terms of ethnocentric indignation are applied to another who is unwilling to relinquish his dog, 'not because of affection ... the often tender familiarity between peasant or shepherd and his dog is unknown in Lapland. So the Laplanders value their dogs because of some old superstition, deriving from some pagan faith, which has not yet been stamped out amongst certain individuals' (p. 249).

D'Aunet's cultural superiority is taken for granted; she would therefore be a much more worthy owner of the dog than this Laplander, whose values are inferior. Not only is he not sentimentally attached to his dogs, as even the most lowly of Frenchmen are; he is superstitious and possibly even pagan. When an offer (presumably very substantial in Lapp terms) is eventually accepted, the vendor is described in terms of avarice reminiscent of those used by Molière to describe Harpagon (*L'Avare*), as one for whom lust for money replaces all human considerations; and this comment is extended to characterise the entire Lapp race (pp. 248–9).

The insensitivity of these comments in the light of d'Aunet's own penchant for material acquisition is highly ironic. Every opportunity is seized to purchase a bargain, often with a view to trade. Shopping sprees are described with minute detail of purchases and prices (see p. 349). In Hjerkinno, for example, she rummages through the clothes in the communal wardrobe (which she sees as fancy dress) and has them packaged for the journey back to France (we are not told on what terms, or indeed if, she purchases them), and also 'three white wolf skins, trophies from hunting expeditions by the son of the household, which he let me have for 35 francs. However well-known the white wolf may be in France, the skins fetch a much higher price there' (p. 87). Animals generally (apart from dogs and seals which are regarded with a great deal of sentimentality) are seen in terms of profit and utility: walruses are seen as a potential yield of ivory, oil and pelt; the practicalities of the potential commercial exploitation of blue foxes from Spitzbergen (p. 201) and reindeer (p. 279) are discussed in detail.

All the above encounters, then, are seen in terms of potential exploitation, and d'Aunet constructs herself very firmly as a part of the French bourgeoisie of the late 1830s, living out Guizot's admonition to 'Get rich' by her contact with the indigenous peoples she encounters. In the context of the 'woman as coloniser', I would now like to return to the concept of the gaze as a 'masculine' mode of subjugation, comparing accounts of spectating at social ceremonies in Lapland (the one a marriage, the other the last rites of a dying woman). These situations are emotive occasions for the participants, and it is revealing to see how d'Aunet and Marmier construct themselves as spectators. D'Aunet attends a wedding at the church in Hammerfest:

> On the day of the wedding ... the couple were accompanied to the church door by a throng of people ... The bridegroom, one of the smallest Lap-landers I have ever seen (he couldn't have been more than four foot tall) wore a robe of grey sackcloth bordered with three bands of coarse blue, red, and yellow cloth, which he seemed very proud of. The bride's bitter ugliness was softened only slightly by her extreme youth. Her small, sunken red-rimmed eyes, her enormous mouth which showed a set of sharp teeth, all far apart, her coarse brown skin, her massive size, her short, dirty hands, made her into a kind of monster. She looked as one would imagine the sister of Caliban, or one of the daughters of an ogre in a fairytale. Her whole appearance was worse than ugly: repulsive ... My ignorance of the Lapp language did not allow me to participate in the general emotion; but looking at the contortions of the physiognomies of this horrible little gathering, I gained an insight into the various and infinite horizons of human ugliness whose existence I had not even suspected until then. (d'Aunet 1854: 147–8)

Once more d'Aunet deliberately distances herself from the proceedings and the individuals. By judging their clothes, appearances and standards of cleanliness by an ethnocentric and class-based standard, she dehumanises the participants in the ceremony (particularly the bride) in order to con-struct herself in a position of superiority (this is a well-worn device of colonialist rhetoric). What is particularly striking is her complete lack of respect and total failure to identify with the situation she is observing: her gaze only demeans and belittles.

The first example of Marmier's gaze also shows him in an incongruous position. When *La Recherche* had attempted to reach Spitzbergen the previous year, he had decided not to accompany the expedition, but to spend some time living among the Laplanders, staying with a local priest. On one occasion, he accompanies the priest to administer last rites to a woman dying of leprosy, some miles away.

> It was a poor Lapp shanty inhabited by two families. On one side were the reindeer skins, which served as a bed; on the other a weaving loom, a few wooden buckets resting on planks, a pot hanging over the fireplace, and that was all. Two women, who had hurriedly thrown on their sackcloth tunics, were sitting on their bed, and in a dark corner, the sick woman was uttering cries of pain. An incurable form of leprosy had eaten away a part of her palate, and her voice, unintelligible for anyone except her son, sounded like

a death rattle ... It was a scene I shall never forget ... it was the most terrible and moving thing I have ever seen. (Marmier 1844–47: I 196–7)

Whereas d'Aunet draws upon the traditional imperialist clichés of filth and úgliness to distance herself from the proceedings, Marmier refuses to exploit even the image of contagious disease. Indeed, at the heart of his discourse is an emotional engagement with those around him. Instead of constructing 'them' as 'other' and therefore 'inferior' to him, he empathises with the proceedings, thereby diminishing the distance between himself and the protagonists. By his own emotional investment in the situation, he invites that of the reader. And if his presence is a priori inappropriate (as 'colonial' observer), his emotional investment makes it much less so.

Significantly, Marmier's sensitivity to the dignity of others sometimes causes him to refuse to observe altogether. At Abo, in Finland, for example, his research into social institutions of the region takes him to a prison. Shocked by the inappropriate decoration and ceremony organised by the governor in his honour, he cuts short his visit 'because I did not have the stomach to observe such a degree of misery any longer, knowing that I was powerless to mitigate [the prisoners'] suffering in any way' (Marmier 1843: I 30).

The aspect of Marmier's contacts with 'others' which is perhaps most striking, is the relationships struck up with individuals. Marmier had taught himself most of the Scandinavian languages in order to gain a deeper understanding of the peoples visited (which does not appear in this context to be a prelude to domination/exploitation). Combined with his propensity for entering into relationships on a premise of respect for the identity of others, this allows for more genuine exchange and an understanding not suggested in d'Aunet's narrative. This is not to say that Marmier's text is entirely free of ethnocentrism. Sometimes, frustration leads him to descend to the level of dismissive generalisations found so frequently in d'Aunet's work. On occasion, he derives humour from his position of 'superiority' in relation to the Laplanders. Thus when he invites his friends Ole Ollsen and his wife on board *La Recherche*, a lot of persuasion is necessary, we are told, to overcome Ollsen's fear that once they were on board, 'he or his wife might be taken away to France, that sad country where there are no herds of reindeer' (Marmier 1844–47: II 353). In contrast to d'Aunet's snide narration of the appropriation of the tent, however, the humour here is gentle, both in the terms in which the incident is related and relative to its context in the narrative. Marmier had met Ollsen the previous year at Hammerfest, and, after an apparently long conversation, had been invited to his tent where he was given a prized Norwegian coin (note the contrast with d'Aunet's comments about the avarice of the Laplanders) with the words: 'You are a good stranger, you don't despise the poor Laplander. Keep this to remind you of me and come and see me in Kitell' (vol. I, p. 193). Ollsen himself sought Marmier out when *La Recherche* returned to Hammerfest the following year, and the story of course finished happily: 'he finally decided to climb the ladder; and once he was on the deck, a good glass of brandy made him the happiest man in the world' (vol. II, p. 353). If the attitude is slightly patronising, this is mitigated by the reciprocity and the evident mutual respect. Elsewhere, Marmier frequently names individuals he has met, and relates conversations he has had with them about their country, the way they live, and about life in France. It is also significant that whereas d'Aunet is usually seen to be buying or taking, Marmier is frequently seen to be giving money, and on the expedition to Iceland in 1836, his propensity for mixing with and learning from local people made him into something of a legendary figure. His renown was such that he figures (albeit in a rather changed form) in one of the major Icelandic novels of the nineteenth century (Gröndal 1861).

A reading of these two texts then confounds the binarism of the man = coloniser / woman = colonised hypothesis. D'Aunet's text reflects specific aspects both of the imposed gender roles of the nineteenth century and certain features of 'écriture féminine', most of which can also be attributed to social factors: lack of scientific knowledge or education, attention to domestic detail, writing of the body (usually of the constraints on the female body). Her representations of alterity, however, show scant respect for 'others'; her attitude in this context is more representative of the entrepreneurial ethos of France at the time than that of Marmier (whose right-wing views in nineteenth-century terms would actually have implied a rejection of capitalism). Certain other aspects of Marmier's text conform to the man = coloniser model, particularly the conflation of exploration and male heterosexual gender identity. This must be considered, however, in the light of the socially imposed gender roles in which male = active, dominant, and female = passive.

Social forces, then, must be seen as crucial to the ways in which both authors construct themselves in relation to their texts and their subjects. However, neither author can be seen merely as the product of particular social forces. The ways in which each chooses to conform, exploit or resist within the framework of those forces leads to a textual and lived individuality outside the binarisms associated both with traveller as coloniser and man as coloniser.

## Ecologies of Desire: Travel Writing and Nature Writing as Travelogue

Richard Kerridge

Will contemporary environmentalism produce a new travel writing? One immediate answer is: why should it? Environmentalism, in many of its ingredients, is not new. Its historical origins are various, but a lot of threads go back into colonialism. To cite two examples: Richard H. Grove (1995) has documented the development of ecological sensibilities and techniques among early colonial administrators, and John M. MacKenzie (1988) has charted the emergence of many conservation practices from colonial big-game management for hunting (pp. 210–310). Travel writing, similarly, has a complex historical relationship with colonialism. Travel writers have frequently been critical of colonial regimes, but many of the familiar conventions of the genre – the rituals of quest and departure, the anecdotal mediation of foreignness to readers at home, the freedom of movement enjoyed by the traveller-protagonist – are interwoven with colonial relations. Both environmentalism and travel writing can be read, in many cases, as continuations, in a post-colonial world, of types of sensibility formed in colonial conditions.

A central claim of contemporary environmentalism is that the present crisis is new. Its scale is unprecedented. Global warming is only its most clearly global manifestation. Local ecological problems, from rainforest fires in South-East Asia and South America to debates over genetically-engineered food in British supermarkets, immediately point us to global routes and systems: of climate, of trade, of infection, of law. Each particular environmental event – each health concern connected with pollution, each natural or human habitat destroyed, each species in danger of extinction – is now, routinely, seen as symptomatic of a single, cumulative, global phenomenon: 'the environmental crisis'. Globalisation is a much-remarked development of contemporary capitalism; environmental problems, as they unfold, seem always to reveal the operations of this capitalism. Environmentalism is frequently an expression of anguish about this process, regret at the penetration of each last remote place; but it is also a perception of systems and interdependencies, calling for new senses of connection to distant localities. This may mean new sorts of travel writing.

Can the older conventions be part of this new orientation? I mean, in particular, the role played by the traveller as heroic venturer, the person whose very daring in entering these places emphasises their difference and impenetrability, while giving the reader a sensation of sudden closeness to the wild and foreign. I mean also the desire for the conservation of 'nature' as something not to be hunted, exactly, but to be visited (or read about, or watched on television) for experiences hard to manage at home (dramas of the chase, spectacles of naked avidity, perhaps, or of the body's materiality). Traditionally, these have been strong among the pleasures taken in travel writing, nature writing and television nature documentaries. Do they now deform environmentalism? Perhaps the contradiction is too damaging: between this desire for the elaborate maintenance of exciting forms of Otherness, and the ecological imperative to acknowledge connections, lift taboos and familiarise the other (to know the detail of what happens to waste, for example). Or perhaps the pleasures of sudden, close encounters with the rare are too valuable, too ingrained and essential, to be disowned.

To explore some of these questions, I want to look at the encounter with the exciting Other, and therein with repressed aspects of the self, in travel writing and in nature writing. This is an important trope shared by environmentalist and colonialist writings; in examining it, I want to ask what form, if any, it might take in a new, environmentalist travel writing.

A characteristic example comes in Paul Hyland's *The Black Heart* (1988), a travel book announced (perhaps ironically) by its title as a neo-Conradian quest-narrative. It is the story of a journey the author took into Central Africa. He recounts what he saw in one forest village:

> A boy begged me to examine his arm. It was blotched with a pale rash. His terror was leprosy. All I could say was, '*Je ne suis pas médecin.*' Litiliyo Wawelo, a French-speaking Baptist, asked me to come and see a sick woman. '*Je ne suis pas médecin,*' I said, but he led me past his chapel of poles and plank benches to the door of a low house. What about the health-team? No, no, it was me he wanted. We entered the shadows. I could see children, a grandmother, flaking mud walls, a swept dirt floor. Squatting on a stool was a woman in anguish, her eyes brimming with fear. I greeted her, '*Mbote na yo, mama,*' in Lingala; '*Mais, citoyenne, je ne suis pas médecin,*' I repeated. She peeled the cloth from her breasts. One was long and heavy; one a wound, crusted, palely exfoliating, above and below a great black nipple. The roof insisted I stoop, the people insisted I examine. I felt sick, fraudulent, a foolish white man. But it was a *mondele*'s judgement they wanted. The eyes above

the abscesses beseeched me. I knew she'd not want my verdict on her cancer. In French I said she must go to the hospital at Yakusu, at once. Litiliyo nodded, translated. He led me out into the heat of the sun. The woman moaned in the darkness. The white man had spoken. (Hyland 1988: 185-6)

The traveller hastily moves on. Two short paragraphs later comes a gap on the page, and a new section beginning 'When we crossed the Zaïre to Yalisombo'. Yet the moment in that hut, as much as any other, is the Conradian 'heart' of the book, the deepest point of its voyage into the interior. Hyland's literal journey continues, but one 'journey', towards identification and the fantasy of making contact and merging with otherness, has to stop here, in a moment of recoil. He never gets further than this. To do so would be to accept responsibilities incompatible with his role as traveller.

As it stands, the moment is a set-piece of confrontation, climax and recoil: a trope of late-Romantic doubt in the face of the infinite, glossed with European post-colonial diffidence. Its ready acceptance of defeat, its retreat into detachment, contrasts markedly with the bustle and scientific industry ostentatiously displayed in the high imperial narrative of exploration which is its ancestor, Paul Du Chaillu's *Explorations and Adventures in Equatorial Africa* (1861). But what might Hyland actually have done? It is not easy to construct plausible alternatives to his retreat. He might have abandoned his journey to help the woman get to hospital. He might engage himself in politics, campaigning for new conditions of trade and fairer distribution of wealth and medical supplies. This would be a relinquishment of the traveller's position; an absorption into the world he is visiting. To put it another way, this would be to allow his travel experience to change him. He would become Object as well as Subject. The membrane of his Englishness, protecting the set identity he must carry unchanged from departure to return, which is his contact with the reader, would be dissolved. His voyage would have so much changed him that he would be unable to return to his old life; it would cease to be a voyage.

It is unfair to single out Paul Hyland with these drastic requirements, since the appeal in this episode is that of any spectacle of suffering which makes the viewer pause. Photographs in charity advertisements are chosen for this effect. Faintly implicit in such a pause is the fantasy, or potential, that the moment could be a turning-point; that the spectacle could move us so much that we would cease to be external viewers and would enter the scene represented.

Nearly always this does not happen, and instead there is an impasse, full of the tension of the viewer's refusal. The moment is ended by the resumption of the journey or the turning of the page. One of the conventions of travel writing is that, although the traveller seeks encounters with otherness, these encounters have only so much space to occupy. The itinerary is fixed, and the timetable for closure – for return and re-entry into the atmosphere of home – is drawn up in advance. Paul Hyland did not have to go to Africa to face the sort of appeal that the woman presented, but it is a traditional place to go on such a quest – and travel is a way of having the encounter while keeping it in the realm of otherness and fantasy.

Travel writing deserves hard questioning in these terms when it presents the journey as a search for an experience that will change the protagonist, only to edge its way around the opportunity and bring the traveller home, unscathed, unchanged. With particular clarity, travel writing displays a combination of desire and anxiety common to numerous forms of subjectivity. The desire is to see and know, to convert the otherness of the world into the familiar and homely, even to dissolve the boundaries between self and world, so that there will be nothing menacing lurking in unexplored places, and the world will not terrify with the things it permits to happen. The anxiety is that the self will be captured, contaminated, absorbed, unable to extricate itself, and that its present consciousness will become imprisoned in a body that has become other.

The traveller offers to be a proxy, venturing into foreign space on behalf of the reader at home, but always maintaining contact with base, through the narrative-address to that reader. He has stepped out of the web of attachments that normally holds him in place, in order to search for something lost or repressed in ordinary life – but only to look at it, or brush against it. These protagonists are Romantic in their liking for standing at thresholds, gazing into or glimpsing the unknown. Desire or fear quickens when something seems about to emerge and cross over from otherness to the known. Anxiety grows when it is the traveller himself who seems pulled towards this threshold.

Western travellers have traditionally felt disquiet at the mixture of otherness and familiarity to be found abroad. Colonialism required of its European administrators a combination of intimate knowledge of the colonised people and hierarchical aloofness from them. Complicated boundaries and rituals were devised to protect this doubleness. Tensions in colonialist subjectivity often appear to be signs of an effort to resist being pulled too far in either direction.

Attraction was usually followed by recoil. Violent punitiveness on the part of colonial administrators has often been seen as frantic reassertion of separateness by a compromised self. Intense attractions that took Europeans in the colonies by surprise have been interpreted as evidence of repressions at home. Rudyard Kipling, Rider Haggard, Joseph Conrad, D. H. Lawrence, E. M. Forster and Paul Scott have all been read in these terms. Kaja

Silverman, for example, in *Male Subjectivity at the Margins* (1992), investigating beleaguered masculinities in a variety of contexts, finds in T. E. Lawrence a particularly agonised and ecstatic drive towards both absorption – giving one's self up to the world, in relinquishment of the position of Subject – and mastery, the stern reinforcement of that position as sealed and complete (pp. 299–338).

The terms of Silverman's inquiry come from Lacanian psychoanalysis; and, following her, I will draw on some of them here. Silverman uses Lacan's distinction between the 'eye' and the 'gaze' to describe a masculinity held in place by a 'scopic field': an interplay of attractions and pressures including a powerfully expectant 'gaze' coming from many directions. Any of these forces may become too strong, drawing or throwing this masculinity off balance. Analysing Fassbinder's *Gods of the Plague*, Silverman suggests that pictorial images of women may themselves return a gaze intimidating to a masculinity whose desiring look issues from 'a subjectivity which pivots upon lack' (p. 143).

Can we apply this to Paul Hyland, and to the position of the observer in travel writing and nature writing of the colonial tradition? Hyland is embarrassed when the woman exposes herself to him. He too is exposed, most of all to himself, as unable to be what the villagers perceive him to be. The encounter is a meeting of mutually unaccommodating looks. Hyland's eyes are drawn to the woman's body, while she and the villagers look expectantly at him.

Lacan defines the gaze as follows:

> I mean, and Maurice Merleau-Ponty points this out, that we are beings who are looked at, in the spectacle of the world. That which makes us consciousness institutes us by the same token as *speculum mundi*. Is there no satisfaction in being under that gaze ... that circumscribes us, and which in the first instance makes us beings who are looked at, but without showing this?
>
> The spectacle of the world, in this sense, appears to us as all-seeing ... The world is all-seeing, but it is not exhibitionistic – it does not provoke our gaze. When it begins to provoke it, the feeling of strangeness begins too. (Lacan 1979: 74–5)

The gaze comes at us from all around (in the mirror-image it comes from myself), while the eye is our own look, directed outwards: 'I see only from one point, but in my existence I am looked at from all sides' (Lacan 1979: 72). Elizabeth Grosz (1990) explains: 'The gaze is thus, like the phallus itself, the drive under which the subject's certainty and identity fail. [For Lacan] ... the possibility of being observed is always primary. To occupy a place in the scopic field is to be able to see, but more significantly, to be seen' (p. 79).

The relationship between the eye and the gaze is revealed with particular intensity when the subject is caught out – is seen, or forced to see himself – in the act of looking. Such a moment is a crisis of subjectivity. Revealed here is the failure Grosz mentions. Lacan describes it:

> A gaze surprises him in the function of voyeur, disturbs him, overwhelms him and reduces him to a feeling of shame. The gaze in question is certainly the presence of others as such. But does this mean that originally it is in the relation of subject to subject, in the function of the existence of others as looking at me, that we apprehend what the gaze really is? Is it not clear that the gaze intervenes here only in as much as it is not the annihilating subject, correlative of the world of objectivity, who feels himself surprised, but the subject sustaining himself in a function of desire? (Lacan 1979: 84–5)

Silverman (1992) interprets this to mean that 'if the gaze always exceeds the look, the look might also be said to exceed the gaze – to carry a libidinal supplement which relegates it, in turn, to a scopic subordination. The gaze, in other words, remains outside desire, the look stubbornly within' (p. 130). This may describe the relationship between the gaze Hyland is conscious of receiving – from the villagers, the woman and himself – and the fascinated look he directs at the woman's body. His inability to meet the gaze that takes him to be '*médecin*' or 'white man', and the inability of the villagers to modify their expectations of him, together produce a gap which exposes the desire in his look, and threatens to reveal the motives for his presence.

His response is repeated disavowal. The incident asks him, squarely, why he is there; and the only answer is that he is there to look. He cannot declare this, to the villagers or to the reader. With his refrain of '*Je ne suis pas médecin*' (what are you then?), he disavows responsibility, presenting himself as passive. He did not choose to go into the hut, but was made to do so. Even his bodily posture was not his own choice but was demanded of him by the roof. This defensiveness surrounds a moment in which his bluff as questing traveller has been called. Here is what he has come to see.

He has given it a mystifying title, 'the black heart', but it is matter-of-factly revealed to him: 'She peeled the cloth from her breasts.' The sentence could be a line of pornography, and the test he faces has a momentary, disturbing resemblance to a challenge to perform sexually. Her disrobing, or unveiling, puts a momentary end to deferment. Outer layers have been removed, one by one. Hyland has penetrated the jungle as far as this village, and entered the darkness of the hut. Now her clothes part to reveal a final surface which will not admit him.

This is the moment of truth which the quest-narrative ostensibly aims for, at which anticipation, speculation and fantasy are met with actuality. The longed-for or dreaded object materialises to present an impenetrable surface, a set of details, something that can be seen or touched. The risk of anti-climax is extreme, and quest-narratives traditionally protect these moments by disguising them and making them into absent centres, so that the traveller sees the object of the quest without recognising it. Only later, when it is no longer present for scrutiny, is its identity revealed.

If Hyland does correspond here to Lacan's figure surprised in the function of voyeur, what is the attraction that holds him? Julia Kristeva's principle of *abjection* raises some possibilities. Abjection is her term for the simultaneous horror and fascination prompted by that which is both self and other: that which was inside the self and is now outside. A primal instance of the abject is food spat out by a young child, or bodily waste expelled. These wastes become objects of disgust, but also draw the eye. They are both 'unapproachable and intimate'; the abject sets up 'a vortex of summons and repulsion'; it is 'above all ambiguity', 'a composite of judgement and affect, of condemnation and yearning' (Kristeva 1982: 6, 1, 9–10).

Kristeva sees abjection as having its origins in a pre-Oedipal rejection of the mother, a function of the earliest emergence of subjectivity. The disgust and panic aroused by the abject are 'safeguards', responses of recoil, jerking the subject back from its own boundaries. The part which has been expelled has a power of attraction which threatens to draw the remainder of the self after it, dissolving subjectivity: 'the jettisoned object, is radically excluded and draws me towards the place where meaning collapses ... And yet, from its place of banishment, the abject does not cease challenging its master ... it beseeches a discharge, a convulsion, a crying out' (p. 2).

Having been discharged, it beseeches that more matter should be discharged after it. Apertures in the body are prime sites of abjection: gaps, orifices, wounds. Abjection is horror at a mortality in which the body is permeable and will eventually itself become other and Object. The body in its entirety will eventually cross the border of the self to become waste, taking everything with it:

> There I am at the border of myself as a living being. My body extricates itself, as being alive, from that border. Such wastes drop so that I might live, until, from loss to loss, nothing remains in me and my entire body falls beyond the limit – *cadere*, cadaver. If dung signifies the other side of the border, the place where I am not and which permits me to be, the corpse, the most sickening of wastes, is a border that has encroached upon everything. It is no longer I who expel, 'I' is expelled. (Kristeva 1982: 3–4)

Depicted here is a consciousness which comes alive in moments of shocked and excited recognition. Kristeva's privileging of moments of overflow and revelation – of abrupt, stabbing sensation as evidence of life – is a late-Romantic enthusiasm for standing at thresholds. Her account of abjection celebrates the heroism of life at the border. This is a subjectivity menaced by the porousness of the self, its constant dissolution and re-formation, its material continuity with the world. Abjection is a horrified recoil from a self seen in connection with its own waste. The idea of the abject expresses a fascination with the expelled other, but not a willingness to reclaim that other as familiar and ordinary; the willingness that environmentalism, which asks us to take responsibility for waste, would require.

The abject is stared at fixedly but secretly. It excites because of its status as repressed and forbidden. Contact with it is loss of frontier between self and other. The self shuns this as a feared defilement. Hyland's eye is drawn to the woman's body, to its openings of breast and wound, to glimpses of its interior. His narrative eye zooms in then flinches. To see her he enters 'the shadows', stepping into the underworld, as if to be brought before a priestess out of Rider Haggard. Later, he emerges into sunlight, leaving the woman in 'the darkness' he still attributes, without irony, to Africa. In there she is like a secret, a thing kept, but kept locked away.

Hyland recognises his inability to keep her in light, in the space he too inhabits, where her body might cease to be a terrifying thing. Instead she is eroticised and seen only in dramatic glimpses. He concludes – and here there *is* apologetic irony – that 'The white man had spoken'. This is an echo of colonialism, but a relieved abdication of colonial power. Unwilling to take any post-colonial responsibilities, the 'white man' remains an aloof subject, but one now defined by helpless detachment, not authority.

One of Suzanne Kappeler's devices, in *The Pornography of Representation* (1986), for defamiliarising the pornographic objectification of women is to take John Berger's influential essay 'Why Look at Animals?' and substitute 'women' for 'animals' (pp. 63–81). She argues that women, as objects of male attention, have been assigned a cultural space similar to that given to animals. Taking my cue from Kappeler, and accepting her sense of continuum, I shall turn now to ways in which nature writing seeks and manages the sort of confrontation described above.

Nature writers are particularly well-defended in their encounters with attraction and repulsion. They are able to get close to foreignness using a number of pretexts or alibis: the highly specific quest of discovery, scientific neutrality, professional expertise, ecological emergency. All of these give the writer a genuine, often urgent reason, first for being there and then for stepping back and moving on.

Travel is one way of encountering otherness while avoiding its most disconcerting demands. Looking at animals is another. In each case, intensity is sought outside home, outside the protagonist's most daily and demanding forms of inter-subjectivity with others. The intensity discovered may be voyeuristic, entirely confined to that separate space: abroad not home, nature not civilisation, animals not people. If so, the result may be a safe release of accumulated desire, enabling the traveller to return to normality purged and relieved. But if the experience is not merely voyeuristic, then the boundaries between home and abroad, sympathy for animals and sympathy for people, will begin to dissolve – as environmentalism demands that they should. The experience will have changed the traveller.

Books about encounters with wild animals have been popular throughout the colonial and post-colonial period, but have received little literary critical analysis. The genre has strong historical links with colonialism. Romantic nature writing (such as the Wordsworthian, with its search for settings for sudden intimations of contact and continuity between self and world) could not be transferred unproblematically to the new colonial territories, since its yearnings for unselfconscious life in nature, and for the lost primitive self, compromised the clarity of its sense of colonial mission. But it could be bolstered with the methodical procedures of scientific classification, so that moments of awe became acceptable as pauses, moments at the end of the day or at the completion of tasks, thickly surrounded by accumulating data and by the anecdotal excitements of the expedition. This is the procedure both of a popular writer such as Du Chaillu, and of the serious scientific narratives of Charles Darwin. Colonial hunting stories, such as R. M. Ballantyne's *The Gorilla Hunters* (1869), opportunistically written to draw on Du Chaillu's popularity, attempt to intersperse occasional reflection with hectic adventure.

The disruptive potential of the Romantic sublime, the moment in which the infinite is glimpsed, was brought still further under control in Victorian and Edwardian books for boys which presented natural history as a manly outdoor pursuit, closely allied to hunting, and a natural preparation for work in the colonies. John MacKenzie (1988) observes that, under the influence of such narratives, 'the study of natural history [was] transformed into a whole system of youth training in the early twentieth century' (p. 48). A good illustration of the narrow space reserved for the contemplative sublime in this genre is an incident near the end of Sir Percy Fitzpatrick's *Jock of the Bushveld* (1907), a much-reprinted book of big-game hunting stories. The first-person narrator, who, with his dog Jock, has featured in numerous hunting exploits, tells us near the book's end of a time when, dozing in the bush, he wakes abruptly, aware of the presence of a magnificent waterbuck. The animal comes close enough to touch. The narrator has his rifle at hand, but: 'There was no thought of shooting ... Just to watch him: that was enough' (p. 444). The vulnerability of the Wordsworthian exposure to the infinite becomes here a complacent act of relinquishment; a gorged hunter graciously refusing one more kill. Even so, the moment becomes taut enough, the pressure of the scene's refusal to acknowledge his masterly presence severe enough, for him to shout, breaking the spell and frightening the buck away. Can the makers of *The Deer Hunter* have been influenced by *Jock of the Bushveld*?

Contemplation of the sublime is thus installed as due reward for a day's work done; the moment of fulfilment that marks the book's turning away from absorption in hunting, into denouement. The moment can stand, nevertheless, as representative of the turn, documented by MacKenzie, from hunting to conservation; illustrating the sometimes intimate connection between the two. Although nature writing was an obvious place for some of the first expressions of concern about ecological crisis to appear, and although it connects these concerns with some of the most radical elements in the Romantic tradition, it has also some long-established habits of containment.

Books of nature writing usually offer a mixture of travel writing, contemplation in the Romantic tradition (in Britain the Wordsworthian, in America the Thoreauvian), and scientific natural history. Wildlife writing encompasses early colonial narratives of exploration, stories of hunting, accounts of collectors' expeditions and environmentalist writing. Common to all these is the quest: for animals rumoured to exist, for the elusive, the rare, the exceptionally fierce or beautiful, the critically endangered species.

Traveller-narrators, exposing themselves to the isolation and discontinuity of self that travel brings, usually make a firm assertion of self from the outset, establishing a strong narrative voice. This is one of the generic attractions of travel writing. Animals do not threaten to interrupt this voice. They do not (or are not usually thought to) demand the range of responsibilities of the observer that people demand. They seem to allow the observer to look intimately at them from a position of self-contained subjectivity. Animals ask for no inter-subjectivity (or none that dominant Christian and Enlightenment traditions have been prepared to recognise). Whether the narrator's concern is to hunt them, discover and study them or save them, they give that narrator a distance and monologic authority which people, as the object of such attentions, would challenge.

A standard procedure of post-structuralist criticism is to look for binary structures: oppositions and encounters between any dominant subjectivity and its most powerful Other. The Other is a part of the self, a set of drives, needs or desires, which has been repressed to enable the subjectivity to take shape. This Other from within is projected on to various external others: other people, other races, other creatures.

Fascination and hope in these theories attaches to the prospect of some explosive return of this Other, or some possibility of crossing into space where the Other resides. For Freud this space is the unconscious, unreachable but able to send messages and phantom emissaries. For Kristeva the pre-Oedipal semiotic continues to erupt into the domain of the symbolic. For Bakhtin, the carnivalesque is potentially revolutionary because its licensed forms of riot may carry the crowd towards an irrevocable crossing of social boundaries. In all these cases, excitement grows as thresholds approach. Liminality is a source of intensity.

Michel Foucault has criticised what he calls 'the repressive hypothesis': the theory that Victorian rules governing sexuality, for example, were simply repressive. Foucault (1981) argues that such rules incite as well as repress, incitement and repression being parts of the same operation (pp. 3–49). The limits of the normal can be defined only if the transgressive is brought into being, displayed as spectacle. Radicalism and conservatism alike will direct their attention, hopefully or warningly, to the places outside these limits, the wild spaces roamed by what has been repressed at home. Radicalism fantasises hopefully, conservatism fearfully and vengefully, that this Other will cross the boundaries to return, but normativity requires that it should precisely remain in place, visible but outside the city limits.

Nature writing would seem to offer a classic instance of this positioning of 'wildness'. In the now emerging environmentalist literary criticism, or 'ecocriticism', much of the focus is on 'nature' held in place in this way. Ecology, however, is concerned not with purity and isolation but with inter-dependency and inter-penetration. An ecological vision sees the global ecosystem as a totality without sealed spaces. There is a debate in ecocriticism between those whose interest is primarily in wilderness as separate space, to be approached only with reverence and difficulty, and those who, while they have a place for this, are more concerned with things that cross boundaries.

Pollution is a malign crossing of boundaries, a return of the abject in harmful form. Commodification of the wild is more ambiguous. Bringing wildness into the midst of domestic space, in the form of writing and photographic or television images, means familiarising it, dispersing its aura, releasing it as a floating signifier which promiscuously acquires numerous meanings. Wildlife tourism, in its less rugged forms, means effortless travel into the midst of wilderness, which has the same effect. The wild becomes less wild, and the purist searches for true wildness further afield.

This debate is not quite the same as the one between 'deep ecology' and 'social ecology', or the one between environmentalists who value nature as an uncommodifiable space outside capitalism and those who are prepared to make use of the commodification of nature. But together these divisions reveal a central fault-line in contemporary environmentalism. I will look at some recent nature writing on either side of this division. Some holds the wild object of its quest at a distance, only to be seen in glimpses, while some moves beyond this deployment of erotic liminality, and begins to travel back and forth across boundaries, allowing the familiar to be strange and the strange familiar.

A good example of the first category is Rick Bass's *The Lost Grizzlies* (1995), which tells the story of three expeditions attempting to discover with certainty that there are still grizzly bears in the Colorado mountains, where they have been declared extinct since the 1970s. The quest is ambiguous, since it may be that the grizzlies' best chance of survival lies in remaining undiscovered. In achieving its end, the expedition may endanger the thing it craves: a neat materialisation of the characteristic paradox of quest literature. Desire is aroused by that which is rumoured and remote, and brought to a pitch of excitement by the proximity of the still-invisible object. The moment when that object comes into view, its unveiling, is the climax and the beginning of anti-climax. At that point begins the familiarisation of the desired thing, its conversion from rare to common.

A strong influence on Bass's book, given explicit homage in the narrative (Bass 1995: 40), is Peter Matthiessen's *The Snow Leopard* (1979), another search for a rare mountain-creature. Famously, Matthiessen avoids the problem of anti-climax by never seeing the snow leopard, though there are several charged moments when he feels he is about to see it. The word never becomes flesh. Matthiessen's other 'search' is for his recently dead wife, and, in its refusal to materialise, and the diffuse and constant presence it has because it does not pin itself to a particular place and time, the snow leopard at moments seems to stand for her; Matthiessen's acceptance of its non-appearance signals a new stage of his bereavement. Redmond O'Hanlon, similarly, sets out ostensibly in search of a creature he never finds: the probably extinct Borneo rhinoceros in *Into the Heart of Borneo* (1984), or the legendary Congo dinosaur *Mokélé-mbembé* in *Congo Journey* (1996). These creatures provide a never-to-be-reached threshold which draws the traveller on, away from things which might detain him.

Bass does eventually see a grizzly, however, and therefore has to find a different technique to avoid the conversion of the longed-for thing into a familiar thing. He uses an absent centre. When he sees the bear he does not recognise it, or does not dare to know what it is. He has just noticed some deer which seem uneasy:

A great wind-weathered fallen fir-tree lies on its side halfway between me and the skittery does, which are now only thirty yards away. When I am ten yards from that fallen tree – which I am all but ignoring, focusing on the deer – a creature leaps up from behind it, seemingly right in my face, a brown creature with great hunched shoulders. It's a bear with a big head, and for the smallest fraction of time our eyes meet. (Bass 1995: 214)

The word 'bear' is delayed for a sentence, and the all-important word 'grizzly' comes two pages later, long after the bear has gone. Once the animal is absent, it can be named; already, even minutes later, it is protected from loss of mystique. Did he really see it?

The searchers' approach to bear territory has been marked by stages of initiation. Moving from the suburbs into the foothills, they pass through zones of increasing alienation from the urban and domestic. In the outer circles of wildness they are depressed by litter, and by the mere presence of hikers. Further in, they enter a high meadow reached only by climbing down a dangerous rock chimney. Such a place should be pristine, but to their dismay they find a hunter's glove, possibly dropped from the air. This small out-of-place object, abruptly appearing from another world without initiation, has the power of a taint or defilement. What they thought of as wild space suddenly is not. 'I look at him as if to say, We did not get far enough in' (p. 58). A similar uncanniness attends objects from the wild which are encountered in urban space – particularly a bear's head, perhaps a grizzly's, in a town bar (pp. 75–7). By insisting that boundaries should not be easy to cross, the writing reinforces the duality between wild and familiar spaces.

'We did not get far enough in.' Distance, in or out, becomes a pre-occupation. Another meeting with a grizzly, in Bass's *The Book of Yaak* (1996), elicits the repeated exclamation, 'Too close; too damn close … We were all too damn close' (pp. 56–7). Getting too close could mean death for the man or for the bear; and the paradox, again, is that if the searchers succeed in establishing that grizzlies are present, they will then argue that the animals should be approached as little as possible. 'If we find the bears – *when* we find them – we must turn our backs and walk away' (Bass 1995: 56). Once contacted, the grizzlies are to remain positioned as wild and unfamiliar, beyond the boundary.

Liminality registers in marks and traces which indicate that humans, or bears, are near. The grizzlies' proximity becomes tangible in a number of signs: spoor, claw-marks, skulls, bedding-litter, hairs, scats (excrement). Absence vies with presence in the aura of these objects, which the explorers make into totems. The signs are at first equivocal and later more certain, until, on the penultimate expedition, the party gets near enough to hear the warning teeth-clicking of a group of bears, which still do not show themselves (p. 151). After Bass has finally seen the bear, its receding presence also is marked by traces. He finds three huge scats, still moist, which he carries back for identification purposes (pp. 221–2). Each scat is a tablet brought down from the mountain, a token of the bear and a reclaimed portion of the abject, which Bass is prepared to handle with the intimacy he was unable to extend to the animal itself.

The desire of Bass's expedition to encounter these rare creatures is flirtatious. The men want to see the bear, but they want seeing it to be difficult, to be promised and denied, to be anticipated and remembered rather than held in the present. Intermediary objects, things that have touched the bear, are caressed and examined with an intensity displaced from the animal itself, which remains in position across the boundary. In the case of the grizzly bear, the reasons for all this are eminently practical, but Bass is showing a typical formation of desire in nature writing, and in the culture of wildlife conservation.

Another device which marks boundaries and zones of transition on wildlife expeditions is the ordeal, early in the journey, which initiates the traveller into what is presented as a necessary hardness. Sometimes this involves witnessing human suffering, sometimes animal suffering. Either way, the message is that if the journey is to continue the traveller must accept the position of passive onlooker, unable to intervene.

Annie Dillard foregrounds the absence, in herself, of an expected emotional response. In an Ecuadorian village she sees a trussed deer awaiting the pot, injuring itself in its struggles. Dillard describes this as 'a sight which shocked the men' (Morris and O'Connor 1994: 417). These men, her North American travel-companions, expect her to show the feminine responses of pity and distress. She refuses to allow herself to be so constructed by their gaze. 'If it had been my wife,' says one man, 'she would have dropped *everything* … she would not have *stopped* until that animal was out of its suffering' (p. 420).

Dillard offers no argument in the face of this scolding, but implicit in her passive response is the suggestion that it is precisely her gendered knowledge of hardship and suffering that governs her reaction to the deer. Her recognition of priorities is clearer than that of the self-indulgent men, who displace their sense of responsibility on to an idea of femininity, thus preserving their own emotional distance while criticising Dillard for main-taining hers. Dillard hints that her close understanding of nature has made her philosophical about certain kinds of suffering – and she is conscious of the limits imposed by her position as cultural tourist.

In aid, she calls up the memory of a press report about a man named Alan McDonald who, twice in his life, suffered traumatic burns (pp. 420–1). The challenge posed by the deer is made small, trumped by a larger suffering safely remote in a press cutting. Such shuffling of the atrocity pack indicates her unease; as does the intensity with which her description searches the animal's body. Dillard seems to feel the readers' inquiring gaze. As if in compensation, to reassure us of her capacity to be affected, she offers an excessive response to the more distant case, telling us that she reads the clipping every morning.

Hyland moved on. Dillard dwells longer, considering the problem, but evades its particular claims by invoking suffering as a generality. The puzzle of her absence of feeling about the deer is subsumed in the larger mystery of all suffering. Job-like but finally coy, she breaks off with a rhetorical question: 'Will someone please explain to Alan McDonald in his dignity, to the deer in Providencia in his dignity, what is going on? And mail me the carbon' (pp. 421–2).

If you are not going to intervene, your expression of feelings should be kept to a minimum: that seems to be the requirement of honesty for both Dillard and Hyland. Yet the way each spectacle becomes the core of the piece of writing belies this resolution. The surfaces presented by suffering – the woman's breast, the deer's neck – are searched as if for some special detail, some opening, that will bring to life the onlooker's feeling. Data are stored, to be searched again when the event is at a safe distance, or to be passed on, almost without comment, to the reader. Absent, exiled, fantasised feeling activates these passages. Both narrators decline to give any emotional lead, save, in Dillard's case, a negative one hinting at what we too should not allow ourselves to feel. The space left vacant by the narrator's passivity becomes space the reader is under pressure to fill.

A similar effect occurs near the beginning of Redmond O'Hanlon's *Congo Journey*. I have already cited his use of improbable, perhaps mythical quest-objects which are never found. But O'Hanlon finds ways of acknowledging impasse and keeping himself open to a diversity of responses.

He is travelling up the Congo by steamer, on the first stage of his journey into the interior, when he witnesses the capsizing of a canoe attempting to dock at the steamer's side. A teenage boy is carried away by the current, presumably to drown. The disaster happens quickly, so that O'Hanlon is more clearly helpless to intervene than were Hyland and Dillard. Perhaps (to be severe) this is why he allows himself to become more agitated than they do. He receives a lecture from his Congolese companion:

> 'So he's drowned,' said Marcellin, looking out across the water at a village on the opposite bank. 'This is the best-governed country in Africa, our people are the best educated. There's no war, no famine. But it's still Africa. Where you're going we'll hear wailing women all day long. If you make a

fuss like that every time someone dies, my friend, you won't last. You'll be wasting my time. We won't complete our mission.' (O'Hanlon 1996: 79)

This is Africa, and Africa signifies a harsh reality of irrevocable material events. The correct response for the western visitor, it is urged here, is a mental toughening, a closing of the portals of emotional sympathy, since this sympathy can only be self-indulgence and self-flattery. With his authority as an African, Marcellin insists that the experience must be treated as an initiation into the realities of African life. Against Marcellin's adulthood, O'Hanlon's demands for action and rescue are cast as childish (Marcellin 'pulled me against him like an errant child').

O'Hanlon happily represents himself as unheroic and childish throughout. His declared motive for going to the Congo (apart from *Mokélé-mbembé*) is that he is searching for a world glimpsed in childhood, in books of African birds, when he crept into the forbidden territory of his father's study (p. 13). While the mild Freudianism and country-parsonage cosiness of this are disarming (and the story has an air of fabrication in any case), it does register his quest as both a reconstruction of childish adventure and a search through ordeal for an adult world into which he can finally cross. He never does so, but moves back and forth.

His writing is in a comic travel writing tradition. Gerald Durrell achieved popularity as the naturalist as clown. Eric Newby, in *A Short Walk in the Hindu Kush* (1958), was the public-school Englishman getting into unlikely scrapes but retaining an absurd composure and thereby domesticating the most exotic and frightening situations. Jerome K. Jerome's Edwardian comedy of the Englishman abroad seems also to be somewhere in the background. The tale of O'Hanlon's Amazon journey appears under the old-fashioned schoolboy-story title *In Trouble Again* (1988). His books mock and ruefully celebrate his charmed life, his capacity to walk into terrifying situations, his habit of dragging more dignified friends along with him.

O'Hanlon puts this tradition to unusual effect. The childishness or clowning he willingly attributes to himself as a westerner abroad enables him to refuse the toughening demanded of him, without claiming any superiority in his refusal. He is not intimidated, by the authenticity of the natives, into adopting their viewpoint about suffering, but neither does he claim priority for his own. The implication is that their attitude has authority as an outcome of their experience; but his experience has been different and entails different responsibilities.

An episode in *Into the Heart of Borneo* (1984) is strikingly similar to Hyland's ordeal. Like Hyland, O'Hanlon is called into a dark hut to look at a woman's injury, in this case a horribly poisoned foot. He too looks into

the wound's opening, and holds his focus for longer than Hyland, attempting to fight back his aversion and familiarise what he sees. Outside the hut
he wavers and seems seriously to consider abandoning his journey in order
to get the woman to hospital (pp. 108–10), but as his guides and the other
Iban villagers discuss this, asserting its impracticality, the possibility
recedes. Between O'Hanlon's raw, appalled response, with its fantasy of
providing rescue, and the courteous pragmatism of the villagers, there is
impasse. The arguments are broken off rather than resolved, but O'Hanlon
does not hurry away like Hyland, or appeal rhetorically to his creator like
Dillard. With O'Hanlon there is a sense that such conversations will always
be resumed.

The childish persona enables O'Hanlon to display a wide-eyed sexual
curiosity, which, in a traditional colonial move, positions indigenous people
as exciting body revealed to O'Hanlon's naive but masterly mind – but also
begins to expose the vulnerabilities and desires which have brought
O'Hanlon to Borneo or the Congo. In *Into the Heart of Borneo* he develops
a deliciously horrified fascination for the *palang*, a bamboo pin driven
crosswise into the penis to increase the woman's pleasure. In *Congo Journey*
this interest is momentarily transferred to the rigid penis-bone of the
angwantibo bushbaby. In both books O'Hanlon is a marvelling spectator and
chronicler of the sexual exploits of his native guides. Their sexual vitality
and promiscuity is further evidence of their materiality and mortality. When
it comes to his own body, however, he is comically frightened of all forms
of penetration: by leeches, chiggers and other insects, snakes, grotesque
foods. Such flirting with nightmares abruptly changes into real panic when
he has to share a bed with his promiscuous companions and becomes
terrified that the bed bugs and floor-maggots may be carriers of HIV
(O'Hanlon 1996: 319–21, 340–44). The threat rears up that Africa will do
something irrevocable to him, absorb him, enter his body, never let him go.
Material presence seems to mean vulnerability; in finally arriving, and being
made flesh, he will become mortal and penetrable. A memory comes of his
friend Bruce Chatwin, another famous traveller, who died of AIDS.

Chatwin's apparition increases O'Hanlon's agitation, then gradually
calms him. The dead friend as dream-figure brings memories of home and
restores O'Hanlon's sense of continuity with life in England. Chatwin's
AIDS, we are told, was first diagnosed because of a rare infection con-
tracted on his travels, but that was only the first *evidence*: the AIDS itself
may have been caught at home or abroad. O'Hanlon is reassured that the
membrane of Englishness he carries everywhere is still unbreached, but at
the same time he is denied his familiar trick of using this Englishness as
a refuge from adulthood and mortality. Mortality becomes a presence in
his Englishness. This is the climax and passing of his panic.

It would be trite for this to be identified as the 'heart', or the great lesson that Africa teaches him. O'Hanlon is not exultant in this way (the main weakness of his tone is that in its comic or frantic breathlessness it has too little space for solemnity). Although his narratives are loosely constructed around a goal and a destination, O'Hanlon repeatedly breaks this orientation. He has frequent impulses to branch off on another trip, and *Congo Journey* ends in urgent reiterations of its old unanswered questions. There is little attempt at staged or ritualistic withdrawal from the wild territory: only, as a sort of decompression chamber, a hotel room still up-river where O'Hanlon finds himself, all his money spent, still arguing.

The token he brings back into domestic space is not a tablet, or a scat standing in for a living thing, but neither is it human and engaging of the fullest responsibilities. It is a baby gorilla, given to O'Hanlon after native hunters have killed its mother. O'Hanlon brings it out of the forest to hand it over to a wildlife refuge. He is here following, and attempting to correct, the example left by Du Chaillu, whose *Explorations and Adventures in Equatorial Africa*, concerned with the same region, lies behind this book as much as does Conrad or Darwin. Du Chaillu records that he attempted several times to keep baby apes captured by his expedition, all of which soon died (Du Chaillu 1861: 205–10, 243–4, 260–1, 283–8). O'Hanlon's gorilla survives, against expectations, apparently because of the fiercely protective care he lavishes on it, hugging it to his body and allowing it to soak his shirt with diarrhoea. He does this in defiance of the opinions of his African team-mates. Marcellin says, 'Really the whites are terrible. They brought the guns here and now they say don't kill your wildlife. They're cruel one minute, sentimental the next' (O'Hanlon 1996: 392). O'Hanlon does not deny this; his clinging to the baby animal is an acknowledged perversity, a flagrant act of tokenism, a boyish parody of motherhood and, in a small, circumscribed way, a willingness to be touched.

I have discussed these books out of a desire to find a sense of possibility in the genre of nature writing; what has perhaps emerged is its comparative conservatism and timidity. I would like to close by contrasting the resources available to recent television documentary in this area, which offers an extraordinary richness of visual images while allowing the observer to seem disembodied. The more intimate the camera becomes with the creatures filmed, achieving viewpoints impossible for any human body to occupy, the more the human viewer ceases to be part of the spectacle, or to feel responsibility for it. The animals appear oblivious to the presence of the camera; the television viewer's emotional response to the animals does not become an object of scrutiny, because the camera eye remains disembodied and clearly differentiated from that of any visible presenter.

But nature writing, so far, seems only able to effect this disembodying trick by becoming impersonal, scientific and undramatic: a relapse into an anachronistic posture of the Linnaean taxonomist, now acceptable only in the form of pastiche. If the writer does not accept these conditions, but wishes to offer the pleasures of narrative, the travelogue must contain a narrating consciousness whose emotions will be included in the spectacle. The implied phenomenology is one not only of the intrusive egotism of the voyager but also of a kind of impertinence of language itself; the exemplary attitude would be one in which wildlife would have no significance in human discourse, but simply remain separate and for itself.

**Part IV**

# Postmodern Travelogue

# The Road to Brixton Market: A Post-colonial Travelogue

Gabriel Gbadamosi

There are zones in London where the unspoken rules of traffic are suspended and you go with a different flow, or get stopped to wait for someone's conversation on the street. Go up Coldharbour Lane, especially in summer, Electric Avenue or Atlantic Road, and you enter the Bermuda Triangle of Brixton market, one of those places where you pass from the fluent curses of the London traffic to the stop–start acceleration of shouts in the street, stand–offs and stylish getaways. As the road slips from mainstream London road culture it hits an interchange with the pulse of Jamaican street life, the go–slows of Lagos.

The other day a Jamaican friend came back from Atlanta and we cruised through Brixton in a monster Mercedes with cool tunes and bass, the one-way ride out of the ghetto. You can create your own sense of place, give your life a new kind of movement. You can live large. And not only movement, but the way people communicate with each other changes. There is a buzz of community, of jostling preachers, socialist newspaper sellers, street vendors and hustlers, an exchange and display of often very singular identities. But don't bump black man's car in Brixton because, along with the altered sense of place, the quality of road rage changes in the traffic jams of spoken and unspoken cultures.

Put your foot down hard on the accelerator and the road to Brixton market pulls London, Africa and the Caribbean into itself, eating up the distances between them as shouts, traffic signs and pumping music get blurred and pulled apart, or merged, by fast cars accelerating into the wind. Before we jump a red light – and bump hard words – what's going on? In order to stop and look I need to bring my post-colonial travelogue through Brixton market into focus by turning to the fieldnotes and journals of the large-scale migrations at the end of empire that brought people here. And I need to negotiate the fluid borders of genre, from factual biography to fictionalised accounts of that movement, in beginning to read the signals of and responses to movement among people making sense of their experience in a new place.

Things happen to words in the context of movement. They go underground, as in this example from Sam Selvon's novel of post-war migration to Britain from Africa and the Caribbean, *Lonely Londoners*. It describes Sir Galahad's, alias Henry Oliver Esquire's, response to being newly arrived in London from Trinidad while travelling to the Bayswater area on the tube:

> 'The only thing,' Galahad say when they was in the tube going to the Water, 'is that I find when I talk smoke coming out my mouth.'
>
> 'Is so it is in this country,' Moses say. 'Sometimes the words freeze and you have to melt it to hear the talk.'
>
> 'That is a old, old one,' Galahad say. (Selvon 1985: 35)

But an old irony can run new subtexts of migrant experience in cold climates: being frozen out of conversations, losing your ability to speak, fuming till the smoke comes out of your mouth. Rage is in the subtext. Sir Galahad's uncertainty, his apprehension of dragonish obstacles to the quest for a new life in this country – not least the cold welcome from Moses with which the novel opens – together with the note of experience in Moses's cryptic redeployment of an old saw to fit a loose, newly-arrived Caribbean jaw to the socially frozen one of 'this country' on the tube, are two responses to movement. Rage, although held in check by the broadly comic fabric and episodic structure of Sam Selvon's novel, is also a response to that experience of the social 'melting pot' of cosmopolitan London. But rage is anti-social if it ends in a crash, and to be avoided in negotiating the new, unspoken rules of the road – in making sense of what Moses Aloetta experiences at the end of the novel as a dark epiphany of migration, 'a great aimlessness, a great restless, swaying movement that leaving you standing in the same spot' (p. 141).

In the literatures of migration and travel that accompany the end of empire, there is often a feeling of dislocation, disorientation, the frustration of movement, of being wound up with finding that time stopped with decolonisation and its disappointments and the whole thing's a bust like a sprung watch mechanism. A post-colonial travelogue demands new rules of the road – new geographies and readings, points of departure, trajectories of meaning, enigmas of arrival. It needs some balance and perspective to keep, as the British would say, its sense of humour, as Sam Selvon does for Moses in his novel. Before then it hardly knows whether it's coming or going, much less on what passport. Bombing round Nigeria by taxi, a commission in his pocket from a British publisher, Adewale Maja-Pearce's *In My Father's Country* (1987), subtitled *A Nigerian Journal*, explores a double irony in ideas of travelogue and identity:

For many years after I left Nigeria I didn't admit to anyone that I couldn't speak my father's language. It was like a dark, shameful secret which cast doubt on my 'Africanness'. The matter was further complicated by the fact that I was, after all, half English ... But in England I was taken to be a foreigner. I was continually being asked where I was from. I would invariably say Nigeria; but it would have been equally accurate, in some ways more so, if I had said England. That I didn't was telling. By rejecting my Englishness, I was colluding in a subtle form of racism. (Maja-Pearce 1987: 14–15)

Adewale is known to me as an editor for the Heinemann African Writers series, Africa correspondent for *Index on Censorship* and a fellow Nigerian Englishman (though *his* English is Scots and mine Irish). A difference that fascinates: he was brought up in Lagos, I'm from London. So I pay special attention when, even ironically, he enters that dark territory of identity: Who are you? Where are you going? What do you have to say? How, beyond racisms, across cultures, do you locate and orient your life?

Language, in Adewale's account, frames a gnawing anxiety about his 'Africanness'. This is an old bone – the dog's sincere, but the plastic's inauthentic. And I don't think Adewale means to accept an essentialist position on 'Africanness' any more than one on 'Englishness'. Rather, I want to crack it between us – by kola nut as the Nigerians would say – by linking language to another, more closely related, facet of what seems to boil down to cultural identity: food. Adewale himself gives a clue in recounting 'a popular refrain' chanted by children in Nigeria (in English) at him and his brothers:

> *Oyinbo* pepper,
> If you eat pepper
> You go yellow more more.
>
> (Maja-Pearce 1987: 15)

*Oyinbo*, he recalls, means 'white man': you ate *white man* pepper and you and your skin turned yellow. Actually what it means in the mouth of an adult is those people that have this colour skin. It's amusing. But what's interesting here is a curiously childlike idea that by eating certain foods you not only change your skin colour but you actually change who you are – it makes you a 'white man'. Food does intersect with cultural identity. For culture, who doesn't know that food is up there, with language?

The point is made, with a child's precision, in Jane Tapsubei Creider's autobiographical account of a Nandi childhood in Kenya, *Two Lives: My Spirit and I* (1986). In one chapter, 'Life on a British Farm', she and her family find themselves fleeing British expansionism. It is the children (not the adults) who mix with the other refugee peoples driven out by the

British – Masai, Sebei, Teso and so on – and arriving among the Luyia. The Mount Elgon Masai, she finds, 'spoke a language which was almost like Nandi, but with a very strong accent and with many different words' (p. 42). She calls them 'half-and-half Nandi' and pities them because 'they can't talk like real people' (p. 42). They are, nevertheless, a cultural and linguistic bridge between the Nandi and the surrounding Luyia, who, to her horror, eat fish: 'A fish is a small snake. They get it from the water alive, kill it, cook it and eat it with porridge' (p. 41). She describes how one day she asks some Masai children a question: '"How do you eat? Do you have a problem eating because of your accent?" "No ... we eat just fine"' (p. 42), (a Canadian transliteration, she says in the acknowledgements, of her Nandi syntax). She sets them a test of eating 'a sour, lemon-like fruit'. She and her brother notice two things: earrings shaking in a little girl's ears – the sourness of the fruit – and that 'they talked when they had food in their mouths (something we wouldn't do)' (p. 42). The language of food is how these children tell people apart from themselves. What's at stake is made very clear: 'In my mind, anyone who was not a Nandi was not a real human being. I would always feel pity for such people' (1986: 40). Given the context of these encounters, this is a language of 'ethnic cleansing' allied to the hygiene of Nandi dietary rules. This is the pity, palatable in a child, which now perplexes the world in the so-called 'ethnic clashes' in East and Central Africa, amounting to pitiless genocide in Rwanda.

I want, then, to take refuge in an alternative account of food, language and identity by looking at life in a British market over the last twenty-five years. Moving away from the aggressive, colonial expansionism of the farm, I want to claim the British market to which both my parents came as migrants, on the eve of the post-colonial settlement in Africa, as the site of more fluid exchanges between cultures. Life in such a market is, for me, mediated by relations of affection (the earrings shaking in a little girl's ears; my parents found each other) rather than tolerance – an official policy of extracting the wealth from a 'multi-culturalism' secured by strict immigration controls. For me a street market's the place where you can go and forget your troubles on a Saturday afternoon in among the crowded colours of the food stalls. Because my parents were happy in each other there. I love walking in a *London* street market because it's full of Londoners: Irish, West Indian, Indian, African and, among others, some English, too. This is *my* post-colonial travelogue.

My first market was Lambeth Walk, made 'world famous' by the song and dance of the same name, 'Doing the Lambeth Walk, Hey!', and a post-war 'mass observation' study of typical working-class British society. I remember walking along, a typical Celtic Yoruba, at four or five or six, saying to my mum I didn't like cabbage, I didn't want cabbage, I wouldn't eat cabbage …

'Look at the rats. *They're* healthy. Eat your cabbage.'

'I hate cabbage. I don't want … What rats?'

'The ones with sleek, glossy black coats – from eating the cabbage stumps they throw in the gutter. It's good for you. Eat up your cabbage.'

Which is the story of how she never got me to eat cabbage (except disguised in an Irish stew) and despaired at the unending struggle to make her children's hair sleek, glossy and black. Black hair was beyond her. With six happy, healthy, cabbage-eating babies, she never knew how to take care of the tangled African mops that always ended up going to the (Maltese) barber.

Please imagine my relief when the 1970s came in with the 'Afro' hairstyle (and my relief when it went out). The 1960 were a time for me when street markets sold solid English cabbages, my hair and skin went unoiled and I hadn't yet read Simi Bedford's *Yoruba Girl Dancing* (1991) in which *she too* describes having her hair cut in Lagos – before leaving for boarding school in Britain – because *they* won't know how to oil it. Imagine the scene, now in Britain, trussed up in a winter hat and coat and being taken along for a fitting for the new school uniform. The hat and coat have to come off:

> There was a slight gasp from the saleswoman and we all stared at my reflection in the looking-glass. I was a frog on stilts, pink medallions decorated my arms and legs where I had scratched the skin from my bites, and already in the crisp English air my skin had become dry and grey and flaky. My hair no longer resembled a snug fitting velvet cap; unoiled, it looked as if it had been hurriedly knitted onto my head with many dropped stitches where my scalp showed through. (Bedford 1991: 66)

When Lambeth Walk closed down, we moved (along with the Pie & Mash shop) to Brixton market with its gaudy-coloured covered arches arranged into 'Avenues' (1st, 2nd, 3rd … ) and open-air food and second-hand clothes stalls. As an area, Brixton has seen waves of immigrants, mainly from the West Indies and, more recently, Africa. In addition, it attracted the 'local colour' of a variety of subcultures: artists, students, the downwardly mobile, the very poor and a British prime minister as an upwardly mobile Conservative councillor. As a market, I've seen it change over the last twenty-five years from selling fruit & veg of the mainly cabbage kind to dealing in foods from Asia, Africa and the West Indies. When I remember Simi Bedford's 'frog on stilts', and me in the barber's mirror like a slump-town rat, I see in Brixton market a rich detritus; a narrative connecting cabbage stumps to oiled, glossy black hair and young south London traders' accents to the flirting *patois* of elderly West Indian ladies: a more mixed and healthy diet for the cultures and identities it nourishes.

One Saturday afternoon I made a list of some of the foods to be found. Here it is: cassava, yam (many kinds), mango, ackee (poisonous before it's ripe), sweet potato, sugar cane (six-footers), choochoo (cristafine, from Costa Rica), water coconut, ewedu (my sister's favourite), egusi (melon seed), horse eye (a hard soup nut), goat's feet, pig's trotters (for Irish stew), tilapia (east African fish), salt-fish, palm-oil, kola nut (red and green, they get you high), plantain, ogerie tola (from Sierra Leone) *and* two teas:

### SOROSIE HERB
Good for: Blood Pressure, Purifying blood,
Nerve settling & restoring appetite

### MINT TEA
Good for: Upset stomach, feel bad stomach,
making tea

Perhaps the prize find was the plantain imported from the West Indies, being sold under the Ghanaian name *apim* to all and sundry by East African Asians. I also found tins of corned beef, used for making *moi moi* with black-eyed beans (a Nigerian dish my mum used to make and I used to love), which set me wondering, whatever happened to corned beef? Something that went out with post-war austerity, I suppose. But, the point is, hasn't the British diet changed? Not to mention the kiwi-fruit and avocados I didn't think to list but don't remember being around in my salad days. If I celebrate Brixton market it's because this diversity nourishes me.

Since the 1970s in Britain, I seem to have lived through a series of end-on-end economic recessions (having missed out on the yuppie-boom of the 1980s). Sometimes, the only thing booming in Brixton seems to be the second-hand clothes market. If post-war reconstruction and optimism brought one wave of immigrants, world-wide recession seems to have brought another. Where I became used to hearing and distinguishing the many forms of Caribbean *patois*, I might now as easily hear Ibo, Asante or the roundly indistinct 'r' of Sierra Leone. What's more, West Indian *patois* has now developed its own British variants, cut round my way with a Kent accent. Where, before, I might have thought to travel to find my Yoruba or Irish cultural routes out of the south London poverty trap, I now find the world is *here*, and rich. Brixton, where I live, is a source for me in writing about *my* culture: African, British, Irish, Black. I can, and do, travel; but I can stay here and chart my knowledge of these streets.

Once, the term *been-to* was used in West Africa to debunk the hauteur of the 'bantu' who had 'been to' Europe, for qualifications, commerce or pleasure. Now it might be more to the point to introduce the term *been-back*, as in: Have you been back to Africa? Presumably to refresh oneself at the springs of cultural authenticity. The point is, people are now *here*; working here, living here, being here. Many never go back. This is a major shift, part demographic, part cultural. It is part of a still larger pattern of exchanges and transformations towards the end of this century affecting the language, identity and work of many 'Africans', including writers. Language is no longer (if it ever was) a guarantee of paternity so much as a map of influences and – why not? – choice of menus.

Diet and literacy, or food and books, are among the basic issues affecting our well-being and they figure largely in Biyi Bandele-Thomas's novel, *The Man Who Came In From the Back of Beyond* (1991). Biyi is a British-based Nigerian writer and the book was published in London. It is set in Nigeria, in Kafanchan, a railway junction town at the approximate geographical centre of the country. As a setting, Kafanchan might be read as being at the centre of a newly emerging *Nigerian* identity, having drawn to it peoples from all major ethnic groups at the height of its railway boom. Then again, it, along with its inhabitants, might simply be seen as slump-town marginalia to the rigidities of those ethnic groups, liminal to all of them. It was Biyi's home town before Brixton and is home to the novel's main protagonist, David, alias Bozo. Conflicting cultures in diet and education emerge at an interesting moment in the book when Mrs Abednego, David's mother, a Catholic, buys a box at auction that turns out to contain books: 'nothing but books. Books and books and books and books. Oh, David, she had thought gleefully to herself, here's your food' (p. 37).

The food hamper turns out to be a Pandora's box of knowledges subversive of her own Catholicism, all of which David reads. A sample of its contents includes: Sadducean theses against the authenticity of Christ's resurrection (imagine!); Greek atheists, Democritus and Leucippus; the Roman, Titus Lucretius Carus; and the works of Arius (Christ a similar, not one, substance with God).

The result: David, alias Bozo, 'voluntarily ex-communicated himself' (p. 37), a moment recalling James Joyce's *Stephen Hero* in Stephen's struggle against the 'strong and intricate' tyranny of his Catholic Jesuit education (p. 134). The struggle here's with 'food': a change in diet, and something 'disagrees'.

It's a feature of post-colonial literatures, this 'mixed diet' of cultures and educations, most clearly seen in symptomatic crises of language-use and identity. Biyi's novel has more to say on the point of educational constipation in bouts of verbal diarrhoea. Mrs Abednego is talking with

Mr Abednego about David, alias Bozo, alias, for his father, 'son-of-a-bitch':

> 'Little woman,' he would bellow in the fake British accent which he always
> adopted when conversing with anybody he considered intellectually below
> him. 'Little woman, you are mistaken, that son-of-a-bitch was born three
> months before independence. I should know better; I am his father.'
>
> 'Abed … ' Mrs Abednego would begin.
>
> 'Call me Abe,' he would say.
>
> 'But you are not Abraham,' she would protest.
>
> 'You are stark illiterate,' he would tell her pompously. 'I finished my
> standard four, so I should know better than a bush woman like you.'
>
> 'OK, Ape,' she would say. (Bandele-Thomas 1991: 27)

Just to unpack this a little: 'I should know better' often means in Nigerian
English, 'I should know better, *and do*' – the opposite of what it usually
means in this country and, therefore, a mistake in Mr Abednego's 'fake
British' English. The irony's on him; a case of the emperor's twisted
underclothes. To stay with this image of clothing – another basic requirement along with food and literacy – Mr Abednego calls his wife 'stark
illiterate'. Coupled with the further accusation against her of being a 'bush
woman', it conjures an image of nakedness: to be uneducated is, in a sense,
to be unclothed, uncivilised, in the bush, *stark naked*. In the novel Mr
Abednego is impotent – from the moment of seeing his wife naked and
bleeding, at the birth of David. His impotence barely clothed by language,
who is the 'bush' figure in the word rift of 'Abed' to 'Abe' to 'Ape'? Mr
Abednego's 'fake British' English constitutes a kind of bush tangling up
the 'Ape-ing' of him by his wife. As such it sustains a recognisable trope
of racism – the ape-bush figure – reduplicating itself through a standard
four education.

Where does this leave David, alias Bozo, in *his* struggle with upbringing
and education? Lost, preaching the subversive fare of revolution: 'He stood,
in a way, as a representative of the mood of his generation, an iconoclast,
a sceptic by societal osmosis, a cynic by experience, bitter in practice'
(p. 60). But, finding his feet when thinking of writing song lyrics, a rather
interesting realisation emerges of what kind of language to write in: 'In
pidgin of course, our real lingua-franca, the language of the ghetto' (p. 60).
Pidgin – referred to in Nigeria as more or less 'spicy' depending on its
ingredients and inventions – has become the 'stew', or scouse (perhaps, so
far, a 'bitter' one) out of which a new, Beatles-era consciousness is being
formed not only for the likes of Bozo in his liminal position in Kafanchan,
but potentially (excuse me as I leap out of the fiction) across West Africa,
and beyond.

Pidgin is by no means the only pot in which something is bubbling. Biyi, that other denizen of Kafanchan and London, has actually written a novel within a novel within a novel, using very disparate styles in an aggressive mastery, and deformation, of English idioms as well as pidgin. Full of syntactical fireworks, recherché vocabulary and *fun*, here's a shopping list on page 4, taken from a lesson (in English) on what is a simile:

'No you twittering idiot, it's not an oxymoron,' someone said.
'Metonymy.' 'No Pauline, it's a paradox.' 'You mean parable.' 'Shut up you two, it's a synecdoche.' 'It's an antithesis!' 'An antonomasia!' 'An apostrophe.' 'A denouement.' 'Litotes.' 'It's an epithet.' 'An alliteration.' 'A euphemism.' 'Rhetorics.' 'An aphorism.' 'An apothegm.' 'An onomatopoeia.' 'A hyperbole.' 'An assonance.'
Someone even called it a ballad.

Really it's a game with language everyone seems to be enjoying. Just to reinforce the point, Simi Bedford's *Yoruba Girl Dancing* (1991) opens with this observation: '"Africans can talk oh!" Aunt Rose often said. She was right, in our house we spoke four languages, and two of them were English' (p. 1).

Whatever the position, it's clear that 'African' writers have a mixed diet of languages. In languages of, perhaps, 'the ghetto', it has been possible, in the post-colonial context, to arrive at internationalist, even anti-nationalist, perspectives. Adewale's anxiety, with which this discussion began, at not speaking his father's language, belongs to a period politics of fomenting cultural nationalisms in Africa and elsewhere, which often reproduced in themselves conditions which underwrote the colonial project: a sweeping simplification and division of identities: divide and rule. His anxiety shadows the failures of the post-independence political order in Africa. On the other hand, eschewing the 'ethnic' authenticities (and certainties) of that order, particularly as part of the large-scale migrations of Africans to a diaspora, has given creative writers a more fluid, more cosmopolitan set of identities both for Africa internally and for Africans in the world. Let us accept that as our culture, we are being given a lot. Why should *any* writer seek to present credentials in a mother-tongue or a father's language in order to prove authenticity? If not using impeccable English allows an 'African' writer to escape having to represent impeccable Englishness rather than something more, so much the better.

Simi Bedford again makes the point. Her book *is* written in sharp, impeccable English. She describes the moment when, after six years of boarding school, her father pays a visit with his brother to see how an English education is going:

I put out my hand and looking from one to the other said brightly in my best English, 'How do you do, which one of you is my father?' …

'The transformation has been too complete,' said Uncle Yomi.

'I think so,' said my father …

But they would never know what it had cost me. (Bedford 1991: 130–1)

Yes, there has been a transformation – a major shift of *peoples*, along with language, culture and identity. Brixton market is my metaphor for attempting to trace in an information age complex web-sites of exchange, points of arrival and new departures, the strands of linguistic and cultural crossing, for people. Each person must find their own position on entering such a market and is, to some extent, free to make choices concerning their own experience and identity. Many things can go wrong when that market contracts, foreclosing on the pleasures and freedoms of exchange. World recession is something we will all have to count the cost of. One part of such a calculation has been described by Frantz Fanon in *Black Skin, White Masks*, first published in 1952, ironically stating the cost of a colonialism founded on the mono-culture of sugar-slavery: 'The Negro of the Antilles will be proportionately whiter – that is, he will come closer to being a real human being – in direct ratio to his mastery of the French language' (p. 18).

This fallacy cuts both ways, in respect of the African language as well as the European. It represents the death of markets in favour of savage monopolies on the languages available to 'real human beings'; a return to the xenophobic monologue.

Now, as Africa disappears from world geopolitical concerns, it's important to insist that Africa itself does not disappear. Africa is also *here*, in its diaspora, interacting with other presences in a context very different from the early modern slave societies of the Americas still today struggling out of that mistake. My question is, what new forms, what metaphors, might emerge to take us forward into the next century, beyond the 'third world' and 'cold war' ghosts of my childhood? I have not stopped listening because I need to know: what kinds of conversations are happening at bus stops on the road to Brixton market?

# Bruce Chatwin: Connoisseur of Exile, Exile as Connoisseur

David Taylor

In 1985 Bruce Chatwin and Paul Theroux followed a venerable imperial tradition by lecturing at the Royal Geographical Society on their respective visits to Patagonia. Before embarking on a characteristically rich selection of anecdotes, Chatwin (1993) asserted that 'if we are travellers at all, we are literary travellers. A literary reference or connection is likely to excite us as much as a rare animal or plant' (p. 7). It may be objected that this would apply equally well to virtually any travel writer since Mandeville (see von Martels 1994), but Chatwin's infusing of physical terrain with romance connotations remains striking. Even so tendentious a thesis as the influence of Anthony Mundy's 1596 translation of Primaleon of Greece on both the Spanish explorer Magellan and Shakespeare, with references to the monstrous Patagon that inspired the creation of Caliban, establishes a kind of parity between different temporal and literary realms that allows moves between them to be governed by something akin to an intellectual pleasure principle.

Paul Theroux similarly speculates that the descriptions of the 'Big-Feet' giants in the 1519–22 journal of Antonio Pigafetta influenced the language of *The Tempest*; but the somewhat irascible ambience of his work lacks the supple fabulation and numinal intensities of Chatwin's prose. The belligerence and condescension of Theroux's persona have regularly been cited by post-colonial criticism as evidence that 'travel narrows' (Clifford 1997: 355n; see also Pratt 1992: 217–21; Caesar 1995: 205n). Chatwin's reception has been much more hospitable, arguably grossly sycophantic, but the implications of his permanent formal strategy of fragmentary, strangely uncoordinated gatherings of data remain to be assessed.

The charge must be addressed that Chatwin's texts are generically continuous with the taxonomies of the colonialist, and that their crystalline felicities serve as the equivalent to an ethnographic neocolonialism for a post-colonial world. From this perspective, his writing explicitly transposes the connoisseur's acquisitive gaze from auction house on to geographical space; and a continual erasure of context renders neutral the status of all objects and events in an idiosyncratic project that reifies and possesses the odd, the arcane and the eccentric. A rhetoric of apparent diversity is ultimately in the service of a phenomenology of dominance that the recurrent nomadic motif does little or nothing to abate.

In this chapter, I wish to counter such an indictment by stressing the conscious anachronism of Chatwin's persona of connoisseur, the redemptive potentialities of his aestheticist stance, and his complex embrace of a postmodern ethics of exile. This cannot, however, be equated with a contemporary ideal of transnational nomadism common to both travel and writing (Kaplan 1996), credulously endorsing Chatwin's own dubious ethnographic theorising and calculated biographical self-promotion. A large proportion of his travelling remains undocumented; indeed, the available versions of his life have caused disputes centring on the degree of myth-making of much commentary and anecdote: his eyesight, for example, has been repeatedly emphasised as both disability (resulting in a temporary bout of blindness) and almost talismanic power (the collector's 'Eye' celebrated in 'The Bey'). The development of this persona of celebrity-traveller and its transposition to his writing is closely bound up with Chatwin's social and literary success in the 1970s and 1980s. Despite his own repeated attestations of self-doubt and failure, he was widely acclaimed during his lifetime: a multiple prize-winner, an inveterate socialite and name-dropper, supported by a network of friends and well-placed acquaintances, who have continued after his death (from AIDS in 1989) vigorously to promote his putative mystique (with, of course, no little reflected lustre on themselves). At the very least, a salutary scepticism towards such hyperbole as Rushdie concluding his memoir (1991) with 'Speaking for myself, I fell in love' (p. 236) (a late variant on 'Reader, I married him'), or O'Hanlon's (1996) saccharine hagiography of Chatwin on his death-bed (p. 344) is long overdue.

Chatwin's total oeuvre – two travel books, three novellas, and scattered notebooks and journalistic ephemera – is clearly not that of a major writer: the much-vaunted comparison with Flaubert ought to make this abundantly clear. Nothing he wrote ever approaches the quality of the French writer's Egyptian journals let alone *Madame Bovary*. However, as Lawrence might have said, never trust the traveller, trust the tale: Chatwin's writing in this area remains an impressive development of the formal possibilities of post-imperial travelogue. The British ancestry is nowhere more apparent than in the compensatory assumption of a cosmopolitan hauteur. An aestheticist posture is made possible only through being in certain material ways a late beneficiary of empire (educated at Marlborough; one of the youngest ever directors at Sotheby's; internationally-sponsored protégé of Cape). There is no explicit political analysis of this legacy; indeed, it is arguably most insistently present in a systematic denial of origin (who after all would think of Chatwin, born in Sheffield, son of a Birmingham lawyer, as a northern writer?). Nevertheless, the problems of historical evaluation raised by 'the elegant and melancholic stance of the dandy' (Chatwin 1983: 11) are fully deserving of close and respectful attention. What does it mean in the closing years of this century for the connoisseur to be (or present himself as) an exile?

*Patagonia Revisited* extends the chance delights of the privileged anecdotalist beyond zoology and botany on to human encounters:

> We are also both fascinated by exiles. If the rest of the world blew up tomorrow, you would still find in Patagonia an astonishing cross-section of the world's nationalities, all of whom have drifted towards these 'final capes of exile' for no other apparent reason than the fact that they were there.
>
> On any one day in Patagonia, the traveller could expect to encounter a Welshman, an English gentleman-farmer, a Haight-Ashbury Flower Child, a Montenegran nationalist, an Afrikaner, a Persian missionary for the Bahai religion, or the Archdeacon of Buenos Aires on his round of Anglican baptisms. (Chatwin 1993a: 7–8)

Appreciation of those who left home and stayed away results in a celebration of the particularity of roots, occupations and beliefs. Pejorative resonances of this condition are substituted for a satisfaction at the apparently motiveless choice to reside in the obscurity of Patagonia, beneath which lies Chatwin's own relation to the act of exile and its relevance to his writing. Departure from England for Chatwin was followed by inevitable return, and the enthusiastic acclaim here for these compartmentalised micro-biographies of an inhabitance virtually without reason marks his distance from the encounters he offers. The delighted lingering over detail defines an absence of 'apparent reason' where none is given by Chatwin: the exiles' motives, if known, are withheld, and are generally subservient to their place in an elegant categorisation that specifies but limits their presence. No qualification is made of the dramatic but incorrect assertion that Patagonia was an obscure and historically arbitrary destination (half a millennium after the importance of the Cape route for global circumnavigation was first established), while the sequential bracketing of individual lives conceals the gradual and complex sedimentation of any number of colonial moments. Instead, the careful motion between the disparate and the congruous reflects the pattern established for the ninety-seven sections of *In Patagonia* (1979) itself, where Chatwin's childhood notion of a region safe from atomic warfare – 'somewhere to live when the rest of the world blew up' (p. 7) – is maintained as the background for a lifetime's ongoing 'search for the miraculous' (Chatwin 1990: 282).

Similarly, the multiplying 'references', 'excitements' and 'fascinations' available to the alert traveller seem discordant with the historical actualities of exile. Chatwin's own journeying, though extensive and often prolonged, was voluntary, even impulsive: the physical hardships, at their most explicit in the posthumous and unrevised *Photographs and Notebooks* (1993b), were self-imposed. Despite his genuine exuberance in discovery, Chatwin was engaged in a form of travelling that was pursued for material gain, and for consolidating his vocation as a writer. *In Patagonia* and *The Songlines*, the two clearest examples of travel writing, combine an intellectual fascination for exile with a fastidious emphasis on a preferred literary identity: the purposelessness of journeying is elevated to an almost Kantian dis-interestedness, while transposing the pathos of refugee status, and enforced and unending movement on to the act of writing itself. *In Patagonia* presents its exemplary cast of individuals, including its author, as embedded in 'a story of exile, disillusion and anxiety' (p. 7).

Yet in all aspects of Chatwin's life and work, the anachronistically aesthetic co-exists with the ruthlessly commercial: as Wilde (1966) says, 'It is only an auctioneer who can equally and impartially admire all schools of Art' (p. 1047). The longer texts of Chatwin's short career were uniformly and assiduously aimed at gaining literary success, and he occupied the unusual position of earning fame primarily as a travel writer – despite his protestations of apartness – rather than being a recognised figure who made occasional contributions to the genre, such as D. H. Lawrence, Graham Greene or Evelyn Waugh. Yet Chatwin repeatedly espoused the belief that his own writing offered a generic alternative to the traditional classification: 'it always irritated me to be called a travel writer' (Chatwin 1987: 27). This will for exemption has been amplified in most commentaries, which release his writings from any particular defining label, opting instead, much as their author would have wished, for claims of their unique *sui generis* quality. The acclaim with which *In Patagonia* was greeted generally asserted the book 'helped to change the idea of what travel-writing could be' (Clapp 1997: 25). Indeed, the discussion of Chatwin to date, largely conducted as journalism, has awarded him a literary prominence based upon this presumed singularity. The status of Chatwin's art has been in question far less than the nature of the texts themselves. For Nicholas Murray (1995), he is 'a writer who defies easy classification' and 'appears … to be entirely resistant to neat critical placing' (p. 9), while for Francis Wyndham, introducing the *Photographs and Notebooks* (1993b), his works are 'intriguingly impossible to categorize' (p. 10). The distinguishing effects of Chatwin's style will be considered later, but the many assertions of his exceptional originality must be contested. These founder in a broader consideration of the assimilative power of the genre: he enriches but does not originate contemporary travel writing's hybrid scope of journalism, anecdote, fictional techniques, stylistic bravura and the generic staple of the phantom quest.

At the opening of *In Patagonia* the 'piece of brontosaurus' (p. 6) sent back from South America by cousin Charley Milward, the sailor and adventurer, and exhibited in a cabinet by Chatwin's grandmother, excites the imagination of young Bruce into making fabrications about monsters, his ancestor and the Land of Fire. The hairy lump of skin turns out to be a fragment of mylodon or Giant Sloth, found by Milward in a cave in Chilean Patagonia, in turn visited by Chatwin towards the end of the book, where 'immensely pleased' he sees 'some strands of the coarse reddish hair' and so had 'accomplished the object of this ridiculous journey' (p. 182). The majority of the book's disparate sections appear to stand distinct from any close relation to this quest narrative, while the muddle of motivations – the search for tales of lost relatives, the hunt for a mythical beast, and the completion of childhood ambitions – jostle indecisively for precedence. (O'Hanlon similarly exploits the motif of self-imposed and unfulfilled pursuit, with diverse and implausible motivations for his temporary exile.) Plausible individual motive is notably absent, inviting explanation on a broader cultural level, and the inexorable but unspoken conclusion that England – its ennui, its prejudices, its dispiritedness – itself is the reason for departure.

The mini-autobiography, 'I Always Wanted to Go to Patagonia' (1996: 3–14) artfully continues the confusion, selecting and displaying an array of exceptional people and events with no binding relevance to the later trip to South America. Rather, the given span of Chatwin's life is granted a consistency in its reach from his schoolboy self, 'an addict of atlases ... always being ostracised for telling tall stories' to the returned voyager, the ambition of Patagonia finally achieved: 'I thought that telling stories was the only conceivable occupation for a superfluous person such as myself' (pp. 8, 14). The all-encompassing sleight of hand in 'stories' indicates Chatwin's own fraught location between art and the conditions for its inspiration, but his deft, sometimes brazen, oscillations between fact and fiction belong to general convention. Thus, his writing is more typical than he and his acolytes propose: the geographical territory is less arcane, and the residual context of romance less innovative. Its distinctiveness lies not in merging fact and fiction, but in the striking combination of the persona of aesthete-traveller with an ostentatious fastidiousness of style.

This very exquisiteness may itself become oppressive, as he himself commented of his career at Sotheby's: 'I began to feel that things, however beautiful, can also be malign. The atmosphere of the Art World reminded me of the morgue' (1996: 11). To journey through the temporal and spatial shifts of Chatwin's writing is to confront streams of data – the jostling objects, ideas, and stories carefully recorded by the eye and mind of the former antiques dealer in a dislocated jumble. The vagaries of history appear in lists similar to the inventories of objects repeatedly placed before the reader. One cannot fail to notice the extraordinary frisson of the simple act of cataloguing. Sympathy sways against the aesthete-murderer who narrates the tale, 'The Estate of Maximilian Tod' (1996: 54–69); yet the fiction derives its momentum from the stylistic techniques of annotation. Similarly, in *Utz* (1989), the perverse attachment of a Prague collector to his Meissen porcelain is lovingly detailed, if ultimately discarded. Chatwin's notation of travel experience is distilled from the aesthetic of the connoisseur developed in such experiments with the Wildean morality tale; the question remains of whether its marmoreal stasis possesses a significant utopian dimension or must be seen as ultimately appropriative, a site of fetishistic cruelty towards both self and world.

Chatwin himself was keen to assert continuities with the aesthete-traveller Robert Byron. In his introduction (1981) to *The Road to Oxiana*, 'the masterpiece' (p. 9) of 1930s travel books, he insists on his own imitativeness: 'I still have notebooks to prove how slavishly I aped both his itinerary and – as if that were possible – his style' (p. 10). Byron certainly prefigures the later writer's temporal and spatial leaps of connection, comparison and coincidence, and his juxtapositions of natural forces and cultural anachronism; although an unspoken admiration for the vigour of Byron's aestheticism and persistent allusions to his homosexuality seem a more pressing context for this enthusiasm. Indeed the differences are equally striking: Chatwin's honed-down miniaturism and brittle asexual prose are distinct from Byron's lapidary moments of immediate consciousness (on homoeroticism in the genre, see Boone 1995); in contrast, the supposedly impersonal Flaubert (1972) confides 'here one admits one's sodomy, and it is spoken of at table at the hotel' (p. 84).

Sympathy for his predecessor's subject-matter and lifestyle induces Chatwin to elide the differences between their respective periods, and underestimates the degree to which his own constitutive structural discontinuities are as much a reaction against modernist techniques of narration as against the nineteenth-century travel book. The voyaging of Byron no less than Kinglake is supported by an imperial infrastructure of bankers-drafts and military sanctions: 'by what strange privilege an Englishman with a brace of pistols and a couple of servants rides safely across the Desert owes its origin partly to the strange wilfulness of the English gentleman ... but partly too to the magic of the Banking system' (Kinglake 1992: 141). Furthermore, in Byron, the foregrounded aestheticism has immediate corollaries in personal freedom (hence its lauded connection with a robust anti-fascism); in Chatwin, style seems to contract and entrap in quasi-punitive fashion to become a microcosm of the workings of power rather than an oppositional space of resistance to it.

The arc from Chatwin's childhood to the final sea voyage in *In Patagonia* holds its series of recollections in the manner of his grandmother's glass-fronted cabinet with its Japanese homunculi and paintings of Dutch burghers: an aesthetic of interiors implies distant contacts. This effect is evident in the contemplative gaze cast on the north shore of the First Narrows, Tierra del Fuego:

> At the water's edge oyster-catchers were needling for shellfish in piles of ruby-coloured seaweed. The coast of Tierra del Fuego was an ashy stripe less than two miles away.
>
> Some trucks were lined up outside the tin restaurant, waiting for the tide to refloat the two landing craft that ferried traffic across. Three ancient Scots stood by. Their eyes were bloodshot-pink and nursery-blue and their teeth worn to little brown pinnacles. Inside, a strong juicy woman sat on a bench, combing her hair while her companion, a trucker, laid slices of mortadella on her tongue.
>
> The advancing tide pushed mattresses of kelp up the scarp of the beach. The gale blew out of the west. In a patch of calmer water a pair of steamer ducks burbled their monogamous conversation *tuk-tuk...tuk-tuk...tuk-tuk* ... I threw a pebble their way but could not disturb their absorption in each other and set their thrashing paddle-wings in motion.
>
> The Strait of Magellan is another case of Nature imitating Art. A Nuremberg cartographer, Martin Beheim, drew the South-West Passage for Magellan to discover. His premise was entirely reasonable. South America, however peculiar, was normal compared to the Unknown Antarctic Continent, the Antichthon of the Pythagoreans, marked FOGS on mediaeval maps. In this Upside-down-land, snow fell upwards, trees grew downwards, the sun shone black, and sixteen-fingered Antipodeans danced themselves into ecstasy. WE CANNOT GO TO THEM, it was said, THEY CANNOT COME TO US. Obviously a strip of water had to divide this chimerical country from the rest of Creation. (Chatwin 1979: 105–6)

In this characteristic passage of elegant, concise and briskly paced sentences, access to landmark is given as consistently measured representation. The careful appreciations of the observant traveller are remembered and relocated as isolated textual moments. Vision here enjoys exceptional agility, its record roaming across the details of landscape at great distance one moment, only to pinpoint local minutiae of the human body the next. This breadth of motion, in its precise photographic truncation, hints at the commonplace of the travel experience – the unpredictability of human encounter – while simultaneously confining it within a highly selective and tonally consistent notation.

Chatwin's assured nominal retrieval of physical data is typically accompanied here by recurrent accretions of history, geography and mythology. Lyrical evocation of the natural gives way to a prosaic yet fluid movement through fact and fiction, consonant with the previous specificity and clarity. The swift telescoping of present and past exhibits Chatwin's imaginative facility for positioning earlier beliefs within a continuously available travelogue. The convictions of the Renaissance explorers and the conscious fabulism of their writers are delivered as clear and intimately informed anecdote while the figures of Magellan and Beheim enter the same time-span as contemporary inhabitants; arresting detail lends them the immediacy of present encounter, and even a certain matter-of-fact familiarity.

Yet the complex artistic effects of Chatwin's strength of recollection include an implicit denial of the human detail of history. Rather we note the abrupt transitions between sentences consciously held apart as objects, with little or no coalescence between them. This controlled halting of the data results in a kind of annulment of temporal perspectives. The briefest sketches of individuals are made to stand for complete narratives of human experience, in this case the likely hardships of Scottish émigrés in Patagonia, with explicit allusion to the convention of taking pleasure in maps and the delimitation of foreign geography. This accentuation of broad generic traits reaches something of an extreme in Chatwin, notably the over-riding of specific experiences of conflict in favour of a savouring of esoteric vocabulary and polished cadences. (The Scots are segregated from the indigenous people, and the question of whether their emblematic status is necessarily at the expense of the native is never broached.)

The Chatwinian convention is to elide particularity, in contravention of the post-colonial insistence on overt recognition of cultural difference. A technique poignant in the representation of objects is disconcertingly reductive of persons, who are divested of contextualising discussion or life-narrative; this trait contradicts the contingency of journeying itself, the complex and unpredictable encounters arising from the lack of controlled itinerary. A style so committed to aesthetic purity cannot but highlight its extremity of manipulation.

Elsewhere in *In Patagonia* we hear the story of Jemmy Button, born in '(t)he year the nations of Europe settled the course of the nineteenth century on the plain of Waterloo' and 'who would make a modest contribution to settling the course of the twentieth' (p. 120):

> The boy was out fishing with his uncle when they sighted the Apparition.
>
> For years the People of the South had murmured about the visits of a monster. At first they assumed it was a kind of whale, but closer acquaintance revealed a gigantic canoe with wings, full of pink creatures with hair sprouting ominously from their faces ...
>
> Heedless of danger, the boy persuaded the uncle to paddle up to the pink man's canoe. A tall person in costume beckoned him and he leapt abroad. The pink man handed the uncle a disk that shimmered like the moon and the canoe spread a white wing and flew down the channel towards the source of pearl buttons.
>
> The kidnapper was Captain Robert FitzRoy, RN, Chief Officer of HMS *Beagle*, now winding up her first survey of southern waters. (Chatwin 1979: 121)

In this paradigm of colonial narrative, the apparent openness of the initial moment of encounter results in an act of kidnapping. A series of thoughts and perceptions, impossible to verify or disprove, are re-created as an exploration and recuperation of history. The imagined motion through time and the intimate portrayal of the boy's mind grant cross-cultural directions and spaces through which the narrative may proceed. The final paragraph gives an accurate account of the routine event of abduction, yet its dramatic touches block rather than illuminate their larger significance. Any gaps between its divergent registers of vocabularies are never overcome. There is (an illusion of?) extraordinary access to history, and yet ultimately we are more struck by what has been withheld than what has been given. Chatwin evades explicit consideration of the problematic of power in such cultural translation (on abduction in Frobisher see Greenblatt 1991: 109–18), but may here be applauded for acknowledging that the perspectives remain incommensurate. Two histories – of innocence and incursion – intersect but cannot be unified.

In examining the central stylistic tropes that unite Chatwin's writings this essay aims to identify a self-conscious voice that in its persistent rhetoric of beliefs and observations implies its own exile. The distinctive 'bleak, chiselled style' (1990: 366) is considered here as an extended metaphor of self-description beyond his painstaking accumulation of the object world. It is the emphatic presence of style per se throughout the texts that holds attention as an object apart from the catalogues of phenomena that momentarily engage the narrative eye. The assiduous control challenges the reader to negotiate its playful staccato jumps and shifts between the frozen, static residue of experience. The confidence of the polished, positioned sentences runs against the abrupt uneven passage through the disparate objects, ideas, histories and people of his accounts. Images and convictions are situated both as highly realised literary artefacts and as segmented fleeting statements. Brought into acute visual focus one moment, without further explanation, they vanish the next. For all their trust in the potential of minutiae, the narratives are in constant flight from prolonged involvement. While tracking the continual specificities of diverse matter, in a key paradox, the reader is routed away from the demands of local knowledge towards the general implications of a style and its negotiations of the cultures it preserves as art. As it passes from one manicured experience to the next, the style infers a calculated distance from what it portrays, but a distance that implies awareness of the self-control that ought to attend the act of representation. The innovative transience of the depicted objects gauges a highly ambivalent relation to this very impulse, prompting continuous withdrawal rather than the apparently solicited expansion.

The sense of plenitude that prevails as one reads is thus attended by a sense of what is missing: practicalities of travel go largely unreported, as do arrangements for meetings and interviews. Despite the air of urgency and authority in the passages of intellectual speculation – historical, literary, anthropological – there is no serious engagement with academic data, no apparent comprehension of the professional's fixed coherent project with its rigorously established result: the narrative dynamic prefers to evade scrutiny by endlessly shifting between disciplines and genres. It remains to be seen whether its implications can withstand political analysis so easily.

The intellectual thesis on nomadism proposed in *The Songlines* is at best idiosyncratic. Throughout Chatwin's oeuvre a rejection of academic procedure is accompanied by a certain plaintive tentativeness of tone that seeks to pre-empt sustained interrogation. The 1969 'Letter to Tom Maschler' states 'I want the book to be general rather than specialist in tone' (1996: 75) and rejects 'The Nomadic Alternative' as 'too rational a title for a subject that appeals to irrational instincts' (p. 75); insisting that the dialectical arguments of the Aborigines 'know no bounds of complication' (p. 77), though that of course is no reason why a study of those beliefs should be similarly indeterminate, 'straining the bounds of scientific rigour (as I undoubtedly have)' (1988: 285).

*The Songlines* (1988) opens with the disarming declaration: 'Obviously, I was not going to get to the heart of the matter, nor would I want to' (p. 14). Yet this rejection of contemporary western intellectual rigour is undermined by its own permanent reliance on European cultural analogies: 'people would inevitably be reminded of something else', when considering the Australian tracks, such as European stone circles, feng-shui dragon-lines, the Nazca etchings (p. 313). 'Bruce' and the Russian *émigré* and land rights activist Arkady continually debate the Aboriginal myths with the aid of a dialogue form derived from Diderot's *Jacques Le Fataliste* (Murray 1995: 89). Protracted and at times precious parallels are drawn with western culture: the ancient tracks are 'as moral as the New Testament' (p. 79), Celtic mythology, Rilke (excruciatingly) (p. 13), a 'bush-telegraph-cum-stock exchange' (p. 63), Genesis (p. 14), a 'sphagetti of Iliads and Odysseys' (p. 16), Beethoven's Opus III (p. 16), Kipling's *Just So Stories* (p. 24) and so on.

Among the specialists employed to bolster his assertions, Chatwin highlights the 'highly original thinker' Ted Strehlow, author of *Songs of Central Australia*, and believer that 'every aspect of Aboriginal song had its counterpart in Hebrew, Ancient Greek, Old Norse or Old English', that we may 'find in song a key to unravelling the mystery of the human condition' (p. 77). This procedure of authentication has the odd effect of making contemporary ethnographic and archaeological speculation seem as pre-rational as the mythology it supposedly explicates.

Animal mimicry in Aboriginal ritual leads Chatwin to the 'Father of Ethnology', Konrad Lorenz, the book's appointed *genius loci*, whose re-location of animal 'paradigms' of behaviour into human beings attributes 'the question of questions: the nature of human restlessness' (p. 181) to genetic encodings within the nervous system. The dubious corollaries of this thesis are evident in Lorenz's chilling if insightful account of soldiers in battle: 'One soars elated above the cares of everyday life … Men enjoy the feeling of absolute righteousness even when they commit atrocities' (p. 240). Chatwin uses the more appealing analogy of 'the mother who fights in fury to defend her child': she 'is – one would hope! – obeying the call of instinct, not the advice of some maternal guidance leaflet. And if you allow the existence of fighting behaviour in young women, why not also in young men?' (p. 240). Yet the shortcomings of this juxtaposition (what about the mother who kills someone else's child?) raise the issue not merely of the instance itself, but of a broader lack of scruple in the over-riding of epistemological accuracy in favour of aesthetic interest.

Thus the Aboriginal tracks are somewhat breezily accounted for by the fact 'that Natural Selection has designed us – from the structure of our brain-cells to the structure of our big toe – for a career of seasonal journeys *on foot* through a blistering land of thorn-scrub or desert' (pp. 181–2). Yet if there is an instinct to travel, why not an equally valid one to exterminate inferior races? Chatwin is elsewhere explicitly interrogative of Lorenz (see 'Variations on an Idée Fixe', a 1979 review of *The Year of the Greylag Goose* [1996: 140–8]), but any broader intellectual thesis to be drawn from his work is vitiated by a comparable biological determinism: Lorenz's plaudit – 'What you have just said is totally new' (1988: 249) – is one of the few occasions where Chatwin's narrativised vignettes are manifestly specious.

The argument of *The Songlines* is less coherent than the aestheticising drive that assembles the choicest details of the summoning of the world through song: an intellectually coherent system concretely realised in the spectacular landmarks of Australia. The characteristic stance of the narrative persona is inherently problematic, presupposing access to privileged knowledge from which the enlightened liberal is excluded, and implicitly denigrating the everyday experience of land activists (both white and Aboriginal) in Australia. Again Chatwin is involved in the recognition and exhibition of oddity, creating characters whose exiled textual forbears are in *In Patagonia*. His self-representation is notably inaccurate, the terse, slightly impatient questions and statements inconsistent with the infamous but engaging monologist of biographical account, while the caricatured versions of specific personalities representing white Australia nearly involved him in legal difficulties (Murray 1995: 90). Whether condemned or pedestalised, they demonstrate Chatwin's weakness in orthodox characterisation: 'the collector evolves a moral system from which he squeezes out people' (1996: 172). The land activists, the witty lawyer, the long-suffering teacher, the racist barflies seem a cast acquired out of narrative duty for their textual photogenicity, conveniently allowing referential flights back to their author's roots in Europe: the Land Council worker, Marian, emerging from a shower becomes a 'Piero madonna' (1988: 112), the iron-pumping policeman whose favourite reading is Spinoza (p. 152).

The language of the dramatic dialogues is frequently at odds with the situations themselves, where the persona glides easily away from bar-room ugliness. Indeed, Chatwin predictably values the exiles of Australia less as complete individuals than for the jarring exceptional details which make up their lives:

> Her name was Goldie. In her ancestry were Malay, Koipanger, Japanese, Scot and Aboriginal. Her father had been a pearler and she was a dentist. Before moving into her apartment, Flynn wrote a letter, in faultless Latin, requesting the Holy Father to release him from his vows. The couple moved to Alice Springs and were active in Aboriginal politics. (Chatwin 1988: 60)

In this case, mobility is deracination, homelessness within an alien terrain, and the diversity of white Australia is left notably unexplored.

Even the mythic resonances of the Aborigines are marred throughout with a certain déjà vu, clichés drawn from both high and popular culture. Celebration of their supposedly timeless vitality mystifies the Aboriginal heritage (the hunting trip [ch. 31] is conflated with earlier anecdotes of the Nemadi in Walata [pp. 142–7]), while simultaneously removing Aborigines from social and economic involvement in contemporary Australia. The 'frank and smiling face' of the Aboriginal Alan Nakamurra implausibly 'reminded me of my father's' (p. 108), typical of the somewhat desperate attempts to forge connections with the Aboriginals by way of substitution for proximity to their beliefs. An emphasis on the secrecy surrounding their lore provides no apparent barrier to Chatwin's own privileged access to their rituals. For all the overt expressions of sympathy, the Aborigine is reduced to supporting data for a somewhat hackneyed quasi-mystical thesis which renders all renditions of personal specificity superfluous. The question remains of whether the artist is still behind the text, a *deus absconditus* paring his fingernails.

The lengthy extracts from the drafts and notebooks offer fragments of decontextualised international culture. Their thesis is of instinct, but the style reeks of premeditated craft and brittle sophistication. These choice gobbets argue indefinitely and somewhat vaguely for an aesthetics of movement, in a kind of private arcana, hovering wryly between general cohesion and absolute irrelation. Far from providing an interlude, they serve as a distillation of intellectual and rhetorical technique: an agile but tricksy diversity, of an ironic collating mind. Chatwin acknowledged 'I cannot provide a history of nomads. It would take years to write' (1996: 75). Responsibility for authenticating research is disingenuously transferred to the reader. All these equations possess a provisional quality. It is not that coherence is necessarily an impossibility, but that they are substitutions for an argument rather than the argument itself. In the London Library, Chatwin the researcher gives up: 'The man sitting next to me was snoring with a literary journal spread over his stomach. To hell with migration! I said to myself' (1988: 307). The effect of the marshalled extracts is less as eclectic fractions of debate than of an indirect mythologising of Chatwin himself. This self-image becomes highly metonymic in relation to both the thesis on Australian myth and Australia itself, and propels the focus of attention back to Europe (where nearly half the book takes place). A certain confessional quality to the work brings a therapeutic scenario into play as he confides to his surrogate persona, Arkady, that the purpose of his visit was '(p)robably a very obvious idea. But one I have to get out of my system' (p. 18), yet it is finally acknowledged that his writing is '(t)he usual mess' (p. 315).

Yet for all its flaws, *The Songlines* is an integrated, highly self-conscious 'performance' which anticipates and pre-empts many of the criticisms to which it is obviously vulnerable (most obviously, as Michael Ignatieff commented, the book parades 'a pretty grandiose metaphysics of your own restlessness' [cited Murray 1995: 92]). Its formal ingenuity allows it to sidestep its intellectual failings and faults of characterisation with its highly crafted and self-reflexive techniques of fragmentation. The text retreats from conclusiveness by proffering a highly conventional fictional 'happy ending': it is difficult if not impossible to ascertain the degree of irony in the (entirely fictitious) final romantic attachment between Arkady and Marian and the cancellation of the threatening railway. According to Clapp (1997), Chatwin 'thought the book a failure and that he should have revised it' (p. 216). Yet the reading experience of its final form possesses a tautological strength: to proceed incrementally through its disjunctions is to enact if not to resolve Chatwin's own nomadic obsessions.

The fidgeting bulletins that make up Chatwin's paragraphs are intermittently punctured with awareness of the political, human catastrophes that have stemmed from the travel of invasion and dominance. *The Viceroy of Ouidah* presents a convenient example:

> Two days before the celebration there was a moment of alarm when Lieutenant-Colonel Zossoungbo Patrice of the Sûreté Nationale burst in on Papa Agostinho's siesta and banned the celebration.
>
> The colonel was twenty-four, and had long curly eye-lashes and knife-edge creases to his green paratrooper fatigues. Two grenades, the shape of scent bottles, were slung from his belt. (Chatwin 1982: 22)

The style's continual reprocessing of event, and counter-balancing gambits, may appear nonchalantly detached; but embedded within the luxuriating perceptions of the former antiquarian's inventories of exotica are delicate but clear-sighted recognitions of local structures of power, past and present. These disturb aestheticising recollection: grenades shaped like scent bottles may still explode. Where the colonialist lingers, defines and expands, Chatwin's truncated, mobile rendering of data bids for an unappropriative contact with the object in view. Yet can the post-imperial observer surpass merely ironic versions of post-colonial futility? It is at least arguable that the history of complicity of these very devices with colonial violence, indeed, of the very pleasure given by finely wrought language, must condemn these texts as mere ciphers for an ultimately reactionary nostalgia.

The elision of the basic fact of being-there, the economic privilege allowing the incursion of the western traveller, renders these effects of tessellation and mosaic not only disingenuous but even sinister in their artful incongruities. Generically, the precedent of the Naipaulian travelogue (and before that Conrad) weighs heavily – an embittered perception of history as always and only farce within the post-colonial context. The over-ornate rhetoric of the novella lends itself to a kind of arrogant self-preening that its modifying devices can qualify but not altogether overcome;

the fictional narrator is granted an implied disengagement if not omniscience rather than defined through a set of perceptual relations which for all their studied brevity remain constitutive of the enlightened wanderer.

The *Photographs and Notebooks* give both a more rounded human being, as the difficulties of the harassed traveller become pretext and spur to a distinctive lyricism. These are much more personalised, relatively uninhibited in their use of the first-person, more inclusive of the sheer frustration of travel. Curiously, the drafts are not themselves fragmentary but serve as a prelude to further excision and honing; collage is arguably a means to both self-protection and control. Overt aggression is a form of vulnerability.

> Hausa house is mud-coloured and on the outside the texture of a good-natured bath towel. Inside, a pillar supporting a vault of thornbush logs – gummy smell. Door made from the gate of a crate of canned pineapples from the Côte d'Ivoire. Stepped on an old champagne bottle. And a plate of water that could have been made by a maiden of the Neolithic age. And an old French military camp bed recovered lovingly with camel leather. It is home. I am happy with it. (Chatwin 1993b: 72)

A West African dwelling is approved as a nexus of intermingled cultural and historical details, which perhaps include an implicit celebration of the passing of the colonial era in the symbolic retrieval of the objects of the former oppressor. But it remains uncertain whether or not what is being celebrated is the colonial period itself rather than the fact of its passing. The rapid scanning of phenomena encourages more than a sense of their disparate interest, rather than unifying them as components of a larger argument. Imported luxury items – 'bath towel', 'champagne bottle' – are neither self-recriminating nor condescending. In this inclusive postcolonial hybrid, the syntax is less pristine, and there is less temporal jumpiness. Diffusion is presented without the characteristic sheen of the revised style. There is an unusual proximity to an inhabited environment, yet one that remains depopulated, without interaction. The curious, almost unprecedented retention of the first person allows the reading that it is the voice of the dwelling itself, the retort of the absent occupants: 'It is home. I am happy with it.'

> A fat Frenchman and his very thin wife – with an appendage, a sister in a pink jumper. The *patron* has demanded payment in advance – 'This is Africa' he says. He is right.
>
> At dinner. There is a negress *habillée en rose* with her hair piled up as a cathedral bell and her legs gleaming black like the shining black of her shoes and hard as steel. Her heart of steel I imagine too.

Now I have revived, for the morning was depressing and I had a headache – a legacy of Paris. The negress has ordered herself a huge bottle of wine. This comes, as all good French come, from Algeria. (Chatwin 1993b: 40)

The preference for colonial subjects (the 'cathedral bell' simile is respectful) and rejection of the colonisers (the *patron* is 'right' to demand 'advance payment') is in disengenuous conjunction with the continued centrality of the 'legacy of Paris' even in drunkenness: a Francophilia is evident throughout both the biography and journalism. There is nothing comparable in a British context to the succinct and probing analysis of French racism in 'The Very Sad Story of Salah Bougrine' (1990: 241–62).

Chatwin is casual about 'the vision of decayed colonial splendour' (1993b: 53): 'The French always exported the very worst of their culture to the colonies. Yet the combination is not displeasing. Meat sellers with hurricane lamps. Umbilical hernias protrude from the bellies of children like some strange tropical fruit' (1993b: 66). There are precedents for this kind of effect – Flaubert's (1972) predilection for *chancres* (e.g. p. 65) – but there is still the pointed conjunction of the 'worst' as exemplified in the appalling consequences of medical neglect providing the most vivid instance of an aesthetic effect 'exported to the colonies'. This foregrounds an element of voyeuristic contempt while daring the reader to assent that 'the combination is not displeasing'. Yet the connoisseur's demand for the authentic must necessarily include human suffering as the only genuine constant of the post-colonial environment. Pain must be not only trans-cribed as evidence of one's own aesthetic transcendence, but transmuted into pleasurable complicity.

Chatwin's elegant omnipresence through his slight but distinctive output is clearly vulnerable to the charge of avoidance of the more immediate dynamics of cultural encounter, explanation and opinion, his stylistic virtuosity a refusal to engage with the actualities of human and political contact. The same criticism recurs within the texts, in the form of carefully positioned (if somewhat occasional) outbursts to counter the overall rhetorical stance. Intelligent, ironic reflection over fragments is ultimately deemed as the appropriate contemporary idiom for the traveller. Rushdie (1991), Chatwin's companion in the Australian outback, remarks on a propensity for 'autobiography of the mind' (p. 239); the notations expressing the specificity of the observer rather than vice versa. The palimpsest effect and the endemic repetitions give the sense of retreading the same paths in different countries, yet it seems inappropriate to regard the oeuvre simply in terms of one sustained voyage of self-discovery.

Bhabha (1994b) recognises in Rushdie a 'monstrous inventory of ill-assorted persons, places, and things that become part of a luminous order as soon as he places them together' (p. 29). This seems technically close to Chatwin, yet the postmodern verve implied is toned down, celebration modulated. The melancholy of passage from one fixed moment to the next may be his most outstanding achievement, the post-imperial observer acknowledging irreconcilable distance from what he sees but no longer possesses. In the context of the perpetual dislocation of the 'sterile wanderer' (Chatwin 1979: 133), the 'art style is the signature of a particular man and a window on the age in which he made it' (1996: 178). The dispassionate surfaces continually intimate at a depth of feeling for some cultural absolute perceived as lost: whether one reads this politically as empire, theologically as the divine, or aesthetically as the numinal, Chatwin as 'voyeur in life' (p. 171) retains an almost ontological apartness. Perhaps it will be possible to read into this dispassionate poignancy 'an allegory for the final years of a winded century' (1983: 4).

# Transatlantic Crossings: Recent British Travel Writing on the United States

Steve Clark

The last two decades have witnessed a veritable outpouring of British travel writing on the United States, including Stephen Brook's *New York Days, New York Nights* and *L.A. Lore*; Mick Brown's *American Heartbeat*; Andy Bull's *Coast to Coast*; Nik Cohn's *The Heart of the World*; Pete Davies's *Storm Country*; Simon Hoggart's *America: A User's Guide*; Geoffrey Moorhouse's *Imperial City*; Michael Pye's *Maximum City*; Jonathan Raban's *Old Glory*, *Hunting Mr Heartbreak* and *Bad land*; Richard Rayner's *Los Angeles without a Map*; Hugo Williams's *No Particular Place to Go*; Nigel Williams's *From Wimbledon to Waco*; and Gavin Young's *From Sea to Shining Sea*. This chapter will examine the sub-genre in terms of reversal of power. If, as Raban (1987) claims, 'four hundred years of imperial experience had given the travelling Englishman a very clear idea where he stood in the world – bang at its moral centre' (p. 254), now he is no longer a privileged observer, but supplicant to and arguably parasitic on a more recently ascendant empire: 'a visiting Englishman strolling amid the mighty throng on Fifth Avenue, may reflect that it must have been quite like this for an Indian, in London from Calcutta or Bombay, when he found himself ambling along Piccadilly just before the First World War' (Moorhouse 1989: 336).

The discursive persona adopted shows strikingly little variation: white, male, highly educated, upper middle class, divorced, customarily both celibate and childless. (Exceptions such as the anglicised American, Bill Bryson's *The Lost Continent*, or the female cyclist, Josie Drew's *Travels in a Strange State*, foreground the basic homogeneity of stance). One might speculate that a century earlier, this cadre of professional writer-journalist would readily have found employment in colonial administration; if travel writing serves as a kind of litmus test of national character, these texts provide a test-case for defining a post-imperial identity. This is customarily characterised by a pervasive sense of decline: I shall argue that it is founded as much on rivalry and displacement, in a new 'world geography', in which, as Bryson notes (1995), America is 'about where Ireland is' (p. 19).

In the post-war era of Pax Americana, the undisputed dominance of the United States has made it, as Ihab Hassan (1990) observes, 'a dangerous or ambiguous other to all nations even in the West'; thus, a 'Middle Power Complex' has emerged in all those who 'profoundly dependent on American power ... surrender easily to pique, cavil, defiance, that irascibility that marks Euro-Gaullism' (pp. 72, 75). One might have anticipated the development of a strain of British intransigence parallel to the French: 'Americans can never figure out why they are hated, even by the people who lap up their advertising and their hamburgers' (Hoggart 1992: 18; see also Kuisel 1993). British travel writing, however, is seldom openly critical of or even attentive to the landmarks of post-war Anglo-American relations – the nuclear bases, Suez, Polaris and so on (Watt 1984) – or the military triumphalism of the Reagan–Bush era. Its characteristic insights into both the functioning of American cultural hegemony and the debilitation of British national identity derive from transformations within the genre itself, promoted by the 'melt-down' of imperial self-assurance (Gendron 1992: 265).

To support this contention, I will focus on three aspects of the subgenre: (1) the political corollaries of the American sublime, with its intimations of punitive violence; (2) the failure of the British traveller's attempts at self-transformation, and the continued determining presence of the homeland; (3) the pre-formation of British travellers by American popular culture, their sense of re-encounter rather than discovery and consequent strategies of protective mimicry.

## 1. American Sublimes

> Manhattan was a dozen glittering sticks of light, through which livid storm clouds were rolling, lit from below, sooty-orange in colour, as they swirled past the middling- and upper-storeys of the buildings. The choppy sea in the harbour was like a lake of troubled mercury, and the water glared so fiercely that it was almost impossible to find the tiny red and green sparks of the buoys marking the deepwater channel. Then one's eye adjusted and the city's famous icons began to emerge from the general dazzle of things ... It was brazen in its disdain for the ordinary limits of human enterprise. I watched the storm and the city battling it out, high in the sky. (Raban 1990: 51–2)

Much has been made of the appropriative power of the imperial gaze but here in this set-piece vista, Raban is reduced to a posture of tremulous deference. The American city becomes a 'powerful fortress, impregnable in the New World', with 'the capacity to suggest protection or possibly to intimidate' (Moorhouse 1989: 19–20). There is no simple opposition between the urban sublime ('what's below is man-made, artifice up to the sky' [Pye 1991: 3]) and the natural landscape, but rather a moment of commingling, or imbibing of power from. Light emanates out towards rather than being received from the physical world (Brook [1985] is similarly enraptured by the 'cosmic tableau of light and vapour and wind' [p. 18]). The 'general dazzle' is 'brazen in its disdain' for the 'ordinary limits of human enterprise', most immediately exemplified in the British traveller. (Similarly in *Bad land*, 'the conjured world swelled' before the immigrants, 'free of the restraints of sceptical realism' [Raban 1996: 21].)

The sublimity of the American landscape is itself imbued with similar political analogues. The very failure of comprehension prompted by its sheer scale becomes testimony to a power that cannot be defined. 'You can't say America's good or bad, or right or wrong. You have to say instead that it's bigger than good or bad, bolder than right or wrong – that it's elemental and electric, spiritual and crazed' (Davies 1993: 315). In this encounter, often simply mundane dimension inculcates the requisite humility, 'the sheer bewilderment of the European imagination when it tried to confront the raw wilderness of the American West' (Raban 1986: 39).

The traveller consequently shrinks, an experience of diminution most eloquently expressed by Davies (1993) : 'But here, the sky was purest blue, and the wide land swept away until, standing in the wind, I felt small like dust' (p. 74); 'in the spirit-rich silence your soul melts away, bleeds off into the sky and land until you're nothing but sand and grass yourself, a speck tossed in the rustling voids of eternity through the heart of America' (p. 129); 'I felt tranquil, disconnected, a dot of perfect motion on the glazed ribbon of the road' (p. 193). (Or in Josie Drew's [1994] less elevated mode, 'In my head I looked down upon a map of America, a massive and meaty bulk, and I thought: Where am I? Who am I? I felt like a peanut on the planet, an insignificant pin-prick crawling across a monster nation' [p. 188].) The imagery of the minuscule – dust, speck, dot – easily merges into that of the germ; the status of the traveller is at best ambivalent in the frequently and belligerently proclaimed 'war against the penetration of foreign bodies' (Raban 1990: 192). Even, or perhaps especially, British travellers must wonder whether they are 'counted ... among the staring aliens': 'this Eye-ran ... is that anywhere near where you come from?'; 'when they defined their enemies it was clear they meant me' (Raban 1986: 253, 402; 1996: 310).

This potential vulnerability in turn permits oblique broodings on the punitive and unforgiving nature of America's cultural and political power:

savage, not in a primitivist idealisation of the past, but more as a proleptic intimation of future aggression. The overt response is frequently supercilious and condescending, but the key question remains unvoiced: what would it be like to 'be a corpuscle' (Raban 1986: 34) in the bloodstream of such a giant host culture, and as 'a citizen of a superpower, to maintain democratically the means of planetary extinction' (Amis 1987: 11). The violence directed against an unspecifiable elsewhere (actually quite precise: Iran at the beginning of the 1980s; Iraq at the end) is frequently presented in terms of an outlet for the frustrated and marginalised: merely redneck ravings. Yet these utterances also presuppose a military and economic power so huge that it can scarcely be directly grasped, let alone confronted. Davies readily disparages his host at Ellesworth Airforce Base, Lt Robert Carver ('driving round a death factory with a zombie'), but finds it less easy to accept the domesticity of the control room:

> 'It's kind of an off-green room. Not kind of lime green, not really grass green – it's a light pastel green. It's not ugly. I wouldn't paint my house that colour, but it's not ugly. And there are red chairs. There's carpet, and nice fluorescent lighting, they have a nice bed module they've put in – and there's a small refrigerator, and a microwave, and a little TV, thirteen inches, colour. So you can watch the ball game. It's a good working environment.'
>
> God save us. You can toss a burger in the microwave, and watch Wrigley Field flare to fire and ash as you turn a key and the world ends. (Davies 1993: 296)

Intense localism produces ferocious xenophobia; the military–industrial complex is a suburban affair. The same 'whole mythic notion of what America is, of family values, of hard work and trust, of fellowship and community' (p. 17), which Davies has previously uncritically celebrated, is precisely what is most dangerous. 'In Austin I went to see *Terminator 2*. It's the perfect American dream for the end of the century – a violent and indestructible robot with a heart of gold' (p. 317).

## 2. Nuclear Intimations

America's continental scale means 'emigration is almost always internal' (Hoggart 1992: 17); 'Even to the Americans, it seemed, America was exotic' (Brown 1994: 6); 'America is more like a world than a country' (Amis 1987: 9). The corollary of this is the dispensability of elsewhere: all that is not America has no right even to exist. Raban (1986) meets a preacher who 'made his globe spin' so 'the colours of the countries swirled and England was lost in China or Japan' (p. 472); and Brook (1985) witnesses a New York teacher, who after 'a cogent account of nuclear war' then 'carried a globe round the class asking his charges to point to Great Britain. Very few had any idea' (p. 114).

'I left London for Los Angeles on the morning that the ground war in the Gulf began. By the time I had unpacked my bags the war was just about over' (Brook 1993: 179). It is striking how little the British partake in the 'post-Gulf hysteria', given the fact that, as Davies (1993) observes, 'we were out there too. Two boys from my village were there' (p. 29). It was an all-American victory, but implicitly one also over the autonomy of its allies: a sense of potential violence was directed against them too.

Davies (1993) repeatedly moves from Midwest tornados on to a desert storm on the other side of the globe: the local fire chief comments on his wrecked town, 'I thought I was in Baghdad' (p. 144).

> [T]he inevitable analogy people reached for, over and over, was war: 'It looks like we was bombed'. But it was more malevolent, more deranged, more deliberate. It was like a giant went through Minatare with a baseball bat, picking each swipe at each house with a conscious intent – then kicking the wreckage about afterwards, just to make good and sure. (Davies 1993: 170–1)

The Gulf War 'looked to an outsider like America was saying, "We killed a hundred and fifty thousand sand niggers and *we don't give a damn*"' (p. 29). During victory celebrations:

> A knot of drunken yahoos were firing rockets from a pick-up across the street. Seeing me reading the sign there, they started firing them at me ...
>
> I walked across the square and down the street back to Jeno's Motel, the sharp screams and cracks of the orange-sparking rockets following me, exploding against walls and windows and on the side-walk, around my head and around my feet, to a scratched and sullen soundtrack of braindead whooping.
>
> When you're looking for the heart of America, you better be able not to flinch ... Actually I was thinking, that's it, I'm out of here. (Davies 1993: 301)

The vignette brings together the night sky over Baghdad, the 'soundtrack' of Reaganite America, and the rapidity with which any 'outsider' becomes potential victim. The Indians fear their 'final disappearance beneath the earth-trashing arrogance and craziness of the flooding white tide' (p. 267): after a deluge, a town official's video 'silently, ominously played on, the water rushing in a white foaming tide over the dirty wreckage of the earth' (p. 209). 'She said she could no more worry about the past than she could sit down and worry about nuclear war. Which would, of course, be the ultimate white tide' (p. 214).

McCrea, Rayner's employer at a pool-cleaning firm, comments of his 'framed photograph of a nuclear mushroom' that 'the chastisement will be great, but man must understand' (Rayner 1992: 129). His wife takes up the theme:

> She pointed her knife at the photograph in the corner of the room.
> She said, 'Nuclear war.'
> 'Nuclear war?'
> She nodded.
> 'But that's terrible.'
> 'Oh yes Richard, it is terrible,' she said. 'But it has to come. It will come. The Word has been spoken. It has been through me.'
> Marlene said I needn't be embarrassed. I shouldn't be afraid of her message. I should confront the reality of my situation. It would make me a happier individual. (Rayner 1992: 131)

Raban (1990) dwells upon 'how Europeans had always seen American nature – as shockingly bigger, more colourful, more deadly, that anything they'd seen at home' (p. 153). The 'irrepressible profusion and savagery' of the 'fire ants', the 'brown recluse spider', the 'snapping turtle' which could 'amputate whole hands of fingers' (pp. 150, 153) reveal a 'lurking kind of American savagery' which is 'as unexceptionable, as platitudinous as ... the hamburger and Coca-Cola' (p. 156). This is later explicitly linked with the 'experimental bombs and warheads' produced at Huntsville ('like the Krupp factory on the Ruhr' [p. 188]) and then with the landscape of the Florida Keys:

> This, more than my Guntersville backyard, was exactly the kind of nature that made Crevecoeur frightened for America's human future. It set a fine example of stealth and rapine. Properly equipped, in snakeboots and pith helmets, and armed with a hunter's carbine, you could learn a lot in there, about such things as techniques of camouflage, strategic defoliation, the advantages of the pre-emptive strike and the deterrent effects of Mutually Assured Destruction. (Raban 1990: 370)

The terrifying and malignant implications of the American capacity to wage nuclear war cannot be directly addressed. On a visit to an abattoir, with a 'steel cabinet the size of my London living room', Raban (1986) notes that the factory was capable of depopulating 'in less than twenty years, the whole of the British Isles' (p. 199); Brook (1993) similarly finds 'echoes of the concentration camps' in the 'airless chambers' of the Haunted House in the 'empire of Goofy and Donald' (p. 328). The only alternative to these anecdotes of vertiginous unease is semi-parodic melo-dramatic vignettes. Nigel Williams (1995) wonders whether 'fear was the reason I had stayed away from America for so long' where 'One minute you have your arms around each other like old friends, and the next you're banged up with a screaming madman who seems to be trying to kill you for no particular reason' (pp. 8, 40). Davies (1993) is beset by a concluding fantasy of a 'leering, rotten-toothed psycho' with a shotgun: 'The barrel spat fire; my right hand exploded in a sudden spray of blood and bone over the inside of the windscreen' (p. 314). Such moments of grotesquerie cannot be dismissed with 'only kidding' when they so accurately reflect an actual balance of power.

## 3. No Place Like Home

The space of the continent so often evoked is peculiarly duplicitous: it embodies an urge to return to a historical origin which itself never existed, a moment when the land was uninhabited, fit reward and redemption for the exile and refugee. (An Edenic vantage which in characteristic colonial fashion presupposes the erasure of the native inhabitants.) The status of the British writer commenting on other immigrant groups is ambivalent: there is an implicit priority and lineage claimed – though the Spanish, French, Dutch, and even Scandinavians might protest – which produces both identification with and disavowal of the category of 'emigrants – a crew of people dingy enough to take a little of the shine out of the words' (Raban 1990: 7). There is an attempt at self-distancing from the 'poor of Europe', but the structural analogue to the contemporary British traveller is too strong: 'when your nose was pressed hard against the glass, it was almost yours, this other life that lay in wait for you with its silverware and brocade' (pp. 59, 63).

Moorhouse (1989) notes that 'no one ever seems to have held a St George's Day Parade', and that 'White Anglo-Saxon Protestants' are invariably 'held in suspicion by almost everybody else' (p. 82). Perhaps because 'it was the British they were originally supposed to bear arms against' (Hoggart 1992: 102), and a 'lingering hostility to the old colonial power' (Moorhouse 1989: 259) lurks in keyring motifs: 'Fucking jerk, Fuck you, You're an asshole, Eat shit' (Davies 1993: 21), and the jeers of Bart Simpson, with 'his finger upraised in a gesture of crude dismissal' (Brown 1994: 32).

There is a recurrent temptation to claim immediate participation in American culture. Hoggart (1992), for example, breezily claims 'the people who live there are not especially different from us. Their languages, laws and religion are derived from ours ... While I lived in the States, I was only half-aware of being a foreigner' (p. 9). Sante (1991), the Belgian, in contrast, is calmly lucid about the 'colonial lineage' that 'carries no resonance and only exists as a vestige' for a New York 'cast in the future tense' (p. x).

The new wave of immigration, primarily Korean and Vietnamese, has such an intentness and lack of inhibition that all attempts to belittle and contain it backfire: Raban (1990) is poignantly envious of the Korean capacity to be 'living the movie' in Seattle, validated by the *'Home Run'* of paternity (pp. 324, 300); Young's (1995) Vietnamese acquaintances are too busy to take time off to visit him because 'The future: that's where *their* dream lies' (p. 24); and Brown (1994) finds that the Asians have 'no past, all future. They want to make it' (p. 36).

Talking about flight from political oppression, economic opportunity and accelerated integration raises questions about the degree of assimilation of the traveller's own voice. This is apparent in the complex ambivalence of the device of comparison, *x* in America is like *y* at home: 'the old world sneaks into every unregarded gap that it can find' (Raban 1996: 23). Rather than descriptions being presented 'only in terms of their difference to objects in Britain' (Mills 1991: 86), however, a double defamiliarisation is operative. The readily available reference point initially attempts to domesticate the American context, but is transplanted and surreally juxtaposed in a manner that inevitably undermines the authority of the commentary. The passengers at Grand Central Station 'make the crowds at the major European commuting stations, like Waterloo and the Gare de l'Est, look distinctly sluggish and just a little dowdy by comparison' (Moorhouse 1989: 197); instead of tornado warnings, 'on TV back in Wales, cosy duffers and smiley girls deploy play-school graphics to tell me, basically, if it's going to rain or not' (Davies 1993: 51); in the Mineshaft club, sexually explicit photos are displayed like 'souvenir pictures pinned up after a ball on the QE2 or after the wizard social that followed the cricket match on the green' (Brook 1985: 163).

Bryson (1994), in contrast, thrives on the giganticism of 'parking lots the size of Shropshire' (p. 46); cheerfully endorses disparaging stereotypes ('It was the worst food I had ever had – and remember, I've lived in Britain' [p. 29]); and feels no inclination habitually to internalise tableaux of melancholy diminishment:

> In Britain it had been a year without summer. Wet spring had merged imperceptibly into bleak autumn. For months the sky had remained a depthless grey. Sometimes it rained, but mostly it was just dull, a land without shadows. It was like living inside Tupperware. And here suddenly the sun was dazzling in its intensity. (Bryson 1994: 14)

The unqualified nature of the antithesis ('dull' versus 'dazzling') and the ultimate circumscription ('inside Tupperware') throw into sharp relief the anachronistic rhetorical demeanour of the British traveller.

The discursive stance of condescension – 'dry little British jokes, fine

little British caste distinctions, and surprisingly formal British manners'
(Mulvey 1990: 31) – has long roots. Mulvey notes that 'verbal self-
promotion and self-assertion ... were a redundancy for an aristocracy who
could always attract favourable attention by displays of modesty, even self-
deprecation'; thus 'proclamations of ignorance and inexpertness were covert
statements of status' (p. 185). Understatements, wryness, perception of
ironies, self-deflating asides, mock-humility and serious pathos become the
stylistic norms against which the scale of America is to be measured,
arguably simply a travesty of a new continent, a new kind of experience
whose irreducibility ensures that 'not even the most fastidiously cultivated
European would be able to patronise them any more' (Moorhouse 1989:
347–8).

The most familiar variant of transatlantic crossings is the nineteenth-
century topos of 'the American visiting Europe – the theme of Innocent
or Ingenue abroad' (Kowalewski 1992: 12), although even in the classic
Jamesian drama, the customary affluence of the visitor testifies to the
growing strength of the United States (Stowe 1994). For the contemporary
British traveller, American difference is manifested most clearly in confidence, abundance and privilege: his own qualities of naivete, gaucheness,
and insufficiency are projected on to the host culture. Raban's title, *Old
Glory* (1986), applies to the position of the British ('smarting under a half-
articulated sense of their national dislocation and national impotence'
[p. 402]), rather than that of the Southern states (which have gained
massively in both economic and political influence during recent decades).
Bryson's *The Lost Continent* similarly gestures at a notional decline in
small-town values, but alludes more precisely to the break-away by the
thirteen colonies during the War of Independence. Davies (1993) is lectured
on American 'Entropy' – 'When you lose your energy, you don't get it
back' ... 'Greece. Rome. Portugal. Spain. France. Britain. Us' (p. 291) –
but it is the post-war British sensibility which is more convincingly that
of 'an imperial nation that has lost its way ... resigned, wry, concerned
with higher things' (N. Williams 1995: 152).

## 4. Rites of Passage

Each and every traveller might be seen as 'an English agent newly
parachuted in' (Hoggart 1992: 30). This transition tends to be presented,
with varying degrees of explicitness, as a form of rebirth. For Raban,
(1986) descent into the 'dank and cellarlike' lock was 'a kind of symbolic
induction, a rite of passage into my new state as a river traveller' (p. 65);
the transatlantic passage becomes 'a strange and frightening sea-ritual,
which would ineluctably transform you' (Raban 1990: 8). The European

self must be cast off and a new and liberating identity assumed: 'Before it was anything else, America was the voyage itself' (p. 9), a process of negation of previous constraints, of the 'European sense of deference' (p. 10). (Drew [1994] amusingly parodies the portentous 'symbolic death' with an extended digression on campsite bathing facilities: 'from my experience this cleansing ritual is not always simple' [pp. 176–7].) Raban claims that 'the soul is put to trial and shriven; a new self is born in glory at the end of the rite' (1987: 265), but this transformation is better regarded as a form of protective mimicry by 'European man, who has for decades been trying to imitate the American dream' (Moorhouse 1989: 18).

In some obvious ways it is difficult for the visitor to do otherwise than eat American, drive American, dress American; Raban (1986) hopes 'that if I acquired a few symbols of pioneer self-sufficiency, it would bring about a transformation of my character and turn me into a proper outdoor adventurer' (p. 49). But the element of conscious duplication and space for self-contempt remain paramount. The traveller is stigmatised by his origins, which re-emerge as a implicit point of latent comparison and chastisement. Raban feels 'rueful to see myself travestied by this foolish character on television', but is nevertheless obliged to acknowledge the 'cheesey pallor' and 'urban fatigue' of the 'clowning greenhorn' on the screen as his own (p. 76). More traumatically, a motel overhead mirror prompts the lament, 'Who on earth could bear to wake to the sight of their own nakedness so splayed and deranged?' (Raban 1990: 150).

The projected identity, the craved transformation, is not into a new individual, but into a familiar type. Englishness must be shed as an embarrassment and an inhibition, to be replaced by the mass man of the mass culture, now to be envied and emulated, 'the person you would eventually become when, and if, you reached the far shore' (p. 8). This 'dizzy sense of social weightlessness' means the traveller is 'invited to experiment, to fantasise, to play with strange and colourful self-images'.

The department store, Macy's, becomes the focal point of this capacity for metamorphosis, 'a world constructed for creatures with infantile attention spans, for whom every moment had to be crammed with novelties and sensations' (p. 69). This magical realm evokes by contrast 'that other world of clothing coupons and short rations', temporal as well as geographical: British post-war austerity, in which Raban himself necessarily partook.

I kept barging into a figure who darkly resembled Henry James's inconceivable alien. I first spotted him in the Victorian men's club: a lank and shabby character in scuffed shoes and concertina trousers whose hair (or what little that was left of it) badly needed pruning. He could have done with a new set of teeth. Had I seen him in the subway station, shaking a polystyrene cup under my nose, I'd have given him a couple of quarters and walked on fast, but in Macy's there was no escaping him. He jumped out at me from behind a rack of padlocked fur coats, and was waiting for me at the bookstore. Wherever he was, he looked equally out of place and I grew increasingly ashamed of him. (Raban 1990: 69–70)

Here we have not the tramp as existentialist but existentialist as tramp, evoking not the metaphysical anxiety of the doppelganger, but an unsparing self-indictment on strictly material grounds. (Later as a 'pretend beggar', Raban has the experience of being 'willed into non-existence by total strangers' through their 'frank contempt' [p. 80].) 'Luxurious artifice' has the power of 'making you feel rotten about yourself': similarly Nigel Williams (1985) finds that 'when solidified', American dreams 'have the habit of shaming European ambitions' (p. 30). Commercial psychology is not the antithesis but the consummation of the 'theological rhetoric in which so much of the European colonisation of America was conducted' (Raban 1990: 41; cf. 1996: 9): signs of election are required in 'an American haircut and a new pair of shiny oxblood Italian loafers'.

'There was a new life waiting in America for all the rubbish in the attics of genteel England', Raban observes (1990), which awaits the 'labour of the alchemist' that will 'stiffen' them 'with exclusiveness and nobility' (p. 68). The 'hoard of moth-eaten Edwardiana' that was 'ransacked' and transported from Liverpool on the *Atlantic Conveyor* (pp. 68–9) accompanied Raban himself on his voyage: 'doubly imitation Anglo, a replica not of the real thing but of how Americans imagine the real thing to be' (Raban 1992: 126). 'The selling of the past has become a mania with the British' (N. Williams 1995: 157), and cultural identity has itself become an object for the American consumer. This is epitomised in the style of Ralph Lauren, whose 'essential symbolism ... was not drawn directly from England, but from P.B.S. television – from "Masterpiece Theatre" and its repertory of soap operas with introductions by Alistair Cooke' (Raban 1990: 96). Lauren is accused of 'eradicating the last trace of historical reality from his fiction' (p. 98): his work, however, may be seen as a vivid dramatisation of the loss of the power that underpinned the 'lives of the English upper class in the heyday of Empire and the Raj' (p. 97).

Raban protests that 'I wanted to see what a new life might look like', but this misses the point that the 'shabby keepsakes of lost empire' have been changed, changed utterly (p. 73): it is not a lifestyle over which Raban can claim proprietorial rights. These goods represent not 'genteel undemocratic dowdiness', but exactly the same impulse of eclectic cultural appropriation on the basis of economic and military power that America now practises. They may now appear as 'emptily fantastic as the culture of the Ch'ing

Dynasty or Tutankhamun', but those, along with the Edwardian Raj, were empires of mythic stature (p. 74). Lauren offers not a 'makeshift reconstruction', but 'a brand-new American invention, as vividly of its own moment as the Reebok and the Space War machine' (p. 99).

Raban stubbornly avoids the implications of his own argument: the 'new American pastoral' (p. 96) is presented as a flight from technology, the city, mass production rather than as the privilege of a dominant culture (the 'Macy empire' [p. 104]). Macy's parade prompts reflection on the 'extraordinarily mythopoeic character of life in this strange country' (p. 122). Irony directed against Macy as a 'solitary American hero' turns back against itself: 'The sale of dry goods and notions was of course something you could set aside alongside the conquering of the frontier or the pursuit of the white whale' (p. 124). To which, one must reply in the affirmative, in so far as both have been victorious in their respective centuries.

## 5. Imbalances of Power

Karen Lawrence (1994) observes that 'travel literature, by both men and women writers, explores not only political freedoms but also cultural constraints; it provides a kind of imaginative resistance to its own plot' (p. 19). From this perspective, the British traveller never leaves home: 'the overspilling cornucopia of America's advance' (Davies 1993: 141) merely provokes an ever more insistent contrast with what is implicit but usually denied (see Cocker 1992: 12–13, 16; George 1996: 2; Caesar 1995: 5). Butor (1994) claims that 'my departed home and country will soon become as seductive as the finally visited country of my dreams' (p. 61), but the experience that the British visitor brings is one of 'slow dereliction' (Raban 1986: 250); 'a story of cultural defeat, something an Englishman is only too well able to understand' (N. Williams 1995: 47); 'that familiar drizzling sense of failure' and 'a surrender to the passivity and helplessness which these areas breed, a kind of reciprocal dejection' (Brook 1993: 25, 263). Young (1995) finds New York 'too much a city full of ghosts' (p. xiii); even the ostensibly streetwise Cohn (1992) laments a past Broadway of which he himself had no experience. (The Belgian Sante [1991], in contrast, dismisses 'nostalgia' as 'a state of inarticulate contempt for the present and fear for the future' [p. xi].) The elegiac tendency at times comes perilously close to a lament for lost youth; but is partially redeemed by its clear cultural analogues: hope, possibility, energy, glimpsed but subsequently disavowed from a vantage of depletion and fatigue. Brown confesses to

> a curious nostalgia for an era which I had never known, an intangible sense
> of longing and regret, as if I had somehow inherited my parents' memories,

or rather the emotional responses which came with their memories, along
with the colour of my hair, my eyes, my disposition. Miller's music seemed
to have been playing for ever in a world tantalisingly beyond my own experience, but which had irrevocably shaped the one into which I had been
born: a world of war, heroic self-sacrifice, the certainties of right and wrong
(the world of the gas mask and steel helmet which gathered dust in the
shed, the remnants of the Anderson shelter in the back garden). (Brown
1994: 34–5)

The comparatively domestic setting ('shed', 'back garden') accentuates
rather than detracts from the 'heroic self-sacrifice' of a previous generation.
The 'longing and regret' are, however, transposed from a British past on
to an American present: like Cohn, Brown stresses the absence of the
golden era, the classic sound (in plain contradiction of the continued global
ascendancy of American popular music).

The travellers usually come from a generation too young to have had
direct experience of the Second World War, and one might have expected
more conscious reflection on the actual post-war balance of power between
Britain and the United States: 'We're too rich … We're the top animal.
We've fixed things. And now we've got freedom rocking the world' (Brown
1994: 236). There is strikingly little consideration, however, of the foreign
excursions of the Reagan–Bush era – Panama, Grenada, Nicaragua – and
the consequences of such activities as the US bombing of Tripoli, where
acquiescence, as Mortimer (1988) comments, means 'Britain has lost its
identity and is in danger of becoming a tasteless mid-Atlantic mess, like
the food in an international airport hotel' (p. 414). From this perspective
'the east coast of the United States and the English home counties had
blurred into one. London was a city just a little east of Boston' (Raban
1986: 100). Or Orwell's Airstrip One, as is suggested by the continual
reminiscences from veteran fliers of the Second World War.

The more openly expository accounts come closest to addressing Anglo-
American relations, albeit in a problematic historical perspective. Hoggart
(1992) chooses to present Suez as 'the moment when the American people
finally realised that their country was now alone as leader of the western
world, the head of the family' (p. 14) rather than as a British humiliation.
(It emerges as a kind of repressed memory in Raban's [1986] 'gibbering trail
of free association': 'what the hell. *Suez? who is? where the zoo is*' [p. 336].)
The 'popular notion on the British Left, that the United States sees our
island as little more than a convenient aircraft carrier' is brushed aside by
Hoggart (1992) as 'unrecognisable to any American', which does not of
course refute it (p. 14). His journalistic insider's personalising of the political
('Dukakis couldn't read the American mind' [p. 97]) leads to judgements

not merely questionable but clearly ludicrous: 'If one superpower, the Soviet Union, chooses to abdicate, then the authority of the rival superpower is necessarily undermined as well. If Cambridge announced that, owing to decades of failure, it was going to give up competing in the Boat Race, then who would care about the Oxford team?' (p. 206). Everyone, if Oxford possessed an arsenal of thermo-nuclear warheads.

Moorhouse's study of New York (1989) bears the epigraph: 'we will discover this new imperial city of today, celebrating its peak of arrogance', in a manner which 'an Englishman should know as well as anyone and better than most' (p. 355). 'The United States gladly accepts its role as a superpower and would not be anything else, but it is loath to acknowledge that a superpower (of whatever brand) is merely a deodorised imperialist – and that sometimes it smells as powerfully as anything of the kind that went before' (p. 335). The displacement is explicit: contemporary European culture is acknowledged to consist of 'merely mediocre imitations of American post-war structures' (p. 352) and 'London, the old imperial capital, appears to be suffering from a pernicious anaemia now' (p. 355).

Moorhouse speaks what the others must repress, but at the cost of a kind of etiolation and mismatch of voice, that implicitly proclaims the redundancy and anachronism of its very virtues: clarity, order, balance. The 'rounded and thoughtful human being' (p. 211; cf. Brook's 'genteel, high-toned orderliness' [1993: 63]) and prose emergent therefrom, are manifestly inappropriate to registering, acknowledging and perhaps celebrating the dynamism of that culture. A variety of personae are offered within Moorhouse's (1989) calm expository prose – 'stranger' and 'outsider'; 'pedestrian observer' (in both senses); 'foreign scoffers', 'compulsive sight-seer', 'watcher' and 'hypercritical souls' (pp. 19, 23, 27, 28, 29, 31), later even 'stubborn misanthrope' (p. 106) – but all these possible vantages on the skyscrapers of Manhattan are 'staggered at once by their collective might'. The relationship to empire has inevitably transformed the witness, and the motivation of a wide range of narrative devices, obviously indebted to the techniques of the new journalism, is to convey the perspective of a new type of post-imperial observer, both enabled and circumscribed by the encounter with American culture.

## 6. Pop Imperialism

It has become a truism of contemporary post-colonial studies that relations of power may be construed in terms of structures of desire. If 'pop culture ruled the world, and America ruled pop culture' (Iyer 1988: 11), then the subordination of other cultures may be achieved at least partially in terms 'of dreams, of fantasies, of preposterous yet satisfying excess' (Brook 1993: 2). More specifically, there is a recurrence of gestures of masochistic submission: 'Voluntary enslavement before my very eyes' (Brook 1985: 164); 'I was ready to crawl to the Promised Land on my knees. And so it seemed was everyone around me' (Brown 1994: 62); 'I loved Los Angeles, it excited and terrified me, and I'd prostrated myself' (Rayner 1992: 69).

It should be stressed that this ideological insertion, or perhaps more accurately libidinal interpellation, is by no means straightforward. If there is a consummation devoutly to be wished simply in being in America, an expectation of finding one's true self – whether at the Chelsea Hotel or Beale St or downtown Los Angeles – there is also the counter-possibility of difference being painfully enforced. One simply does not belong: the historical links are of severance. 'On 2nd Avenue I saw my dream walking. "Hello, Dream", I said. "Get the hell, motherfucker", said my dream' (H. Williams 1981: 200).

For a slightly older generation, the myths are comparatively high-cultural: Raban re-enacting Huck Finn's voyage down the Mississippi, Young posturing as Philip Marlowe. I wish to close, however, by looking at the impact of cinema and popular music on Rayner and Brown, and contrasting these with Bryson's response.

Rayner (1992) opens his text with the confession that he 'somehow never went to America, even though it had been there from the beginning, lined up for me, a mystery waiting to invade my life' (p. 7); the connotations of 'invade' are obviously not fortuitous. 'I belonged to a generation raised on stories of glamour, stories of violence and excitement, stories of America', a realm absolutely opposed to the provincial constraints of 'Bradford, a soot-caked Victorian city, then capital of the north of England's wool industry' (p. 5). In the upheaval of moving house, American music represents therapeutic release: 'I pressed my face against the cool glass of the windscreen and heard my brother sing Eddie Cochran' (p. 5). The very consolation that American culture offers becomes a focus for paternal resentment and interdiction: '"Yank rubbish", said my father, thrusting the comics into the flames of the kitchen grate' (p. 6).

An epigraph from Gibbon neatly combines desire and popular culture – 'The intervals of lust were filled up with the basest amusements' – and the imperial analogue is later developed in baroque form: 'Los Angeles is like Rome. During the reign of Commodus. Violence, decadence, insanity. It is all here, and the sexually intriguing footnotes are not in Latin' (p. 176). A masochistic attraction to aggression pervades the text: 'When in Rome fuck the Romans before they fuck you' (p. 184). Hostility is accepted and even at times actively solicited: at a disco, 'A fist came out of the crowd and knocked off my glasses. I didn't mind' (p. 22); 'What happens in the end' of 'a story about Americans not understanding this European' is 'They kill the dude' (pp. 169–70); 'Los Angeles, it seemed, was giving it to England in a big way', prompting the reflection that the best way for the English to 'stick together' is by attending each other's funerals (p. 126).

The idea of a 'love affair with America' (N. Williams 1995: 28) is a recurrent motif in British travel writing: 'This could be a way for me to say goodbye. It could also be a love-letter to New York City' (Pye 1991: 6); 'America's like that girl you had that thing with when you were twenty, that girl who drove you crazy' (Davies 1993: 315). Rayner (1992) develops the trope of 'an Englishman, in love with the idea of America' (p. 9) up to and beyond the point of self-parody by personifying it in Barbara, the Playboy-bunny.

Instant infatuation spurs Rayner to abandon his long-suffering partner, Jane, who had been 'wanting us to get married for over two years' (p. 133) in pursuit of a holiday romance, 'on the 1 a.m. from everything real, playing at adventure' (p. 8). But reality cannot simply be identified with a past life which is presented as drab, restricted, boring, among 'the English: a mob of rainsoaked punks who couldn't buy beer when they wanted' (p. 173). 'At college a friend and I used to learn dialogue from movies' (p. 90), and the text continually reprocesses these citations until films become the primary mode of reference and categorisation. Rayner plays a series of elaborate games on the ambivalent status of his narrative: it becomes irrelevant to inquire whether it is fact or fiction, whether the conversation with Bryan Ferry, for instance, ever took place. What matters is that it is situated in the realm of 'adventure' negatively defined as a conscious and deliberate refusal of 'home'.

Movies always imply, however, that someone is running the production: like Patterson, with his love-triangle plot, 'taking sadistic pleasure in his control of the situation' (p. 76). 'What awful sexual despair', it is pondered, 'could lead a man to assault Minnie Mouse' (p. 18): one different in degree perhaps, but not in kind from Rayner's panic-stricken response to deviation from his own preinscribed longings: 'This was not my script. This was definitely not my script' (p. 157).

'I told Barbara I thought my sense of the erotic was entirely derived from movies' to which she replies, sensibly enough, 'What sense of the erotic?' (p. 146). More sinisterly, her initial appeal, looking as if 'she had walked straight out of a surfing movie' (p. 3), is later connected to the theory of 'surf Nazis': through attracting 'the strongest, fittest, most beautiful' since the 1920s, 'it was Los Angeles … not Hitler's Germany, which had given the world a master race' (p. 104). (This apparently facetious intimation of incipient fascism is further supported by Mrs Wechler's complaint of 'long hours' working in a 'concentration camp', and the dance-floor chant, 'The Holocaust is now. Hitler showed us how' [pp. 69, 22].)

The fantasy lineage of the good parent – 'Jack Nicholson, who was exactly like Jack Nicholson' and whose advice 'set me straight' (pp. 174–5) – is contrasted with the actual paternal figure, traumatically exposed in childhood as 'a fraud' (p. 61). Yet if Nicholson's film roles provided 'the moments which formed part of my dream about America', Rayner's perception of and subsequent disillusion with his ex-RAF father derives from idealised expectations founded upon his first movie, *The Dam Busters* (p. 61).

Englishness is not only not unmediated, but also obliged to transform itself into ever more grotesque forms. Working as a 'mechanical man' in the 'Wax Museum', Rayner claims to be 'giving advice on the English characters who might be included in the collection' (p. 21): the English Lorraine 'looked like Diana Dors on mescalin' (p. 11); 'an English producer with an Elvis Presley quiff and a face that hideously resembled a rodent' (p. 40); and an 'English director named Freddie who for some reason planned a film version of *Beowulf*' (p. 170).

> I ordered beers, and heard Kimberley telling Barbara that I was not what she had expected. What might that have been? Slashed jeans and safety pins, a spiky haircut: ageing Sex Pistol? Armani suit and gold collar pin: city whizz kid? Tweed jacket with pipe and scarf flung round my neck: writer type? Or a public school boy, nasal vowels and bow tie: Rupert Everett in *Another Country*? It depended, I supposed, on the movies she'd been watching. (Rayner 1992: 145)

When told of the invitation to 'tie me up' delivered on the beach, Barbara scornfully retorts to Rayner that what was really in bondage is 'Your imagination, your mind' (p. 109), both in its restricted repertoire of roles and in its abject cultural submission. Yet this is an inescapable condition: one is never without an ideological map in this sense; freedom is not leaving the movie but choosing your own script and turning your limitations into strengths.

Furthermore, the relation to America is openly avowed to be one of desire, which in turn redefines the traveller as a 'hysterical adolescent' (p. 8). There is a decisive refusal of guilt in favour of an undifferentiating impulse of pleasure-seeking: 'you're like a child, you have the ego of a baby, you're fucked up, you're a total fuck-up' (p. 180). One notable instance of this naive bewilderment and impulsive hedonism is the willingness to experiment with drugs – 'what is crystal methadrine?' (p. 118) – whereas other travellers shy away from even the mildest of illicit indulgences ('I wish I could but I can't keep it on the boat' [Raban 1990: 396]). Rayner's great achievement is to disavow restraint and maturity in favour of immersion and abandonment, accepting it as a necessary condition of release, even redemption, from an otherwise inexorable cultural diminishment.

Brown (1994) opens by evoking his suburban childhood as an implicit gesture of distance travelled by the author in class as well as geographical terms ('From the perspective of South London, South Memphis seemed impossibly romantic' [p. 57]). 'Cultural shifts' in America had at that time 'sounded in Britain like ricochets of gunfire, messages I had been hearing since adolescence' (p. 5):

> Pop music is a language of hidden codes and meanings. It speaks to those who have ears to listen. It draws maps of emotional landscapes, and sometimes geographical ones too. It plants ideas, dreams, to incubate in the imagination, to be tested and proved. I drew a map of America from songs, came to it like a blind man reading Braille. (Brown 1994: 5)

The self-designation as a 'blind man reading Braille' (appropriate as a reference to musical scores) establishes a context of miraculous redemption for 'those who have ears to listen'. The idea of the elect deciphering 'hidden codes', however, is difficult to reconcile with the popular availability of this music. When Chuck Berry sings 'Anything you want they got it here in the USA', it is acknowledged that 'there was no more persuasive salesman for the American Dream' (p. 52). Brown nevertheless attempts to maintain a qualitative distinction between the manipulation of American advertising, 'the relentless messages to consume, which could seem like harmlessly amusing diversions one minute, but the most insidious and poisonous brainwashing the next' (p. 204), and songs as 'the heartbeat of America, the coded messages of the nation's psyche' (p. 121):

> These songs were pieces of American heaven, describing a vista of possibilities that found no equivalent in English music. They hinted at a vastness, a variegated landscape and range of experiences that demanded to be celebrated, made sense of ... This was indoctrination masquerading as infatuation, perhaps. I felt in a sense, American; my culture more of that country than my own. Now it is called Coca-Colonisation, but it felt like missionary work and I was an eager convert. (Brown 1994: 6)

Brown, disappointingly, fails to develop the implications of this 'indoctrination' or to struggle against the influence of 'Coca-Colonisation'. There is no critique of the element of betrayal, desertion, involved in the 'eager convert' who feels 'my culture more of that country than of my own', and no self-reflexive awareness of how the authority of the British traveller, implicitly drawing on an imperial heritage, itself must be changed by this pre-formation. Instead only the emancipatory possibilities of

'American heaven' are stressed; and the sublime 'vista' and 'vastness' are concentrated into one final epiphany.

> All the way across America I had been conscious of a country disintegrating before my eyes. But here, at last, was the healing Wholeness. The perfect reconciliation of the most profound atavistic desires, dreams and myths – the Civil War South, country music, the Caribbean holiday, mall shopping. A place with no turmoil, no poverty, no strife, no taxes. And there, in the heavens, a camp angel in blue sequins, playing 'Silent Night'. I had found American heaven. (Brown 1994: 242)

The traveller momentarily takes on the role of both the 'camp angel' singing the hymn and the audience undergoing 'perfect reconciliation'. This lyric flourish self-guarded by pre-emptive kitsch opts for a 'healing Wholeness' which not only refuses sceptical distance, but betrays the fundamental ethos of its genre by positing a moment that allows no continuation, no afterwards. (Bull [1993], in contrast, engaged on a similar musical pilgrimage to map 'the soundtrack against which I have lived my life', finds in Nashville 'America at its shallowest, most schmaltzy, money-grabbing and exploitative' [pp. 128, 79].)

Bryson's childhood encounter with European culture has a superficial similarity to that of Brown and Rayner:

> Then one grey Sunday afternoon when I was about ten I was watching TV and there was a documentary on about movie-making in Europe. One clip showed Anthony Perkins walking along some sloping city street at dusk. I don't remember now if it was Rome or Paris, but the street was cobbled and shiny with rain and Perkins was hunched deep in a trench coat and I thought, 'Hey, *c'est moi*!' I began to read – no, *to consume* – *National Geographics*, with their pictures of glowing Lapps and mist-shrouded castles and ancient cities of infinite charm. From that moment, I wanted to be a European boy … I cannot for the life of me think why. (Bryson 1994: 7)

There is double media framing of TV and cinema: adopting an identity is unproblematically presented in terms of 'movie-making' rather than simply watching: a conscious, voluntary activity. The lack of specificity ('Rome or Paris') expands into an anthropological dominance ('*National Geographics*'): there is no such thing as a composite 'European boy'. The most obvious reason 'why' is the power to 'consume', as an economically privileged purchaser, with a secondary sense of 'ignite', consume in flames.

There is an alternative primal scene offered, however:

> I was alone in a curtained room in front of the TV, lost in a private world, with a plate of Oreo cookies on my lap and Hollywood magic flickering on

my glasses ... The one constant in these pictures was the background. It was always the same place, a trim and sunny little city with a tree-lined Main Street full of friendly merchants ... Everybody on TV ... lived in this middle-class Elysium. So did the people in the advertisements in magazines and on the commercials on television and in the Norman Rockwell paintings on the covers of the *Saturday Evening Post.* (Bryson 1994: 37–8)

For Bryson the media are the source of not only the pouting European existential hero, but also a counter-balancing ideal of the 'middle-class Elysium' of small-town family life and community, which he is able to inhabit with equal facility: one does not have to be sacrificed to enter the other. Its level of affluence is always presupposed: there is ready acceptance that 'not having running water in the house is something beyond the realms of the imaginable to most Americans' (p. 70; compare the incredulity at the very existence of outside lavatories [Rayner 1992: 106]). The nostalgia is as pronounced as his British counterparts, only what for them is the future is for Bryson already past: 'it all seems so long ago now, and it was' (p. 20).

For both Rayner and Brown, American culture represents a future and more abundant life, prized as a compensation for present deprivations. It possesses an oppositional status in so far as movies and pop music establish the autonomous tastes and buying power of the teenager, as an implicit refusal of parental authority; more importantly, it intimates a utopian elsewhere and alleviates a culturally pervasive disappointment and fatigue. The counter-argument would be that they have been duped by American 'pop-cultural imperialism' (Iyer 1988: 11): their urge for emancipation involves abject submission to an alien power. British travel writing on the USA displays a belatedness that is moral and political as well as textual: '"You're full of pain ... You see yourself as a second-class citizen, therefore a traveller. You're so full of pain it's pathetic." That was before I became "full of anger" and "full of shit"' (H. Williams 1981: 189). Like Raban's second-rate chanteuse, the sub-genre possesses an 'unintentional, rather terrible, sincerity':

It was smart now to sing of loss and failure and the discovery that life was mostly second-hand. The catch was that the songs were supposed to be sung by successes, international stars of loss and failure. From the mouth of a real loser, they came close to genuine blubbering despair. And in this setting, where the hopefulness of the immigrants who had created it was so close to the historical surface, far from sounding narcissistically wry and self-knowing, they sounded simply and painfully tragic. (Raban 1986: 75)

# Bibliography

## 1. Primary

Amis, Martin (1987) *The Moronic Inferno and Other Visits to America* (1986), London: Penguin.

Arber, Edward (ed.) (1885) *The First Three English Books on America. [?1511–1555 A.D.]*, Birmingham [np].

Ballantyne, Robert Michael (1869) *The Gorilla Hunters*, London: T. Nelson.

Bandele-Thomas, Biyi (1991) *The Man Who Came In From the Back of Beyond*, London: Bellew.

Banks, Joseph (1962; 1963) *The 'Endeavour' Journal of Joseph Banks, 1768–1771*, ed. J. C. Beaglehole, 2 vols, Sydney: Trustees of the Public Library of New South Wales in association with Angus and Robertson.

Bass, Rick (1995) *The Lost Grizzlies*, Boston: Houghton Mifflin.

— (1996) *The Book of Yaak*, Boston: Houghton Mifflin.

Baudrillard, Jean (1988) *America* (trans. Chris Turner), London: Verso.

Bedford, Simi (1991) *Yoruba Girl Dancing*, London: Heinemann.

Biard, Pierre (1612; 1896–1901) *Letter from Port Royal in Arcadia ...* , in Reuben Gold Thwaites (ed.), *The Jesuit Relations and Allied Documents: Travels and Explorations of the Jesuit Missionaries in New France, 1610–1791*, 73 vols, Cleveland, OH, vol. II.

Boswell, James (1953) *Boswell on the Grand Tour: Germany and Switzerland, 1764*, ed. Frederick A. Pottle, London: Heinemann.

— (1955) *Boswell on the Grand Tour: Italy, Corsica and France*, ed. Frank Brady and Frederick A. Pottle, London: Heinemann.

Bougainville, Louis Antoine de (1771; 1772) *A Voyage round the World* (trans. John Reinhold Foster), London: S. Nourse and T. Davies.

Brook, Stephen (1985) *New York Days. New York Nights* (1984), London: Picador.

— (1985) *Honky-Tonk Gelato: Travels through Texas*, London: Hamish Hamilton.

— (1993) *L.A. Lore* (1992), London: Picador.

Brown, Mick (1994) *American Heartbeat: Travels from Woodstock to San Jose by Song Title* (1993), London: Penguin.

Bryson, Bill (1994) *The Lost Continent: Travels in Small Town America* (1989), London: Abacus.

— (1995) *Notes from a Small Island*, New York: Doubleday.

Bull, Andy (1993) *Coast to Coast: A Rock Fan's U.S. Tour*, London: Black Swan.

Burnett, James Lord Monboddo (1773–92) *Of the Origin and Progress of Language*, 6 vols, Edinburgh: T. Cadell, W. Creech, A. Kincaid.

Burton, Richard (1857) *Personal Narrative of a Pilgrimage to al-Madinah and Meccah*, 2 vols, London: Longman.

Byron, Robert (1937; 1981) *The Road to Oxiana*, London: Picador.

Chapone, Hester (1773; 1823) *Letters on the Improvement of the Mind*, Edinburgh: John Anderson.

Chatwin, Bruce (1979) *In Patagonia* (1977), London: Picador.

— (1981) introduction to Byron, *The Road to Oxiana*, 9–15.

— (1982) *The Viceroy of Ouidah* (1980), London: Picador.

— (1983) 'An Eye and Some Body', introductory essay to Robert Mapplethorpe, *Lady Lisa Lyon*, New York: Viking Press, 9–14.

— (1987) 'An Interview with Bruce Chatwin', with Michael Ignatieff, *Granta* 21, 21–38.

— (1988) *The Songlines* (1987), London: Picador.

— (1989) *Utz* (1988), London: Picador.

— (1990) *What am I Doing Here* (1990), London: Picador.

— (1993a) with Paul Theroux, *Patagonia Revisited* (1985), Worcester: Michael Russell.

— (1993b) *Photographs and Notebooks*, ed. and intro. Francis Wyndham, London: Jonathan Cape.

— (1996) *Anatomy of Restlessness: Uncollected Writings*, ed. Jan Borm and Matthew Graves, London: Jonathan Cape.

Chesterfield, Philip Dormer Stanhope, Earl of (1774; 1992) *Correspondence*, ed. David Roberts, Oxford: OUP.

Cohn, Nik (1992) *The Heart of the World*, London: Chatto and Windus.

Columbus, Christopher (1968) *The Journal of Christopher Columbus* (trans. Cecil Jane; rev. L. A. Vigneras), London: Hakluyt Society.

Courtenay, John (1774) *A Poeticall Epistle from an Officer at Otaheite to Lady Gr\*\*v\*n\*r*, London: T. Evans.

Craven, Elizabeth, Lady (1789) *A Journey through the Crimea to Constantinople. In a Series of Letters from the Right Hon. Elizabeth Lady Craven, to his Serene Highness the Margrave of Brandebourg, Anspach, and Bareith. Written in the Year MDCCLXXXVI*, London: G. G. J. Robinson.

— Margravine of Anspach (1814) *Letters from the Right Honorable Lady Craven, to His Serene Highness the Margrave of Anspach, during her Travels through France, Germany, and Russia in 1785 and 1786*, London.

— (1826) *Memoirs of the Margravine of Anspach, Written by Herself*, 2 vols, London: Henry Colburn.

Creider, Jane Tapsubei (1986) *Two Lives: My Spirit and I*, London: Women's Press.

Crone, R. G. and R. A. Skelton (1946) 'English Collections of Voyages and Travels 1625–1846', in Edward Lynam (ed.), *Richard Hakluyt and his Successors. A Volume Issued to Commemorate the Centenary of the Hakluyt Society*, London: Hakluyt Society.

d'Aunet, L. (1854; 1872) *Voyage d'une femme au Spitzberg*. Paris: Hachette.

— (1856) *Un mariage en province*, Paris: Hachette.

Davies, John (1786) 'A Discovery of the True Causes why Ireland was never brought under Obedience of the Crown of England, until the Beginning of his Majesty's happy Reign' (1612), in *Historical Tracts: By Sir John Davies*, ed. George Chalmers, London: John Stockdale.

Davies, Pete (1993) *Storm Country: A Journey to the Heart of America* (1992), London: Mandarin.

Davies, Robyn (1982) *Tracks* (1980), London: Paladin.

de Buffon, Georges-Louis Leclerc (1812) *Buffon's Natural History* (trans. William Smellie), 20 vols, London: T. Cadell and W. Davies.

de Charlevois, Pierre François Xavier (1769) *A History of Paraguay* ... , 2 vols, Dublin: D. and W. Saunders, B. Grierson, J. Potts, D. Chamberlaine and J. Williams.

Defoe, Daniel (1719) *The Life and Strange Suprizing Adventures of Robinson Crusoe*, London: W. Taylor.

— (1724–27) *A Tour thro' the Whole Island of Great Britain*, 3 vols, London: G. Strahan.

Doughty, Charles (1888) *Travels in Arabia Deserta*, Cambridge: CUP.

Douglas, Norman (1923) *Siren Land* (1911), London: Martin Secker.

Drew, Josie (1994) *Travels in a Strange State: Cycling across the USA*, London: Little, Brown and Co.

Du Chaillu, Paul B. (1861) *Explorations and Adventures in Equatorial Africa*, London: John Murray.

Ferguson, Adam (1767) *An Essay on the History of Civil Society*, Edinburgh and London: A. Kincaid, J. Bell, A. Millar, T. Cadell.

Fielding, Henry (1997) *Journal of a Voyage to Lisbon* (1755), ed. Ian A. Bell and Henry Varsey, Oxford: OUP.

Fitzpatrick, Sir Percy (1974) *Jock of the Bushveld* (1907), London: Longman.

Flaubert, Gustave (1972) *Flaubert in Egypt: A Sensibility on Tour* (1850), ed. and trans. Francis Steegmuller, London: Bodley Head.

Fordyce, James (1809) *Sermons to Young Women*, 3rd US from 12th London edn, Philadelphia and New York: M. Carey and I. Biley.

Freud, Sigmund (1973), 'A Disturbance of Memory on the Acropolis' (1936), in *The Standard Edition of the Complete Psychological Works of Sigmund Freud*, trans. and ed. James Strachey, London: Hogarth Press and the Institute of Psycho-analysis, vol. XXII, 239–48.

Gildon, Charles (1698) *Phaeton: or, the Fatal Divorce*, London: Abel Roper.

Gröndal, B. (1861) *Sagan af Heljarsloodarorrustu*, Copenhagen: Sveinsson.

Haggard, H. Rider (1887) *She: A History of Adventure*, London: Longmans.

Hakluyt, Richard (1925–28) *The Principal Navigations Voyages Traffiques and Discoveries of the English Nation* (1598–1600), intro. John Masefield, 8 vols, London and Toronto: Dent.

— (1935) *The Original Writings and Correspondence of the Two Richard Hakluyts*, Hakluyt Society, second series, no. LXXVII, 2 vols, London: CUP.

Harris, Wilson (1985) *The Secret Ladder* (1963), London: Faber.

Harrison, William (1587) 'A Historical Description of the Islandes of Britayne, etc.', in R. Holinshed, *The First and Second Volume of Chronicles*, 2 vols, London: J. Harrison, G. Bishop, R. Newbene, H. Denham and T. Woodcocke.

Hawkesworth, John (1773) *An Account of the Voyages undertaken by Order of His Present Majesty for making discoveries in the Southern Hemisphere*, 3 vols, London: W. Strahan and T. Cadell.

Herodotus (1992), *The Histories* (trans. Henry Cary from the text of Baehr), London: Folio Society.

Hill, Aaron (1709) *A Full and Just Account of the Present State of the Ottoman Empire*, London.

Hoggart, Simon (1992) *America: A User's Guide* (1990), London: Fontana.

Home, Henry, Lord Kames (1776) *Sketches of the History of Man*, 2 vols, Edinburgh: W. Creech.

Hume, David (1784) *Essays, Moral, Political and Literary* 2 vols (1753), London: T. Cadell.

Hyland, Paul (1988) *The Black Heart: A Voyage into Central Africa*, London: Gollancz.

Iyer, Pico (1988) *Video Nights in Kathmandu, and Other Reports from the Not-So-Far-East*, London: Black Swan.

Johnson, Samuel (1988) *The History of Rasselas, Prince of Abissinia* (1759), ed. J. P. Hardy, Oxford: OUP.

Joyce, James (1977) *Stephen Hero*, London: Granada.

Kinglake, Alexander W. (1992) *Eothen, or Traces of Travel brought home from the East* (1845), intro. Jonathan Raban, London: Centennary Publishing.

Kingsley, Mary (1897) *Travels in West Africa: Congo Français, Corisco and Cameroons*, London: Macmillan.

Kpomassie, Tete-Michel (1987) *An African in Greenland* (trans. James Kirkup), London: Secker and Warburg.

Lane, Edward W. (1836) *An Account of the Manners and Customs of the Modern Egyptians*, 2 vols, London.

Lawrence, T. E. (1935) *Seven Pillars of Wisdom: A Triumph*, London: Jonathan Cape.

Lévi-Strauss, Claude (1973) *Tristes Tropiques* (1955) (trans. John Weightman), London: Jonathan Cape.

Maja-Pearce, Adewale (1987) *In My Father's Country – A Nigerian Journey*, London: Heinemann.

Malinowski, Bronislaw (1922) *Argonauts of the Western Pacific: An Account of Native Enterprise and Adventure in the Archipelagos of Melanesian New Guinea*, London: Routledge.

— (1929) 'Practical Anthropology', *Africa* 11(1): 22–38.

— (1930) 'The Rationalisation of Anthropology and its Administration', *Africa* 111(4): 405–30.

— (1935) *Coral Gardens and Their Magic*, 2 vols, London: George Allen and Unwin.

— (1967) *A Diary in the Strict Sense of the Term*, London: Routledge.

Mandeville, Sir John (1967) *Mandeville's Travels*, ed. M. C. Seymour, Oxford: Clarendon Press.

Marbeau, J.-B.-F. (1834) *Politique des intérêts, ou essai sur les moyens d'améliorer le sort des travailleurs sans nuire aux propriétaires … par un travailleur devenu propriétaire*, Paris: Mame.

Marmier, X. (1844–47) *Voyages de la commisssion du Nord en Scandinavie, en Laponie, au Spitzberg et au Feroe, pendant les années 1838, 1839 et 1840 sur la corvette 'La Recherche'. Relation du voyage*, 2 vols, Paris: Bertrand.

— (1843) *Lettres sur la Russie, la Finlande et la Pologne*, Paris: Delloye.

Maxwell, Constantia (1923) *Irish History from Contemporary Sources (1509–1610)*, London: George Allen and Unwin.

*Metropolitan Nuncio, The, OR Times Truth-teller, commenting Verity, condemning Falsity, reproving the Wilful, pittying the Ignorant …* , Numb. 3 (From Wednesday, June 6, to

Wednesday, June 13, 1649).

Millar, John (1779) *The Origin of the Distinction of Ranks*, 3rd edn, London: John Murray.

*Moderate Intelligencer, The; Impartially communicating Martiall Affairs to the Kingdom of England*, Numb. 215 (From Thursday, April 26, to Wednesday, May 2, 1649).

Montagu, Lady Mary Wortley (1763) *Letters of the Right Honourable Lady M—y W—y M—e: Written, during her Travels in Europe, Asia, and Africa, to Persons of Distinction, Men of Letters, &c. in different Parts of Europe. Which contain, among other curious Relations, Accounts of the Policy and Manners of the Turks; drawn from Sources that have been inaccessible to other Travellers*, 3 vols, London: T. A. Becket and P. A. de Hondt.

— [spurious] (1767) *An Additional Volume to the Letters Of the Right Honourable Lady M—y W—y M—e: Written, during her Travels in Europe, Asia and Africa, to Persons of Distinction, Men of Letters, &c. in different Parts of Europe*, London.

— (1965–67) *The Complete Letters of Lady Mary Wortley Montagu*, ed. Robert Halsband, 3 vols, Oxford: OUP.

— (1977) *Essays and Poems, and 'Simplicity, a Comedy'*, ed. Robert Halsband and Isobel Grundy, Oxford: Clarendon Press.

— (1992) *Letters*, ed. Clare Brant, London: Dent.

Montaigne, Michel (1886) *The Essayes of Michel Lord of Montaigne* (1603) (trans. John Florio), ed. Henry Morley, London and New York: George Routledge and Sons.

Moorhouse, Geoffrey (1989) *Imperial City: The Rise and Rise of New York* (1988), London: Sceptre.

More, Thomas (1966) *Utopia* (1516) Menton: Scholar Press.

Mortimer, (1988) 'My Voyage Around Reagan's America', in Philip Marsden Smedley and Jeffrey Klinke (eds), *Views from Abroad: The Spectator Book of Travel Writing*, London: Grafton.

Naipaul, V. S. (1987) *The Enigma of Arrival*, London: Viking.

Nash, Thomas (1972) *The Unfortunate Traveller, and other Tales* (1595), ed. J. B. Stearne, London: Penguin.

Newby, Eric (1974) *A Short Walk in the Hindu Kush* (1958), London: Picador.

*New General Collection of Voyages and Travels, A* (1743–47), 4 vols, London: Thos. Astley.

Nichols, Philip, Preacher (1626) *Sir Francis Drake Reuiued: Calling vpon this dull or Effeminate Age, to folowe his Noble Steps for Golde and Siluer, By this Memorable Relation, of the Rare Occurrances (neuer declared to the World) in a Third Voyage, made by him into the West-Indies, in the Yeare 72. & 73. when Nombre de Dios was by him and 52. others only in his Company, surprised*, London: Printed by E.A. for Nicholas Bourne.

O'Hanlon, Redmond (1994) *Into the Heart of Borneo* (1984), London: Picador.

— (1988) *In Trouble Again*, London: Hamish Hamilton.

— (1996) *Congo Journey*, London: Hamish Hamilton.

*Otaheite* (1774), London: C. Bathurst.

Polo, Marco (1931) *The Travels of Marco Polo*, ed. John Masefield, London: Dent.

Pope, Alexander (1956) *Correspondence of Alexander Pope*, ed. George Sherburn, 5 vols, Oxford: Clarendon Press.

Porter, Sir James (1768) *Observations on the Religion, Laws, Government and Manners of the Turks*, London: J. Nourse.

Purchas, Samuel the Elder (1613; 2nd edn enlarged 1614) *Purchas his Pilgrimage*, London: Featherstone.

Pye, Michael (1991) *Maximum City*, London: Sinclair-Stevenson.

Raban, Jonathan (1986) *Old Glory: An American Voyage* (1981), London: Picador.

— (1990) *Hunting Mr Heartbreak*, London: Picador.

— (1996) *Bad land: An American Romance*, London: Picador.

Ralegh, Walter (1596) *The Discoverie of the Large, Rich and Bewtifvl Empyre of Gviana, With a relation of the great and Golden Citie of Manoa (which the Spanyards call El Dorado) And of the Prouinces of Emeria, Arromaia, Amapaia, and Other Countries, with their riuers, adioyning. Performed in the yeare of 1595. by Sir W. Ralegh Knight, Captaine of her Maiesties Guard, Lo. Warden of the Stanneries, and her Highnesse Lieutenant generall of the Countie of Cornewall*, London: Robert Robinson.

Rayner, Richard (1992) *Los Angeles without a Map* (1989), London: Flamingo.

Rycaut, Paul (1668) *The Present State of the Ottoman Empire*, London: J. Starking and H. Brome.

Santé, Luc (1991) *Low Life*, New York: Random House.

Schomburgk, Richard (1922) *Travels in British Guiana 1840–1844* (trans. Walter Roth), 2 vols, Georgetown: Daily Chronicle.

Selvon, Sam (1985) *Lonely Londoners*, London: Longman Caribbean Writers.

Seward, Anna (1780) *An Elegy on the Death of Captain Cook*, London: J. Dodsley.

Shelley, Mary (1985) *Frankenstein* (1818), London: Penguin.

Smollett, Tobias (1979) *Travels through France and Italy* (1766), ed. Frank Felsenstein, London: OUP.

Spenser, Edmund (1790) *A View of the Present State of Ireland*, ed. W. L. Renwick, Oxford: Clarendon Press.

Stark, Freya (1982) *The Southern Gates of Arabia: A Journey in the Hadbramant* (1936), London: Century Books.

Stedman, John Gabriel (1992) *Narrative of a Five Years Expedition against the Revolted Negoes of Surinam* (1796), ed. Richard and Sally Price, Baltimore: Johns Hopkins University Press.

Sterne, Lawrence (1768) *A Sentimental Journey through France and Italy*, London: T. Becket and P. A. De Hondt.

Swift, Jonathan (1970) *Gulliver's Travels* (1726), ed. Robert A. Greenberg, New York: Norton.

— (1984) 'A Modest Proposal for preventing the Children of poor People from being a Burthen to their Parents or the Country, and for making them Benificial to the Public' (1730), in Angus Ross and David Woolley (eds), *Jonathan Swift*, Oxford and New York: OUP.

Theroux, Paul (1983) *The Kingdom by the Sea: A Journey around the Coast of Great Britain*, London: Hamish Hamilton.

Thesiger, Wilfred (1959) *Arabian Sands*, London: Collins.

— *The Travels of the Jesuits into Various Parts of the World* (1743), 2 vols (trans. John Lockman), London: John Noon.

Waring, Thomas (1651) *An Answer To certain Seditious and Jesuitical Queres, etc*, London: William Du-Gard.

Waugh, Evelyn (1930) *Labels: A Mediterranean Journal*, London: John Murray.

Williams, Hugo (1981) *No Particular Place to Go*, London: Jonathan Cape.

Williams, Nigel (1995) *From Wimbledon to Waco*, London: Faber and Faber.

Wollstonecraft, Mary (1796) *Letters written in a Short Residence in Sweden, Norway and Denmark*, London.

Young, Gavin (1995) *From Sea to Shining Sea: A Present-day Journey into America's Past*, New York: Random House.

## 2. Secondary

Abu-Lughod (1989) *Before European Hegemony: The World-System A.D. 1250–1350*, Oxford: OUP.

Adam, Ian and Helen Tiffen (eds) (1991) *Past the Last Post: Theorizing Post-colonialism and Post-modernism*, London: Harvester.

Adams, Percy G. (1962; rev. 1980) *Travelers and Travel Liars, 1660–1800*, Berkeley: University of California Press.

— (1983) *Travel Literature and the Evolution of the Novel*, Lexington: Kentucky University Press.

Adler, Judith (1989) 'Origins of Sightseeing', *Annals of Tourist Research* 16: 7–29.

— (1989a) 'Travel as Performed Art', *American Journal of Sociology* 94(6): 1366–91.

Ahmad, Aijaz (1992) 'Orientalism and After: Ambivalence and Metropolitan Location in the Work of Edward Said', in *Theory. Class, Nations, Literatures*, London: Verso, 159–219.

— (1995) 'Postcolonialism: What's in a Name', in de la Campa et al. (eds), 11–32.

— (1996) *Lineages of the Present: Political Essays*, New Delhi: Tulika.

Amin, Samir (1989) *Eurocentrism* (trans. Russell Moore), New York: Monthly Review Press.

Anderson, Benedict (1983) *Imagined Communities: Reflections on the Origin and Spread of Nationalism*, London: Verso.

Anderson, Warwick (1992) 'Medicine as Colonial Discourse', *Critical Inquiry* 18: 506–29.

Andrews, Kenneth R. (1984) *Trade, Plunder and Settlement: Maritime Enterprise and the Genesis of the British Empire 1480–1630*, Cambridge: CUP.

Andrews, Malcolm (1989) *The Search for the Picturesque: Landscape Aesthetics and Tourism in Britain, 1760–1800*, Stanford: Stanford University Press.

Appaih, Kwame Anthony (1991) 'Is the Post in Postmodernism the Post in Postcolonial?', *Critical Inquiry* 17: 336–57.

Ardener, Edwin (1985) 'Social Anthropology and the Decline of Modernism', in Joanna Overing (ed.), *Reason and Morality*, London: Tavistock, 47–70.

Arens, William (1979) *The Man-Eating Myth: Anthropology and Anthropophagi*, Oxford: OUP.

Armstrong, Nancy (1987) *Desire and Domestic Fiction: A Political History of the Novel*, New York: OUP.

Arneil, Barbara (1996) *John Locke on America: The Defence of English Colonialism*, Oxford: Clarendon Press.

Austin, J. L. (1984) *How to do Things with Words* (1962), Oxford: OUP.

Babcock, Barbara (1993) 'Feminism/Pretexts: Fragments, Questions and Reflections', *Anthropological Quarterly* 66: 59–66.

Bachelard, Gaston (1969) *The Poetics of Space* (1958) (trans. Maria Jolas), Boston: Beacon Press.

Bartowski, Frances (1995) *Travelers, Immigrants, Inmates: Essays in Estrangement*, Minneapolis and London: Minnesota University Press.

Batten, Charles L. (1978) *Pleasurable Instruction: Form and Convention in Eighteenth-Century Travel Literature*, Berkeley: University of California Press.

Baumann, Zygmunt (1996) 'From Pilgrim to Tourist – or a Short History of Identity', in Stuart Hall and Paul du Gay (eds), *Questions of Cultural Identity*, London: Sage, 18–36.

Bayly, C. A. (1989) *The Imperial Meridian: The British Empire and the World 1780–1836*, London: Longman.

Behar, Ruth and Deborah Gordon (eds) (1995) *Women Writing Culture*, Berkeley: University of California Press.

Behdad, Ali (1994) *Belated Travellers: Orientalism in the Age of Colonial Dissolution*, Durham: Duke University Press.

Bell, Ian A. (1996) 'To See Ourselves: Travel Narratives and National Identity in Contemporary Britain', in Ian A. Bell (ed.), *Peripheral Visions: Images of Nationhood in Contemporary British Fiction*, Cardiff: University of Wales Press, 6–26.

Belsey, Catherine (1985) *The Subject of Tragedy: Identity and Difference in Renaissance Drama*, London and New York: Methuen.

Berger, John (1980) *About Looking*, London: Writers and Readers Publishing Cooperative.

Bhabha, Homi K. (1986) 'The Other Question: Difference, Discrimination and the Discourse of Colonialism', in Francis Barker et al. (eds), *Literature, Politics and Theory: Papers from the Essex Conference 1976–84*, London: Methuen, 148–72.

— (1987) 'Interrogating Identity', in Lisa Appignanesi (ed.), *Identity*, London: Free Association Press, 5–12.

— (1994a) *The Location of Culture*, London: Routledge.

— (1994b) review of Salman Rushdie's 'East, West', *Guardian Weekly*, 16 October: 29.

Birkett, Dea (1989) *Spinsters Abroad: Victorian Lady Explorers*, London: Blackwell.

Bishop, Peter (1989) *The Myth of Shangri-La: Tibert, Travel-Writing and the Western Creation of Sacred Landscape*, Berkeley: University of California Press.

Black, Jeremy (1986) *The British and the Grand Tour*, London: Croom Helm.

— (1992) *The British Abroad: The Grand Tour in the Eighteenth Century*, Stroud: Alan Sutton.

Blake, Susan L. (1992) 'A Woman's Trek: What Difference Does Gender Make', in Chauduri and Strobel (eds), 19–34.

Bland, L. (1981) 'The Domain of the Sexual: A Response', *Screen Education* 39: 56–68.

Bloom, Lisa (1993) *Gender on Ice: American Ideologies of Polar Exploration*, Minneapolis: Minnesota University Press.

Blunt, Alison (1994) *Travel, Gender and Imperialism: Mary Kingsley in West Africa*, New York: Guilford Press.

Blunt, Alison and Gillian Rose (eds) (1994) *Writing Women and Space: Colonial and Postcolonial Geographies*, New York: Guilford Press.

Boehme, Elleke (1995) *Colonial and Post-Colonial Literature: Migrant Metaphors*, Oxford: OUP.

Bohls, Elizabeth A. (1995) *Women Travel Writers and the Language of Aesthetics 1716–1818*, Cambridge: CUP.

Bongie, Chris (1991) *Exotic Memories: Literature, Colonialism and the Fin de Siècle*, Stanford: Stanford University Press.

Boon, James (1983) 'Functionalists Write Too Much: Frazer/Malinowski and the Semiotics of the Monograph', *Semiotica* 4: 131–49.

Boone, Joseph (1995) 'Vacation Cruises; or the Homoerotics of Orientalism', *PMLA* 110: 89–107.

Boorstin, Daniel (1985) *The Image: A Guide to Pseudo-events in America* (1961), New York: Athenaeum.

Bottomley, Gillian (1992) *From another Place: Migration and the Politics of Culture*, Cambridge: CUP.

Boucher, Philip P. (1992) *Cannibal Encounters: Europeans and Island Caribs, 1492–1763*, Baltimore and London: Johns Hopkins University Press.

Brah, Avtar (1996) *Cartographies of Desire: Contesting Identities*, London: Routledge.

Brantlinger, Patrick (1985) 'Africa and the Victorians', *Critical Inquiry* 12: 166–222.

— (1988) *Rule of Darkness: British Literature and Imperialism, 1830–1914*, Ithaca, NY: Cornell University Press.

Bree, Germaine (1968) 'The Ambiguous Voyage: Mode or Genre', *Genre* 1: 87–96.

Bristow, Joseph (1991) *Empire Boys: Adventure in a Man's World*, New York: Harper Collins.

Brown, Laura (1982) *English Dramatic Form*, New Haven and London: Yale University Press.

— (1993) *Ends of Empire: Women and Ideology in Early Eighteenth-century English Literature*, Ithaca, NY: Cornell University Press.

Buford, Bill (1984) 'Editorial', *Granta* 10, 'Travel Writing': 5–7.

Burnett, Paula (ed.) (1986) *Caribbean Verse in English*, London: Penguin.

Butor, Michel (1994) 'Le voyage et l'écriture', *Romantisme* 4 (1972): 4–19; trans. as 'Travel and Writing', *Mosaic* 7 (1974), 1–16; and in Kowalewski (ed.), 53–70.

Buzard, James (1993a) *The Beaten Track: European Tourism, Literature and the Ways to 'Culture' 1800–1918*, New York: OUP.

— (1993b) 'A Continent of Pictures: Reflections on the "Europe" of Nineteenth Century Tourists', *PMLA* 108: 30–44.

Caesar, Terry (1995) *Forgiving the Boundaries: Home as Abroad in American Travel Writing*, Athens: University of Georgia Press.

Cain, P. J. and A. G. Hopkins (1993) *British Imperialism: Innovation and Expansion 1688–1914*, London: Longman.

Calloway, Helen and Dorothy O'Hellel (1992) 'Crusader for Empire: Fiona Shaw/Lady Lugard', in Chaudhuri and Strobel (eds), 79–97.

Campbell, Jill (1994) 'Lady Mary Wortley Montagu and the Historical Machinery of Female Identity', in Beth Fowkes Tobin (ed.), *History, Gender and Eighteenth-Century Literature*, Athens: University of Georgia Press, 64–85.

Campbell, Joseph (1949) *The Hero with a Thousand Faces*, Princeton: Princeton University Press.

Campbell, Mary B. (1988) *The Witness and the Other World: Exotic European Travel Writing, 400–1600*, Ithaca, NY: Cornell University Press.

Carrington, Dorothy (1947) *The Traveler's Eye*, New York: Pilot Press.

Carter, Paul (1987) *The Road to Botany Bay: An Essay in Spatial History*, London: Faber.

Casson, Lionel (1994) *Travel in the Ancient World* (1974), Baltimore: Johns Hopkins University Press.

Chambers, Douglas (1996) *The Reinvention of the World: English Writers 1650–1750*, London: Longman.

Chambers, Iain (1994) *Migrancy, Culture, Identity*, London: Routledge.

Chambers, Ross (1994) 'Strolling, Touring, Cruising: Counter-Disciplinary Narrative and the Literature of Travel', in James Phelan and Peter J. Rabinowitz (eds), *Understanding Narrative*, Columbus: Ohio State University Press, 17–42.

Chaudhuri, Nupur and Margaret Strobel (eds) (1992) *Western Women and Imperialism*, Bloomington: Indiana University Press.

Cheyfitz, Eric (1991) *The Poetics of Imperialism: Translation and Colonisation from 'The Tempest' to 'Tarzan'*, New York: OUP.

Clapp, Susannah (1997) *With Chatwin: Portrait of a Writer*, London: Jonathan Cape.

Clark, David (1972) *Plane and Geodetic Surveying*, 2 vols, London: Constable.

Clifford, James (1982) *Person and Myth: Maurice Leenhardt in the Melanesian World*, Berkeley: University of California Press.

— (1983) 'On Ethnographic Authority', *Representations* 1: 118–46

— (1986) 'On Ethnographic Self-Fashioning: Conrad and Malinowski', in T. C. Heller M. Sonsa and D. E. Welbery (eds), *Reconstructing Individualism: Autonomy, Individuality and the Self in Western Thought*, Stanford: Stanford University Press.

— (1988) *The Predicament of Culture: Twentieth-Century Literature, Ethnography and Art*, Cambridge, MA: Harvard University Press.

— (1989) 'Notes on Theory and Travel', in James Clifford and Vivek Dhareshwar (eds), *Travelling Theorists, Inscriptions* 5: 177–88.

— (1990) 'Notes on (Field)Notes', in Roger Sanjek (ed.), *Fieldnotes: The Making of Anthropology*, Ithaca, NY: Cornell University Press, 47–70.

— (1991) 'Response', *Social Analysis* 29:145–58.

— (1997) *Routes: Travel and Translation in the Late Twentieth Century*, Cambridge, MA: Harvard University Press.

Clifford, James and George E. Marcus (eds) (1986) *Writing Culture: The Poetics and Politics of Ethnography*, Berkeley: University of California Press.

Cocker, Mark (1992) *Loneliness and Time: British Travel Writing in the Twentieth Century*, London: Secker and Warburg.

Cohen, Erik (1979) 'A Phenomenology of Tourist Experiences', *Sociology* 13: 179–201.

Conrad, Peter (1980) *Imagining America*, New York: OUP.

Cosgrove, Dennis and Stephen Daniels (1988) (eds), *The Iconography of Landscape*, Cambridge: CUP.

Coward, Rosalind (1985) *Female Desires: How They are Bought, Sold, and Packaged*, New York: Grove Press.

Cribb, T. J. (1993) 'T. W. Harris – Sworn Surveyor', *Journal of Commonwealth Literature* 29: 33–46.

Crick, Malcolm (1994) *Resplendent Sites, Discordant Voices: Sri Lankans in International Tourism*, Chur: Harwood Academic.

Cronon, William (ed.) (1996) *Uncommon Ground: Rethinking the Human Place in Nature*, New York: Norton.

Culler, Jonathan (1988) 'The Semiotics of Tourism', in *Framing the Sign: Criticism and its Institutions*, Oxford: Blackwell, 153–67.

Daniel, Norman (1966) *Islam, Europe and Empire*, Edinburgh: Edinburgh University Press.

Darwin, John (1988) *Britain and Decolonisation: The Retreat from Empire in the Post-war World*, London: Macmillan.

— (1991) *The End of the British Empire: The Historical Debate*, Oxford: Blackwell.

Davis, Lance E. and Robert A. Huttenback (1986) *Mammon and the Pursuit of Empire: The Political Economy of British Imperialism 1860–1912*, Cambridge: CUP.

Davis, M. (1965) *The Undecidable*, New York: Raven Press.

de Certeau, Michel (1988) *The Writing of History* (trans. Tom Conley), New York: Columbia University Press.

de la Campa, Roman, E. Ann Kaplan and Michael Sprinker (eds) (1995) *Late Imperial Culture*, London: Verso.

Deleuze, Gilles and Felix Guattari (1983) *Anti-Oedipus: Capitalism and Schizophrenia* (1972) (trans. Robert Hurley et al.), London: Athlone Press.

— (1987) *A Thousand Plateaus: Capitalism and Schizophrenia* (1980) (trans. Brian Massumi), Minnesota: Minneapolis University Press.

— (1994) *What is Philosophy* (trans. Graham Burchell and Hugh Tomlinson), London: Verso.

Dening, Greg (1992) *Mr Bligh's Bad Language: Passion, Power and Theatre on the Bounty*, Cambridge: CUP.

Derrida, Jacques (1976) *Of Grammatology* (trans. Gayatri Spivak), Baltimore: Johns Hopkins University Press.

— (1997) *The Politics of Friendship* (1994), London: Verso.

Devall, Bill and George Sessions (1985) *Deep Ecology*, Layton, UT: Gibbs Smith.

Dirks, Nicholas B. (ed.) (1992) *Colonialism and Culture*, Ann Arbor: Michigan University Press.

Dodd, Philip (ed.) (1982) *The Art of Travel: Essays on Travel Writing*, Totowa, NJ: Frank Cass.

Donaldson, L. E. (1993) *Decolonizing Feminisms. Race, Gender and Empire Building*, London: Routledge.

Dube, Suarabh (1998) 'Travelling Light: Missionary Musings, Colonial Cultures and Anthropological Anxieties', in Kaur and Hutnyk (eds).

During, Simon (1987) 'Post-Modernism or Post-Colonialism Today', *Textual Practice* 1: 32–47.

Eade, John and Michael Sallnow (1991) *Contesting the Sacred: The Anthropology of Christian Pilgrimage*, London: Routledge.

Eagleton, Terry (1991) *Ideology. An Introduction*, New York: Verso.

Edmond, Rod (1997) *Representing the South Pacific: Colonial Discourse from Cook to Gauguin*, Cambridge: CUP.

Edward, Philips (1988) *Last Voyages: Cavendish, Hudson, Ralegh*, Oxford: OUP.

— (1995) *The Story of the Voyage*, Cambridge: CUP.

Eisner, Robert (1991) *Travelers to an Antique Land: The History and Literature of Travel to Greece*, Ann Arbor: Michigan University Press.

Ermath, Elizabeth D. (1983) *Realism and Consensus in the English Novel*, Princeton: Princeton University Press.

Evans, J. (1993) 'First Missionaries, Then Marketeers': Review of *The Oxford Book of Exploration, Guardian*, 2 November.

Fabian, Johannes (1983) *Time and the Other: How Anthropology Makes its Object*, New York: Columbia University Press.

Fanon, Frantz (1986) *Black Skins: White Masks* (1952), London: Pluto.

— (1983) *The Wretched of the Earth* (1961) (trans. Constance Farrington), New York: Grove Press.

Fausset, David (1993) *Writing the New World: Imaginary Voyages and Utopias of the Great Southern Land*, Syracuse, NY: Syracuse University Press.

Feferman, Solomon (1991) 'Kurt Godel: Conviction and Caution', in S. G. Shanker (ed.), *Godel's Theorem in Focus*, London: Routledge.

Feifer, Maxine (1986) *Going Places: Tourism in History from Imperial Rome to the Present*, New York: Stein and Day.

Fielder, John (1991) 'Purity and Pollution: Goonininup/The Old Swan Brewery', *Southern Review* 24: 34–42.

Fieldhouse, D. K. (1966; 1982) *The Colonial Empires*, London: Weidenfeld and Nicolson.

— (1981) *Colonialism 1870–1945: An Introduction*, London: Weidenfeld and Nicolson.

— (1984) 'Can Humpty-Dumpty be Put Back Together Again: Imperial History in the 1980s', in R. F. Holland and G. Rizvi (eds), *Perspectives on Imperialism and Decolonization: Essays in Honour of A. F. Madden*, London: Cass, 9–23.

Foster, Shirley (1990) *Across New Worlds: Nineteenth-Century Women Travellers and their Writings*, Hemel Hempstead: Harvester Wheatsheaf.

Foucault, Michel (1981) *The History of Sexuality. An Introduction* (trans. Robert Hurley), London: Penguin.

— (1986) 'Of Other Spaces', *Diacritics* 16: 22–7.

Franklin, Wayne (1979) *Discoverers, Explorers, Settlers: The Diligent Writers of Early America*, Chicago: Chicago University Press.

Frawley, Maria H. (1994) *A Wider Range: Travel Writing by Women in Victorian England*, Cranbury and London: Associated University Press.

French, Marilyn (1985) *Beyond Power: Women, Men and Morals*, London: Cape.

Frow, John (1991) 'Tourism and the Semiotics of Nostalgia', *October* 57: 125–51.

Frye, Northrop (1957) *Anatomy of Criticism: Four Essays*, Princeton, NJ: Princeton University Press.

— (1976) *The Secular Scripture: A Study of the Structure of Romance*, Cambridge, MA: Harvard University Press.

Fuller, Mary C. (1995) *Voyages in Print: English Travel to America 1576–1624*, Cambridge: CUP.

Furedi, Frank (1994) *The Ideology of Imperialism*, London: Pluto.

Fuss, Diana (ed.) (1996) *Human, All Too Human*, London: Routledge.

Fussell, Paul (1980) *Abroad: British Literary Travelling between the Wars*, Oxford: OUP.

— (1988) 'Travel, Tourism, and "International Understanding"', in *Thank God for the Atom Bomb and Other Essays*, New York: Ballantine, 151–71.

Gallagher, Catherine (1992) *Nobody's Story: Women's Vanishing Acts in the Market-Place*, Berkeley: University of California Press.

Gallagher, John (1982) *The Decline, Revival and Fall of the British Empire*, ed. Anil Seal, Cambridge: CUP.

Galvin, Fernando (1993) 'Travel Writing in British Metafiction: A Proposal for Analysis', in Theo D'haen and Hans Bertram (eds), *British Postmodern Fiction*, Amsterdam and Atlanta: Rodopi, 77–87.

Geertz, Clifford (1973) *The Interpretation of Cultures*, New York: Basic Books.

— (1983) *Local Knowledge: Further Essays in Interpretative Anthropology*, New York: Basic Books.

— (1988) *Works and Lives: The Anthropologist as Author*, Stanford: Stanford University Press.

— (1992) 'Local Knowledge and its Limits: Some Ober Dicta', *Yale Journal of Criticism* 5: 129–36.

— (1995) *After the Fact: Two Countries, Four Decades, One Anthropologist*, Cambridge, MA: Harvard University Press.

Gellner, Ernest (1994) *Encounters with Nationalism*, Oxford: Blackwell.

Gendron, Charisse (1992) 'Perspectives on Abroad in Spender's and Hockney's China Diary', in Kowaleski, 264–83.

George, Rosemary Marangoly (1996) *The Politics of Home, Postcolonial Relocations and Twentieth Century Fiction*, Cambridge: CUP.

Gillies, John (1994) *Shakespeare and the Geography of Difference*, Cambridge: CUP.

Gilroy, Paul (1993) *The Black Atlantic: Modernity and Double Consciousness*, London: Verso.

Gledhill, John (1994) *Power and its Disguises: Anthropological Perspectives on Politics*, London: Pluto.

Godel, Kurt (1967) 'On Formally Undecidable Propositions of Principia Mathematica and Related Systems I', trans. and ed. Jean van Heijenoort, in *From Frege to Godel: A Sourcebook in Mathematical Logic, 1879–1931*, Cambridge, MA: Harvard University Press.

Goody, Jack (1992) 'Local Knowledge and the Knowledge of Locality: The Desirability of Frames', *Yale Journal of Criticism* 5: 137–47.

Graburn, Nelson (1978) 'Tourism: the Sacred Journey' in Valerie Smith (ed.), *Hosts and Guests: The Anthropology of Tourism*, Oxford: Blackwell, 17–31.

Green, Martin (1980) *Dreams of Adventure and Deeds of Empire*, London: Routledge and Kegan Paul.

— (1991) *Seven Types of Adventure Tale: an etiology of a major genre*, Pennsylvania: Penn State University Press.

Greenblatt, Stephen (1978) *Renaissance Self-Fashioning: From More to Shakespeare*, Chicago: Chicago University Press.

— (1981) 'Invisible Bullets', *Glyph* 8: 40–61; rev. in *Shakespearean Negotiations: the circulation of social energy in Renaissance England* (1988), Cambridge: CUP, 21–65.

— (1991) *Marvelous Possessions: The Wonder of the New World*, Chicago: Chicago University Press.

— (1993) (ed.), *New World Encounters*, Berkeley: University of California Press, intro. vii–xviii.

Gregory, Derek (1994) *Geographical Imaginations*, Oxford: Blackwell.

Gregory, Derek and James Duncan (eds) (1999) *Writes of Passage: Travel Writing, Place, Ambiguity*, London: Routledge.

Grewal, Inderpal (1996) *Home and Harem: Imperialism, Nationalism and the Culture of Travel*, Durham: Duke University Press.

Grosz, Elizabeth (1990) *Jacques Lacan: A Feminist Introduction*, London: Routledge.

Grove, Richard H. (1995) *Green Imperialism: Colonial Expansion, Tropical Island Edens and the Origins of Environmentalism, 1600–1860*, Cambridge: CUP.

Gruesser, John C. (1990) 'Afro-American Travel Literature and Africanist Discourse', *Black American Literature Forum* 24: 5–20.

Grundy, Isabel (1992) '"The Barbarous Character We Give Them": White Women Travellers Report on Other Races', *Studies in Eighteenth-Century Culture* 2: 73–86.

Hall, Stuart (1991) 'The Local and the Global: Globalisation and Ethnicity', in Anthony D. King (ed.), *Culture Globalisation and the World System*, London: Macmillan, 19–40.

Halsband, Robert (1956) *The Life of Lady Mary Wortley Montagu*, Oxford: Clarendon Press.

Hamalian, Leo (ed.) (1981) *Ladies on the Loose: Women Travellers of the Eighteenth and Nineteenth Century*, New York: Dodd, Mead.

Hanfi, Zawar (1972) *The Fiery Brook: Selected Writings of Ludwig Feuerbach*, New York: Anchor.

Hanke, Lewis (1959) *Aristotle and the American Indians*, Bloomington: Indiana University Press.

Hanne, Michael (ed.) *Literature and Travel*, Amsterdam and Atlanta: Rodopi.

Haraway, Donna J. (1989) *Primate Visions*, London: Verso.

— (1991) *Simians, Cyborgs and Women: The Reinvention of Nature*, London: Free Association Books (1991).

Hartog, François (1988) *The Mirror of Herodotus: The Representation of the Other in the Writing of History* (trans J. Lloyd), Berkeley: University of California Press.

Hassan, A. (1990) '"As I Write": Narrative Occurrences and the Quest for Self-Presence in the Travel Diary', *Ariel* 21: 33–47.

Hassan, Ihab (1990) *Selves at Risk: Patterns of Quest in Contemporary American Letters*, Madison: University of Wisconsin Press.

Hedetoft, Ulf (1985) *British Colonialism and Modern Identity*, Aalborg: Aalborg University Press.

Hegel, G. W. F. (1967) *Philosophy of Right* (trans. T. M. Knox), Oxford: OUP.

— (1975) *Hegel's Logic: being part one of the Encyclopaedia of the Philosophical Sciences* (trans. William Wallace), Oxford: OUP.

— (1977) *Phenomenology of Spirit* (trans. A. V. Millar), Oxford: OUP.

Helgerson, Richard (1992) *Forms of Nationhood: The Elizabethan Writing of England*, Chicago: Chicago University Press.

Helms, Mary (1988) *Ulysses' Sail: An Ethnographic Odyssey of Power, Knowledge and Geographical Distance*, Princeton: Princeton University Press.

Herbert, Christopher (1991) *Culture and Anomie: Ethnographic Imagination in the Nineteenth Century*, Chicago: Chicago University Press.

Herndl, Carl G. and Stuart C. Brown (eds) (1996) *Green Culture: Environmental Rhetoric in Contemporary America*, Madison: Wisconsin University Press.

Hesse, Barnor (ed.) (1998) *Discrepant Multiculturalisms*, London: Zed Books.

Hobsbawm, Eric (1995) *The Age of Empire 1875–1914* (1987), London: Weidenfeld and Nicolson.

Hobson, J. A. (1988) *Imperialism: A Study* (1902), Unwin: London.

Hoffer, Peter and N. E. N. Hull (1981) *Murdering Mothers: Infanticide in England and New England*, New York: New York University Press.

Holland, R. F. (1985) *European Decolonisation 1918–1981*, London: Macmillan.

hooks, bell (1995) *Killing Rage: Ending Racism*, London: Penguin.

Housee, Shrin and Sanjay Sharma (1988) 'Too Black and Too Strong: Anti-racism and the Making of South Asian Political Identities in Britain', in Jordan and Lent (eds), *Storming the Millennium: The Politics of Change*, London: Lawrence and Wishart.

Hulme, Peter (1986) *Colonial Encounters: Europe and the Native Caribbean 1492–1797*, London: Methuen.

Hutcheon, Linda (1994) 'The Post always rings Twice: the Postmodern and the Postcolonial', *Textual Practice* 8: 205–38.

Hutnyk, John (1987) 'The Authority of Style', *Social Analysis* 21: 59–79.

— (1988) 'Castaway Anthropology: Malinowski's Tropical Writings', *Antithesis* 2: 43–54.

— (1989) 'Clifford Geertz as a Cultural System', *Social Analysis* 25: 91–107.

— (1996) *The Rumour of Calcutta: Tourism, Charity and the Poverty of Representation*, London: Zed Books.

— (1997) 'derrida@marx.archive', *Space and Culture* 2: 95–122.

— (forthcoming) 'Capital Calcutta Coins, Maps, Monuments', in Bell and Haddour, *City Visions*, London: Longman.

Hyams, Ronald (1976; 1993) *Britain's Imperial Century*, London: Macmillan.

— (1990) *Empire and Sexuality: The British Experience*, Manchester: Manchester University Press.

Hymes, Dell (1974) *Reinventing Anthropology*, New York: Vintage.

Illich, Ivan (1981) *Shadow Work*, Boston and London: Marion Boyars.

Islam, Syed Manzural (1996) *The Ethics of Travel: From Marco Polo to Kafka*, Manchester: Manchester University Press.

Jakle, John A. (1985) *The Tourist: Travel in Twentieth-Century North America*, Lincoln: University of Nebraska Press.

JanMohamed, Abdul R. (1985) 'The Economy of Manichaean Allegory: The Function of Racial Difference in Colonial Literature', *Critical Inquiry* 12: 58–87.

Jarvis, Robin (1997) *Romantic Writing and Pedestrian Travel*, London and Basingstoke: Macmillan.

Kapferer, Bruce (1988) 'The Anthropologist as Hero: Three Exponents of Post-Modern Anthropology', *Critique of Anthropology* 8: 77–104.

Kaplan, Caren (1996) *Questions of Travel: Postmodern Discourses of Displacement*, Durham, NC: Duke University Press.

Kappeler, Suzanne (1986) *The Pornography of Representation*, Cambridge: Polity Press.

Kaur, Raminder and John Hutnyk (eds) (1998) *Travelworlds: Journeys in Contemporary Cultural Politics*, London: Zed Books.

Kaur, Raminder and Virinder Kalra (1996) 'New Paths of South Asian Identity and Musical Creativity', in Sharma, Hutnyk and Sharma, 217–31.

Kerridge, Richard and Neil Sammells (eds) (1998) *Writing the Environment: Ecocriticism and Literature*, London: Zed Books.

Khare, R. S. (1992) 'The Other's Double – the Anthropologist's Bracketed Self: Notes on Cultural Representation and Privileged Discourse', *New Literary History* 23: 1–24.

Kiernan, V. G. (1969) *The Lords of Humankind: Black Men, Yellow Men and White Men in the Age of Empire*, London: Hutchinson.

—— (1978) *America: The New Imperialism from White Settlement to World Hegemony*, London: Zed Books.

King, Russell, John Connall and Paul White (eds) (1995) *Writing across Worlds: Literature and Migration*, London: Routledge.

Knapp, Jeffrey (1992) *An Empire Nowhere: England, America and the Literature from 'Utopia' to 'The Tempest'*, Berkeley: University of California Press.

Knight, Diana (1997) *Barthes and Utopia: Space, Travel, Writing*, Oxford: Clarendon Press.

Knox-Shaw, Peter (1986) *The Explorer in English Fiction*, New York: St Martin's Press.

Kobak, A. (1988) *Isabelle: The Life of Isabelle Eberhardt*, London: Chatto and Windus.

Koepping, Klaus Peter (1989), 'Mind, Body, Text: Not Quite Satirical Reflections on the Trickster', *Criticism, Heresy and Interpretation* 2: 37–76.

Kowalewski, Michael (ed.) (1992) *Temperamental Journeys: Essays on the Modern Literature of Travel*, Athens: Georgia University Press.

Kratz, Corinne A. (1994) 'On Telling/Selling a Book by its Cover', *Cultural Anthropology* 9: 179–200.

Krippendorf, Jost (1987) *The Holiday Makers: Understanding the Impact of Leisure and Travel*, Oxford: Heinemann.

Kristeva, Julia (1982) *Powers of Horror: An Essay on Abjection* (trans. Leon S. Roudiez), New York: Columbia University Press.

Kuisel, Richard F. (1993) *Seducing the French: The Dilemma of Americanisation*, Berkeley: University of California Press.

Kulikoff, Alan (1986) *Tobacco and Slaves: The Development of Southern Cultures in the Chesapeake, 1680–1800*, Chapel Hill: North Carolina University Press.

Lacan, Jacques (1979) *The Four Fundamental Concepts of Psycho-analysis*, ed. Jacques-Alain Miller (trans. Alan Sheridan), London: Penguin.

Lawrence, Karen R. (1994) *Penelope Voyages: Women and Travel in the British Literary Tradition*, Ithaca, NY: Cornell University Press.

Leed, Eric J. (1991) *The Mind of the Traveler: From Gilgamesh to Global Tourism*, New York: Basic Books.

Lestringant, Frank (1997) *Cannibals: the Discovery and Representation of the Cannibal from Columbus to Jules Verne* trans. Rosemary Morris, Berkeley, CA: University of California Press.

Lew, Joseph W. (1991) 'Lady Mary's Portable Seraglio', *Eighteenth-Century Studies* 24: 432–50.

Lewis, Bernard (1993) *Islam and the West*, Oxford: OUP.

Lewis, Reina (1996) *Gendering Orientalism: Race, Femininity and Representation*, London: Routledge.

Loomba, Ania (1991) 'Overworlding the "Third World"', *Oxford Literary Review*, special issue, 'Neocolonialism', 13: 164–6.

Lopez, Barry (1986) *Arctic Dreams: Imagination and Desire in a Northern Landscape*, London: Macmillan.

Low, D. A. (1994) 'The Contraction of England: An Inaugural Lecture 1984', in *Eclipse of Empire*, Cambridge: CUP, 1–21.

Low, Gail Ching-Liang (1996) *White Skins/Black Masks: Representation and Colonialism*, London: Routledge.

Lowe, Lisa (1991) *Critical Terrains: French and British Orientalisms*, Ithaca, NY: Cornell University Press.

Lowenthal, Cynthia (1990) 'The Veil of Romance: Lady Mary's Embassy Letters', *Eighteenth-Century Life* 14: 66–82.

MacCannell, Dean (1976) *The Tourist: A New Theory of the Leisure Class*, New York: Schrocken.

— (1992) *Empty Meeting Grounds: The Tourist Papers*, London: Routledge.

McClintock, Anne (1994) *Imperial Leather: Race, Gender and Sexuality in the Colonial Context*, London: Routledge.

Mackay, David (1985) *In the Wake of Cook: Exploration, Science and Empire 1780–1801*, London: Croom Helm.

MacKenzie, John M. (ed.) (1984) *Imperialism and Popular Culture*, Manchester: Manchester University Press.

— (1988) *The Empire of Nature: Hunting, Conservation and British Imperialism*, Manchester: Manchester University Press.

McKeon, Michael (1987) *The Origins of the English Novel, 1600–1740*, Baltimore: Johns Hopkins University Press.

McNay, L. (1994) *Foucault and Feminism*, Cambridge: Polity Press.

McQuire, Scott (1995) *Art, Culture, and Power*, Wauran Ponds: Deakin University.

— (1997) *Visions of Modernity: Representation, Memory, Time and Space in the Age of the Camera*, London: Sage.

Manning, Greg (1993), review of Greenblatt's *Marvelous Possessions*, *Australasian Journal of American Studies* 12: 81–4.

Marcus, George (1988) 'Parody and the Parodic in Polynesian Cultural History', *Cultural Anthropology* 3: 68–76.

— (1995) 'Ethnography In/Of the World System: The Emergence of Multi-sited Ethnography', *Annual Review of Anthropology* 24: 95–140.

Marcus, George and Michael Fischer (1986) *Anthropology as Cultural Critique: An Experimental Moment in the Human Sciences*, Chicago: Chicago University Press.

Marcus, Julie (1991) 'Something about Clifford', *Social Analysis* 29.

Markham, Sir Clements (1896) *Richard Hakluyt: His Life and Work. With a Short Account of the Aims and Achievements of the Haklyut Society*, London: Hakluyt Society.

Marshall, P. J. and Glyndwr Williams (1982) *The Great Map of Mankind: British Perceptions of the World in the Age of Enlightenment*, London: Dent.

Marx, Karl (1968) *Selected Works*, London: Lawrence and Wishart.

Maseo, Miyoshi (1993) 'A Borderless World? From Colonialism to Transnationalism and the Decline of the Nation-State', *Critical Inquiry* 19: 726–51.

Massumi, Brian (1992) *A User's Guide to Capitalism and Schizophrenia: Deviations from Deleuze and Guattari*, Cambridge: MIT.

Mathy, Jean-Phillipe (1993) *Extrême-Occident: French Intellectuals and America*, Chicago: Chicago University Press.

Matos, Jacinthan (1992) 'Old Journeys Revisited: Aspects of English Post-War Travel-Writing', in Kowalewski (ed.), 215–29.

Matthiessen, Peter (1979) *The Snow Leopard*, London: Chatto & Windus.

Melman, Billie (1991) *Women's Orients: English Women and the Middle East, 1718–1918*, London: Macmillan.

Miller, Christopher L. (1985) *Blank Darkness: Africanist Discourse in French*, Chicago: Chicago University Press.

Miller, Daniel (1987) *Material Culture and Mass Consumption*, Oxford: Blackwell.

— (1994) *Modernity: An Ethnographic Approach: Dualism and Mass Consumption in Trinidad*, Oxford: Berg.

— (1995) 'Consumption and Commodities', *Annual Review of Anthropology* 24: 141–61.

Miller, Donald F. (1992) *The Reason of Metaphor: A Study in Politics*, New Delhi: Sage.

Mills, Sara (1991) *Discourses of Difference: An Analysis of Women's Travel-Writing and Colonialism*, London: Routledge.

Minh-ha, Trin T. (1996) 'Other than Myself/My Other Self', in Robertson et al. (eds), 9–26.

Mintz, Sidney W. (1985) *Sweetness and Power: The Place of Sugar in Modern History*, New York and London: Sifton.

Mommsen, Wolfgang J. and Jurgen Osterhammel (eds) (1986) *Imperialism and After: Continuities and Discontinuities*, London: Allen and Unwin.

Montrose, Louis A. (1991) 'The Work of Gender in the Discourse of Discovery', *Representations* 1–41; reprinted in Greenblatt (ed.) (1993), 177–217.

Morgan, Susan (1987) 'An Introduction to Victorian Women's Travel Writings about South-East Asia', *Genre* 20: 189–207.

Morris, Mary and Larry O'Connor (eds) (1994) *The Virago Book of Women Travellers*, London: Virago.

Morris, Meaghan (1988) 'Panorama: The Live, the Dead, and the Living', in Paul Foss (ed.), *Islands in the Stream: Myths of Place in Australian Culture*, Sydney: Pluto, 160–87.

Mudimbe, V. Y. (1988) *The Invention of Africa: Gnosis, Philosophy and the Order of Knowledge*, Bloomington: Indiana University Press.

Mulvey, Christopher (1983) *Anglo-American Landscapes: A Study of Nineteenth Century Anglo-American Travel Writing*, Cambridge: CUP.

— (1990) *Transatlantic Manners: Social Patterns in Nineteenth-Century Anglo-American Travel Writing*, Cambridge: CUP.

Murray, Nicholas (1995) *Bruce Chatwin* (1993), Seren: Brigend.

Nagel, Ernest and James R. Newman (1959) *Godel's Proof*, London: Routledge.

Nandy, Ashis (1983) *The Intimate Enemy: Loss and Recovery of Self under Colonialism*, Delhi: OUP.

Nerlich, Michael (1987) *Ideology of Adventure: Studies in Modern Consciousness 1100–1750* (trans. Ruth Crowley), 2 vols, Minneapolis: Minnesota University Press.

Newton, Esther (1993) 'My Best Informant's Dress: The Erotic in Fieldwork', *Cultural Anthropology* 8: 3–23.

Nietzsche, Friedrich (1979) 'On Truth and Lies in an Non-Moral Sense', in *Philosophy and Truth*, trans. and ed. Daniel Breazeale, Atlantic Highlands: Humanities Press.

Nugent, Stephen (1991) 'Tell me about your Trope', *Social Analysis* 29: 130–5.

Nussbaum, Felicity (1982) *'The Brink of All We Hate': English Satires on Women 1660–1750*, Lexington: Kentucky University Press.

— (1995) *Torrid Zones: Maternity, Sexuality and Empire in Eighteenth-Century Narrative*, Baltimore: Johns Hopkins University Press.

Obeyesekere, Gananath (1992) '"British Cannibals": Contemplation of an Event in the Death and Resurrection of James Cook, Explorer', *Critical Inquiry* 18: 630–54.

O'Gorman, Edmund (1961) *The Invention of America: An Inquiry into the Historical Nature of the New World and the Meaning of History*, Bloomington: Indiana University Press.

Ousby, Ian (1990) *The Englishman's England: Taste, Travel and the Rise of Tourism*, Cambridge: CUP.

Pagden, Anthony (1982) *The Fall of Natural Man: The American Indian and the Origins of Comparative Ethnology*, Cambridge: CUP.

— (1993) *European Encounters with the New World: From Renaissance to Romanticism*, New Haven: Yale University Press.

Papastergiadis, Nikos (1993) *Modernity as Exile: The Stranger in John Berger's Writing*, Manchester: Manchester University Press.

Parker, Kenneth (1996) 'Fertile Land, Romantic Spaces, Uncivilised Peoples: English Travel-Writing about the Cape of Good Hope', in Schwarz (ed.), 198–231.

Parks, G. B. (1928) *Richard Hakluyt and the English Voyages*, New York: American Geographical Society.

Pemble, John (1987) *The Mediterranean Passion: Victorians and Edwardians in the South*, Oxford: Clarendon Press.

Penrose, Boies (1952) *Travel and Discovery in the Renaissance 1420–1620*, Cambridge, MA: Harvard University Press.

Perry, Ruth (1992) '"Colonizing the Breast": Sexuality and Maternity in Eighteenth-Century England', *Eighteenth-Century Life* 16: 185–213.

Philips, Jim (1993) 'Reading Travel-Writing', in Jonathan White (ed.), *Recasting the World: Writing after Colonisation*, Baltimore: Johns Hopkins University Press, 241–55.

Phipps, Peter (1998) 'Tourists and Terrorists', in Kaur and Hutnyk (eds).

Porter, Bernard (1987) *Britain, Europe and the World 1850–1986: Delusions of Grandeur* (1983), London: Allen and Unwin.

— (1996) *The Lion's Share: A Short History of British Imperialism* (1975), London: Longman.

— (1994) *Britannia's Burden: The Political Evolution of Modern Britain 1851–1990*, London: Arnold.

Porter, Dennis (1991) *Haunted Journeys: Desire and Transgression in European Travel-Writing*, Princeton: Princeton University Press.

— (1993) 'Orientalism and its Problems', in Patrick Williams and Laura Chrisman (eds), *Colonial Discourse and Post-colonial Theory: A Reader*, Hemel Hempstead: Harvester Wheatsheaf, 132–49.

Prakash, Gyan (ed.) (1995) *After Colonialism: Imperial Histories and Postcolonial Displacements*, Princeton: Princeton University Press.

Pratt, Mary Louise (1985) 'Scratches on the Face of the Landscape; or, What Mr Barrow Saw in the Land of the Bushmen', *Critical Inquiry* 12: 119–43.

— (1986) 'Fieldwork in Common Places', in Clifford and Marcus (eds), 27–50.

— (1992) *Imperial Eyes: Travel-Writing and Transculturation*, London: Routledge.

Price, Sally and Jamin, Jean (1988) 'A Conversation with Michel Leiris', *Current Anthropology* 29: 157–74.

Raban, Jonathan (1987) *For Love and Money: Writing, Reading, Travelling*, London: Collins Harvill.

Rapport, Nigel (1990) 'Surely Everything Has Already Been Said about Malinowski's Diary!', *Anthropology Today* 6: 6–9.

Rediker, Marcus (1987) *Between the Devil and the Deep Blue Sea: Merchant Seamen, Pirates and the Anglo-American World*, Cambridge: CUP.

Rennie, Neil (1995) *Far-Fetched Facts: The Literature of Travel and the Idea of the South Seas*, Oxford: OUP.

Richardson, Miles (1975) 'Anthropologist – the Myth Teller', *American Ethnologist* 2: 517–33.

Robertson, George et al. (eds) (1996) *Travellers' Tales: Narratives of Home and Displacement*, London: Routledge.

Robinson A. H. and B. B. Petchenik (eds) (1986) *The Nature of Maps*, Chicago: Chicago University Press.

Robinson, Jane (1990) *Wayward Women: a Guide to Women Travellers*, Oxford: OUP.

— (1995) *Unsuitable for Ladies: An Anthology of Women Travellers*, Oxford: OUP.

Robinson, Ronald, John Gallagher and Alice Denny (1981) *Africa and the Victorians: The Official Mind of Imperialism* (1961), London: Macmillan.

— (1986) 'Imperial Theory and the Question of Imperialism after Empire', R. F. Holland and and G. Rizvi (eds), *Perspectives on Imperialism and Decolonisation: Essays in honour of A. F. Madden*, London: Frank Cass, 42–54.

Rojek, Chris (1993) *Ways of Escape: Modern Transformations in Leisure and Travel*, London: Macmillan.

Rosaldo, Renato (1989) 'Imperialist Nostalgia', *Representations* 26: 107–22.

Rose, Gillian (1993) *Feminism and Geography: The Limits of Geographical Knowledge*, Oxford: Polity.

Ross, Andrew (1994) *The Chicago Gangster Theory of Life*, London: Verso.

Rossi, Paolo (1970) *Philosophy, Technology and the Arts in the Early Modern Era*, New York: Harper Torchbook.

Rushdie, Salman (1991) 'Travelling with Chatwin' and 'Chatwin's Travels', in *Imaginary Homelands*, London: Penguin/Granta, 232–6, 237–40.

Sahlins, Marshall (1978) 'Culture as Protein and Profit', *NYRB* 25: 18, 45–53.

— (1979) 'Cannibalism: an Exchange', *NYRB* 26: 4, 45–7.

— (1983) 'Raw Women, Cooked Men and Other "Great Things" of the Fiji Islands', in Paula Brown and Donald Tuzin (eds), *The Ethnography of Cannibalism*, Washington DC: Society for Psychological Anthropology, 72–93.

Said, Edward W. (1979) *Orientalism* (1978), London: Routledge.

— (1984) 'Travelling Theory', in *The World, the Text, the Critic*, London: Faber, 226–44.

— (1986) 'Orientalism Reconsidered', in Francis Barker et al. (eds), *Literature Politics and Theory. Papers from the Essex Conference 1976–84*, London: Methuen, 210–29.

— (1989) 'Representing the Colonized: Anthropology's Interlocutors', *Critical Inquiry* 15: 205–25.

— (1993) *Culture and Imperialism*, London: Chatto and Windus.

— (1994) *Representations of the Intellectual. The 1993 Reith Lectures*, London: Vintage.

Sanday, Peggy Reeves (1986) *Divine Hunger: Cannibalism as a Cultural System*, Cambridge: CUP.

Sartre, Jean-Paul (1983), preface to Fanon, *The Wretched of the Earth* (trans. Constance Farrington), London: Penguin.

Sayyid, Bobby (1997) *A Fundamental Fear*, London: Zed Books.

Schaffer, Kay (1990) *Women and the Bush: Forces of Desire in the Australian Cultural Tradition*, Cambridge: CUP.

Schivelbusch, Wolfgang (1986) *The Railway Journey: The Industrialisation of Time and Space in the Nineteenth Century*, Berkeley: University of California Press.

Schwarz, Bill (ed.) (1996) *The Expansion of England: Race, Ethnicity and Cultural History*, London: Routledge.

Seeley, Sir John R. (1909) *The Expansion of England: Two Courses of Lectures*, London: Macmillan (1st edn 1883).

Seelye, John (1977) *Prophetic Waters: The River in Early American Life and Literature*, New York: Oxford University Press.

Sellers, Susan (ed.) (1994) *The Hélène Cixous Reader*, London: Routledge.

Shanin, Teodor (1983) *Late Marx and the Russian Road: Marx and the Peripheries of Capitalism*, New York: Monthly Review Press.

Sharma, Sanjay, John Hutnyk and Ashwani Sharma (1996) *Dis-Orienting Rhythms: The Politics of New Asian Dance Music*, London: Zed.

Sharpe, Jenny (1993) *Allegories of Empire: The Figure of Woman in the Colonial Text*, Minneapolis: Minnesota University Press.

Shaw, Rosalind and Charles Stewart (1994) 'Introduction: Problematizing Syncretism', in *Syncretism/Anti-Syncretism: The Politics of Religious Synthesis*, London: Routledge, 1–26.

Shaw, Stanford (1976) *History of the Ottoman Empire and Modern Turkey*, 2 vols, Cambridge: CUP.

Shurmer-Smith, P. and K. Hannam (1994) *Worlds of Desire, Realms of Power: A Cultural Geography*, London: Edward Arnold.

Silverman, Kaja (1992) *Male Subjectivity at the Margins*, London: Routledge.

Sked, A. (1989) *Britain's Decline*, Oxford: Blackwell.

Smith, Bernard (1960) *European Vision and the South Pacific 1760–1850: A Study in the History of Art and Ideas*, Oxford: Clarendon Press.

Smith, Tony (1981) *The Pattern of Imperialism: the United States, Great Britain, and the Late-industrialising World Since 1815*, Cambridge: CUP.

Smith, Valerie (ed.) (1978) *Hosts and Guests: The Anthropology of Travel*, Philadelphia: Pennsylvania University Press.

Spengemann, William C. (1977) *The Adventurous Muse: The Poetics of American Fiction, 1789–1900*, New Haven: Yale University Press.

Spivak, Gayatri C. (1987) *In Other Worlds: Essays in Cultural Politics*, London: Methuen.

— (1990) *The Post-Colonial Critic*, ed. Sarah Harasym, New York: Routledge.

— (1993) *Outside in the Teaching Machine*, London: Routledge.

— (1995) 'Ghostwriting', *Diacritics* 25: manuscript.

— (1996) *The Spivak Reader*, ed. Donna Landry and Gerald Maclean, New York: Routledge.

Spufford, Francis (1996) *I May Be Some Time: Ice and the English Imagination*, London: Faber.

Spurr, David (1993) *The Rhetoric of Empire: Colonial Discourse in Journalism, Travel Writing and Imperial Administration*, Durham, NC, and London: Duke University Press.

Stafford, Barbara Maria (1984) *Voyage into Substance: Art, Science, Nature and the Illustrated Travel Account 1760–1840*, Boston: MIT.

Stagl, Justin (1996) 'Nicolai Nicolayevich Miklouho-Maclay: or the Dilemma of the Ethnographer in the pre-Colonial Situation', *History and Anthropology* 9: 255–65.

Stagl, Justin and Christopher Pinney (1996) 'Introduction: From Travel Writing to Ethnography', *History and Anthropology* 9: 121–4.

Steinem, Gloria (1985) *Moving beyond Words*, London: Bloomsbury.

Stocking, George W. Jr (1985) 'Anthropology and the Science of the Irrational: Malinowski's Encounter with Freudian Psychoanalysis', *Malinowski, Rivers, Benedict and Others: Essays on Culture and Personality*, Madison: University of Wisconsin Press.

— (1991) 'Maclay, Kubary, Malinowski: Archetypes from the Dreamtime of Anthropology', in G. W. Stocking (ed.), *Colonial Situations: Essays on the Contextualisation of Ethnographic Knowledge*, Madison: University of Wisconsin Press, 9–74.

Stout, Janis P. (1983) *The Journey Narrative in American Literature: Patterns and Departures*, Westport, CT: Greenwood University Press.

Stowe, William W. (1994) *Going Abroad: English Travel in Nineteenth-Century America*, Princeton: Princeton University Press.

Strathern, Marilyn (1987) 'Out of Context: the Persuasive Fictions of Anthropology', *Current Anthropology* 28.

— (1991) 'Or, Rather, On Not Collecting Clifford', *Social Analysis* 29: 88–95.

Stratton, Jon (1990) 'Writing Travel', in *Writing Sites: A Genealogy of the Postmodern World*, London: Harvester Wheatsheaf, 43–92.

Street, Brian V. (1975) *The Savage in Literature: Representations of 'Primitive' Society in English Fiction 1858–1920*, London and Boston: Routledge and Kegan Paul.

Sulieri, Sara (1992) *The Rhetoric of English India*, Chicago: Chicago University Press.

Tarski, A. (1956) *Logic, Semantics, Metamathematics. Papers from 1923 to 1938*, Oxford: Clarendon Press.

Taussig, Michael (1980) *The Devil and Commodity Fetishism in South America*, Chapel Hill: University of North Carolina Press.

— (1987) *Shamanism, Colonialism and the Wild Man: A Study in Terror and Healing*, Chicago: Chicago University Press.

Thomas, Nicholas (1994) *Colonialism's Culture: Anthropology, Travel and Government*, Princeton: Princeton University Press.

Thornton, Robert (1985) '"Imagine Yourself Set Down … ": Mach, Frazer, Conrad, Malinowski and the Role of the Imagination in Ethnography', *Anthropology Today* 1: 7–14.

Tidrick, Kathryn (1981) *Heart-Beguiling Araby*, Cambridge: CUP.

— (1990) *Empire and the English Character*, London: I. B. Tauris.

Tiffin, Chris and Alan Lawson (eds) (1994) *De-Scribing Empire: Post-colonialism and Textuality*, London: Routledge.

Todorov, Tzvetan (1984) *The Conquest of America: The Question of the Other* (trans. Richard Howard), New York: Harper and Row.

Tomaselli, Sylvana (1985) 'The Enlightenment Debate on Women', *History Workshop* 20: 101–24.

Tomlinson, John (1991) *Cultural Imperialism: A Critical Introduction*, London and Baltimore: Johns Hopkins University Press.

Turner, Katherine S. H. (1995) 'The Politics of Narrative Singularity in British Travel Writing, 1750–1800', unpublished D Phil dissertation, University of Oxford.

Turner, Victor (1974) *Dramas, Fields and Metaphors: Symbolic Action in Human Society*, Cornell: Cornell University Press.

— (1977) *The Ritual Process*, Ithaca, NY: Cornell University Press.

Uberoi, J. P. S. (1962) *The Politics of the Kula Ring: An Analysis of the Findings of Bronislaw Malinowski*, Manchester: Manchester University Press.

Urbain, Jean-Didier (1991) *L'idiot du voyage. Histories de touristes*, Paris: Plon.

Urry, John (1990) *The Tourist Gaze: Leisure and Travel in Contemporary Societies*, London: Sage.

Van den Abbeele, Georges (1992) *Travel as Metaphor from Montaigne to Rousseau*, Minneapolis: Minnesota University Press.

van Gennep, Arnold (1909; 1960) *The Rites of Passage* (trans. Monika B. Vizedom and Gabrielle L. Caffee), Chicago: Chicago University Press.

Viswanathan, Gauri (1989) *Mask of Conquest: Literary Study and British Rule in India*, London: Faber.

von Martles, Zweder (ed.) (1994) *Travel Fact and Travel Fiction: Studies on Fiction, Literary Tradition, Scholarly Discovery and Observation in Travel Writing*, Leiden: E. J. Brill.

von Neumann J. (1966) *Theory of Self-Reproducing Automata*, ed. A. W. Burks, Urbana: University of Illinois Press.

Wade, Peter (1993) 'Sexuality and Masculinity in Fieldwork among the Columbian Blacks', in Diane Bell, Pat Caplan and Jahan Karim (eds), *Gendered Fields: Women, Men and Ethnography*, London: Routledge, 199–214.

Washburn, Wilcomb E. (1962), 'The Meaning of "Discovery" in the Fifteenth and Sixteenth Centuries', *American Historical Review* 68: 1–21.

Watt, D. Cameron (1984) *Succeeding John Bull: America in Britain's Place 1900–1975*, Cambridge: CUP.

Wayne, Helena (ed.) (1995) *The Story of a Marriage Vols 1 and 2: The Letters of Bronislaw Malinowski and Elsie Masson*, London: Routledge.

Weiner, Annette B. (1988) *The Trobrianders of Papua New Guinea*, New York: Holt, Rinehart and Winston.

Whitford, Margaret (1989) 'Rereading Irigaray', in Teresa Brennan (ed.), *Between Psychoanalysis and Feminism*, London and New York: Routledge, 106–26.

Whitten, Norman E. Jr (1991) 'Pretext of a Modernist Predicament', *Social Analysis* 26: 96–109.

Wilde, Oscar (1966) 'The Critic as Artist', in *Complete Works*, London: Collins.

Wilson, Edward O. (1992) *The Diversity of Life*, London: Penguin.

Wolf, Eric (1982) *Europe and the People without History*, Princeton: Princeton University Press.

Wolff, Janet (1995) 'On the Road again: Metaphors of Travel in Cultural Criticism', in *Resident Alien: Feminist Cultural Criticism*, London: Polity, 1–22.

Wood, Frances, (1995) *Did Marco Polo go to China?*, London: Secker and Warburg.

Woodward, David (ed.) (1987) *Art and Cartography*, Chicago: Chicago University Press.

Young, Michael (1979) *The Ethnography of Malinowski: The Trobriand Islands, 1915–1918*, London: Routledge and Kegan Paul.

— (1984) 'The Intensive Study of Restricted Area, Or, Why did Malinowski Go to the Trobriand Islands?', *Oceania* 55: 1–26.

Young, Robert M. (1990) *White Mythologies*, London: Routledge.

— (1995) *Colonial Desire: Hybridity in Theory, Culture and Race*, London: Routledge.

Youngs, Tim (1994) *Travellers in Africa: British Travelogues 1850–1900*, Manchester: Manchester University Press.

— (1997) 'Punctuating Travel: Paul Theroux and Bruce Chatwin', *Literature and History* [Placing Travel] 6: 73–88.

Zizek, Slavoj (1989) *The Sublime Object of Ideology*, London and New York: Verso.

Zweig, Paul (1974) *The Adventurer: The Fate of Adventure in the Western World*, Princeton: Princeton University Press.

# Index